THE DOWNFALL OF THE
LIBERAL PARTY
1914–1935

The Downfall of the Liberal Party
1914-1935

TREVOR WILSON

Cornell University Press

ITHACA, NEW YORK

329.942
W 69 d
60290
Jan. 1968

Printed in Great Britain

FOR JANE

PREFACE

This book is intended as a piece of narrative history. It does not seek to " namierize " the Liberal Members of Parliament, or to view through the microscope the party in the constituencies. Such specialised studies must in time be undertaken. But before they are, it is necessary to establish the chronology of the Liberal party's break-up. Hitherto the actual course of events, and the part played in it by leading individuals, have not been set down. That is what is attempted here.

Two main sources have been drawn on : collections of private papers, and the newspaper press. The importance of the former will be obvious. What needs to be stressed is the importance of the latter. The newspaper press is the great untapped source for the writing of recent British political history. Its value for a book of this kind is not easy to exaggerate.

I have received much assistance in writing this book : from the Nuffield Foundation, which enabled me to make a return visit to the United Kingdom in 1964 ; from reference libraries, particularly that in Manchester; from historians and political workers who have discussed with me the events dealt with here ; and from individuals and institutions who have allowed me to consult private papers in their possession. (Details of this last group will be found in the bibliography.) In addition, I owe long-standing debts of gratitude to Willis Airey and R. M. Chapman in Auckland, R. B. McCallum and Kenneth Tite in Oxford, and W. J. M. Mackenzie in Manchester. I also wish to thank Hugh Stretton for his trenchant advice on matters of style ; and Brian Chapman, John Grigg, H. J. Hanham, Malcolm Jack, Richard Ollard, and Jane Wilson for reading and commenting on various sections of the book. (All of them, I am sure, dissent from much that I have written).

NOTES ON TERMINOLOGY

i. I have referred throughout to the " Conservative "
party, instead of using " Unionist " in the early
chapters and " Conservative " in the later. The two
names " Conservative " and " Unionist " were
synonymous.

ii. I have used " Liberal " and " Liberalism " with
capitals when referring to the members and organised
forces of the Liberal party, and " liberal " and " liberalism " without capitals when referring to the body of
ideas regarded as constituting liberalism in Western
Europe.

iii. I have employed " whig " in the manner which
had become habitual by 1914, that is to describe any
right-wing Liberal, not just Liberals who belonged to
landed families.

CONTENTS

CONTENTS

ILLUSTRATIONS

INTRODUCTION

Yet I am enough of a traditionalist to see with regret the end of power which goes back directly to 1832 and the great epoch of reform, and, indirectly to the Revolution of 1688. The funerals of historical entities are melancholy events.

Harold Laski to Oliver Wendell Holmes, 30 May 1926[1]

THE purpose of this book is to tell the story of the British Liberal party during the years in which, from being the ruling party in the land, it ceased to be a contender for office and exhausted all avenues to revival. When war broke out in 1914 the Liberals governed Britain and held 261 seats in Parliament. By 1935 they were down to a score of members, with no prospect of improving their position and a good chance of losing some of the seats they held. This account stops at 1935 because nothing happened during the next twenty years to alter the pattern already established; and the story of the Liberal party since 1955 requires separate presentation. By the same token, the decade before 1914 is not dealt with here, because it constitutes a different era needing to be treated by itself.

Not everyone will approve of this starting-point. It is commonly believed that the Liberal party began to fall well before 1914. I recall discussing this matter with some fellow-undergraduates when I was first becoming interested in the subject. One of them set the ball rolling by asking " When did the Liberal party reach the point of no return ? " (He was an American student). Their answers covered many years. One considered the Liberal party doomed from the time of the Home Rule split in the 1880s ; another from the foundation of the Independent Labour party in the 1890s, or anyway the Labour Representation Committee in 1900 ; another from the

[1] *Holmes–Laski Letters*, edited by Mark Howe, vol. II, pp. 843–4.

election of Labour M.P.s in 1906; another from the political upheavals of the period 1910–1914 ("The Strange Death of Liberal England"). Thus to satisfy every view about when and why the Liberal party met its doom, one might as well go back to the time when there was a party bearing the name Liberal at all.

This temptation has been resisted. The account given here is confined to the period when the Liberal party was clearly disintegrating. Such was not the case before 1914. If the party passed through troubled times between 1885 and 1905, its electoral victories from 1906 to 1910 appeared to show it fully recovered. Between 1911 and 1914 it again encountered difficulties : Nonconformity, at least for the moment, had passed its peak, the situation in Ireland was full of menace, Labour was talking of ending its alliance with the Liberals, there was much industrial unrest, and by-elections seemed to show that the Liberals would lose the next election to the Conservatives. All of these are reasons for believing that the Liberal party might soon have been out of office. They do not show that it was doomed to near-extinction. The fact that Nonconformity was losing ground did not mean that it might not soon recover it. And although the Conservatives were capturing seats in by-elections, it was not certain that before long they would capture office. There seemed no limit to their folly during these years. They had lost two elections in 1910, soon after their prospects had begun to look rosy, by encouraging the House of Lords to wildly irresponsible conduct. In 1914 the crisis in Ireland was acting to their advantage; but they might still have carried their disregard for law and order over this issue to a point which would shock moderate opinion and lose them another election.

The most menacing problem for the Liberals before August 1914 was relations with Labour. The Liberal party contained a substantial element of wealthy businessmen, many of whom held individualistic views on economic matters and looked askance at the trade union movement ; in Scotland, particularly, Liberal-Labour relations had for some years been awkward. To maintain a working alliance with Labour, the Liberals would probably have been obliged to shed some of these more " conservative " elements. But such a shedding process had occurred

before without causing irrevocable disaster. The real danger
to the Liberals was that in seeking to retain their " whigs "
they might lose contact with Labour. Yet in 1914 this was not
happening. The social reforming wing of the Liberal government was making the running. " Advanced " thinkers were
still looking to Liberalism to implement their ideas. And
Labour had put forward no major policy items which the
Liberal party was unable to implement.

Nor in purely electoral terms was there any sign that Labour
was supplanting the Liberals. In the general elections of 1910,
and in by-elections from 1911 until the outbreak of war, Labour
fared abysmally in contests with the Liberals. Twice in by-
elections during these years Liberals contested Labour-held
seats, and on both occasions Labour came bottom of the poll.
Thus even in constituencies where Labour could not be dismissed
as a " hopeless " party (because it happened to be in occupation), it could not hold its own against the Liberals. By and
large, the Labour parliamentary party still existed in 1914 by
Liberal indulgence—that is, because the Liberals deemed it
advantageous to give Labour a free run against the Conservatives in certain seats. There is no way of knowing what would
have happened before the war if Labour had set itself up in
rivalry to the Liberals. On the basis of electoral evidence up to
1914, both would have suffered, but Labour would have fared
much worse than the Liberals. Whether, in that event, Labour
would have persisted in hopeless battles, or would have made a
new (and probably more favourable) agreement with the Liberals,
is a matter for speculation. It did not appear inevitable that
Labour would persist in the former course.

The whole notion that " Liberal England " died " strangely "
between 1910 and 1914 is based on the assumption that during
these years the nation experienced a cataclysm of internal
violence to which the war provided a fitting climax. The elements in this cataclysm were the intransigence of the House of
Lords, wide-scale industrial unrest, the excesses of the suffragettes, and the imminence of bloodshed in Ireland. But did
these add up to a " pattern " of violence, rather than an accidental convergence of unrelated events ? Some of the problems
were passing : the Upper House had been put in its place, and
the strike-wave seemed to be receding. The other problems

were not manifestly insoluble. The suffragette question, and perhaps even Ireland, might have been settled before this with a firmer lead from the government; and even now they were not past redemption. To make the argument that Liberalism was already strangely dead carry conviction, it is necessary to employ a palpable sleight of hand : to imply that the outbreak of war in August 1914 was the culmination of this pattern of internal violence, that " international anarchy " was part and parcel of " domestic anarchy ". The argument fails in two respects. There was domestic unrest, but no anarchy. And the events on the continent which dragged Britain into war were extraneous to British affairs. They sprang from circumstances outside the British experience, and outside the control of British statesmen. As far as the onset of war was concerned, Britain and the Liberal party were innocent bystanders.

To make clear the view taken here about when the Liberal party " reached the point of no return ", it may be permissible to resort to allegory. The Liberal party can be compared to an individual who, after a period of robust health and great exertion, experienced symptoms of illness (Ireland, Labour unrest, the suffragettes). Before a thorough diagnosis could be made, he was involved in an encounter with a rampant omnibus (the First World War), which mounted the pavement and ran him over. After lingering painfully, he expired. A controversy has persisted ever since as to what killed him. One medical school argues that even without the bus he would soon have died ; the intimations of illness were symptoms of a grave disease which would shortly have ended his life. Another school goes further, and says that the encounter with the bus would not have proved fatal had not the victim's health already been seriously impaired. Neither of these views is accepted here. The evidence for them is insufficient, because the ailments had not reached a stage where their ultimate effect could be known. How long, apart from the accident, the victim would have survived, what future (if any) he possessed, cannot be said. All that is known is that at one moment he was up and walking and at the next he was flat on his back, never to rise again ; and in the interval he had been run over by a bus. If it is guess-work to say that the bus was mainly responsible for his demise, it is the most warrantable guess that can be made.

Thus this story begins as the vehicle leaves the road and starts across the footpath ; or, to move back from analogy to history, as the German war machine broke loose across western Europe, and the British government became irresistibly involved.

PART ONE

The Liberal Party and the War

1914–1918

1. THEMES

Oh the war ! If it would only cease !

Lord Haldane to his mother, 7 January 1915 [1]

THE outbreak of the First World War initiated a process of disintegration in the Liberal party which by 1918 had reduced it to ruins. As Liberals were often the first to recognise, the onset of war jeopardised the existence of a party whose guiding principles were international conciliation, personal liberty, and social reform. On the fateful 4th of August 1914 Christopher Addison, a junior member of the Liberal government, foretold his party's demise in words which, with one variation or another, were to be repeated many times in the following years. Addison was talking with Sir John Simon, the Attorney-General, about possible resignations from the government, and Simon said that he was reluctant to see too many ministers resign because that would necessitate a coalition government, " which would assuredly be the grave of Liberalism." Addison gloomily replied that in the opinion of most Liberals, and certainly of himself, Liberalism was in its grave already.[2] A few months later a prominent Scottish Liberal wrote privately : " I meet many good Liberals in Midlothian and elsewhere who are prone to take the view that we pacifists made a mistake and the Jingos were right all along ".[3]

For a Liberal government to lead Britain into war, and to direct a wartime administration, seemed almost a contradiction

---

[1] Haldane Papers.

[2] Christopher Addison, *Four and a Half Years*, vol. I, p. 35.

[3] Alex Shaw (M.P. for Kilmarnock from May 1915) to A. G. Gardiner, 9 December (1914), Gardiner Papers. Shaw's reference to " we pacifists " designated Liberals who had opposed increases in armaments before the war. He was not an anti-war Liberal on pacifist or other grounds, and served throughout the battle of the Somme.

in terms. Its task of international pacification had automatically disappeared. And it had little hope of preserving intact those principles and practices identified with Liberalism : free trade, protection of minorities, the " pacification " of Ireland, liberty of the individual, and voluntary service in the armed forces. Yet once a Liberal government began to modify its ideals under stress of war, how long would it be before the liberal position was abandoned altogether and that of the Conservatives adopted ? In short, war and the conduct of war threatened to eliminate liberalism as a coherent political position.

While some liberal principles were being suspended for the duration, others seemed unlikely (except to devout Liberals) ever to become important again. Issues on which Liberals possessed a distinctive and militant attitude, like temperance, denominational education, and Welsh Church disestablishment, suddenly seemed irrelevant both now and for the future. The one attempt made to further temperance as a cause during the war failed ignominiously, and an Education Act was passed in 1918 without a whisper of the denominational controversies which had once roused Liberals. As for the central liberal tenet of free trade, even individualistic Liberals like J. M. Robertson and Lord Murray of Elibank began to doubt its revival. Murray in 1916 warned a director of the Liberal *Westminster Gazette* that the paper should avoid discussing " whether or not we should trade with the Germans after the war."

> Personally [he wrote] I think that as the Emperor William has been responsible for our adopting conscription, so may he be responsible for our changing all our tariff traditions and our adopting a commercial imperial federation working in association with the Allied Powers. At any rate, I would advise the paper to be very cautious in committing itself to any opinions on tariffs at this stage. The prosecution of the war and a consolidated Government at home are the only policies which the mass of the public demands.[1]

---

[1] Murray to Sir Donald Maclean, 29 June 1916, Elibank Papers. As it happened, free trade did revive in force after 1918. But this does not alter the fact that Liberalism suffered great damage during the war owing to disbelief in its revival.

On these questions which alone concerned " the mass of the public " there was no distinctive liberal position, and no standard round which the party could rally.

As " the prosecution of the war " pushed aside liberal issues, so it undermined the organisations associated with the Liberal party. By 1918 the powerful forces within the Irish and Labour movements which favoured co-operation with the Liberals, so providing Asquith with a parliamentary majority between 1910 and 1914, had been disrupted.[1] Even more serious was the damage suffered by the great force of religious Nonconformity. Charles Royle, a Stockport butcher of humble origin who was deeply involved in Nonconformist and temperance activities, has written of one branch of Nonconformity, the National Brotherhood movement :

> When the war commenced in 1914 our members began to join up and before it was finished over 600 had been enrolled as serving the King.
>
> We found to our great regret that it was one thing for them to go and although the big majority came back to the town [Stockport] only a small number resumed their membership of the Brotherhood. Is it to be wondered at, after the devastating influences of such an experience, that men should have little room for things of a religious nature.[2]

Nonconformity, it should be stressed, was not just a pressure group which looked to the Liberals for aid on some issues. Its religious dynamic expressed itself in political terms. One of its chief periodicals, the *British Weekly* (edited by Sir William Robertson Nicoll), called itself " a journal of social and Christian progress." Nonconformity had seen the Liberal party as the instrument, politically, of " social and Christian progress ", and Liberalism had correspondingly been underpinned by the force

---

[1] In November 1910 the chief Liberal organiser, Sir Jesse Herbert, estimated that at the election then in progress the Liberal government would secure a majority both in England and Wales, " counting Liberal & Labour together." (Herbert to the Master of Elibank, 9 November 1910, Elibank Papers). Before the war the *Liberal Yearbook* always classified Liberal and Labour M.P.s together, and only ceased doing so in 1919.

[2] Charles Royle, *Opened Doors*, p. 37. Mr. Royle was a Liberal M.P. briefly in the 1920s, and his son (the present Lord Royle) was a Labour M.P. from 1945 to 1964.

of Nonconformist conviction. But central to the Free Church ideal of " Christian progress " was peace between nations. As the *British Weekly* said on 6 August 1914 : " We of the Free Churches are bound under the most tremendous penalties to set the example of peace and good will." It had long been clear, it continued, that the present military system of Europe must come to an end, either by general disarmament, or by mutual destruction. " The Free Churches have worked for disarmament, and who can blame them ? " In this way they had hoped that this bloodshed, this devastation, this outbreak of deadly passions, these strong perils casting their shadows far into the future, might be averted.

The purpose of this article was not to urge neutrality, but to explain the necessity for intervening in the war. Yet the terms in which it was expressed suggested the blow which Nonconformity had suffered. (A few days earlier, before the violation of Belgium, Robertson Nicoll had written to Lloyd George utterly opposing intervention). At the beginning of December 1914 Sir George Riddell, the newspaper owner, found Nicoll " very broken by the war. He said that he had been at a Free Church meeting on Friday and that some of the dissenting ministers are still peace-at-any-price people. On the other hand, some are very militant. For example, one wanted Nicoll to insert in the *British Weekly* a little story of which the point was that we should pray for the destruction of the Germans."[1] These differences disintegrated Nonconformity, especially as a political force. Whereas by 1918 prominent divines like Maude Royden were moving over to the Labour party, others like Dr. Shakespeare had followed Lloyd George into Conservative company. Nicoll took the latter course. He even, in December 1914, favoured inserting the dubious paragraph about praying for the destruction of the Germans. Thereafter he strongly advocated severe restrictions on enemy aliens, conscription for the armed forces, and a Lloyd George premiership—all of them causes associated with the Conservatives rather than the Liberals. By June 1915 his journal was being spoken of in the same breath as Lord Northcliffe's *Times*. Haldane wrote to his mother : " The ' Times ' is now joining with the ' British Weekly ' in a movement to turn out the poor

[1] *Lord Riddell's War Diary*, p. 44.

P.M. & substitute Ll. George."[1]   When Nicoll died in 1923, Lloyd George spoke of him warmly as a good friend and a great help during the war.   The two of them, Lloyd George said (" with much bitterness "), had made enemies because when they decided—reluctantly—to go into the war they went in heart and soul, whereas other Liberals agreed to participate but sought to satisfy their anti-war proclivities by carrying on the struggle in a meagre and unsatisfactory way.   (Significantly, Lloyd George here seemed to be using " Liberals " as synonymous with " Nonconformists ").   To Lloyd George, Nicoll's attitude had been vitally important in securing Free Church support for the war, and so in deciding the outcome of the conflict.[2]

But if the war effort had prospered, Nonconformity had been the loser.   It had become too closely associated with a regime Conservative in complexion and nationalistic in outlook. Whereas the Church of England might survive, and even prosper from, identification with the nation in arms, such identification did violence to the genius of Nonconformity.   Yet those Free Churchmen who resisted this trend seemed helpless to save their cause.   They had struggled so hard to avert war that with the outbreak of hostilities they had lost their bearings, and almost their *raison d'être*.   J. Allen Baker, who was a leading Quaker, a London social reformer, and a Liberal M.P., is a case in point.   Before 1914 his unremitting efforts had been devoted increasingly to international conciliation, and in this cause he had travelled widely and been welcomed by the Kaiser, the American President, and the British Foreign Secretary.   Then in August 1914 his world collapsed about him.   From being a considerable force in the land he became a quite unimportant figure. He died in 1918, heartbroken and almost forgotten.   In a sense the fate of Nonconformity was the fate of the Liberal party.[3]

---

[1] Haldane to his mother, 11 June 1915, Haldane Papers.

[2] *Lord Riddell's Intimate Diary of the Peace Conference and After*, p. 406.

[3] There is an affectionate life of Baker (*J. Allen Baker: A Memoir*) by E. B. Baker and P. J. Noel Baker.

II

For the Conservative and Labour parties, these years presented no such menace. From the outset the war redounded to the advantage of the Conservatives. It seemed to vindicate their pre-war conduct, particularly their hostility to Germany, their advocacy of a tariff policy directed (amongst other things) against German trade, and their demand for increased armaments and peacetime conscription. Further, the war produced in Britain a mood of acute, sometimes frenzied, nationalism which was bound to help the Conservatives as being the more nationalistic, " patriotic " party. And the actual conduct of war demanded encroachments on the liberty of the individual which were more acceptable to Conservatives than to Liberals ; for, as the *Manchester Guardian* said on 8 May 1916, love of personal freedom was of the essence of liberalism, and resort to compulsion in accord with the traditions of conservatism.

Initially Labour secured no comparable advantage from the war. The party was divided into a majority supporting British intervention and a minority, including the I.L.P. section, opposing it. Its internal dissensions on this matter, and its " internationalist " outlook in the past, cost it many adherents, to whom it now seemed insufficiently patriotic. These losses led, among other things, to the formation of the right-wing British Workers League (later called the National Democratic party), which captured Merthyr Tydfil from Labour at a by-election in November 1915.[1] C. B. Stanton, the victor in this contest, had formerly been a Labour candidate and miners' leader. And J. A. Seddon, who became chairman of the National Democratic party, had been a Labour M.P. and chairman of the T.U.C. not long before.

Yet the war proved in the long run of the greatest benefit to Labour. In the first place, it wrought such havoc upon the Liberals that it provided Labour, as the party nearest them in political complexion, with the chance to appropriate their position of principal left-wing party. Despite the small importance of the pre-war Labour party, it proved of the utmost advantage for it simply to have existed in 1914—existed, that

[1] The Labour candidate in this by-election had strong I.L.P. affiliations.

is, as a parliamentary, non-revolutionary party with important, if still limited, trade union associations and with many attributes of radical Nonconformity. As a consequence the Liberal party only had to suffer a shattering disaster for Labour to take over its role as chief contender for office with the Conservatives.

The war not only inflicted such a disaster on the Liberals but provided Labour with the impetus to seize its opportunity. The impact of the war on the nation's economy so increased the importance of the trade unions, and so stimulated their political consciousness, that it correspondingly enhanced the position of the Labour party, which had all along derived much of its limited importance from its association with organised labour. Primarily it was not the numerical strength of the Labour party in the House of Commons or the calibre of its members available for office, but the need for trade union co-operation in the war, which caused Labour to receive posts in the wartime coalitions. Certainly if Labour's following in the House of Commons alone was considered, it had little claim to equal representation with the Liberals in Lloyd George's five-man war cabinet.[1] What secured it this position was its enhanced political potential, resulting from its connection with the trade union movement.

Participation in these wartime governments did not, moreover, deprive Labour of what was to be a prime advantage after the war : freedom from responsibility for the deeds of governments up to that time. Labour had supported the Asquith administration before the war, and from 1915 to 1918 held office in the coalitions, yet it was only marginally associated with these governments. Indeed during the war it combined membership of them with independence of, and even hostility to, the other parties making them up. In the short term Labour was to suffer for its detachment from Lloyd George's " victorious " administration. But in the long run it was to prove an advantage that, unlike the Liberals, Labour was not directly responsible for the alleged errors or misdeeds of the past. In consequence many of those who thought the British government in some measure culpable for the outbreak of war, or who hoped to

[1] The Liberal in this war cabinet, it might be added, was Lloyd George himself, whose affiliations with the Liberal party were by this time uncertain.

redeem the sacrifices of the war by constructing a new social order, abandoned the Liberals as supposedly tarnished by failure and threw in their lot with Labour.

III

The way in which the onset and conduct of war disrupted the Liberals may be shown by the behaviour of various sections of the party. The allegiance of one group was irrevocably shaken by the decision to participate at all. The war to them was not the product of German militarism but of " pre-war diplomacy ", a system which they equated with the balance of power, armaments-building, and binding agreements between rival power groupings. In their view, Britain's Liberal government had gravely erred by joining in this system, and so had helped to bring about the war. As one Liberal "pacifist" M.P., Philip Morrell (employing all the judiciousness he could summon up), put the matter in October 1916 :

> I was opposed to the policy of the Triple Entente, which in my judgment was one of the principal causes leading to war, and so far from thinking that the outbreak can be attributed entirely to the exceptional wickedness of one nation or one man, I held, and still hold, that whatever may have been the special guilt of Germany, which I do not for a moment extenuate or excuse, all the Governments of the Great Powers of Europe, not excluding our own, were in different degrees responsible for the outbreak.[1]

For these Liberals, the impending subjugation of Western Europe by German militarism in August 1914 was no sufficient ground for intervening in the war. According to P. A. Molteno, " no vital interest " of Britain " has been attacked ". According to Joseph King, Britain was obliged to " protest " against the German assault on Belgium but not to go to Belgium's aid. In the opinion of the British Neutrality League (a body formed on the eve of war and including several Liberal M.P.s) there was no likelihood that Germany would annex Belgium, and if it did so this would only make Germany " weaker than she is now, for she would have to use all her forces for holding her conquests down." In any case, as Arnold Rowntree put it, if Britain

[1] *Manchester Guardian,* 30 October 1916.

did intervene successfully against Germany, Russian despotism would become dominant in Europe.[1]

Underlying this extraordinary mixture of high-mindedness, self-interest, and wild delusion was the conviction that neither the circumstances in which Germany attacked in 1914, nor the military victories likely to follow, should influence Liberals on the question of intervention. According to Arthur Ponsonby, the British case set out in the White Paper on the outbreak of war was overwhelming. But the causes of the war were not to be found in the events related there. They went much farther back, to a policy with which he had profoundly disagreed—a policy of armaments, the balance of power, and secret diplomacy. It was, he claimed, a diplomats' not a people's war.[2]

It is little wonder that Liberals taking this view, and believing that their leaders had helped to cause the war, became disillusioned with their party. (It is also not surprising that the M.P.s in this group were often repudiated by the Liberal associations in their constituencies). Not all of them ceased to be Liberals ; a small section, usually wedded like Francis Hirst and Arnold Lupton to *laissez-faire* economics, remained in the party as a dissident, critical element.[3] Others, including Lord Morley and John Burns who resigned from the cabinet on the question of intervention, drifted out of politics altogether. " For the moment," Morley wrote to a Liberal editor in 1915, " our common ground on public things is broken to pieces. We don't speak the same language ".[4] But by far the greater section of Liberal " pacifists " remained politically active yet severed their ties with the Liberal party. In the next few years C. P. Trevelyan (who also left the government in August 1914), Ponsonby, King, C. R. Buxton, and H. B. Lees-Smith transferred their allegiance to Labour and became openly hostile to the Liberals.

[1] *Parliamentary Debates*, 5th series, House of Commons (hereafter referred to as *H. C. Deb.*), vol. 65, column 1846 (3 August 1914); *Manchester Guardian*, 3 and 4 August 1914.

[2] *H. C. Deb.*, 65,2089 (6 August 1914) ; *Manchester Guardian*, 7 August 1914.

[3] Lupton, a Liberal M.P. between 1906 and 1910, received a prison sentence during the war for activities considered prejudicial to recruiting. Hirst was editor of the *Economist* from 1907 to 1916.

[4] Morley to J. A. Spender, 16 March 1915, Spender Papers.

IV

As it happened, the number of Liberal "pacifists" at the outbreak of war proved much smaller than seemed probable only two or three days before. As the left-wing periodical the *Nation* said on 17 October 1914 : "the policy of the British Government receives a more whole-hearted and reasoned support than has been given to the policy of any war that has ever been waged by the nation." "Radicals, Socialists, and Syndicalists ", it went on, had been rallied to support of the war by the events leading to its outbreak. As war spread across Europe " internationalist" Liberals like Josiah Wedgwood and Gilbert Murray, and radical journals like the *Nation* and *Manchester Guardian*, were shocked out of a neutralist attitude by " the stupefying panorama of German arrogance " and the prospect of " brute force " overrunning Europe. In Wedgwood's view, social reformers had been called from their task by a more elementary battle for liberty, and if that battle was lost everything they cared for would be lost with it.

But not all Liberals who took this view in 1914 held to it thereafter. Doubts about the Liberal government's responsibility for the coming of war, banished for the moment, sometimes revived as the events of August 1914 became obscured by the carnage of the next four years, and as the claims of Liberals who attributed the war to " secret diplomacy " gained rather specious verification from the publication of the wartime secret treaties by the Russian Bolsheviks. Moreover, many of the Liberals who had reluctantly agreed to British intervention were at one with the " pacifists " regarding the methods by which the war should be conducted. They held that Britain must fight the war on the basis of liberal principles, and that the abandonment of these principles would constitute a triumph for " prussianism ". So while they might not accept Morrell's views about responsibility for the war, they frequently agreed with him about the principles which should govern wartime administration. Liberals, he said in the speech of 1916 already quoted, should not abandon in this conflict the principles of individual liberty—free trade, free service, freedom of opinion—which had made Britain one of the best-governed and most prosperous countries in the world. And he went on :

The system of conscription, like the system of [Tariff] Protection, with which it is closely allied, is in every country where it exists one of the most potent instruments of privilege and oppression. It gives to the military authorities a power over the lives of other men, and especially the lives of the workers, which is destructive of all true progress. It leads inevitably to that spirit of militarism of which the pernicious effects, as developed in Germany, are now very visible to us.

Many non-pacifist Liberals agreed with him about upholding liberal ideals in wartime. This can be seen (if in exaggerated form) from the attitude of W. M. R. Pringle and J. M. Hogge, the " terrible twins " who harried Lloyd George in the later years of the war. Both Pringle and Hogge supported British intervention. Pringle, speaking in Parliament on 3 August 1914 following the German ultimatum to Belgium, dissociated himself from former colleagues like Ponsonby. In the coming conflict between blood and iron and international morality, he said, those holding to liberal traditions must take the side of morality. His speech was considered important, as pointing to the abandonment of neutralism by many Liberal M.P.s because of the threat to Belgium. Yet although supporters of the war, he and Hogge stoutly resisted, first under Asquith and then under Lloyd George, measures of compulsion and restrictions on personal freedom. Even something as mild as a proposal by the Liberal government, early in 1915, to take the whole time of the House of Commons aroused their ire as infringing the rights of private members. Why would the government not trust them, Hogge demanded, when they were all trying their level best to support it in the great issues in which it was involved. The government, he complained, " take no notice of private Members of this House and of their own supporters—an excellent Liberal example." And he added, with no little exaggeration : " I would remind the Prime Minister that already the Cabinet have shut the mouth of the Press in this country, and they are now proposing to shut the mouths of private Members in this House." [1]

To Liberals of this way of thinking, Asquith during the first two years of the war was guilty of repeated deviations from the

[1] *H. C. Deb.*, 69, 66–7 (3 February 1915).

liberal position : in the sphere of personal liberty by the Defence of the Realm Act and the press censorship, in the sphere of government by the admission of a Conservative element, including Sir Edward Carson, into the ministry, in the sphere of free trade by the McKenna duties of 1915 and the " Paris Resolutions " of 1916, in the sphere of Ireland by the mismanagement which led up to and followed the Easter Rebellion of 1916, and above all in the sphere of voluntary service by the resort to conscription. To Liberal fundamentalists the war was no excuse for these actions. They denied, as Simon did when he resigned from the government over conscription, that any serious deficiency in the war effort existed under the voluntary system ; and if shown that deficiencies did exist they were prepared to argue, as did Reginald McKenna and Walter Runciman while resisting conscription in the cabinet, that the whole concept of total war implicit in the measure meant a struggle beyond Britain's resources. Pringle, taking up a contrast which Asquith had made between his government and that of the younger Pitt, asserted :

if Pitt and his successors were successful it was because they, in spite of all criticism, in spite of all failures, in spite of all complaints, adhered with the utmost strictness to the traditional policy of this country, namely, never to enter upon a Continental war on the basis of unlimited military liability. That we have done in the present case.[1]

It is clear that Liberals of this school had not wholly overcome their misgivings about Britain's involvement in war. Initially they had not appreciated how large a sacrifice of liberal principles it might entail. On theoretical grounds they would scarcely admit that the war could be conducted more effectively by compulsory than by voluntary means. And where their view was successfully challenged, they were so alarmed by the danger of permanent restrictions on liberty that they preferred, however they might rationalise their attitude, that the conduct of the war should suffer.

Consequently as the war proceeded an increasing number of Liberals began condemning their leaders, and indeed their party as a whole, for " betraying " liberal ideals. And they often inquired despairingly whether Liberalism would ever

[1] *ibid*, 81, 2630 (2 May 1916).

rise again after such misfortunes—queries which followed on directly from the doubts expressed on the outbreak of war about Liberalism's powers of survival. Lady Toulmin, wife of an M.P., wrote in mid-1916 that it was difficult for a life-long Liberal to speak with moderation about the state of Liberal politics. Unity had been maintained in the government by the surrender of all their party held dear : a voluntary army, the right of asylum, respect for conscience, education, Home Rule, and international law as touching the rights of neutrals. Other parties had surrendered nothing and had gained all along the line. " Will it ", she asked, " need another twenty years in the wilderness to purify and purge the Liberal party of the poison it has swallowed with such docility during the last months ? " For many a year, she concluded, " there shall be doubt, disappointment, and pain ; never glad, confident morning again." These statements, affirmed the president of the women's Liberal organisation in Yorkshire, expressed the view of thousands of sincere rank and file Liberals, who had been rendered dumb by recent events but were eagerly awaiting an opportunity to battle for the principles of faith. Some of them were asking whether they could honestly remain associated with a party whose sanction had been given to active work against liberal principles.[1]

Not all the Liberals who took this pessimistic view went so far as to abandon the party. Pringle and Hogge served out their political careers as Liberals, the former becoming reconciled to Asquith after the war, the latter remaining hostile to the end. But whether or not they left the party, they weakened it by endorsing the view that it was no longer a fit custodian of liberal principles. A party whose shortcomings were so loudly proclaimed by its own adherents had little chance of keeping its following intact or securing the allegiance of new entrants to politics—especially when another party unblemished by these supposed lapses was seeking to replace the Liberals as the principal left-wing party.

[1] *Manchester Guardian*, 5 and 10 August 1916.

V

So far attention has been directed to the Liberals whose allegiance was shaken by the decision to go to war or by the methods employed to conduct it. But another section turned against the party for precisely opposite reasons : because they considered it unwilling to surrender traditional ideas in face of the clear demands of war. To this group, the war and its efficient conduct took precedence over all other questions, including the principles of their party. And efficiency to them involved those measures of state direction and compulsion advocated by Conservatives and resisted by orthodox Liberals—measures like conscription for the armed forces, coercion of trade unions, punitive action against conscientious objectors and enemy aliens, and abandonment of free trade. Further, they were not prepared to wait for these measures while other Liberals were being convinced of their necessity. They wanted them immediately, even if it meant alienating the mass of Liberals and making an alliance with the Conservatives. Whereas most Liberals who supported the war tried to make their liberalism and their " patriotism " march hand in hand, or anyway to sacrifice only as much of their liberalism as the needs of patriotism absolutely demanded, many in this group did not. By placing the war before everything else they in effect abandoned their liberalism, moving over, in their ideology, their policy, and their political associations, into the Conservative camp.

No one made this transition more whole-heartedly than Lloyd George. For him the change was considerable. Although never peace-at-any-price, he had resisted intervention in August 1914. On 3 August one of his fellow ministers, C. F. G. Masterman, " spoke strongly of the way in which George had fought in the Cabinet all through the week for peace." And Lloyd George himself said that he " had done his utmost for peace but events had been too strong for him." He had even declined to treat a minor violation of Belgium as a *casus belli*, and it was only the full-scale invasion which had ended his resistance.[1]

But once Lloyd George (like Robertson Nicoll) was in the

[1] Scott's diary, 3 August 1914, C. P. Scott Papers.

war he would admit of no half-measures. As he wrote a few years later : " it was not ' my war '. . . . But being in it, I realised that the only safe way out was through the gates of victory, and that victory was only to be won by concentrating all thought and energy on the making of war ".[1] The truth was that the struggle obsessed him. He showed utter disregard for military leaders who (in his view) failed to comprehend the needs of the war as well as he did : hence his conflicts with Lord Kitchener, Admiral Jellicoe, Field-Marshal Haig, and Sir William Robertson. And he rejected out of hand liberal practices and principles—not to mention Liberal statesmen—when he considered them a hindrance to the war effort. Whereas Asquith showed little relish for the measures of compulsion he felt obliged to introduce, Lloyd George was not at all squeamish. Sometimes he made a peremptory effort to reconcile support for conscription with belief in liberalism, as when he claimed that the great battles for liberty in the past, like the French Revolutionary wars and the American Civil War, had been fought by conscript armies. But as the *Manchester Guardian* (a paper generally sympathetic to him) pointed out on 8 May 1916, what worried Liberals was not that he eventually supported conscription but that he had adopted it too readily, and had not appeared averse to doing so. That is, he had seemed prone to rely on force rather than persuasion, and to substitute compulsion for organisation. In so doing he had moved away from the liberal and towards the conservative position. What was more, although the *Manchester Guardian* did not say this, he had moved into the company of Conservatives and of those right-wing Liberals seeking an understanding with the Conservatives, and had not appeared anxious to conciliate the left-wing Liberals with whom he had once been associated.

In the long run, the defection of these Liberals who were prepared to abandon a liberal position and ally themselves with the Conservatives was probably less damaging than the withdrawal of members claiming that Liberalism had been betrayed by its leaders. Many in the conscriptionist group were untypical of the party as a whole, comprising what *The Times* on 13 December 1916 called " the substantial men in the party " :

[1] Lloyd George to Gilbert Murray, 26 October 1927, Gilbert Murray Papers.

members of landed and political families like Winston Churchill and F. E. Guest, mill and mine owners like Sir Arthur Markham and Sir Frederick Cawley, commercial figures who had become newspaper owners like Sir Henry Dalziel, and leading members of the chemical industry like Sir Alfred Mond. (The disproportionately large number of recipients of titles in this group may have been connected with the award of honours to persons who contributed substantially to party funds). The breaking-away of this group, like the secession of the whigs in the 1880s, was most injurious to the party—and not least to its finances—but not mortally wounding. It was less dangerous to lose a group moving from liberalism to conservatism than to lose radicals who claimed that they were preserving their principles unimpaired, and leaving the party in order to safeguard them.

Yet the withdrawal of the former section still did the party a great deal of damage. By their advocacy of sterner measures in prosecuting the war, and their demand for more dynamic leadership than Asquith provided, they won at least partial assent from many Liberals who, though unhappy about allying with the Conservatives, agreed that a major war could not be conducted by established liberal methods or the established Liberal leader. Further, although their defection robbed the party of only two of its most prominent individuals, namely Lloyd George and Churchill, they were the two on whom (according to Halévy) " the eyes of the public were fixed " before the war, " the men of to-morrow " as Asquith had appeared to be only a man of the present.[1] And Lloyd George's defection rendered the radical section leaderless for the second time in thirty-five years, depriving it once again of the man whom it had regarded as its particular spokesman—" the Radical leader ", as the *Nation* sadly described him, " to whom democracy was accustomed to look as its representative man."[2]

---

[1] Elie Halévy, *A History of the English People in the Nineteenth Century,* vol. 6, p. 236.

[2] *Nation*, 6 May 1916.

VI

While the war was dissolving the allegiance of Liberals on both the left and right of the party, it was reducing the remainder to near-helplessness. Faithful to Liberalism, they yet could see no way to stave off the disaster threatening it, and often seemed to lack even the will-power to act on its behalf. Their impotence was in sharp contrast to the growing assertiveness not only of the leaders but even more the rank and file of the Conservative and Labour parties.

Fundamentally this loss of initiative sprang from an inability to reconcile liberal ideals with effective prosecution of the war. But the difficulties of Liberals were aggravated by the behaviour of Asquith and his closest associates, both as leaders of the party and as directors of the war effort. Most Liberals were prepared to sacrifice their principles when the necessities of war imperatively demanded it. But too often Asquith seemed to call for such sacrifices less on account of the military situation than because of acute political pressure threatening his government. While some Liberals were prepared to accept his lead on all occasions, others could not overlook the political manœuvring which so often preceded his departures from a liberal position.

There was a further cause of misgiving among Liberals which had nothing to do with political principle or party allegiance : the question of Asquith's fitness as war leader. The war did not go well during his premiership ; failure attended the Allied effort in Gallipoli and Mesopotamia, on the Russian front and the western front, in Serbia and Roumania. Even some of his supporters considered him partly responsible for these setbacks. His wartime administrations seemed wanting in foresight and energy, and he did not create the impression of being a visionary, dynamic leader. Nor were these misgivings confined to advocates of compulsion or opponents of the Liberal party. The diary of the radical Addison reveals how, during the first year of the war, his admiration for Asquith was changed first to uneasiness and then to antipathy by what seemed his leader's habitual fumbling and indecision.[1]

[1] See the first volume of his *Four and a Half Years*.

For Liberals occupying this middle position—anxious both for their party and for the war, and doubtful of Asquith either as custodian of liberal principles or as director of the national effort—no line of action seemed open. Should they assail the government on some outstanding issue, they would bring Asquith down, for without Liberal support he was unlikely to survive a day. Notwithstanding the presence of the Conservative leaders in his government from May 1915, he enjoyed no real following among the Conservative rank and file. Only because he was leader of the Liberal party, and because it was difficult to envisage a ministry being formed without Liberal support, did he retain office for so long. Nor did he hesitate to threaten resignation if his followers became too restive. The party was profoundly shaken in May 1915 by his decision, at Conservative insistence, to form a coalition ministry; it required a twenty-minute exhortation from him to dissuade a meeting of over a hundred Liberal M.P.s from passing a resolution hostile to the change.[1] On this occasion he warned them quite frankly that if the resolution was adopted he would leave office. And the same threat, even if not explicitly repeated, faced his followers whenever they felt like challenging his actions.

The difficulty of Liberals in this situation was stated by one M.P. during the upheaval over the first conscription bill. H. W. Massingham, the editor of the *Nation*, had written bitterly that only thirty of the " 200 Liberal Anti-Conscriptionist members " had actually voted against the bill, and this M.P., signing himself " One of the 200 ", put the case for those who had not. If all of them had voted against conscription, he said, Asquith would have resigned and Lloyd George taken his place, and Massingham himself had said that this should be avoided. The party had been foolish to tie its hands by agreeing to a coalition, but it would be even more foolish to commit suicide by forcing Asquith to resign over conscription.[2]

Fear of unseating Asquith lest a worse fate befall them played a signal part in reducing the Liberals to impotence during the early years of the war. At first sight it seems surprising that neither Massingham nor " One of the 200 " rejoiced at the prospect of Lloyd George as Premier, considering his qualities

[1] *Daily News*, 20 May 1915.   [2] *Nation*, 22 January 1916.

THEMES

of wartime leadership. But he combined these qualities with others less attractive to Liberals : blatant disloyalty to his colleagues, open intriguing for office, and a ready acceptance of compulsion and Conservative allies. Only great disgust with Asquith would cause " middle " Liberals to consider replacing him by Lloyd George. A few did so. The *Manchester Guardian*, claiming that the war must take paramountcy over party or person and that Asquith was ill-equipped as war leader, welcomed Lloyd George as Premier. Indeed, it had called on him seven months earlier to abandon the government and join Churchill and Carson in opposition. Yet when he eventually became Prime Minister, even this newspaper admitted to a pang of regret at seeing him leading a largely Conservative government. It warned him—as it proved, in vain—" to walk warily and to permit no sort of provocation, should provocation come, to goad him into antagonism to the party to which he still owes allegiance, and to preserve for the future of Liberalism all the treasure of his soul."[1]

Many Liberals who agreed generally with the *Manchester Guardian,* and even endorsed its strictures against Asquith, felt that the dangers of a Conservative-dominated government under Lloyd George were too great to justify a change of ministry. Nor was it only party prejudice which caused this attitude. They feared that once in power the Conservatives would use the war to attain objectives deeply repugnant to them : permanent curtailments on liberty, coercive measures against labour, the final alienation of Ireland, imperialistic war aims, and a punitive peace settlement. Nor could Liberals welcome a change of government which in part would be attributable to the defamatory, rabble-rousing, fundamentally anti-democratic tactics of the press barons, and which might advance those individuals towards political power. In the event not all of their fears were to be realised. But the Conservative party's behaviour in the pre-war years and during the first years of the war makes it difficult to claim that any of them were groundless.

The essential helplessness of Liberals who regretted Asquith's performance yet feared his supersession is illustrated by a *Nation* article called " The Coalition and After ", written on the eve of

[1] *Manchester Guardian*, 21 April and 7 December 1916.

41

his fall. " We are afraid ", it said of the Asquith coalition,
" . . . that from the first it proclaimed its unfitness for the
task." All through it had been a " mere mechanical combination of Front Bench men " fettered by party interests and personal susceptibilities, with Asquith acting as a kind of referee
seeking compromises between opposing principles. The nation
was in no mood for delay. It would insist on a change of method,
and would respect no one, from the Prime Minister down, who
failed to provide it. Yet this article did not go on to demand
a new administration, but to warn against any likely replacement. The Asquith coalition was a " poor, uninspired " government, but its successor might be worse—not so much in ability
as in character. And it asked :

> What precisely does the country expect from the type of
> politician who has followed the strange banner that has
> been raised now from the centre of the ranks of the Coali-
> tion, and now from the circumference [i.e. by Lloyd George
> and Carson respectively] ? A strong or a united Cabinet ?
> A satisfied Army ? A well-ordered plan of campaign ? A
> good peace ? A contented Alliance ? A re-settled Europe ?
> There is no such prospect.[1]

For Liberals who felt like this, there was no way of escape.
They could only look on, with growing despair and no real will
to resist, as their party disintegrated and forces hostile to it
wrested power from the failing hands of Asquith and his semi-
Liberal regime.

VII

This survey of the effects of the war on the Liberal party would
not be complete if it was confined to the rank and file. For
the war also had a most adverse effect on the party's upper
strata. In a number of ways it helped to disrupt the group of
individuals who made up the Liberal leadership, destroying the
reputations of some and providing others with the chance to
enhance their positions by allying with their party's enemies,
so creating profound distrust between former close associates.
Hence by the end of the war the Liberal leadership, as a reasonably coherent body of individuals working generally together

[1] *Nation*, 2 December 1916.

in the interests of the party, had ceased to exist. Such leaders as the party retained were either elder statesmen apparently no longer in touch with the pressing issues of politics, or younger figures who had failed in the testing experience of the war. Those prominent Liberals who had improved their standing had also apparently severed their links with the main body of their party.

The extent to which this development injured Liberalism, and for that matter the part played by prominent individuals in the triumphs and failures of political parties, is open to dispute. But few would doubt that the disintegration of the body of outstanding leaders which the Liberal party possessed in 1914 was of substantial importance in its loss of confidence and public support. The defection of Lloyd George alone wrought it great harm. He had been heir apparent to the Liberal leadership and a driving force behind the social reforming movement in the pre-war Liberal government, and it was particularly damaging that he should become an object of distrust among Liberals who had been his personal followers and large sections of organised labour once sympathetic to his brand of liberalism. In part their antipathy was the result of his eager adoption, as explained earlier, of measures repugnant to orthodox Liberals. But this is not the whole explanation. Lloyd George, it appeared to many Liberals, welcomed the Tory embrace for its own sake, and not merely because he saw in Tory ideas the best way of winning the war; welcomed it, that is, because he realised that by forming an alliance with the Conservatives he could unseat Asquith and seize the premiership. In short, Liberal hostility sprang largely from the conviction that he was conspiring with the enemies of his party for his personal advantage.

What is to be said of this ? In the first place it is unnecessary to believe that Asquith fell from office simply because of an intrigue between Lloyd George and the right-wing press. Whatever Asquith's abilities as a wartime administrator, even some of his colleagues were critical of him. McKenna, usually considered a prime Asquithian (certainly he loathed Lloyd George), nevertheless voiced misgivings about his chief : he was reported in April 1916 as speaking of Asquith's " failure to come to decisions ", and as saying " that he would favour a change in the head of the Government if he could see an alternative."[1]   Curzon, a Conservative member of the first coalition who also disliked Lloyd George, wrote during the crisis of December 1916 : " we know that with [Asquith] as Chairman, either of the Cabinet or War Committee, it is absolutely impossible to win the War ".[2]   And Edmund Gosse, only a month before Asquith's fall, related that " one of [Asquith's] closest friends told me last night [that the Prime Minister] plays bridge *three times a day* ! "[3]   Now even if this information was correct, it might mean no more than that Asquith found in bridge-playing the relaxation which Churchill in a later war secured by after-lunch naps.   But clearly to the " close friend " it meant nothing of the sort.   He saw it as evidence of slackness and lethargy.   And his belief, whether justified or not, served to undermine his confidence in Asquith.   By contrast, Lloyd George from the outset revealed a prescience regarding the needs of the conflict and readiness to sound a note of stern resolve which equipped him for the role of war leader.   Thus, whatever the part Lloyd George played in Asquith's downfall, it was not by intriguing against his chief that he acquired the stature of potential leader of the nation.   At best, the " intriguing " was designed to convert potentiality into reality.

What however must be said is that during the war a situation developed in which Asquith required Lloyd George's support to remain in office, and that in ever-increasing degrees that support was withdrawn.   Far from attempting to defend his chief against traducers in parliament and the press, Lloyd George identified himself with the position of those who were denouncing Asquith to his advantage.   For example, when Simon criticised people who were constantly indulging in " sterile controversies " about the past and " unworthy panic " about the future, and another minister, McKinnon Wood, deplored the attitude of pessimists who never looked at what had been done but always at what had not,[4] they were speaking primarily against Asquith's critics in the press.   Yet the attitudes they condemned bore a striking resemblance to those publicly adopted by Lloyd George.

---

[1] *Lord Riddell's War Diary*, p. 172 (account by Robertson Nicoll of a conversation with McKenna).

[2] Lord Newton, *Lord Lansdowne*, p. 453.

[3] Gosse to Haldane, 31 October 1916, Haldane Papers.

[4] *Manchester Guardian*, 10 and 12 July 1915.

Further, Lloyd George never rebuked the newspapers which were denouncing his leader, or said that he would refuse the benefits which they were trying to secure him. His silence did not spring from reluctance to take issue with newspapers. In a speech at Conway on 6 May 1916 he furiously denounced a section of the press, " mischief makers " who should be stamped out and who had discharged " a wave of poison gas " at him. But the newspaper so described was not a right-wing journal campaigning against Asquith ; it was the Liberal, pro-Asquith *Daily News,* which had accused Lloyd George of disloyalty to his chief. The manner in which he assailed it made very apparent his failure to criticise Conservative papers which were abusing his leader while sparing him their strictures.

In short, the war having placed Lloyd George in a position to displace Asquith, he did not scruple to seize this opportunity for his advancement. In this respect it is quite beside the point to recall that in December 1916, following Asquith's resignation, he urged Bonar Law to take the premiership. By that time it had become, in part thanks to his activities, too unpleasant a post for anyone but himself to occupy (as well as being a position which large sections of the public and press considered him alone fitted to occupy). Bonar Law had already shown considerable alacrity in abandoning his claim to posts on which Lloyd George had set his heart, like the Ministry of Munitions in May 1915 and the War Office in June 1916. There was no likelihood in December 1916 that the Conservative leader would lay his neck on the chopping-block from which Asquith's head had just rolled. Had Lloyd George really been reluctant to occupy the premiership, he would have shown it during the long period when Asquith was being subjected to unprecedented attacks on his behalf. Far from doing so, he craved for power so blatantly that he aroused the distrust of nearly all the leading Conservatives. Indeed it required an incipient rebellion of Conservative back-benchers late in 1916 before Bonar Law was finally driven to align with him against Asquith.

As to the merits of Lloyd George's conduct in helping to expel his leader and the main body of Liberals from office, no final judgement is possible. Few will doubt that he was a better war leader than Asquith or that, however dubious his methods, he acted from motives of patriotism as well as self-interest.

There seems to have been as much conviction as calculation in his brief, striking appeal to Bonar Law on 2 December 1916, after Asquith had rejected their proposals : " The life of the country depends on resolute action by you now."[1] Yet it still appears that he might have attained effective control of the war without employing the methods he did, had he not been bent on discrediting and replacing, instead of working with, a leader to whom he was profoundly indebted. His contribution to Britain's war effort was outstanding, and yet in the course of it he helped to bring disaster on the Liberal party—a disaster far greater than it need have been had Lloyd George been a man of more scruple and a stronger sense of gratitude.

This is not to say that his ingratitude and lack of scruple were a product of the war. The overweening ambition, the instability of attachment to party and colleagues, and the friendliness towards a type of Conservative least trusted in Liberal circles, were all in evidence before 1914. But hitherto his schemes for a coalition with the Conservatives, and his hankering after an alliance with men like F. E. Smith, had proved abortive and even fanciful. It was the onset of war which made them practicable, and so brought out those facets of his many-sided personality which were to sever his connection with the Liberal party.

Lloyd George was not the only leading Liberal lost to the party at this time. Asquith's attempts to survive politically during the first two years of the war caused him to alienate some of his closest colleagues. This was especially true of Haldane and Churchill. To avoid a Conservative onslaught in May 1915, Asquith agreed to form a coalition in which Haldane was given no office and Churchill so minor an office that he resigned six months later. Both of them deeply resented his failure to stand by them, and neither was to join hands politically with him again. Certainly, Churchill's defection from the Liberal party might have occurred anyway : he was felt to share Lloyd George's political instability and leaning towards the Conservatives, and when war broke out preceded him in urging the formation of a coalition. Nevertheless, his separation from the Liberals was definitely encouraged by Asquith's con-

[1] Lord Beaverbrook, *Politicians and the War*, p. 406.

duct. And Haldane seems to have been lost principally because
of the treatment he received in May 1915. Driven out of
politics during the war, he proved ill-disposed thereafter to
accept Asquith's overtures to re-enter Liberal politics. Harold
Laski found him in 1921 " very anti-Asquith " on account of
the way he had been treated in 1915, and " conducting a twofold
flirtation, in part with the Labour party and in part with
Lloyd George."[1]   In due course the former " flirtation "
resulted in his entry into the Labour party and the first Labour
government.

The defection of leaders to other parties and political groupings was the clearest manifestation of the way in which the war
disintegrated the Liberal leadership. But the party was
further weakened by a sharp decline in the reputation of those
leaders who remained. Runciman's career was abruptly checked
by his failure to cope with shipping problems, Grey's was
profoundly injured by misfortunes in his wartime diplomacy,
and Augustine Birrell's was shattered beyond repair by the
effects of the war on the Irish situation. But the principal
casualty, especially in view of his standing in the party and
the country, was Asquith himself. When war broke out he was
regarded, for all his deficiencies, as a powerful figure adept at
resolving differences between ministers, and capable of decisive
action in at least some of the crises he encountered. By the
end of the war his reputation lay in ruins. He was widely
believed to have failed utterly in face of a great challenge, and
to have clung to office long after his deficiencies had become
apparent. To many who knew him, he seemed by the end of
the war a shadow of the leader of old, his grasp and will-power
shaken irrevocably by the personal loss he had suffered, the
venomous campaign waged against him, the active disloyalty
of some of his colleagues, the humiliating retreats to which he
had been driven, and the utter finality of his eventual expulsion
from office. In a sense Asquith more than anyone reflected the
fate of the Liberal party in the war years. Whereas leaders like
Lloyd George, Churchill, Haldane, Birrell, Morley, and Burns
had by 1918 departed into retirement or fresh political company,
Asquith was at least head of the party as he had been in 1914.
But with the falling-off in his powers and the air of ineffective-

[1] *Holmes-Laski Letters*, vol. 1, p. 314.

ness and almost non-participation which characterised his conduct, he scarcely resembled the leader who had broken the House of Lords and brought a nation united into war. Far from his retention of the leadership providing a ray of hope for his hard-pressed followers, it seemed almost a further handicap for a party weighed down by difficulties enough.

2. THE PROSPECT OF A COALITION

I call for a Vendetta—a vendetta against every German in Britain, whether " naturalised " or not. As I have said elsewhere, you cannot naturalise an unnatural beast—a human abortion—a hellish freak. But you *can* exterminate him. And now the time has come. . . .

I am ignoring the Government. This is a nation's job. I do not trust the Government—I do not trust Lord Haldane. I believe that if the Kaiser visited us to-day, they would give him a State reception.

> Horatio Bottomley (" *Now For The Vendetta!* ")
> in " *John Bull*", 15 May 1915

IN the short term, the Liberal party emerged relatively unscathed by the crisis attending the declaration of war. Both cabinet and party had been threatened with disruption during the first two days of August 1914, when scarcely a Liberal organisation met without passing a resolution favouring neutrality, and the list of Liberals opposing intervention was long and impressive. Then came the German ultimatum to Belgium and the impending subjection of Western Europe by "Prussian" militarism, and the Liberal government was saved. Only two ministers and one under-secretary resigned, and the flow of resolutions from Liberal bodies ceased altogether. Yet within nine months Asquith, against his declared intention and in consequence of an ultimatum from Bonar Law, was forced to dissolve the Liberal government and form a coalition with the Conservatives. This was a major event in the Liberal retreat. " I confess I have had a sleepless night of misery over H's decision of yesterday ", Margot Asquith wrote to Haldane. " Our *wonderful* Cabinet *gone* ! ! *Smashed* ! "[1] And Riddell wrote in his diary : " The Liberal party looks as if it were dead. . . . The Liberals are mad to see the prospect of a Coalition."[2]

Asquith's surrender in May 1915 showed that, despite his

[1] Margot Asquith to Haldane, 18 May 1915, Haldane Papers.
[2] *Lord Riddell's War Diary*, p. 88.

continued majority in the House of Commons (i.e. with Labour and Irish Nationalist support), the power of the Liberals had declined severely since the outbreak of war. There were several reasons for this. In the first place, as mentioned earlier, though the government survived the crisis of August 1914, the war cast a long shadow of gloom over its hopes and aspirations and caused a minor section of Liberals to go into opposition. Secondly, though hardly anyone had anticipated a war of such intensity, the government was soon being accused of failing to make sufficient preparation for the struggle. It was blamed in addition for the early setbacks of the war, particularly the munitions crisis on the western front and the bungled operation in the Dardanelles. And most of all, it was felt to lack the grip, the *élan*, and the determination which the conflict demanded. This feeling was expressed by the *Manchester Guardian* when it discussed Lloyd George's abortive attempt at wartime control of the liquor traffic :

> One thing is pretty clear [it said on 1 May 1915]. Mr. Lloyd George, to whose bold and contriving mind had been entrusted the preparation of the measure, would have produced something worthy of the Government and of the occasion. Unhappily he failed to convince the majority of his colleagues, and thus it comes about that we are left with only the remains of what should have been a great measure.
>
> . . . The fact that the Government has not dared to challenge the nation to rise above itself is one among many signs that, in spite of loud lip professions and sounding expressions of resolve to put the war through, the war is, in fact, not being taken seriously. . . . How can any slacker be blamed when the Government itself is slack ?

Eleven days later it returned to this question. The government having failed to take up the challenge of liquor,

> will they give us more of energy, initiative, and organisation in the equipment and the preparation of war ? We have little sympathy with the personal attacks which have disfigured certain portions of the press. But the nation recognises one or two men in the Government and in the Opposition who appear to show resource, resolution, and leadership. These men it will have to guide it. . . .

What was required, it said on 19 May when the coalition was being formed, was not merely a change of men but a change of spirit—" an altogether new degree of energy, resolution, and courage."

The difficulties encountered by the government suggest that in part the Liberals were simply unlucky to be in power at this time. Any government holding office prior to the war and during its disillusioning first months was likely to be accused of inadequate preparation for the struggle, and to be assailed by problems over munitions and strategy—not to mention personal difficulties with Lords Kitchener and Fisher. And the criticisms levelled at Asquith might have proved equally applicable to Bonar Law, who rarely shone forth as a dynamic or far-sighted leader. Yet in one respect the Liberals laboured under a major disadvantage from which a Conservative government would have been exempt. The Conservatives, in or out of office, remained peculiarly the party of nationalism and " patriotism ", the party that was expected to show capacity in running a war. The Liberals were identified with principles like internationalism and free trade which caused them —however unjustly—to be considered over-sympathetic to pacifists and aliens, and lacking in the nationalistic fervour necessary for wartime government. That is, they were frequently regarded as being, by their very nature, ill-equipped to conduct a war. The way in which the prevailing frenzy over spies and aliens was employed as a weapon for belabouring ministers showed what a handicap their liberal inheritance could be at such a time.

In sum, from early in the conflict the Liberal government found itself in serious difficulties—greater difficulties than a Conservative regime would have encountered in identical circumstances. But one factor emerged at the same time which should have proved to the Liberals' advantage : the qualities of wartime leadership revealed by Lloyd George. The *Manchester Guardian,* said, without noticeable exaggeration, on 20 May 1915 (by which time Asquith was re-forming his government) :

No Ministry now formed can hope to render its full service to the nation which does not give full and free scope to the contriving genius and the powerful initiative of Mr. Lloyd George. . . . For the particular work which now above

all needs to be done—the organisation of the whole industrial resources of the nation for the purposes of the war—
there is no one in or out of office who can approach him in
capacity.

This was a scarcely-anticipated element in the situation which
might have gone far to offset the difficulties of the Liberals.
For if Lloyd George was an essential member of any wartime
government, then presumably his party must remain dominant
while the war lasted.

Yet this proved to be anything but the case. The reason
was Lloyd George's tenuous association with the Liberal party.
He was bent on advancing both the war effort and his political
career, and mobile in his party allegiance if it meant furthering
either. Even before the war he was considered insecurely
attached to his party and spoken of as a likely successor to
Joseph Chamberlain,[1] who had begun as a Liberal social reformer
and then deserted to the enemy. It was common knowledge
that in 1908 Lloyd George compelled Asquith to make him
Chancellor of the Exchequer by threatening to take his political
services elsewhere,[2] and Morley even then warned Asquith to
beware of a " stab in the back " from Lloyd George.[3] One
sign of the instability of his party allegiance was his craving
for a coalition. In 1910, when the House of Lords crisis was
at its height, he had put forward an incredible scheme for a
coalition government whose programme would include a form
of compulsory military service.

The war opened a new phase in Lloyd George's career, by
creating a situation in which he possessed essential qualities
lacking in Asquith. These qualities he did not employ to
strengthen the Liberal government but to further the formation
of a coalition in which he would have the Conservatives as allies.
Already by the end of 1914 he was profoundly dissatisfied with
the way his colleagues were conducting the war and more than
ready to make this known to the Conservatives, so weakening
the government and encouraging its opponents to attack it.
For several months before the Liberal government's fall he

[1] cf. A. G. Gardiner, *Prophets, Priests, and Kings*, pp. 129–37.
[2] E. T. Raymond, *Mr. Lloyd George*, p. 104, says : " A certain antagonism
between the two statesmen dates from this time."
[3] So Morley told Laski in 1920 ; *Holmes-Laski Letters*, vol. 1, pp. 278–9.

was " believed to favour a Coalition,"[1] and a number of his supporters were publicly agitating for it. F. Handel Booth, an erratic, jingoist Liberal who had defended Lloyd George with much partisanship on the Marconi Committee in 1913, spoke out in favour of a coalition in February and May 1915. And on the evening of 17 May (in effect the last day of the Liberal government) Sir Henry Dalziel, a newspaper proprietor and Liberal M.P. very friendly to Lloyd George, called for a coalition government to direct the country through this " national crisis ".[2] His wishes were already being met. Earlier that day Bonar Law had gone to Asquith and demanded a coalition as the only alternative to a Conservative assault on the government, and he had done so in company with Lloyd George—an embryo coalition in itself, particularly as Lloyd George (according to Churchill) threatened resignation if Asquith did not agree.[3]

So Lloyd George's great abilities in war, far from helping the Liberal government, contributed to its fall. He was so detached from most of his colleagues that his achievements did not redound to their credit but rather highlighted their short-comings, thus enhancing the case for a new government in which his talents would be better supported.

II

The change of government was not merely a Liberal retreat. It was a triumph in party warfare for the Conservatives. This has been obscured by the circumstances in which the change took place.

It is usual to attribute the formation of the coalition to a double crisis in the war ; or rather, since the appearance of Beaverbrook's *Politicians and the War,* to attribute it to one crisis and deny the importance of the other. The two crises were the " shell scandal ", that is the alleged shortage of munitions on the western front, and the resignation of Fisher, the First Sea Lord, on account of his dislike of the Dardanelles operation originated by Churchill, the First Lord of the Admir-

[1] *New Statesman,* 22 May 1915.   [2] *H. C. Deb.,* 71, 2104–5.
[3] Churchill called Lloyd George " the powerful politician whose action had compelled the formation of the Coalition ". (*The World Crisis,* vol. 2, pp. 365, 383.)

alty. Beaverbrook and his followers argue that the first crisis was not important at this stage, and did not become a public issue until after the coalition was formed. According to Mr. Robert Blake, by the time the shell scandal became a matter of public outcry " the Liberal Cabinet was already dead." [1] This view has been accepted by non-Beaverbrook historians, Mr. Roy Jenkins saying that the " situation at the Admiralty and not the shell crisis . . . was the real cause of the fall of the Liberal Government "—a statement endorsed by Asquith's daughter. [2]

Yet the argument from chronology has no substance. There is plenty of evidence that the shell shortage was a live issue before the Liberal government fell. Bonar Law (and not only he) made strong reference to the matter a month earlier : " It is common knowledge—I knew it not as guess-work, but as knowledge—that were short of ammunition months ago."[3] And on 17 May, almost as the change of government was taking place, there was an anguished discussion in Parliament about the lack of munitions. According to Handel Booth : " We are all thinking of a certain position. . . . If you could look inside the hearts of most hon. Members of this House to-day, you would find that the one word impressed upon them was the word ' shells.' "[4] And Asquith that day wrote a memorandum, stating his reasons for the change of government, in which he gave the shell shortage equal weight with the Fisher resignation. A coalition was necessary, he said, in order to avoid the threatened parliamentary attack over the " resignation of Lord Fisher, which I have done my best to avert, and the more than plausible parliamentary case in regard to the alleged deficiency of high-explosive shells ".[5]

But the point that needs to be stressed here is that it was not the actual crises which drove Asquith to form a coalition, but the use which the Conservatives were threatening to make of them. And this was only the latest phase in a Conservative campaign against the government. Asquith wrote that " for some time past " he had been coming to the conclusion that it

[1] Robert Blake, *The Unknown Prime Minister*, p. 241.

[2] Roy Jenkins, *Asquith*, p. 355, and review by Lady Violet Bonham Carter in *The Times*, 2 November 1964.

[3] *H. C. Deb.*, 71, 326 (21 April 1915).   [4] *ibid*, 2107.

[5] Asquith Papers.

would be necessary to form " a ' broad-based ' Government ". His reason was that : " Under existing conditions, criticism, inspired by party motives and interests, has full rein, and is an asset of much value to the enemy." On the same day J. A. Pease, the Minister of Education, reported that " quite apart from the Winston-Fisher episodes " Asquith had been feeling for quite a while that he would " be compelled to make the Tories assume a share of responsibility because of the horrible campaign now being carried on by the Harmsworth and other papers."[1] And the *Liberal Magazine* for June 1915 attributed the change of government both to the crises in the war, and to the contemptuous disregard shown by a section of the Conservative press for the party truce.

The war had provided the Conservatives with a splendid opportunity for their political advancement. Of it they were not slow to take advantage. Admittedly they agreed to a political truce regarding by-elections which they maintained to the end of the war. But from early in the conflict a section of Conservative M.P.s, and much of the right-wing press, embarked on a form of party warfare by making crude and often ill-founded attacks on particular ministers. These ministers they harried mercilessly and maliciously. Haldane, their prime victim, was accused of a shameful fondness for the Germans, as shown by the fact that he had in the past sought an accommodation with Germany. Churchill was condemned for illegitimate interference in naval matters. And McKenna was thought to lack zeal in the hunt against enemy aliens. Before long the attack included Asquith as well, and by April 1915 the *Liberal Magazine,* a judicious and responsible journal for all its party origin, felt called to complain :

> It is not easy at times to remember or to believe that the Party Truce is still in existence. We have no complaint to make of the Unionist leaders or organisations, but in no small or unimportant section of the Unionist Press attacks and criticisms on the Government are being made, the clear object of which is, if possible, not to help towards winning the war, but to discredit Liberal Ministers.

By the time this was written the press campaign was seeking not merely to injure ministers but to bring about a reconstruc-

[1] Addison, *Four and a Half Years,* vol. 1, pp. 78–9.

tion of the government, so that Asquith would lose office and Lloyd George take his place.

Initially, as the *Liberal Magazine* stated (with almost excessive impartiality), this campaign against ministers did not emanate from the Conservative leaders but from the right-wing press and irresponsible back-benchers like W. Joynson-Hicks. Indeed Bonar Law complained of the difficulties of an opposition " at a time like this " when it was necessary " to put aside all ordinary party considerations and to think only of the interests of the country ", and stated that he was being " constantly criticised by my own friends, in letters, because we do not criticise the Government enough."[1]   Yet if he did not lead the attack on Liberal ministers, neither did he repudiate or openly discourage it.   As was so often the case, Bonar Law seemed content to follow at a distance those he was supposedly leading, avoiding the excesses of his more vociferous supporters yet never becoming separated from them.   At the beginning of 1915 he was at pains to say that he was not in the government's confidence or responsible for its decisions, and thereafter, although less extreme than some of his supporters, he echoed their denunciations of ministers.   He joined in the attack on McKenna over the aliens question, criticised Asquith for complacency in contrast with Lloyd George, and in the end involved himself completely in his followers' insensate crusade against Haldane and Churchill.   So when he abruptly threatened a Conservative onslaught on the government if Asquith did not agree to a coalition, he was not executing an about-turn from party truce to party warfare.   His action marked the point at which a series of attacks on ministers culminated in an attack on the ministry as such.

The principal historians of Bonar Law's career, Beaverbrook and Mr. Blake, have rather ignored the element of party warfare evident in these actions, particularly in his conduct towards Haldane. They have been concerned to present him in a more favourable light than Asquith, whom they argue was, unlike Bonar Law, influenced by considerations of narrow party advantage when forming the coalition. It is not easy to admit such a difference between the two leaders. Bonar Law's treatment of Haldane constituted party politics in its crudest form,

[1] *H. C. Deb*, 71, 324 (21 April 1915).

and there can be little doubt that Asquith was profoundly influenced by this example. It was said that his " one betrayal of open bitterness of feeling in the recent crisis " occurred when he realised that he would have to concede the Conservatives' demand for Haldane's exclusion. " Poor Henry he wept to me when he told me," Margot Asquith wrote to Haldane.[1]

Mr. Blake, in his biography of Bonar Law, makes slight reference to this inglorious incident. Haldane, he tells us, " had once observed that Germany was his spiritual home, referring in fact to the cloudy metaphysicians of that country, to whose works he was addicted ; but this was a fatal admission to have made, now that public feeling condemned everyone who had ever, in any context, spoken well of Germany. Bonar Law made his exclusion an absolute condition [of forming the coalition government] ".[2] Contrary to this, it was not remotely the case that " public feeling condemned everyone who had ever, in any context, spoken well of Germany." Bonar Law himself, not in the more spacious days before the war but after the outbreak of hostilities, had announced that he was not ashamed to say he had always been fond of German literature, and had loved the old German spirit of which it was the expression. Only at the beginning of that year (1914), he went on, he had taken one of his sons to Germany to learn its language and literature.[3] No tirades of abuse fell on the author of these remarks from the *Daily Mail* or *Daily Express*, and no one expected that they would. The press campaign, far from condemning every manifestation of sympathy for Germany, was quite selective in its choice of victims, and one of the principles of selection was party interest—the denigration of important Liberals so as to undermine the Liberal regime. If Asquith sometimes acted from party motives when constructing the new ministry, he was only following a precedent set by Bonar Law when, for no reason except party, he made Haldane's exclusion " an absolute condition " of forming the government at all.

It may of course be argued that these attacks on Liberal

---

[1] *Manchester Guardian*, 27 May 1915 ; Margot Asquith to Haldane, 24 May 1915, Haldane Papers.

[2] Blake, *The Unknown Prime Minister*, p. 252.

[3] *Liberal Magazine*, October 1914.

ministers, culminating in the attack on the Liberal government, were not motivated by a desire for party advantage but by concern for the national welfare. Yet even Bonar Law's sympathisers have hardly suggested that the war effort was advanced by the expulsion from office of Haldane and Churchill. And it is difficult to believe that, without the stimulus of long-standing party rancour, the Conservatives would have thought otherwise. The Lancashire Conservative leader, Lord Derby, admitted as much in a letter to Grey, who had protested against the attacks on Haldane. Haldane, Derby conceded, " is very much disliked by my own political party."

> Although all hatchets are for the moment buried one cannot entirely forget all that went on before this War broke out [a statement which seems to mean that although all hatchets had been buried, some remained unburied]. I think the chief reason for the attack on him at the present moment is due to this feeling of resentment against him.[1]

And whatever the motives behind this campaign against ministers—be it disinterested patriotism, or wartime hysteria, or party gain, or a mixture of all three—it certainly benefited the Conservative party at the expense of the Liberals. Its culmination in the fall of the Liberal government constituted a major victory for the Conservatives and a decisive stage in the Liberal decline.

III

There is much evidence of the dismay caused in the Liberal ranks by the formation of the coalition. Even before Haldane's fate was known there occurred a dangerous revolt of Liberal back-benchers, and Asquith, as related earlier,[2] had to be called in to suppress it. This he was able to do by a strong personal appeal and a threat of resignation. But the discontent remained. " Although there will be no revolt of Liberal members," it was reported, " it must not be inferred that they are satisfied. A great many—perhaps a majority—believe that if the Prime Minister had chosen to use his strength he could have defied the critics of the Government and have crushed all opposition. Among Liberal intellectuals there is a melancholy feeling, very

---

[1] G. M. Trevelyan, *Grey of Fallodon*, p. 276.   [2] See above, p. 40.

frankly expressed, that this is probably the end of the Liberal party for many years to come."[1]   A month later Pease, who had failed to secure a post in the new government, wrote :

> Politically things are settling down a bit but the rank & file of our party resent the way the Coalition came about & suspect Lloyd George had meetings with the opposition & Fisher *before* the P.M. adopted the new policy behind the backs of his colleagues and party.

> There may be a good deal to be said in favour of a non party Government but the way it was brought about looked as if individuals in both parties had been playing for their own hand rather than their countrys interest.[2]

Liberal resentment came to centre, naturally enough, on the treatment of Haldane, who of a sudden found himself " more popular than I ever was with the Liberal Party." Liberals representing every section and viewpoint, including some not particularly friendly to him in the past, signed an address (still preserved in his papers) which praised his contribution to war preparations and deplored his retirement from office.[3]   In addition, Liberal associations sent him " wonderful resolutions ", and a gathering was held in his honour at the National Liberal Club.   There he received a " magnificent reception ": " The hall was packed half an hour before the time. . . .   The Prime Minister wrote a fine letter.   But the real thing was the welcome & the feeling shown.   I never have been in such a position as at present."[4]   The reason for this feeling is clear.   As one Liberal wrote to Haldane : " you have been hounded out of office by your political enemies.   This, at any rate, is how it appears to most Liberals."[5]

One individual who recognised the damage done to the party by the change of government was Lord Murray of Elibank, who a few years before had been an outstanding chief whip.   The present whip, John Gulland, was not in the same

---

[1] *Manchester Guardian*, 20 May 1915.

[2] Pease to A. C. Murray, 19 June 1915, Elibank Papers.

[3] Among the few Conservatives who, most nobly, wrote to Haldane in similar terms was W. M. Aitken—an act which Aitken (later Lord Beaverbrook) was not wont to recall during his subsequent adulation of Bonar Law.

[4] Haldane to his mother, 15 and 26 June and 6 July 1915, Haldane Papers.

[5] F. Maddison to Haldane, 19 May 1915, Haldane Papers.

class, and Murray, as tactfully as possible, tried to convince him of the seriousness of the situation.

I called to see you on Saturday morning [Murray wrote to Gulland] to tell you that some personal friends of mine in the House, particularly Oswald Partington, had, of their own initiative, told me of the very awkward feeling there is in the Party at this moment towards the P.M. and L.G. Partington was particularly anxious that I should lay the matter before the P.M. and yourself. . . .

My own personal opinion, for what it is worth, is that you should hold a Party Meeting in order to rekindle the personal touch between the Prime Minister and his supporters, both in the House of Commons and the House of Lords. I discussed this matter confidentially with the P.M., Edwin Montagu, [Lord] Reading and [Sir Francis] Hopwood. . . . Hopwood, Reading, Edwin Montagu and Eric Drummond are of the opinion that nothing but good could come of such a meeting. . . .

When I was in Scotland the other day, old Radicals said to me : " Why doesn't the Prime Minister come out and tell us what to do and what he wants ? All we hear of is an Indignation Meeting against him behind closed doors, where he is supposed to have made a good impression." Such a Meeting was, of course, a Defensive Meeting, and I am told that it has by no means allayed the irritation that prevails. . . .

As an old friend and colleague of yours, brought up in the atmosphere of the Whips' Room, I cannot help thinking that such a Meeting will very considerably strengthen your own hands in dealing with the extraordinary difficulties that are ahead of you.

Murray concluded by appealing to Gulland to " make use of that wonderful personal magnetism, which I used to find so effective when I was in a difficulty, namely, the personal touch and hold that the P.M. has over his own people when they are brought together."[1]

No meeting took place. Murray recounted the fact in a letter to his brother :

I have been rather in favor of [Asquith's] holding a short

[1] Murray to Gulland, 14 June 1915, Elibank Papers.

Party Meeting, to call upon his men in the two Houses and the country to give their full and unstinted support to himself and the New Government . . . . it is a mistake with the Liberal Party to take " everything for granted ". He was very much inclined to agree with me. . . . Gulland, however, who came back on Monday from his week-end, and Geoffrey Howard, thought the meeting was unnecessary, as it was now rather late, and therefore I do not think it will take place. As a matter of fact, it was really not too late, because he only finished forming his Administration last Friday. . . . I think it is his duty to meet his own people who have supported him all these years, when one Government disappears and another takes its place. Such a meeting would also give L.G. an opportunity of killing the gossip to the effect that he and the Northcliffe Press are working for disintegration. You know well the groundless gossip that gathers force and volume if not immediately dealt with. . . .

I never regarded our two friends in the Whips' Room (J.G. and G.H.) as having good political noses for a situation, but perhaps during the last 3 years they may have developed the political instinct which they previously did not possess. O.P., with his knowledge of Yorkshire and Lancashire, is very strongly of the opinion that such a Meeting ought to have been held.[1]

Although Murray did not say so, this incident revealed Asquith's growing failure to lead or keep contact with his followers. The Prime Minister was under no obligation to accept Gulland's advice against his own judgement. But with the immediate crisis past, he seemed happy to evade an important but difficult undertaking. Whether from absorption in other matters, or inclination to follow the line of least resistance, Asquith during these years neglected to rally his shaken party by exercising his " wonderful personal magnetism".

IV

Why did Asquith give in to the demand for a coalition ? Probably because he recognised that otherwise his chances of retain-

[1] Murray to A. C. Murray, 15 June 1915, Elibank Papers.

ing office were poor. Bonar Law made this point nine days
later : they had felt, he told a Conservative meeting, that the
Liberal government had been losing its hold on the country,
and one course they could have followed was to wait for the
fruit of government to drop into their hands. Whether or not
in stressing the Liberals' failing hold " on the country " he was
referring obliquely to a general election, it was here that his
strength ultimately lay. Even had Asquith been able to withstand a Conservative attack in Parliament, he had little prospect,
in view of the government's loss of prestige since the war (not
to mention before the war), of surviving an appeal to the country.
What part this played in his calculations is problematical, but
it is unlikely that, in the last year of a Parliament which could
not be prolonged without his opponents' consent, the question
of an election was ever far from his mind. Certainly during
the next three years he was a consistent opponent of an appeal
to the country—a noteworthy indication not only of the Liberal
party's decline but of its consciousness of decline. The election
which he was seeking to ward off as late as November 1918
menaced him almost from the first year of the war, for the
House of Commons elected at the end of 1910 could only run
beyond its statutory five years with the consent of the ultra-
Conservative Upper House. Should he reject Bonar Law's
demand for a coalition and decide to stand and fight, the House
of Lords could force him to hold an election which hardly anyone
expected his government to survive.

More than this, perhaps for all its distasteful features a
coalition possessed some attractions for Asquith. With
Britain's most famous soldier in its midst his government was
already something of a coalition. Kitchener of course had been
made War Secretary for military reasons, but he brought to
the ministry a conservative element which for a while restrained
right-wing criticisms. This semi-immunity soon disappeared
owing to Kitchener's inadequacy for his task, which was readily
exposed by individuals like Northcliffe seeking from the war their
own advancement. But by absorbing more Conservatives into
the government and making them responsible for the conduct
of the war, Asquith might recover the shield from attack which
Kitchener ultimately had failed to provide. At the same time
he would be countering attempts to make Lloyd George Prime

Minister by depriving him of an organised opposition with whom he might ally. And while doing this, Asquith would be retaining the premiership and preserving for his party a majority —however precarious—of offices.

But if he did hope that the unpleasantness of forming a coalition would be offset by some advantages, he was soon to be disillusioned. From the outset the coalition proved a barren experiment which probably damaged his party far more than would the outright loss of office. Admittedly he remained Prime Minister for another eighteen months, but the extent of his discredit at the end of 1916 was to be far greater than in mid-1915. And he had been sadly mistaken when he believed that he could abolish " the horrible campaign now being carried on by the Harmsworth and other papers " by bringing the Conservatives into his government. The press campaign had all along been selective in its choice of victims (had not the *Liberal Magazine* said of Lloyd George in February 1915 that " all men speak well of him " ?). Once the coalition was formed these newspapers did not cease their attacks but simply carried further the process of selectivity, denouncing the Asquith government but seeking an alternative ministry from within it. By the same token, Asquith had not eliminated the threat from Lloyd George. There was now no organised party outside the government with whom the latter might coalesce, but there was a Conservative element in the government which, if associated with him, could force its will upon the cabinet or offer itself as an alternative administration.

But the crucial failing of the new government was its lack of any certain following in the country or the House of Commons. The few Liberals pleased with Asquith's action were principally those on the right of the party who were becoming separated from himself and inclined to favour further Conservative inroads into the government. And while Asquith was sacrificing Liberal enthusiasm, he was certainly not acquiring the loyalty of the Conservatives. As Bonar Law's metaphor suggested, they believed that before long the whole " fruit " of government might have been theirs, and they were less grateful for what Asquith had surrendered in the fierce bargaining over offices than resentful at what he had retained. He had been forced to abandon Haldane, but he had kept McKenna, another victim of Conservative wrath, and had even elevated him to the Chancellorship of the Exchequer. McKenna was recognised as " one of Mr. Asquith's men ", so that his promotion could be taken to show that Asquith still " counts [for] more than anybody else in the Government, whatever gossip may say."[1] Again, if he had been obliged to give the Ministry of Munitions, on which all attention centred, to Lloyd George (whom many observers expected would supplant him " before long "),[2] he had succeeded in relegating Bonar Law to a relatively unimportant position. It is not surprising that this arrangement failed to satisfy the Conservatives, or that after their display of party warfare they would not support unreservedly a government which retained so large a Liberal element. Indeed the principal outcome of the change of government was that the Liberals remained in a sufficiently eminent position to warrant attack, without any longer possessing the resources of support or enthusiasm indefinitely to withstand it.

[1] *Manchester Guardian*, 26 May 1915.

[2] *ibid.* The *Manchester Guardian*'s political correspondent wrote : " I think it right to mention here a very strong rumour that we may before long see another great change in the present Government, and that Mr. Asquith may retire from the Premiership and be succeeded by Mr. Lloyd George."

3. "THE MOST INCOMPETENT ADMINISTRATION"

I only wish the Prime Minister would be strong. The Sunday papers had a caricature yesterday of Ll. George coming into his room where he was asleep and stealing his crown.

Haldane to his mother, 12 July 1915 [1]

FROM the outset, the Asquith coalition was beset by crippling difficulties. It was unable to produce any radical improvement in the course of the war : during 1915 stalemate continued on the western front, the Dardanelles expedition had to be abandoned, the situation on the Russian front deteriorated alarmingly, and Serbia was overrun. The last of these setbacks caused particular dismay in Britain, for it appeared partly to have been caused by divisions in British strategy and shortcomings in Grey's diplomacy ; and it cost the government, among other things, the services of Carson, who resigned after only five months of office. By the end of 1915 the *Liberal Magazine* was admitting itself " conscious of the disappointments of the year that is now over," and commenting : " We have made the mistakes which would seem to be inseparable from the conduct of war, we have not achieved in 1915 what we had too confidently reckoned on achieving before the year was out ; but 1916 finds us undismayed ".

Just as outside events dogged the new government, so did disruptive issues of policy. " The attempt to stampede the country into conscription ", complained the *Manchester Guardian* when the coalition was not a fortnight old, " is now in full swing."[2] The addition of a group of conscriptionists to the government gave fresh stimulus to those who wanted compulsion either for industry or the army, and it correspondingly alarmed

---

[1] Haldane Papers.   [2] *Manchester Guardian*, 1 June 1915.

Liberals to whom such proposals meant " the moral defeat of the British system and the victory of German methods ".[1] Thus it only required a minister to speak critically of the voluntary system of recruiting, as did Lord Lansdowne in July 1915, for the government to be thrown into a turmoil. Further, there were personal as well as policy divisions. Precipitated by a Conservative ultimatum, and only completed after weeks of haggling over offices, the coalition did not easily cohere. For a month or more, ministers from the two principal parties usually sat in separate groups on the treasury benches, and it often happened that when a minister from one party addressed the House no ministers from the other party were present to hear him.[2]

Nor did the personal problems of the coalition end here. From early in its existence it was widely believed that Lloyd George intended to break up the government and seize the premiership himself. Certainly his actions were calculated to make its survival difficult. It was he, and not any Conservative minister, who precipitated its embarrassments over conscription. In his first public address as Minister of Munitions, at Manchester on 3 June, he stressed that industrial conscription might in time become necessary, and that although military conscription was not required as yet he accepted it in principle. For all the undoubted merits of these opinions, it was no help to a divided government to publicise them like this. As the *Nation*, until recently his warm supporter, remarked angrily on 5 June :

> Mr. Lloyd George has done for the Government of 1915 what Mr. Chamberlain did for the Government of 1902. He has forced its hand on compulsory service, as Mr. Chamberlain forced the earlier Ministry's hand on Protection. The first Chamberlain did not get Protection, but he broke up his Government. The second may accomplish a similar or a reduced result. Mr. George works on the malleable material of a Coalition, but even such a body may call for some method and deliberation of procedure. We are not aware that the Coalition Cabinet has as yet come to any decision on the policy of putting workmen under martial law, or has even completed an inquiry into it. Why, there-

[1] *ibid*, 29 May 1915.   [2] *ibid*, 30 July 1915.

fore, does Mr. George foreshadow such action or announce his own conversion to it ? That is not government by Cabinet. It is *Daily Mail* statesmanship.

The quality of Lloyd George's statesmanship did not, in the opinion of this journal, rise in the following weeks. At the beginning of July 1915, he shocked the *Nation*—and the Prime Minister—by his treatment of a cabinet colleague. His close associate Dalziel, who was recognised as acting on " pretty high inspirations ",[1] launched an attack on von Donop, the Master General of Ordnance, which was by implication an attack on Kitchener himself. Lloyd George in replying was expected to defend the War Minister, but he did not. He simply said that if he had any trouble with the War Office " I shall without any hesitation, and even without any consideration of etiquette, report the matter to the House of Commons ".[2] When Haldane, now an ex-minister, sought to repair this disloyalty to both a public servant and a cabinet colleague, he was publicly attacked by Lloyd George for doing so. (Margot Asquith told Haldane that this caused a " row " between her husband and Lloyd George). Similar embarrassments continued through the following months. In September, as Parliament was about to re-assemble after the summer recess, Lloyd George gave the newspapers a " preface " he had written for a forthcoming edition of his war speeches.[3] In its scarcely-veiled advocacy of immediate conscription for both army and factory, and in its demand for less hesitancy and postponement in the making of vital decisions, this document seemed to the *New Statesman* " practically an appeal to the country against his colleagues ", and to be clearly intended to precipitate a ministerial crisis.[4] And as the session of Parliament began, so it ended. In December 1915, on the eve of the recess, Lloyd George created " a parliamentary sensation "[5] by offering a series of comments on the course of the war which, to some of his listeners, would

---

[1] *ibid*, 3 July 1915.

[2] *H. C. Deb.*, 72,2104 (1 July 1915). Asquith considered Lloyd George's conduct " quite inexcusable." (Asquith to Crewe, 4 July 1915, Asquith Papers).

[3] The " preface " appeared in the press on 13 September 1915, the day before Parliament met, although the book containing it was not available until early October.

[4] *New Statesman*, 18 September 1915.

[5] *Manchester Guardian*, 21 December 1915.

have come more appropriately from the mover of a vote of censure than from a member of the government :

> Too late in moving here [Lloyd George lamented]. Too late in arriving there. Too late in coming to this decision. Too late in starting with enterprises. Too late in preparing. In this War the footsteps of the Allied forces have been dogged by the mocking spectre of " Too late "; and unless we quicken our movements damnation will fall on the sacred cause for which so much gallant blood has flowed.[1]

" That", wrote Lloyd George nearly two decades later, " summed up my considered opinion at the time on the muddled campaign of 1915. That is my judgement to-day ".[2] It may very well prove to be the judgement of history. But by expressing it in this way he was clearly hampering the survival of what one dissident Liberal called " the utterly incapable Government of which he is a member."[3]

How then did such a coalition survive its divisions and difficulties for more than eighteen months ? Two general causes seem to have preserved it. First, Lloyd George hesitated to break with the government until he was certain of his relations with the Conservative leaders. Secondly, Asquith's anxiety to retain office caused him to back down whenever the rebels in the cabinet reached the point of actually deserting him.

As to the first of these, it is clear that the formation of the coalition did not foster the alliance between Lloyd George and the Conservative leaders which had been developing on 17 May 1915. Instead, it subjected it to severe strain. Both Beaverbrook and Mr. Blake stress the point that the Conservative leaders found Lloyd George at close quarters a disturbing and unattractive companion, for all their agreement with him on matters of policy.[4] Bonar Law, in June 1916, berated him to his face for his ambition and self-seeking, and Austen Chamberlain, just after Lloyd George had become Prime Minister,

---

[1] *H. C. Deb.*, 77,121 (20 December 1915). These remarks were not delivered without careful reflection ; Lloyd George had discussed the " too late " passage with Riddell two days earlier (*Lord Riddell's War Diary*, pp. 143–4).

[2] David Lloyd George, *War Memoirs*, vol. 1, p. 529.

[3] *Manchester Guardian*, 24 December 1915. The author of these views was J. Annan Bryce, Liberal member for Inverness.

[4] Beaverbrook, *Politicians and the War*, pp. 205–8 ; Blake, *The Unknown Prime Minister*, pp. 281–2, 296.

remarked that he took "no pleasure in a change which gives me a chief whom I profoundly distrust—no doubt a man of great energy but quite untrustworthy." Lloyd George, Chamberlain said, "has tired out the patience of every man who has worked with him and most of those who have worked for him ; " he "let his Unionist colleagues down about conscription at the critical moment and then took up the question again when he thought the audience more favourable and the limelight more concentrated on himself."[1] On the other hand the Conservative leaders found McKenna, whom they had freely denounced when they sat opposite him, a more acceptable colleague than his predecessor at the Exchequer, even though they were often at odds with him on questions of policy.

Meanwhile Lloyd George can have been in no doubt about the extent of his estrangement from large sections of the Liberal party and of organised labour. The Liberals "are very disgruntled with L.G.", J. A. Spender said in June 1915. "The Liberal Party are angry with him ", Reading admitted the next month.[2] This meant that he lacked the sure support of any party. As a consequence he could not afford to abandon office. When Carson and Churchill did so and became leaders of small opposition groups in Parliament, they proved to be weakly placed to gain power. They afforded him a warning, if any were needed, that he should not leave office without securing the support not only of the Conservative rank and file but more especially of the leaders and organisation of the Conservative party. So for all his disruptive activities within the coalition, he would not go as far as resigning except on an issue which would oblige the Conservative leaders to do the same. The Irish crisis of July 1916 illustrates this. On the morrow of the Easter Rebellion, the cabinet appointed Lloyd George to seek a settlement of the Irish problem. With great resource he got a scheme accepted both by John Redmond and the Irish Nationalist movement, and by Carson and his followers in Ulster. But in the cabinet, Lansdowne and a few other Tory diehards threatened to resign if the terms were not modified.

[1] Sir Charles Petrie, *The Life and Letters of the Right Hon. Sir Austen Chamberlain*, vol. 2, p. 63. Chamberlain, it will be recalled, in 1922 forfeited both the premiership and the leadership of his party out of loyalty to Lloyd George.

[2] *Lord Riddell's War Diary*, pp. 104, 113.

Under this pressure Asquith abandoned the settlement which Lloyd George had achieved and substituted fresh terms which Redmond could not possibly accept. Lloyd George was disgusted with Asquith's behaviour—" He is very sick with the P.M. over the way he has messed up the Irish business "[1]—but he did not resign. His tame surrender to a " little aristocratic clique "[2] was contrasted unfavourably in Liberal circles with the way in which, on other occasions, he had forced his will on a majority of the cabinet and his own party. But the point was that this was an issue on which he could not hope to take the Conservative leaders with him. Bonar Law would not have followed him out of office simply because Asquith, under Tory pressure, had gone back on an agreement with Redmond.[3]

Conscription, on the other hand, was potentially much more dangerous. If Lloyd George chose to resign on this issue the Conservative leaders, in view of the conscriptionist leanings of their party even in peacetime, could hardly have avoided doing the same. Yet the government survived this issue also, for the second of the reasons suggested above : Asquith and most other Liberal ministers eventually conceded enough to prevent the conscriptionists from resigning. No doubt self-defence was part of their reason for doing so. If the government broke up on this issue, the anti-conscriptionists would have little hope of staying in office. Yet considerations of political survival do not wholly account for their surrender. In war, the Asquithians occupied no certain position of principle on conscription. However reluctantly, most of them were prepared to concede it to incontestable military necessity. Yet as long as they possessed no sure criterion of such necessity, and admitted that they might accept conscription sometime, were they justified in destroying the government and risking a disastrous general election in order to oppose it ? Once it became the timing, rather than the principle, that was at stake, then too devoted a resistance seemed unwarranted. As a result conscription did not lead directly to Asquith's overthrow. But it did wrack the

[1] Addison, *Four and a Half Years*, vol. 1, p. 234.

[2] *Manchester Guardian*, 26 July 1916.

[3] The best discussion of this Irish crisis of July 1916, from which hardly any of the participants on the English side emerged with credit, is in Jenkins, *Asquith*, pp. 395–404.

coalition throughout the whole of its first year of existence ; and its part in destroying such prestige as the government had ever possessed, and in shattering the morale of its Liberal supporters, was incalculable.

II

The determined conscriptionists in the cabinet based their strategy on a simple fact of the constitution which has already been mentioned : that the life of the House of Commons would automatically expire on 31 January 1916 unless extended by an Act requiring the assent of the House of Lords. Lloyd George, Churchill, and a group of Conservative ministers arranged to employ the right-wing majority in the Upper House to force their colleagues either to accept conscription, or to face anni-hilation at an election on the conscription issue.[1] Lloyd George was serving public notice of this intention when on 13 September 1915 he published his famous " preface ". There could be no better indication of his change of position since the outbreak of war than that he, of all people, should have resorted to the remaining powers of the House of Lords to coerce the Liberal majority in the cabinet. And in the end his strategy was entirely successful. In January 1916 a House of Commons still with a Liberal-Labour-Nationalist majority enacted the first con-scription bill.

Lloyd George's decision to force Asquith's hand over con-scription produced a crucial stage in Liberal affairs. In personal terms, relations between the two leaders deteriorated alarmingly, and despite occasional patchings-up never really recovered. The antagonism was mutual. In a conversation of 14 October, " Ll. G. spoke with great bitterness " of Asquith.[2] And the state of feeling on the other side is revealed by two letters of Margot Asquith's.[3] On 15 October she wrote to Lord Murray of Elibank asking him to come and see her : " Politics are VERY

[1] *Manchester Guardian*, 18 September 1915; Scott's diary, 17 October 1915, C. P. Scott Papers.

[2] Scott's diary, 14 October 1915, C. P. Scott Papers.

[3] This does not mean that Asquith's opinions were necessarily his wife's, or that he was influenced by her to anything like the extent which was sometimes supposed. But the letters (particularly the second) do reveal events as well as opinions.

bad Ll. G is behaving like a maniac. He Winston & Curzon are pure wreckers." She implored Murray to see Grey and say to him : " 'You & the P.M must get together & check the Ll. G Winston gang. *No* wobbling over Conscription. The Labour world have had a *promise* from their P.M. & if you & he break your words you go right under & the wreckers Ll. G Winston & Co will score.' "

Murray apparently left London without receiving, or anyway without acting on, this letter. Five days later he received a further epistle from the same source (Asquith's health had just suffered a breakdown which was to keep him out of action for a fortnight) :

I'm *very very* unhappy & wd. have given the *world* to have seen you before you left—

Oh! Why did you go now of all times! ?—

I consider the next 4 days the most critical in my life. Henry is not so ill physically but he is stale & *morally disgusted*. He read me the chapter in New Testament of Simon Peter's betrayal of our Lord & how the Lord looked at Peter & the cock crew—he said " This might have been written of Ll. George—Peter was a Celt "

It is *this* that breaks H. his colleagues treachery—& the good ones Lansdowne Walter Long etc *Stupidity* not seeing that conscription Spells Revolution & then the Times being *allowed* to say what it likes & making Permanent mischief between allies. . . .

Northcliffe & Ll. George trying to hound him out of public life & undermining his authority by constantly saying " We want a leader—we must get rid of K. Grey Sir J. French Asquith " turn after turn these will drive H. into *private life* . . . . for the moment he is absolutely indifferent as to whether he will go on only *not one* syllable must you breathe of this   (It wd. *delight* L.G & Winston if they thought H. was likely to go)[1]

It may be difficult to visualize Asquith making the scriptural parallel recounted by his wife (Lloyd George on such occasions tended to refer to Judas rather than Peter). But it should be appreciated that just then he was showing considerable signs of strain. Only three days earlier he had written, to quote

[1] Margot Asquith to Murray, 15 and 20 October 1915, Elibank Papers.

Mr. Jenkins, " a most uncharacteristic letter " to Kitchener,
warning him that " what is now going on is being engineered
by men (Curzon and Lloyd George, and some others) whose real
object is to oust you. They know well that I give no countenance
to their projects, and consequently they have conceived the
idea of using you against me." [1] This letter, taken with the
remarks to his wife and the breakdown in his health, is evidence
of the desperate position into which he had been driven by
Lloyd George's ultimatum.

For the truth was that Asquith, although claiming to have an
open mind on conscription, detested it—and believed that he
represented his party in doing so. Five days after the appearance of the Lloyd George preface, he wrote to A. J. Balfour,
the Conservative leader least enthusiastic for conscription,
saying that conscription would arouse practically united and
vehement opposition from Labour, and that he had received
" during the last few days from the most trusted & representative
men of the [Liberal] rank & file a number of apparently spontaneous communications, & all in the sense of resolute & dogged
opposition. It is no exaggeration to say that, at this moment,
the two most unpopular & distrusted men in the party are
Ll-George & Mr. Churchill." On the merits of the conscription
issue he wrote :

> You & I know the facts & figures : we have read with
> more or less attention the reports & memoranda of our
> colleagues, & the evidence (such as it was) upon which they
> at any rate profess to be based. . . . My deliberate con-
> clusion is that the voluntary system has stood the ordeal
> of fiery experiment with marvellous success . . . [and] that
> there is no evidence worthy of the name that Compulsion in
> any form would have given, or could have given, more
> satisfactory results. . . .[2]

It is unlikely that Asquith's opinion changed at all during the
next few months. In a conversation of January 1916 he related
Runciman's grounds for opposing conscription and added : "the
Dickens is that I so agree with him." [3]

Yet by then the battle against conscription was already lost.

[1] Jenkins, *Asquith*, p. 378.
[2] Asquith to Balfour, 18 September 1915, Asquith Papers.
[3] Lady Scott's diary, 13 January 1916, Asquith Papers.

From mid-September 1915 he had had three months in which to choose between conscription and an election. His first response was characteristic : he tried to reconcile opposites. In October he launched the Derby recruiting scheme, ostensibly a last great attempt to preserve the voluntary system, but so hedged about with contingent threats of compulsion that it constituted in itself a long step towards conscription. On 2 November Asquith gave his famous pledge that married men attesting under the Derby scheme would not be called up until virtually all unmarried men of military age had joined the forces—either voluntarily or by other means. Lloyd George himself later observed that, given this threat to coerce unmarried men, the Derby scheme was not really a voluntary appeal at all. But its combination of threat and cajolery represented Asquith's last hope of satisfying both parties.

The attempt did not succeed. When the campaign ended in December 1915, a substantial number of unmarried men had still not come forward. The Liberals attempted a last resistance by trying to show that the number was smaller than the conscriptionists claimed, and that another Derby-style canvass might reduce it further ; hence when on 22 December the cabinet met to consider the figures, the discussion (Asquith noted anxiously) " unhappily followed party lines . . . and to judge from to-day's experience we seem to be on the brink of a precipice." [1] But this resistance soon collapsed, aided by a sharp push from Lloyd George (now the only ardent Liberal conscriptionist left in the cabinet following Churchill's resignation in November). Lloyd George was away from London at the time of this cabinet meeting, but on his return he presented Asquith with what was popularly dubbed an " ultimatum ", stating that unless unmarried men were conscripted immediately, he would resign. [2]

[1] J. A. Spender and Cyril Asquith, *Life of Lord Oxford and Asquith*, vol. 2, p. 201. Curiously, Spender on the next page claims that the division over conscription " was by no means on party lines ". Lloyd George aside, the resistance to conscription came principally from the Liberals, and its passage was a setback for them and a triumph for the Conservatives.

[2] Addison, *Four and a Half Years*, vol. 1, p. 156. Lloyd George wrote this communication to Asquith on the evening of Sunday, 27 December, and Asquith presumably received it next morning, the 28th. An account of its contents appeared in the *Daily Mail* on the 29th.

In this situation, Asquith's pledge of 2 November proved to be not a trap but a way of escape. It enabled him to compel unmarried men to enlist, as Lloyd George demanded, not on conscriptionist grounds but to fulfil a promise originally made in an attempt to preserve the voluntary system. When Asquith presented the first conscription bill to Parliament in January 1916, he could announce himself still an adherent to the voluntary system, and claim that " in view of the results of Lord Derby's campaign, no case has been made out for general Compulsion. I, at any rate, would be no party to a measure which had that for its object." [1] He was merely fulfilling his pledge to married men by treating all unmarried men of military age as if they had volunteered—what some Liberals described as saving the voluntary system in general by conscripting one group in particular. But whatever Asquith might say, it was plain that Lloyd George had won. His victory was faithfully reflected by the progress through the House of Lords of the measure extending the life of Parliament. As long as the bill conscripting " unmarried slackers ", as they were popularly called, remained in the Commons, the prolongation bill tarried in the Lords. When the conscription measure completed its passage through the Lower House, the prolongation bill proceeded without delay through the Upper. Thus the two measures went together to receive the royal assent, an appropriate conjunction of events in the opinion of one observer, for, as he put it, in earlier life these bills had been strangely united, and it was fitting that at the end they were not divided. [2]

By his handling of this crisis Asquith avoided a general election and placated the conscriptionists with a measure mild enough to cause the resignation of only one Liberal, Simon. Yet it was a dubious success. Such a half-measure was scarcely worth while unless it represented a real desire for unity and reconciliation amongst his divided ministers ; and this it did not do. Lloyd George had shown no strong inclination to

---

It must be added that Asquith, several weeks later, emphatically denied having received an ultimatum from Lloyd George. It is difficult to see what else he could have done if he was not, by remaining silent on the matter, to confirm knowledge of what ought to have been a ministerial secret.

[1] *H. C. Deb.*, 77,951 (5 January 1916).   [2] *Manchester Guardian*, 28 January 1916.

preserve the coalition or to compromise with particular opponents within it. (It was even suggested that one thing that persuaded McKenna and Runciman to stay in the government was
his blatant efforts to get them out). And Asquith had paid
dearly to keep his government in being : he had submitted to
public threats from his colleagues ; he had agreed to sacrifice
the " unmarried slacker " so as to keep at liberty the " married
slacker ", a solution which really satisfied neither supporters
nor opponents of conscription ; and he had added another to
his record of compromises when compromising politics was
the last thing the nation wanted. And after all this the
peace which the measure brought him lasted barely three
months.

In March 1916 Lloyd George renewed the attack, demanding
the conscription of married men as well, and the cabinet entered
another upheaval. In the following weeks this crisis proceeded
in full view of the public, until on 19 April newspaper headlines
could announce : " Acute Crisis in the Cabinet. . . . The
Differences Between Mr. Asquith and Mr. Lloyd George." [1]
The next day Asquith was forced to tell the House of Commons
that owing to internal differences the break-up of the government
was imminent.

As before, the only thing keeping Lloyd George from resigning
was uncertainty about his Conservative allies. At first most of
them, including Bonar Law, Chamberlain, and Lansdowne,
were reluctant to disrupt the government by so soon demanding
a fresh measure of conscription. Gradually, however, circumstances forced them forward. On 10 April the Army Council
submitted a report calling for new recruiting measures. And
from even earlier, Bonar Law was being subjected to a type of
pressure which it was not his custom long to resist. On 4 March
the press lord, Rothermere, wrote concerning him : " I am
told Bonar Law's position is very insecure. Carson apparently
is taking up a strong line with him and as he only holds his
position by reason of Carson's good will I imagine that at any
moment the bolts of the trap door may be pulled and Bonar
Law disappear from view." [2] Carson's activities soon became
public. From 21 March onwards the Unionist War Committee

[1] *ibid*, 19 April 1916.
[2] Rothermere to Murray, 4 March 1916, Elibank Papers.

—a body led by Carson and reputed to possess the support of 150 Conservative M.P.s—exerted growing pressure on Bonar Law to join forces with Lloyd George in demanding the conscription of married men. At first Bonar Law made a brave show of resisting this pressure, but it was widely recognised that on such occasions he would generally subordinate his opinions to preserve the unity of his party—and, incidentally, to outflank Carson's challenge to his leadership. As the parliamentary correspondent of *The Times*, discussing possible cabinet resignations, observed on 18 April 1916 : " There are grounds, moreover, for thinking that, if it becomes a case of resignation, other factors will intervene besides the merits of the question at issue. It is known, for instance, that Mr. Bonar Law holds certain opinions about his tenure of office in the event of a division among Unionist members of Parliament."

Faced by the gradual defection of the Conservative ministers, Asquith tried once more to find a compromise which would preserve both his cabinet and his consistency. Dogged by his fateful statement in January 1916 that he would be " no party " to general conscription, he sought vainly for something short of full conscription which would satisfy Lloyd George. He was prepared to accept both the automatic conscription of young men as they turned eighteen, and the enforced retention of time-expired members of the regular army.[1] But Lloyd George stood firm on conscripting married men as well, and on this difference the government seemed doomed to break in two. On successive days in April, having arranged to present the ministry's recruiting proposals to the House, Asquith was obliged to admit himself unable to do so. But at the last moment he preserved the coalition once more by an all-but-complete retreat. The cabinet devised a formula which in effect conceded all of Lloyd George's demands, but saved a very little of Asquith's face. Under it, eighteen-year-olds and time-expired men were to be conscripted immediately, but married men were to have a month in which to volunteer ; then, if they failed to do so in sufficient numbers, they also were to be fetched. This unconvincing compromise so enraged both conscriptionists and

[1] In January he had resisted automatic conscription of eighteen-year-olds on the logical ground that this group, having previously been unable to enlist, could not be classed as " slackers ".

anti-conscriptionists outside the government that it no sooner
emerged from the cabinet than Parliament forced its withdrawal.
" Within the short space of two hours there was an ignominious
end of the whole elaborate edifice of bargain and compromise
erected in weeks of ' Cabinet crisis ' and secret conferences." [1]
A few days later the government agreed to the immediate
conscription of all men of military age.

Asquith's handling of this crisis had a most adverse effect
on his political reputation. He seemed to be splitting unimportant hairs and parading inappropriate scruples. He agreed
to conscript eighteen-year-olds who could not be described as
" slackers " when they had been given no opportunity to slack,
whereas married men were to remain free to volunteer as long
as they took only a month about it. If the engineers of the
crisis were really out to dethrone Asquith, as the *Daily News*
declared, his conduct appeared to excuse them ; they understood better than he the requirements of wartime leadership.
As *The Times* put it while the crisis was at its height, the
differences in the cabinet " are really fundamental and not as
they might appear on the surface, differences of method. . . .
One party has its mind unalterably fixed on a final settlement
[of the recruiting problem]. The other is still content to wait
and see." [2]

III

This year-long struggle over conscription took severe toll of
the spirit and unity of the Liberal party.

The ardent Liberal conscriptionists in the House of Commons,
numbering about fifty, became quite alienated from the government, and did not return to their allegiance when at length it
gave them what they wanted. Most of them had actively
supported the formation of the coalition in May 1915, as introducing into the government a healthy element of vigour and
compulsion. But the display of hesitations and divided counsels
over conscription convinced them that this government was no
better than its predecessor. One of this group, W. H. Cowan,
expressed their view in a conversation with Vivian Phillipps, a
supporter and later a private secretary of Asquith, during the

[1] *The Times*, 29 April 1916.   [2] *ibid*, 20 April 1916.

first conscription crisis in September 1915. According to Phillipps's account, Cowan told him that conscription should be carried through immediately, whether Kitchener wanted it or not, and that if organised labour resisted then " so much the worse for them "; the army could " deal with them." Asquith, Grey, and Kitchener would have to go, but it would be worth their loss to put Lloyd George in command. The conscription issue had reached a stage where Lloyd George must win or go, and the country could not afford to lose him. " This ", Phillipps commented on Cowan's remarks, " is evidently the current talk among the conscriptionist gang." [1] In January 1916 the " gang " formed itself into an unofficial Liberal War Committee, popularly known as the Liberal " ginger group ". Its avowed purpose was to stimulate and invigorate, not to harass, the government, but it was recognised as working to replace Asquith by Lloyd George at the head of a predominantly Conservative regime. Cowan and Mond, another " ginger " Liberal, said publicly that the government had lost the confidence of the country, and should face a general election. And Sir Arthur Markham, one of the treasurers of the group, denounced the coalition as " the most incompetent Administration that has ever been in office " and called its leader a " professional politician " whose word was not trusted and who was prepared to stick to nothing but his parliamentary salary. Lloyd George, he declared, was the only man in the cabinet with courage. [2]

While this minority of Liberal M.P.s attacked Asquith for his resistance to conscription, a much larger number were shaken in their allegiance by his gradual and equivocal acceptance of it. Most of them had opposed the formation of the coalition on the general ground that it represented a rebuff to Liberalism and a triumph for the right-wing press ; Dalziel, one of the Liberals who supported the change, spoke of having made " enemies of lifelong friends " by his attitude. [3] But in particular these Liberals deplored the resort to a coalition because it brought conscription nearer, and their fears were immediately confirmed by the conscriptionist agitation and the support given it by Lloyd George. With Liberals, Massingham wrote in late

[1] Phillipps to Gardiner, 20 September 1915, Gardiner Papers.
[2] *H. C. Deb.*, 80,2104–7 (15 March 1916) and 81,2248 (18 April 1916).
[3] *ibid*, 72,597 (15 June 1915).

May 1915, conscription was the " all-dominating anxiety ". If the new cabinet yielded on it " the national unity is at an end, and the Liberal Party not merely suspended but broken for ever ".[1] Evidence of this anxiety was provided by the strong opposition of a group of Liberals to parts of the Ministry of Munitions bill in June 1915, and to the whole of the National Register bill in July. Addison in his diary for 7 June " rejoiced in [his] heart " at the " tremendous explosion " of protest in the House against the aspects of compulsion in the Ministry of Munitions bill. As parliamentary secretary to this ministry, he had taken on himself the duty of " standing up " to Lloyd George on the subject of industrial conscription, and he felt that the Liberal outburst in the House " would be extremely useful in preventing L.G., in his enthusiastic energy, from taking a false step ".[2] The next month there was strong Liberal resistance to the National Register bill, which provided for a census of manpower intended, according to its critics, as a first step towards conscription. To one observer their attitude revealed how much of the " old political Adam " remained in the breasts of the Liberal rank and file, and how suspiciously the Liberals in the House continued to regard the coalition government.[3]

But in the following months, from July to November 1915, there occurred a distinct movement of Liberal sympathy towards the Asquith coalition—even despite the shock caused by the protectionist aspects of McKenna's first budget. This sympathy probably bespoke less love of the coalition than fear of its probable replacement ; for clearly if Asquith fell he would be succeeded by a conscriptionist administration under Lloyd George, now freely described as going the way of Joseph Chamberlain and as conspiring with Northcliffe against the Prime Minister.[4] According to political commentators in September 1915, Lloyd George's advocacy of compulsion "does not carry with him those who would usually be classed as his political followers even among Welsh members." Indeed, " Liberals who a year or two ago would have been counted among his natural followers have for many months spoken of

---

[1] *Nation*, 22 May 1915.   [2] Addison, *Four and a Half Years*, vol. 1, p. 91.
[3] *Manchester Guardian*, 6 July 1915, under the heading " A Revival of Party."
[4] *Lord Riddell's War Diary*, pp. 104, 113, 128, 136–7.

THE CABINET'S CHRISTMAS CAROL.

THE HYMN OF TOO-LATE.

We are too late!
We are too late!
It's really most unfortunate,
I—, I—, alone am worth my salt.
I never, never hesitate
When managing affairs of State;
It's all the other follow's fault—
HE — makes — US — Late.

The cabinet in December 1915—cartoon from the *Sunday Times*.
The members of the Cabinet are, from left to right, Austen Chamberlain, Curzon, McKenna, Arthur Balfour, Lloyd George and Asquith

Sir Alfred Mond and his daughter leaving for Palestine in 1921

C. F. G. Masterman—cartoon by Low

him with hostility and bitterness." The same was true of the other leading Liberal conscriptionist : " Between Mr. Churchill, who is also supposed to be for compulsion, and many Liberals there has grown up a positive estrangement. . . . Many old allegiances will perhaps never be knit up again."[1] Evidence of the severing of " old allegiances " was provided by Pringle in June 1915, only a month after the formation of the coalition. In Parliament a member of the government disputed the accuracy of a statement in the *British Weekly*, and Pringle intervened gratuitously to inquire : " Is the right hon. Gentleman not aware that the ' British Weekly ' is the organ of the Minister of Munitions ? " The next day Lloyd George, parrying an interruption by Pringle, tartly commented : " I do not know what my hon. Friend says, but I know he wants to say something offensive."[2] As long as the only alternative ministry was a Lloyd George-conscriptionist government, the Liberal opponents of conscription found themselves from the middle of 1915 coming round to support of the government they had—at the very time when the Conservatives and " ginger " Liberals were beginning actively to oppose it. These changing attitudes were described by one Liberal M.P. on the day Parliament reassembled in September 1915, with conscription and the Lloyd George " preface " the all-absorbing topics of discussion. He found, he said, " evidence of a most monstrous *volte-face* . . . . it is amazing to find those who fathered the Coalition Government, those who claim to have been the dictators at whose mandate it was appointed, turning against their offspring, and becoming enemies to it." At the same time the majority of Liberals seemed to be going through the reverse process. " When this Coalition Government was formed there was a great deal of suspicion about it on the part of many of my hon. Friends. As matters have turned out they have accepted the Coalition Government, and acquiesced in it. I think it may be said that the Coalition Government has a full measure of their confidence."[3] This last sentence was audibly contradicted in the House, and was clearly an exaggeration even when the coalition stood highest in

---

[1] *Manchester Guardian*, 15 and 18 September 1915.

[2] *H. C. Deb.*, 72,1040 and 1272 (22 and 23 June 1915).

[3] *ibid*, 74,32 (14 September 1915). The speaker was A. MacCallum Scott, Liberal member for the Bridgeton division of Glasgow.

Liberal estimation. It was too feeble and divided an instrument ever to receive the " full " confidence of Liberals. But many did find themselves obliged to support it as the only obstacle to the victory of conscription.

From the end of 1915, however, the coalition's long and painful course of surrender on this issue went far to enfeeble Liberal support. For a time Asquith's followers did not recognise, or refused to admit, how much he was giving away by his various commitments to Lord Derby. Indeed, his crucially important speech of 2 November 1915 seemed to satisfy both supporters and opponents of conscription. But this happy situation could not endure, and his further statement on 11 November, which made plain the extent of his concessions, came as a great shock to his " most loyal and devoted supporters, the anti-compulsionists."[1] " We hope ", complained the *Nation*, which had applauded the 2 November speech as eliminating the danger of conscription, " that the Government have not, as they sometimes seem to do, abandoned the attempt to govern, and adopted the *rôle* of spectator. Certainly their withdrawal from the field in favor of Lord Derby has led to a real and most regrettable confusion on the subject of recruiting."[2] When confusion was removed at the end of the year by a measure of conscription, the hostility of this journal was not dispelled. "With this wanton breach with historic Liberalism [it lamented on 1 January 1916], that great movement practically comes to an end, and a new alignment of parties must gradually take place, with new leaders to conduct it." The reception of the conscription bill in the House of Commons in January 1916 suggests that a good many Liberals, even when they did not vote against the measure, felt some of this resentment. The most enthusiastic response which Asquith elicited from the large body of Liberals came when he said that no case had been made out for general conscription. As he outlined the substance of the bill it was the Conservative benches which broke into " triumphant acclamation ". And when, at the end, he warmly insisted, in face of contradiction, that he was as strong a supporter of the voluntary principle as any one in the House, his followers failed to provide

[1] *Manchester Guardian*, 13 November 1915.

[2] *Nation*, 4 December 1915. This spelling of " favor ", and similar words like " Labor ", was always used by the *Nation* while Massingham was editor.

" the expected chorus of support". Indeed Liberal and Labour cheering was reserved, not for the Prime Minister, but for Simon as he rose to oppose the measure.[1]

The voting on this bill scarcely reflected the upheaval in the Liberal ranks caused by Asquith's surrender. Strong pressure was brought to bear on Liberal members to support the bill, and they knew that if they opposed it the government would fall and an election probably follow. A few heroic souls were prepared to accept this alternative, even if it meant losing their seats. One of them was Llewellyn Williams, a Welsh Liberal who had become bitterly opposed to Lloyd George :

I do not know [he said] what is going to happen. I do not know whether this Government of shreds and patches will continue to hang together. I do not believe that they can last long. . . . I say this deliberately, Radical as I am, I would sooner see a Tory Government in power than the Government we have here—I would sooner accept, if accept one must, a Bill of this sort from a Tory Government that believes in compulsory service than I would accept it at the hands of Gentlemen who profess their unbounded devotion to the voluntary principle while cutting its throat.[2]

But others could not bring themselves to force Asquith from office when the consequence might be even worse than divided government and diluted conscription : the annihilation of the Liberal party at a " khaki " election, and the accession to office of a Lloyd George-Carson administration capable of much greater inroads on personal liberty.

This is not to say that political survival was the only motive of Liberals who now abandoned resistance to conscription. As has been said above, many saw it sincerely as an unwelcome necessity of war. A *Manchester Guardian* correspondent had earlier written : " No party . . . professes itself unconvertible on the subject. However unlikely the necessity of conscription may seem to its opponents, it is at least conceivable. That is

---

[1] *Manchester Guardian*, 6 January 1916.
[2] *H. C. Deb.*, 77,1035 (5 January 1916). Curiously enough, by the following December Williams was doing his best to keep Asquith (" that brave, patient man, the greatest Englishman of all time ") in office. *Manchester Guardian*, 4 December 1916.

admitted."[1]   This overlooked some, like R. D. Holt, who denied absolutely the right of the state to force an individual to bear arms against his will. But it did faithfully represent the minds of a large number of Liberals normally opposed to conscription. Yet even they were in many instances shaken by the methods that Asquith employed to enact conscription between January and May 1916. One who voted against the first conscription bill probably spoke for many who did not when he said that they had seen too much behind the scenes to believe that the matter was being decided on grounds of national interest alone. The conscription campaign, he claimed, was being engineered by men out to gain a personal triumph.[2] Whether or not such suspicions were justified, Asquith undoubtedly encouraged them by his custom of waiting until his enemies had driven him into a corner and then agreeing to measures of conscription seemingly to save his government. Such behaviour was scarcely calculated to overcome what one Liberal journalist, even after the first conscription bill had passed its second reading by an overwhelming majority, could refer to as " the latent distrust of the great majority of the Liberal party towards the measure ".[3]

This distrust was soon transferred from the measure to the men who enacted it. If Asquith hoped that by carrying through conscription in instalments he would placate his party, he was mistaken. Doubtless in January 1916 it seemed sensible to administer only a small dose of conscription and so save the " general principle " of voluntary service ; and it is clear that the " moderate character "[4] of the first measure did reconcile many Liberals to it. But consequently their dismay was all the greater when, in the following months, the voluntary principle disappeared before successive extensions of conscription, each of which appeared not as a courageous act of war but as a concession to political pressure. There can be little doubt that Asquith would have served his party better, and made the resort to conscription ultimately less painful, if from the outset he had boldly called on his followers to accept the reversal of a

---

[1] *Manchester Guardian*, 15 September 1915.

[2] *ibid*, 5 January 1916. These views were expressed by Percy Alden, Liberal M.P. for Tottenham.

[3] *ibid*, 13 January 1916.   [4] Addison, *Four and a Half Years*, vol. 1, p. 159.

historic liberal principle on the broadest grounds of patriotism and national necessity. He would certainly have served himself better. In the end, his display of broken pledges and uncertain purposes had attracted as much hostility as conscription itself. " In his own party ", Massingham claimed in May 1916, " all is chilled and changed ".[1] And it was the hopeless equivocation of his April proposals which decided the anti-conscriptionist *Manchester Guardian*, now despairing of him eithei as war leader or as guardian of liberal principles, to call on Lloyd George to abandon the government and go into opposition.

Others stopped short of this conclusion. On 19 April, when the cabinet crisis was at its height and Lloyd George's resignation apparently imminent, a gathering of one hundred Liberal M.P.s resolved unanimously that Asquith's continuance as Prime Minister was a national necessity, and appointed a deputation to tell him so. But the resolution was worded so as to withhold support from further measures of conscription, even though it was known that he had already consented to some. At most this rally to Asquith proved that a substantial body of Liberal M.P.s still preferred him to Lloyd George. " It is impossible to disguise the fact ", Addison wrote, " that there was very strong and bitter feeling on the part of many Liberals against L.G." The meeting " was nominally in support of the P.M., but really directed against L.G."[2] Such support for Asquith was negative and insubstantial, as shown by the fact that soon afterwards Simon, a member of the deputation, was attacking him for bowing to " political expediency " when he agreed to fresh measures of conscription. It would need more enthusiasm than this to preserve a government whose morale had been so profoundly shaken.

IV

After a first year of almost continuous upheaval, the last months of the Asquith coalition, from May to December 1916, were something of an anti-climax. No other issue focused all discontents and political aspirations as conscription had done. Yet the erosion of strength and confidence continued. Lloyd George proceeded on his disruptive way, attracting some Liberals by

[1] *Nation*, 6 May 1916.   [2] Addison, *Four and a Half Years*, vol. 1, pp. 197–8.

the vigour of his conduct (" in word and in action he has been the real leader of the nation "),[1] repelling others by his self-seeking and unscrupulousness. Through most of June 1916 he was occupied in a struggle to take over the now vacant War Office, in which he was successful, and to take it over with all its old powers restored, in which he was not. In September he caused another political disturbance by appropriating, without consulting Grey or the cabinet, the functions of the Foreign Office. In an extraordinary interview with an American journalist, he denounced as " pro-German " any contemplated attempt by the American government to institute peace talks between the warring powers, espoused the doctrine of a fight to a " knock-out ", and characterised the war in a series of sporting metaphors of astonishing shallowness. The extent to which he had become an independent entity in politics, only nominally associated with his Liberal colleagues, was revealed at this time by operations in the newspaper world which foreshadowed his take-over of the *Daily Chronicle* two years later. About the middle of 1916 it became known that efforts were being made to establish a newspaper " to promote the policies, as the Americans would put it, of Mr. Lloyd George."[2] Simultaneously a group of Lloyd George Liberals, including Mond and Sir Charles Henry, tried to remove Asquith's close friend Spender, who had been criticising Lloyd George, from editorial control of the *Westminster Gazette*. " These people," Spender wrote to Murray, " whether with or without Ll. G.'s connivance, speak quite openly about their plans & have not at all abandoned their notion of getting me out of the W.G."[3] For the moment, however, the attempt to dislodge Spender came to nothing.

While Lloyd George embarrassed the government by these

---

[1] The view of F. Kellaway, Liberal M.P. for Bedford ; *Manchester Guardian*, 25 April 1916.

[2] *ibid*, 10 June 1916.

[3] Spender to Murray, 6 June 1916, Elibank Papers. Murray, a shareholder in the *Westminster Gazette*, did not want Spender removed, but he did believe " that the safety of the country is bound up *in a complete understanding and close association* between the Prime Minister and Lloyd George ", and he enjoined Spender to cease criticising the latter. " I have again taken the W. G. matter in hand vis-a-vis yourself, and pretty strongly ", Murray assured Lloyd George. (Murray to Spender, 7 June 1916 ; Murray to Lloyd George, 18 July 1916, Elibank Papers.)

assertions of independence, Asquith continued to dissipate what Liberal sympathy he retained by his apparent deviations from liberal principles, especially in the matters of free trade and Irish Home Rule. He startled Liberals (outside the " ginger " section) by endorsing the resolutions of the Allied Economic Conference in Paris, which provided in some circumstances for a post-war policy of very high tariffs. And he caused even greater dismay in his party by giving way to Tory pressure in the cabinet and throwing over the agreement which Lloyd George had reached with the Irish Nationalists.[1] So great had been the expectations aroused by this arrangement, as a last chance of reconciling southern Ireland, that even a slumbering body like the executive of the National Liberal Federation had rallied itself to demand that the government implement the scheme immediately. Asquith's surrender to the Tories not only drove into opposition the Irish Nationalists, a vital element in his pre-war majority, but so shocked his Liberal followers that a significant number refused to support him in the division lobby when his Irish administration was challenged by Redmond.[2]

A government so adept at alienating its supporters without converting its enemies could not be expected to survive much longer. " The Govt. is very tottery ", wrote Haldane. " It is their own fault."[3] By mid-1916 there were clear signs that the ministry had just about exhausted the patience of the Commons; on successive days in July it suffered severe rebuffs in the House on minor issues, and only by bowing to a demand for commissions of inquiry into the Dardanelles and Mesopotamian operations did it escape outright defeat. Early in August 1916 a Liberal journalist reported :

Many good and cautious Parliamentary judges believe that a reconstruction of the Government is very probable and very near, and that the reconstruction when it comes will mean a new Prime Minister. In the last week or two Mr. Asquith's prestige has suffered severely. In the last few days the Government has suffered what has amounted

[1] see above, pp. 69-70.

[2] The execution of Roger Casement for his part in the Sinn Fein rebellion, and the use made by the authorities of his diaries to discredit him before execution, also aroused the indignation of many Liberals against the government.

[3] Haldane to his mother, 4 July 1916, Haldane Papers.

to a series of defeats, and on the top of these the Irish affair has placed Mr. Asquith in a very difficult position.[1]

In this situation nothing could save the government except a startling improvement in the course of the war. As Massingham had written in July : " Henceforth, the Coalition will have to live, if it lives at all, on its works and very little on the faith of the Commons."[2] And the works of the coalition, as revealed in the progress of the war, were not of a sort to make good these deficiencies of faith. The Somme offensive, on which great hopes had been placed, petered out after appalling losses in October. And belief in the slow exhaustion of the enemy was rudely dispelled by the devastating German campaign against Roumania in October, bringing on the British government much the same discredit as had followed the overrunning of Serbia a year before. These setbacks on land were accompanied by widespread misgivings about the conduct of the war at sea. In June 1916 there was an outburst of indignation against the Admiralty for the way in which its early Jutland communiqué had created the impression of a British defeat ; and by November concern over the submarine campaign had produced an all-but-universal demand, to which Asquith with misguided loyalty refused to accede, for Balfour's removal from the Admiralty. This growing despair over the course of the war (" Useless to veil the gloom of the hour "[3]) led to a considerable demand in November for a secret session of the House of Commons, not so that the government might review the state of the war in confidence, but so that members could tell it frankly what they thought of it.

Here was Lloyd George's opportunity. If it is true that he willed the doom of the government, it is also true that the government, for good reason or bad, had become so discredited that it no longer had the resources to withstand him. The Liberal press generally was speculating about its downfall. On the same day, 29 November 1916, the *Westminster Gazette* and the *Daily Chronicle* expressed almost identical views about its inadequacy. The former referred to " an appearance of delay and indecision, which may belie the facts, but none the less makes an unhappy impression " and " leaves the public

---

[1] *Manchester Guardian*, 3 August 1916.   [2] *Nation*, 29 July 1916.
[3] *ibid*, 28 October 1916.

disturbed and uneasy ". And the latter warned the government that " unless it shows more grip than it latterly has, it seems to us in serious danger of coming to grief, in spite of the absence of an alternative. The Ministry's arch-defect is inability to make up its mind. It is not so much that it reaches wrong decisions, as that for weeks and even months it fails, in crucial matter after crucial matter, to reach any decision at all." On 2 December, a *Manchester Guardian* correspondent wrote : " I do not think that the Coalition Ministry has any longer the collective prestige to resist attack from within or without. The House of Commons has reached the mood when it is ready to create another Ministry ". And the *Nation*, just after Asquith had resigned, admitted : " The mass of the public. . . . longs for success, or for emergence from the shadow of failure, and divines with a certain truth of feeling that no such guide existed in the divided will and compromising tactics of the Coalition."[1] What was more, although differing greatly in their appreciation of Lloyd George, these journals were at one in recognising the pre-eminent position which he had come to occupy. According to the *Manchester Guardian:* " the course of events probably depends on Mr. Lloyd George, and if, as rumour says, Government changes are coming, it is he who, whether immediately or afterwards, will have to take the responsibility of the Government." And the *Nation*, although severely critical of him, admitted him to be " a true personality of the hour. It has made him ; his audacities of manipulation excite and please, and even inspire men with hope." It is this sense of hope which Lloyd George was able to arouse, and which Asquith could no longer evoke even from many of his followers, which goes far to explain the change of government in December 1916.

[1] *ibid*, 9 December 1916.

4. MIDWAY

I admit (& I find others who are not Georgian doing likewise) that it is impossible to defend the Asquith government. To go on with it meant certain defeat.

. . . I should be happier if I thought we shd have no more personal dealings with a man [Lloyd George] who appears personally disloyal & untrustworthy.

L. T. Hobhouse to Scott, 9 December 1916 [1]

WITH Asquith's downfall so thoroughly prepared, all that was needed to complete it was the formation of an alliance between Lloyd George and Bonar Law. For months it had been said that the only thing keeping Asquith in office was the lack of an alternative ministry. What this meant was that a Lloyd George-Bonar Law government could not be formed because of the ill-feeling between the new Secretary of State for War and the leader of the Conservative party.

But for all Bonar Law's reluctance to ally with Lloyd George, clearly he was not inflexible. In August 1916 he delivered a speech to Conservatives which, although ostensibly defending the government, suggested that he did not expect it to survive long : he remarked *inter alia* that he did not think the present government indispensable or the political situation especially bright, and observed that the House of Commons seemed to be getting tired of itself and of the government. And it was only necessary to look at his behaviour during the conscription crisis of April to see that, if subjected to sufficient pressure from the Conservative rank and file, he would eventually go along with Lloyd George whether he approved of him or not. Late in 1916 this pressure was applied once more. In the " Nigeria debate " of 8 November, Carson and a substantial body of Conservatives revolted against the government and their leader.[2] As Bonar Law noticed with dismay, many of the Conservatives who

[1] C. P. Scott Papers.
[2] The government proposed that enemy property captured in Nigeria should

followed Carson had previously been his own staunchest supporters, and had backed him for the party leadership five years
before.[1] He emerged from the debate " with his teeth chatter-
ing."[2] But it was Asquith, who recounted the fact, who had
cause to shiver. For this was all the prompting that Bonar Law
needed to abandon the discredited Prime Minister and make
terms with Lloyd George. Negotiations began later that month,
and the way was open for the final act in Asquith's overthrow.

What happened thereafter has been described in considerable
detail, and with no little controversy, by a number of historians.
In essentials the story is straightforward enough. As their price
for remaining in the government, Lloyd George and Bonar Law
called on Asquith to establish a " War Council " which would
take over direction of the war. Asquith, after initial hesitation,
rejected this scheme on 4 December 1916, and Lloyd George
and the Conservatives resigned, precipitating the break-up of
the government. Two days later Lloyd George became Prime
Minister.

It is hard to doubt that this was the unexpressed, and perhaps
unacknowledged, object for which Lloyd George and Bonar
Law were working. For the scheme they offered Asquith was
so humiliating and unworkable that at best it made his departure
from office only a matter of time. Lloyd George was to become
head of the small war cabinet which would direct war policy,
and neither Asquith nor any of his supporters was to belong to
it. Indeed, the only control which the nominal Premier and
cabinet might exercise over this body was a veto they would
hardly dare to use for fear of bringing on themselves the collective resignation of the war cabinet.

The unenviable position of the Prime Minister under such an
arrangement was aptly summed up on 4 December 1916 by
The Times in a leading article which soon became a subject of
controversy. Lloyd George, it said, had been urging the formation of a small War Council " fully charged with the supreme

---

be offered for sale both to British subjects and to neutrals. Carson moved that
only British subjects should be eligible.

[1] H. A. Taylor, *Robert Donald*, pp. 115, 128.
[2] So Asquith told Lady Scott. Lady Scott's diary, 8 November 1916, Asquith
Papers.

direction of the war ". Of this council Asquith would not be a member ; nor, " on the ground of temperament ", would " certain of Mr. Asquith's colleagues ". " On the other hand, the inclusion of Sir Edward Carson is believed to form an essential part of Mr. Lloyd George's scheme ". It followed this accurate account of Lloyd George's demands with an oft-quoted sneer at Asquith's position under the new arrangement : the Prime Minister had at last been convinced that he was better fitted " to ' preserve the unity of the nation ' (though we had never doubted its unity) than to force the pace of a War Council."

Later that day, Asquith wrote to Lloyd George referring to this leader as a reason for rejecting his proposals. It has been usual to describe Asquith's letter as an unwarranted criticism of Lloyd George for supposedly inspiring this attack.[1] But if one chooses to read on, instead of between, the lines of Asquith's letter, one finds no reference to Lloyd George's supposed inspiration of this article. What Asquith at least claimed to be discussing was not the source but the substance of this " production "—the suggestion, as he put it, that he was being " relegated to the position of an irresponsible spectator of the War ".[2] And what is noteworthy about this suggestion is that it faithfully represented his position under Lloyd George's proposed arrangement. It is little wonder that he came to the conclusion that he could not " possibly go cn " with the scheme.

It is true that on 3 December, the day previous, he had gone some way towards accepting it. He had just received a resolution from the Conservative ministers calling on him to resign office and forwarding their own resignations, and he apparently turned to Lloyd George's proposal as his only hope of clinging to his position. It has since been argued by Beaverbrook[3] that Asquith misunderstood the Conservative ministers' intention in demanding his resignation, and that (except for

[1] The charge was unwarranted in that Carson, not Lloyd George, supplied the editor of *The Times* with information for the article. But Lloyd George had given Carson the information in the first place, and had been regularly passing confidential information to the press either directly or through intermediaries like Carson, so he must bear considerable indirect responsibility both for the appearance of the article and for any suspicions Asquith may have entertained.

[2] Spender and Asquith, *Life of Lord Oxford and Asquith*, vol. 2, p. 264.

[3] *Politicians and the War*, pp. 412–4.

Bonar Law) their object was to strengthen his hand by forcing Lloyd George to try forming a government and showing that he could not do it. On this it may be said that if any incomprehension existed, it was not on Asquith's part. Plainly nothing but his retention of office stood between Lloyd George and the premiership, and some at least of the Conservative ministers recognised this. Curzon, for example, expected Lloyd George to form a government, if not on his own terms, and said regarding Asquith that " it will be for himself and Lloyd George to determine whether he goes out altogether or becomes Lord Chancellor or Chancellor of the Exchequer in a new Government".[1] Probably the Conservative ministers were torn between despair over the existing situation and antipathy to Lloyd George, and decided to resolve an intolerable state of tension by putting a Lloyd George premiership to the test, without being sure what outcome they hoped for. Thereafter they may have decided that they had been more sympathetic to Asquith than this, but it was not his fault that he did not detect such sympathy. Nor would their sympathy (when coupled with a demand for his resignation) have been much use to him, even if he had been convinced of its existence.

Anyway, Asquith did not contemplate accepting Lloyd George's terms for long. Having veered that way on 3 December, he decided firmly against the next day. For this apparent change of front various explanations have been offered : for example, that he believed Lloyd George to have inspired the attack in *The Times,* or that he had been convinced by Liberals like McKenna that he could retain office without surrendering to the demand for a War Council. But the true explanation may well be the obvious one, that he had come to see Lloyd George's scheme as being not an alternative to his expulsion from office but his expulsion in particularly humiliating circumstances—" a protean compromise ", as Curzon called it in relating the deliberations of the Conservative ministers, " which, in our view, could have no endurance."[2] It is possible to criticise Asquith for not facing up to this from the outset. But it seems unjust to censure him for eventually doing so.

What is certainly incorrect is to claim that a final agreement had been reached between Asquith and Lloyd George on

[1] Newton, *Lord Lansdowne,* p. 453.　　　[2] *ibid.*

3 December, and that Asquith then " went back " on it. When Asquith, on the 4th, at last decided to stand and fight, it was in the knowledge that, even if he accepted the principles of Lloyd George's scheme, he would still not have satisfied his colleague's apparently insatiable demands. Clearly, as long as Asquith was to be excluded from the war cabinet, the membership of this body was of the utmost importance to him. And we have the testimony of Lloyd George as well as Asquith that at no stage did they approach agreement on what the latter termed " the delicate and difficult question of personnel."[1] Nor were they ever likely to. Indeed, failure was more or less assured by Lloyd George's stipulation that " the inclusion of Sir Edward Carson " was an " essential part " of his scheme.[2]

Why was Lloyd George so insistent on making Carson one of the select group who were to wrest control of the war from both cabinet and Prime Minister ? Carson had revealed no great capacity while a member of the coalition government in 1915. Indeed, there have been few individuals who have established a like reputation in British politics with so few positive achievements to their credit. Carson's reputation rests on negatives : whom and what he opposed, and the lengths he would go to in carrying through his opposition. What was more, when Lloyd George became Prime Minister immediately after these negotiations, he made Carson First Lord of the Admiralty but did not include him in the war cabinet. And when seven months later he transferred Carson from the Admiralty to the war cabinet, it was not because he wanted him in the latter but because he wanted him out of the former.[3]

Why then did Lloyd George stipulate to Asquith that Carson must be included in the war cabinet ? The answer would appear to be because Carson was serving a characteristically negative function : his inclusion among the members of the

---

[1] Beaverbrook, *Politicians and the War*, pp. 389, 456.

[2] see above, p. 92.

[3] Carson had proved adamant in resisting Lloyd George's plan to dismiss Jellicoe, the First Sea Lord, so Lloyd George transferred Carson to the war cabinet and then, even though this body was supposed to control the conduct of the war, did not inform him when a few months later Jellicoe was dismissed. Carson first learned of it as a snowed-up passenger at a railway station, where he heard it being discussed by two country-folk. See Addison, *Four and a Half Years*, vol. 2, p. 411 ; *Manchester Guardian*, 7 March 1918.

proposed junta ensured that the negotiations would not succeed. Of all the men in England whom Lloyd George might, without flippancy, have nominated, Carson was the one most difficult for Asquith to accept. Carson's contempt for the Prime Minister, and determination to drive him from office, had been proclaimed throughout the land. It would be humiliation enough for Asquith, while remaining nominal Prime Minister, to be robbed of the direction of war policy. But for Carson to be among the select group which appropriated control would be carrying the process of humiliation beyond limits which could be considered tolerable.

There is little point in criticising Asquith for declining proposals apparently designed to demand rejection. If he is to be criticised, it is for retaining the premiership so long, when he might have made way for a subordinate better fitted than himself for the role of war leader. Shortly before Asquith resigned, Robert Cecil " had the courage to suggest to him that the finest and biggest thing that he could do would be to offer to serve under Lloyd George ". This suggestion Asquith rejected " with indignation and even with scorn."[1] It is difficult not to see a large element of wounded vanity in his response. But it should be remembered that he was being asked to take second place to an individual who had gone to remarkable lengths to drive him from office while remaining a member of his government, and that he had been subjected to a press campaign of unprecedented " virulence and coarseness of phrase "[2] which his proposed successor had condoned if not actively inspired. So oppressed had Asquith become by the manifestations of disloyalty within his government and by the stream of abuse from without that he could not perceive the deeper discontents existing with his conduct of the war, and viewed his impending downfall as solely the result of an intrigue between Lloyd George and the press barons. In this respect the press campaign against him, with its vindictiveness and dishonesty, was wholly unfortunate. Even an occasional Conservative felt moved to protest against it : " I must say ", complained Colonel Mildmay, " that the reckless use of the

[1] Petrie, *The Life and Letters of the Right Hon. Sir Austen Chamberlain*, vol. 2, pp. 60–1.
[2] *Manchester Guardian*, 6 December 1916.

terms ' pro-Hun ' and ' traitor ' positively sickens one."[1]
Subjected to such abuse, Asquith struggled to retain the premiership, lest his supersession should appear to confirm the charges
of slackness and incompetence—not to say sympathy with the
enemy—which were levelled against him. And while he clung
to office, his relations with Lloyd George deteriorated to such
an extent that eventually no government could hold them
both.

On 5 December 1916 this situation reached its irresistible
climax. By deciding to reject Lloyd George's demands and seek
no further accommodation with him, Asquith brought the crisis
to a head. Lloyd George, Bonar Law, and all the other Conservative ministers resigned, and the coalition automatically
collapsed. There was never any prospect that Asquith would
form another government, for with the Conservatives, a vociferous section of Liberals, the Irish Nationalists, and at least
some Labour members against him, he could not muster even
a paper majority in Parliament. Nor, had he possessed one,
would he have stood much chance of creating a fresh administration capable of carrying on the war and withstanding the attacks
of Lloyd George and the Conservatives. The attempt, anyway,
was not made. Asquith resigned from the premiership and the
king, after a token gesture to Bonar Law as Conservative leader,
commissioned Lloyd George on 6 December to form a government. Of his success there was really no doubt. A *Manchester
Guardian* correspondent wrote on the same day, in a passage
whose irony was apparently quite unconscious :

I am told that early in the day Mr. Lloyd George (while
explaining that he did not wish to form a Ministry) had
mentioned an informal estimate of the support he thought
he might command in the House of Commons if he should
be obliged to form a Government. He reckoned, according
to this account, that he would be supported by the whole
of the Unionist party and 70 Liberals. He hoped to be able
to win the support of the Labour party, and that he might
be able to offer concessions to Ireland which would secure
him also the support of the Irish members.[2]

Did Asquith, as Beaverbrook suggests, believe when he

[1] *H. C. Deb.*, 88,1718 (21 December 1916).
[2] *Manchester Guardian*, 7 December 1916.

C. P. Scott

Lloyd George in 1923

resigned from office that he would return within the week " as the only and inevitable Prime Minister ", having put his opponents " to the humiliation of being unable to form a Government "[1]? It is not easy to credit this conjecture. Clearly he thought that Lloyd George would find it harder to construct a ministry than proved to be the case, and probably in moments of optimism he imagined that events would soon discredit Lloyd George and restore himself to power. But plainly he was not leaving office because of any calculations he had made regarding Lloyd George's following, but because he could retain the premiership no longer. His resignation was not a manœuvre to strengthen his hold on office, but a despairing act of recognition that the process of retreat and surrender could go no farther, and that the time had come to abandon a position from which dignity and authority had already departed.[2]

For the Liberal party this constituted a shattering defeat—even though some excellent Liberals considered it necessary for success in the war. Since August 1914 the party had undergone one humiliation after another in attempting to keep a foothold in government. First the Liberal administration had given way to a coalition in which, though the Liberals were a considerable element, they were no longer certainly the dominant element. Many Liberals had resented this change, and had come round to supporting the new government only to keep conscription at bay ; then they had found themselves accepting conscription in order to save the government. Now it transpired that all their sacrifices of persons and principles had been in vain. In December 1916 the Liberal party as such was conclusively ejected from office, and a section of Liberals established an alliance with their party's traditional enemies to which there appeared no certain point of termination. Towards the new, basically non-Liberal regime which Lloyd George had formed, it was difficult for Liberals to behave either with sympathy or hostility. Many of them looked to it for more effective prosecution of the war, and felt bound to assist it in this task ; yet by doing so they enhanced the position of the Conservative party which dominated the government, and increased their

[1] *Politicians and the War*, p. 464.
[2] see appendix at the end of this chapter, pp. 102-3.

own party's discredit. Hitherto Liberals could hope that a startling improvement in the war might rescue them from disaster. Now not even success in battle would make any difference. Indeed, every step the Allies advanced towards victory brought catastrophe closer to the Liberal party.

II

On 8 December 1916, three days after Asquith's fall, a meeting of Liberal members of both Houses took place at the Reform Club. The purpose of the gathering was to hear statements from Asquith and Grey, and to pass a resolution defining the party's attitude to the new situation. The meeting was uneventful. The addresses by Asquith and Grey, while giving their views on the recent crisis and defending their actions, were by common consent statesmanlike and unprovocative. They were also not very illuminating. No discussion followed, apart from a characteristically fractious intervention from Handel Booth. A motion was proposed and accepted without dissent, thanking Asquith for his " magnificent services " to the nation and expressing unabated confidence in him as leader of the Liberal party, and also recording the party's determination " to give support to the King's Government engaged in the effective prosecution of the war." With this accomplished, the meeting came to an end.

In the light of subsequent events, what made this function noteworthy was the people who attended it. Accompanying Asquith and Grey was a phalanx of ex-ministers, whips, and devoted followers whom critics dubbed the " old gang ": men like Gulland, J. M. Robertson, Walter Rea, Geoffrey Howard, and Asquith's brother-in-law H. J. Tennant. Also present was an ex-minister who had preceded Asquith out of office, Sir John Simon. Probably for him the change of government was not without compensations. In spirit he belonged with Asquith on the right of the party, but sometimes he followed the prompting of his cool intellect when it told him that the centre of gravity lay on the left. Consequently his resignation from the government in January 1916 had placed him in a rather false position, making him the ally of radical anti-conscriptionists for whom he possessed no real sympathy and in whose company he had appeared decidedly uncomfortable. So possibly he welcomed the chance of rejoining his late colleagues, now that they too had been driven into the wilderness.

Also represented were the more characteristic opponents of conscription, the radical and "pacifist" wings of the party. The presence of M.P.s like R. D. Holt acts as a reminder that some in this category served out their political careers as Liberals. The presence of others, like R. L. Outhwaite, R. C. Lambert, H. B. Lees-Smith, and Joseph King, points to a different tendency evident in this section. By the end of the war or soon after, they had joined the Labour party and were utterly separated from the Liberals. Indeed only three years after accepting the resolution of confidence in Asquith, these and other ex-Liberals made a determined attempt to prevent him regaining a seat in Parliament.

And while the Liberals who soon after defected to Labour were in evidence at the Reform Club, so were those now moving into alliance with the Conservatives. Lloyd George, although certainly invited, was not present, but a number of Liberals who had joined or were about to join his government attended, like Kellaway and Sir L. Chiozza Money. Also on hand to defend the new Prime Minister was a strong contingent from the Liberal " ginger " group. Its members had anticipated an attempt being made to exclude them from the gathering, and had laid plans to invade it in case of need. But their precautions proved unnecessary. The day had yet to come when such an inclination towards the Conservatives as they were revealing would cause them to be excluded from a Liberal meeting.

One further group present on this occasion deserves mention : those rank and file Liberals who were not peculiarly committed to Asquith against Lloyd George or Lloyd George against Asquith, who wanted both the war and their party to prosper, and who in the ensuing years continued to act—if only rarely as Members of Parliament—as faithful Liberals. Yet already by December 1916 the foundations of their position were being dragged away by the disintegration going on around them. Something of the ineffectiveness to which they were being reduced was revealed by the events of this meeting. For though the party was still united enough to hold a meeting, it was of necessity a very innocuous affair quite out of keeping with the upheaval which had occasioned it. The formal, reserved speeches and absence of debate bore witness to deep divisions in the party which more positive conduct would have brought to the surface. Even the resolution passed at the meeting, for all its positive features, reflected this situation. For it was the positive expression of two divergent positions, and was acceptable to the whole meeting only because it went out of its way to satisfy both points of view. This inconsistency was brought out a few days later by two Liberal M.P.s who reserved seats for themselves on both sides of the House, and when taxed with this action explained that they were seeking to carry out the spirit of the Reform Club resolution, which had pledged them both to support the government and to continue under Asquith's leadership. Doubtless they were being facetious, but the situation on which their jest was based was fraught with danger for the Liberal party.

One small incident of the Reform Club meeting illustrates these diverse tendencies underlying the fragile unity of the party. Just before the meeting began, three Liberal M.P.s arrived together in a taxi. Their subsequent careers are illuminating. The first was Josiah Wedgwood, radical member for a Potteries constituency. He served with distinction in the war and during 1915 was associated with the " ginger " Liberals in advocating conscription, so that he was sometimes classified among Lloyd George's supporters. But this was not his real position : in a debate of May 1918 he criticised the Premier's associations with the Conservatives and hoped that Asquith would soon recover office. In the 1918 election he received the government's imprimatur but refused to stand as one of its supporters, and after the election acted with the opposition Liberals in Parliament. Then, in April 1919, he suddenly broke with the Liberal party altogether, arguing that its leaders were failing to uphold radical causes, and transferred to Labour.

Also occupying a seat in the taxi was MacCallum Scott, member for a working-class division of Glasgow. Like Wedgwood, he belonged to the radical wing of the party, but he was also an admirer of Churchill, about whom he had written two biographical works. For six years after the Reform Club meeting he followed an uncertain course as a radical Liberal

allied to the Conservatives, including a spell as private secretary
to Churchill. He lost his seat in 1922, but remained a Liberal
until late in 1924. Then, shocked by what he considered im-
proper associations between the Liberal leaders and the Conservatives, he abandoned the party and followed Wedgwood
into the Labour fold. (He was adopted as a Labour candidate,
but died in an air crash in Canada in 1928).

The third occupant of the taxi was the subject of MacCallum
Scott's works of biography. By December 1916 Churchill's
career as a radical Liberal lay behind him. A renegade from
the Conservatives, whom he had once represented in Parliament,
Churchill from early in the war seemed bent on working his
way back to his former party. Ideally, he wished to combine
both allegiances by building a bridge between Liberals and
Conservatives, so as not to damage further his reputation for
consistency. In the ensuing years these efforts proved unavail-
ing, and so in 1924, at almost the same time as Scott defected
to Labour, Churchill re-entered the Conservative party.

Thus by 1924 not one of the trio who arrived together at the
Reform Club remained in the Liberal ranks. If they retained
a common attitude to the Liberal party, it was because they
were united in seeking to crush it out of existence.

So even though nothing of import occurred at the Reform
Club on 8 December 1916, there remains a certain poignancy
about the gathering. Particularly is this true about the moment
of its termination : for as the function came to a close and the
participants went their separate ways, the old Liberal party,
which a short time before had won three consecutive general
elections and held office for a decade, was dispersing forever.
Never again did this group of people, or the forces they represented, assemble together at a single Liberal gathering. And
the party which had prospered by their conjunction was now
to fade into insignificance, weakened and at length attenuated by
their separation.

APPENDIX TO CHAPTER IV, p. 97

ASQUITH'S MOTIVES FOR RESIGNING

Since this paragraph was written, Beaverbrook's account has been strongly supported by Mr. A. J. P. Taylor, in a review of *Asquith* by Roy Jenkins (*Observer*, 1 November 1964). He says that " Mr Jenkins, though without new evidence, challenges the version of Lord Beaverbrook ", but that " there is decisive evidence the other way, not referred to by Mr Jenkins. Robert Donald, editor of the *Daily Chronicle*, a Liberal paper, has recorded that Asquith expected Lloyd George to fail : ' then he would have to come in on *my* terms.' "

Mr. Taylor has made a considerable contribution to our knowledge of this period (particularly in his book *Politics in Wartime*), and his judgement is not to be lightly set aside. But the following are grounds for disagreeing with him in this instance :

(a) It is not necessary to possess " new evidence " to challenge the version of *Politicians and the War*. Beaverbrook was providing an interpretation of events and seeking to divine Asquith's intentions : he had no direct evidence about Asquith's motives. Mr. Jenkins's view (and not his alone) is that the facts demand a different interpretation. For example, he argues cogently that in effect the resignation of the Conservative ministers " was directed solely against Asquith ", not (as Beaverbrook claimed) against Lloyd George as well. Mr. Taylor does not dispute this, but argues that " even if true " it was " not creditable to Asquith " because it proved him to be almost bereft of support. Certainly, from one point of view this was not creditable to Asquith. But it does support Mr. Jenkins's view (as against Beaverbrook's) that Asquith resigned because the foundations of power had gone, not because he was being too clever by half.

(b) The interview between Robert Donald and Asquith does not provide " decisive evidence " for the Beaverbrook view. In the passage quoted, Asquith and Donald were discussing, not whether Lloyd George would be able to form a government, but whether the government he formed would be able to last long. They were doing so, not while Asquith was contemplating resignation, but on the day *after* he resigned. And at no stage was Asquith speaking about his *motives for resigning*. Asquith may have said that if, as he seemed to anticipate, Lloyd George failed to form a " stable " government and he was recalled, " then Mr. Lloyd George would have to come in on *my* terms." But this is not the same thing as saying that he had resigned because he considered Lloyd George incapable of forming any kind of government. As a matter of fact, it is not a comment on his reasons for resigning at all. And certainly the interview provides no proof, *before the event*, of what was in Asquith's mind when he decided to relinquish office. It is not unusual for Prime Ministers who have been driven from power to believe that their successors must fail and that they themselves will soon be recalled—in the spirit, one might say, of *après moi le déluge, et, après le déluge, moi*. The interview with Donald seems no more than an example of a defeated man whistling to keep his courage up, and there is support for this in Donald's account of the interview. It begins : " I called on Mr. Asquith at 10, Downing Street, at 4 o'clock. He was sitting at the large table in the Cabinet room, his back to the fire. He looked a very lonely figure and a tired man." (Taylor, *Robert Donald*, pp. 118–23). This is hardly a portrait of an individual who believed that he was engaged in publicly humiliating his rivals, and that " within the week " he would be revealed as " the only and inevitable Prime Minister " of Great Britain.

5. LLOYD GEORGE IN POWER

Asquith has been in Brighton for some time—taking a rest. The Liberal party is much disintegrated.

Haldane to his sister, 2 March 1917 [1]

We have got him.

Beaverbrook on Lloyd George, September 1918 [2]

DURING the last two years of the war, the difficulties facing the Liberal party moved to a climax. Threatened by disruption within and attack on two fronts from without, the party wilted visibly before the dangers encompassing it.

Even more than during the first coalition, the Liberals had no clear role to play. They were at odds with one another over such problems of the war as Lloyd George's conflict with the generals and Lansdowne's plea for a negotiated peace ; and these divisions existed within the rival Liberal sections. Asquith, for example, took the side of the military leaders. Yet one of their strongest critics was the " pacifist " Joseph King, certainly no ally of Lloyd George. And when King voiced his opinions in Parliament (" Is there one general with whom we can say we are satisfied ? "), he was sharply rebuked by Sir Charles Henry and Sir Hamar Greenwood, two strong supporters of the new Prime Minister.[3] Similarly the Lansdowne letter, with its call for a negotiated peace, showed up Liberal differences. Francis Acland considered it " very good indeed—a great step forward "; to him the important thing was that " the war can only end if the people on both sides who want security for the future rather than triumph for the moment can get control in

---

[1] Haldane Papers.
[2] Scott's diary, 23–5 September 1918, C. P. Scott Papers.
[3] *H. C. Deb.*, 88, 1055–9 (15 December 1916).

their different countries & then get together."[1]   Arnold
Bennett, on the other hand, although like Acland hostile to
Lloyd George, did not " think much " of the Lansdowne letter.
" In this I agree with Spender ", he wrote.   ". . . . I do not for
an instant believe in the chance of any decent peace until
Germany has had a really severe & dramatic blow ".[2]   When
Buckmaster, the Lord Chancellor in the first coalition, sought to
rally the directors of the Liberal machine behind the Lansdowne
policy, he found them rigidly opposed.   " I have received a
blank and rather curt refusal from Gulland ", he wrote, " in
answer to my request to be allowed to use the Liberal Agencies
for the purpose of circulating Lord Lansdowne's letter.   I am
not prepared to let the matter drop there."[3]   Asquith in these
circumstances retired into equivocation.   He treated Lansdowne's letter as a call for a definition of war aims, which it
was easy for Liberals to support.

But it was not only on issues of policy that the Liberals were
uncertain.   They were undecided on the most pressing issue of
all, their attitude to the government.   Presumably the party
leaders did not wholly admire the new ministry, or they would
not have kept out of it.   Yet were they its opponents ?   This
was no minor question for Liberals.   Upon it depended a matter
of desperate importance: how far the split in their ranks had
gone.   Was there even a single party any longer, or two separate
and opposed parties ?   If Asquith followed up his refusal to
join the government by declaring war on it, then the Liberals
in Parliament would split into hostile parties : one which voted
with and one which voted against the government.   The menace
of such a division oppressed the Liberal party throughout these
years, and did much to cause its erratic and seemingly purposeless conduct.

II

In a sense, from December 1916 there were two Liberal parties
in Parliament, for one group of prominent Liberals sat on the
front government bench, and another on the front opposition

[1] Acland to his wife, 30 November (1917) and n.d., Acland Papers.
[2] Bennett to Gardiner, 30 November 1917, Gardiner Papers.
[3] Buckmaster to Gardiner, 2 December 1917, Gardiner Papers.

bench ; and when E. S. Montagu crossed from one side to the other (he joined the ministry in July 1917) he was treated as an apostate by the Asquithians.[1] Also, there were two sets of Liberal whips : Lloyd George's, who occupied the government whips' office in company with the Conservatives, and Asquith's, who now moved to the opposition whips' office.

Yet this did not utterly divide the parliamentary party, for there occurred no clear-cut separation of Liberal M.P.s. The whips canvassed, not distinct groups of Liberals, but all Liberal members. And Asquith's chief whip, Gulland, offered the party's assistance to Liberals entering the government should they have to resign their seats and fight by-elections. Moreover, the leading Asquithians denied being in conflict with the government. Liberals, said the semi-official *Liberal Magazine*, " have nothing but the sincerest good wishes for the new Administration "; and Asquith announced that he was not an opposition leader and would give the government " support, organised support ".[2] Even the fact that he sat on the opposition side of the House did not clearly invalidate this claim. The Liberal ministers who had lost office in May 1915, on the formation of the first coalition, had done the same, without necessarily opposing the government of the day. Admittedly after December 1916 circumstances were different, for irrespective of their intentions the occupants of the front opposition bench now constituted a potential alternative government. But the question was whether Asquith, contrary to his protestations, would seek to realise this potentiality by trying to unseat Lloyd George. If so, he must be prepared to force Liberal M.P.s into rival Liberal parties. And despite his strong antipathy to Lloyd George, he could not bring himself to do this. So mild, in fact, was his behaviour towards the government during its first year that in mid-1917 a Liberal journalist expressed the hope that Asquith would " not think it the whole of his duty to provide the Government with a way out, or to

[1] Montagu had already been rebuffed by Asquith a month before, when he joined a government committee on reconstruction. (Letters of 18 and 19 June 1917, Asquith Papers). The *Manchester Guardian*, 19 April 1918, commented that Montagu had been made to feel (" wrongly and absurdly ") that his acceptance of office " was something like an apostasy in respect to his former colleagues."

[2] *Liberal Magazine*, January 1917

106

devise for them a formula for saying something and doing nothing."[1]

The pattern for his conduct was established soon after the formation of the government. In March 1917 Lloyd George, against the wishes of Liberal ministers, introduced a form of tariff protection for the Indian cotton industry. Asquith was expected to resist firmly this affront to liberal convictions, but he failed to do so. The furthest he would go was to propose a temporising resolution, acceptable to and probably pre-arranged with the government, affirming that the matter should be considered afresh after the war. Several Liberal M.P.s criticised his conduct, saying that they had been prepared to make allowances while he was in office but expected something different now that he enjoyed the freedom of opposition. But did he see himself as occupying the " freedom of opposition " ? If so, it was not apparent from a message he sent soon afterwards to a follower in a by-election, calling on the electors " to preserve national unity by returning the official candidate to support the Government in a resolute prosecution of the war to victorious issues."[2]

From this date to the end of the war, Asquith at no time took a stronger line against the government in defence of liberal principles. He remained silent when it instituted a ban on the overseas circulation of the *Nation*, something which even Churchill and Dalziel attacked in " liberal " terms, and although he spoke strongly against the Corn Production Bill (which many Liberals condemned for providing state bounties to agriculture) he would not vote against it. Even when, apparently, a vital part of the liberal creed was at stake, Asquith persisted in this mediatory attitude. In April 1918 Lloyd George flouted Liberal opinion by deciding to extend conscription to Ireland, which hitherto had not been conscripted because it was not self-governing. This decision was partly a response to the military crisis caused by the German offensive in March, but it also represented a surrender to pressure from the Conservative rank and file—pressure which reflected less military necessity than traditional Conservative hostility to Ireland. Bonar Law, characteristically, disagreed with his followers but felt obliged to go along with them, for as he told

[1] *Manchester Guardian*, 15 June 1917.   [2] *ibid*, 2 April 1917.

H. A. L. Fisher : " personally he was against introducing conscription [to Ireland], but the Tories would have withdrawn
support if he hadn't."[1]

This decision provoked an uprising among Liberal and
Labour members of the government. After consulting together
they decided that they could assent to Irish conscription only
if it was to be immediately followed by Home Rule. So
strongly did they press their case that Lloyd George gave way ;
what was more, he announced the fact to Parliament in a speech
warmly favourable to Home Rule. This killed Conservative
enthusiasm for Irish conscription (which anyway was encoun-
tering formidable resistance in Ireland). Rather than have
Ireland advance towards self-government, the Conservatives
preferred that the conscription measure, once it was on the
Statute Book, should be quietly forgotten.

What for present purposes is noteworthy about this dis-
creditable episode is that the Liberal members of the government
were much more forthright in opposing Irish conscription than
was the leader of the Liberal party. Had Asquith assailed the
measure, he would have rallied a substantial Liberal following.
But once again he adopted the role of " a moderating influence
or a ' wet blanket,' according to the view you take of any
particular issue."[2] He told the House that, much as he disliked
the measure, he would not do anything to oppose the government at this time. Granted that he was influenced by the
gravity of the military situation (his principal speech coincided
with Haig's " backs-to-the-wall " Order of the Day), it still
appeared that by letting pass a proposal so repugnant to liberal
convictions, and foregoing such an opportunity to attack the
government, he was abrogating conclusively the role of opposition
leader in wartime. Indeed he later cited his behaviour on this
occasion to refute the charge that he had adopted such a role.
His defence would seem to have been justified, for even the
pro-government *Manchester Guardian* had said that, " notwithstanding all the obvious risks,"[3] he ought to have voted
against Irish conscription.

Yet there were a few occasions when his hostility to Lloyd
George almost got the better of him. As we have seen, these

[1] Fisher's diary, 29 April 1918, Fisher Papers. Fisher was Minister of Education
in the Lloyd George government.

[2] *Manchester Guardian*, 10 April 1918.   [3] *ibid*, 16 April 1918.

were not (oddly enough) instances when the government con-
travened liberal ideals. They sprang from the conflict between
Lloyd George and the military leaders of the nation. As a
Liberal, Asquith might have been expected to side with the
government against the soldiers. But he saw this not as a
struggle between civilians and military but as another manifestation of Lloyd George's lust for power. To him, the Prime
Minister was seeking to overthrow the country's military
leaders in the same unscrupulous, unwarranted fashion that he
had earlier overthrown first Kitchener and then Asquith himself.
Moreover, the Liberal leader recognised that in attacking the
strategy of Haig and Robertson, Lloyd George was implicitly (and
sometimes quite explicitly) condemning the running of the
war during Asquith's own premiership.

Twice on account of Lloyd George's intervention in military
affairs Asquith came to the point of attacking but then drew
back : the first time was in November 1917, on account of
Lloyd George's speech in Paris criticising Allied strategy and
giving reasons for setting up an Allied War Council ; the
second was in February 1918, following the resignation of
Sir William Robertson, Chief of the Imperial General Staff.
Then on a third occasion Asquith did not draw back. In a letter
to *The Times* on 7 May 1918, Major-General Sir Frederick
Maurice accused the government of misleading Parliament
about the strength of British forces on the western front during
the German attack in March. So strongly did Asquith feel
about this that, only a month after refusing to vote against
Irish conscription, he moved for an inquiry into Maurice's
charges, and pressed the motion to a division after Lloyd George
had characterised it as a vote of censure.

This seemed a grave action. Two days before the vote, a
political commentator said of Asquith : " He has never before
taken so positive a step in opposition. He has never, I think,
before put down a notice of motion."[1] And *The Times* called
the actual division " the *début* of an organised Opposition."[2]
This, it said, was the first occasion during the war on which
the opposition whips had acted as tellers against the government
and the opposition front bench had voted against it on an issue
of confidence. Yet reading Asquith's speech in the debate (the

[1] *ibid*, 8 May 1918.   [2] *The Times*, 10 May 1918.

sole contribution to come from his front bench) it is difficult to believe that he took the matter so seriously. At no point did he make an outright attack on the government or say that he believed Maurice's charges to be true. Further, he was at pains to insist that his motion was not a vote of censure. The government had at first suggested that a judicial committee should investigate Maurice's charges—a suggestion which it quickly withdrew—and Asquith devoted his speech to explaining why the investigation should be carried out not by judges but by a select committee of the House. The *Manchester Guardian* on 10 May found his behaviour " most difficult to comprehend." He had treated grave charges against the government as if they were only a matter of procedure. " People do not understand this formalistic attitude to affairs of life and death."

The explanation seems to be that even now he could not bring himself to act as an opposition leader. His later statements bear this out, for he always thereafter denied that his motion had been intended as a vote of censure. Nor did he say this only in public. In a private letter of November 1918, which he cannot have thought would reach a wider audience, he wrote that Lloyd George's description of the Maurice incident as a conspiracy to overthrow the government was a " blackguardly " accusation.[1] But in that case, why did he go to the length of forcing a division ? Nothing in the Maurice incident seemed to call for it. Even if he did not accept Lloyd George's apparent refutation of Maurice's charges, it hardly seemed the business of a Liberal leader to embarrass the government for the sake of an insubordinate soldier. It should be remembered that Maurice's charges, whether true or false, were based on privileged information obtained in the service of the government. Addison was not exaggerating unduly when he called this a " remarkable example of military anarchy."[2] The same point was made to A. G. Gardiner by a former military correspondent of the *Daily News:* " Though I am no longer serving the *Daily News* [he wrote] will you allow me as your quondam Military Correspondent to say how strongly I feel the breach of discipline committed by General Maurice?" Certainly, he said, it was

[1] *H. H. A. Letters of the Earl of Oxford and Asquith to a Friend*, First Series, p. 85.
[2] Addison, *Four and a Half Years*, vol. 2, p. 522.

necessary for Parliament to settle the question of ministers' veracity ; " but Maurice was not the man to put his chiefs right. As long as he is serving, a soldier has to take his likes and dislikes of the politicians, under whom he is serving, lying down. . . . Soldiers are the servants, not the masters of the State. . . . I wonder if you agree. I rather think you do judging from a talk I once had with you about the Ulster troubles."[1] As this last sentence suggests, it was hardly consistent for Liberals who had condemned military insubordination during the Curragh incident to sympathise with it now.[2]

There could be only one reason why Asquith would divide the House in these circumstances : he hoped that an inquiry into Maurice's allegations would damage the government and shake Lloyd George's hold on Parliament and the country. Doubtless he was sincere when he said that he was not attempting to defeat the government (his innocuous contribution to the debate bears this out), but he was embarking on a course which, if successful, would certainly injure it. This was the nearest he got to displaying publicly his feeling against Lloyd George. But it was such a half-hearted display, especially after he had let slip so many better opportunities for attacking the government, that it fell far short of converting him into an opposition leader. The most it can be said to have done was to throw doubt on his claim not to be acting as one.

Given the dislike of the government which this incident revealed, why did Asquith not wage war upon it ? After all, as he admitted during the Maurice debate, some of his followers yearned for him to do so. Probably he was restrained by the fact that, at a time of war and an ill-defined party truce, he was uncertain what his role should be, and quite certain that he did not want to provoke the government into holding an election. But it is clear that the major influence on his conduct was his desire to avoid what one of his whips called " organic

[1] A. M. Murray to Gardiner, 11 May 1918, Gardiner Papers.
[2] This does not mean that the Liberal leaders had no cause for resentment if the government, by presenting misleading information to the House, was concealing its responsibility for the military setback in March. But while this might have justified Asquith in levelling charges against the government, it hardly entitled him, without making such charges, to condone Maurice's action.

division " in the Liberal party.[1] As far as Parliament was concerned it lay in his power, as in no one else's, to bring about the formation of rival Liberal parties. When individuals like Pringle and Hogge, or groups like the Liberal " pacifists ", assailed Lloyd George they spoke only for themselves, and they did not secure the support of the many M.P.s who would join in an attack only if Asquith led it. Furthermore, Asquith's reluctance to take issue with the government decided the conduct of Lloyd George and his followers also. So long as Asquith did not attack, there was no call on the Prime Minister, and little opportunity for him, to make a definite break with his former chief or persuade his supporters to do so. The result was that, for all the tension in the parliamentary party, the Liberals in the House of Commons preserved to the end of the war a tenuous unity.

III

Similarly in the country, there were not yet separate Liberal parties. Admittedly there were many signs of strain. One of Asquith's objects in securing a resolution of confidence from the meeting on 8 December 1916 was to ensure that he remained Liberal leader; for as leader he controlled the headquarters and fund of the party. The party headquarters (the Liberal Central Association) was directed by the chief whip, who also had the party fund at his " quite uncontrolled discretion ". But " according to established custom " the whip himself was appointed by the leader, without reference to the party. This in effect gave Asquith control of the central Liberal machine.[2]

Lloyd George responded by setting up his own headquarters. It soon possessed a staff of over a dozen agents, some of whom were sent to visit Liberal workers in the country. (On occasion they even described themselves as representing " Liberal headquarters " !). At the same time he set to work accumulating

[1] Geoffrey Howard in an address to the executive of the Yorkshire Liberal Federation. Minutes of the Yorkshire Liberal Federation, 31 January 1917.

[2] The quotations are from an unsigned but clearly official document of Asquith's headquarters, dating from about January 1919. It will be referred to hereafter as: "The Liberal Party" document, Asquith Papers.

a political fund. One of its principal sources became apparent when he issued his first honours list, which (according to the *Nation*) bore " its usual character of that falsification of merit which belongs to its secret and evil source."[1] Similar complaints about the sale of honours continued throughout Lloyd George's premiership, though the Liberal leaders rarely joined in them, perhaps because they hoped to regain office before long and so replenish their own party fund.

At the same time as these rival headquarters and funds were being established, an underground struggle was proceeding for control of Liberal newspapers. Lloyd George had an inordinate belief in the power of the press, and yearned to control at least one Liberal daily. None of the four major Liberal newspapers could be counted on to support him in every eventuality. The *Manchester Guardian* was very close to him, but it remained devoted to the Liberal cause and could not suppress misgivings about his ultimate intentions. The *Daily News* and *Westminster Gazette* were plainly hostile, owing to the attitude of their editors. Gardiner, who edited the *Daily News*, was one of Lloyd George's most trenchant critics from a radical viewpoint, and Spender of the *Westminster Gazette*, if more judicious, was also more officially Asquithian. In fact, by visiting Haig at the front in October 1917 Spender sparked off an unfortunate scene between the Prime Minister and the Commander-in-Chief; on their next meeting Lloyd George berated Haig for enter- taining his " personal enemies ".[2] The fourth Liberal paper, the *Daily Chronicle*, was somewhere between the *Manchester Guardian* and the *Westminster Gazette* in outlook. Its editor, Robert Donald, had once been closely associated with Lloyd George, his near-neighbour and frequent golfing companion. But since 1914 they had rather diverged, particularly over conscription and Lloyd George's " personal ambitions ", and the breach widened after Lloyd George became Prime Minister. Evidence of the divergence was provided in May 1918, when Donald hired General Maurice, who had been retired from

[1] *Nation*, 9 June 1917.
[2] See the unsigned, undated memorandum (clearly written by Spender) in the Spender Papers. Haig, according to this account, " retorted warmly " to Lloyd George " that he had no knowledge of Lloyd George's personal feuds and would choose his guests at his own discretion." But thereafter Spender found himself not a welcome visitor at the front.

the army on account of his famous letter, as the paper's military correspondent, and in the following September when Donald wrote an editorial criticising Lloyd George's " small mind " in " petulantly " refusing to congratulate Haig on his recent victories.[1]

Of these four papers, two were unlikely to come on the market: the *Manchester Guardian*, owned by its editor C. P. Scott, and the *Daily News*, owned by the Cadbury family. So Lloyd George directed his attention to the *Westminster Gazette* and *Daily Chronicle*. As the former was an evening paper with a limited London circulation, it might appear surprising that he made so many attempts to capture it. But it enjoyed considerable prestige—the American crime novelist Raymond Chandler, who was once employed by the *Westminster Gazette*, calls it " perhaps the best evening paper the world ever saw "[2] —and its influence was out of all proportion to its circulation. Lloyd George, so Spender was told, held that it was more quoted abroad than any paper except *The Times*, and that it was of great importance to him not to be exposed to its criticisms.[3] Moreover the desperate financial position of the paper made it vulnerable to his attacks. Even before the war it had been losing about £11,000 a year, and since 1914 this deficit had risen sharply. In 1912 the paper had been taken over by a syndicate of wealthy Liberals who felt it should be preserved as an influential Liberal organ whatever its financial shortcomings. But in 1917 these shareholders included two members of the government, Mond and Lord Cowdray, as well as Henry, a devoted follower of the Prime Minister, and they were not likely to prolong it indefinitely as an Asquithian journal.

As early as December 1916 David Davies, Lloyd George's parliamentary private secretary and one of his most active and wealthy Welsh supporters, made overtures to an Asquithian shareholder regarding the purchase of the paper " in the War Government interest ". He met with no response, and let the matter lapse.[4] Then late in 1917 Lloyd George and his allies

---

[1] Taylor, *Robert Donald*, pp. 165–74 ; *Daily Chronicle*, 13 September 1918.

[2] *Raymond Chandler Speaking*, p. 22.

[3] Spender to Asquith, 4 October 1917, Asquith Papers.

[4] Joseph Davies, *The Prime Minister's Secretariat 1916–1920*, p. 56. This book, in common with many commentators at the time, pays tribute to the

—though now without the support of David Davies—made a concerted effort to gain control of the paper, and came so near success that by October Spender's position was " both grave and urgent."[1] To effect a change of editor, Lloyd George had to secure the agreement of two key shareholders, Cowdray and Murray (who were striving to keep the peace between the Liberal camps). The following letter from the Prime Minister to Murray indicates the pressure he was bringing to bear on them. He enclosed a cutting from the *Westminster Gazette* and said of it :

Here is another example of the kind of offensive attack which you and Cowdray are subsidising against your friends. The political part of it I do not mind so long as it is clearly understood that you are out to discredit me and my Colleagues. That I feel certain is not your policy. All the same your paper never misses an opportunity of undermining the influence of the Government amongst Liberals. That, however, is not my chief complaint, but rather against the very offensive personal attack which is made in the paragraph which I have marked. . . . If this kind of hitting below the belt had been indulged in in any other paper, I should never have complained but I do think it hard that it should be done in a newspaper directed, controlled, and " kept " by my own friends.

As a postscript he added in his own hand " I never heard of

---

services which David Davies, M.P. for Montgomeryshire, rendered Lloyd George by rallying Liberal support in December 1916. Davies's services, however, did not save him from a quite appalling letter of repudiation, in June 1917, as a consequence of some rather pompous letters he had written to Lloyd George urging him not to deviate from Liberal paths. " I regret having to tell you ", Lloyd George wrote, " that there is a concerted attack to be made upon me for what is called ' sheltering ' in a soft job a young officer of military age and fitness. . . . I hear that Welsh parents—North and South—are highly indignant and do not scruple to suggest that your wealth is your shield. . . . I am sure you will agree that I am taking the straight course intimating to the Committee set up to re-examine men in the public service that in my judgment you can render better service to your country as a soldier than in your present capacity." (The full correspondence may be found in Frank Owen, *Tempestuous Journey*, pp. 378–82.)

[1] Lord Crewe to Asquith, 6 October 1917, Asquith Papers.

another case where a member of a Govt financed a paper to attack his own Colleagues."[1]

Cowdray as a minister was vulnerable to this kind of pressure. He and Murray sought to restrain Spender, but this was not likely to have satisfied Lloyd George, and anyway Spender was " very touchy about his ' authority ' ".[2] Rather than lose what he considered his " reasonable independence "[3], Spender preferred to resign, and at the beginning of October 1917 he informed Asquith that he would soon have to do so. " I may tell you in confidence that Alec Murray has intimated that the moderate criticism of the Government which the W.G. permits itself places him & Cowdray in an exceedingly awkward position & has asked that it shall cease. I doubt his right to speak for Cowdray[4] but so long as Cowdray is a member of the Government, we cannot look for any help from him." Lloyd George had declared war on him, Spender wrote, by starting a libel action over the offending paragraph, and " hostile shareholders " were demanding that he " promise to refrain from all criticism of the Government or Ll. G. in the future. Needless to say, I shall do nothing of the kind ". But the financial problems of the paper were acute, and unless fresh financial assistance could be obtained his opponents would either close it down or establish a new directorate without him.[5]

> It is open to the shareholders to elect a new board and change the direction of the paper by a bare majority. Several of the shareholders have been approached with offers for their shares in view, no doubt, of this possibility, and the would-be buyers have very confidently expressed their opinion that the Westminster Gazette will fall into their hands before the end of the year.[6]

But before this takeover could occur, the situation changed abruptly and Spender's position was saved. For this turn of events, Lloyd George had only himself to blame. He had been

[1] Lloyd George to Murray, 17 September 1917, Elibank Papers.
[2] Murray to Cowdray, 18 August 1915, Elibank Papers.
[3] Spender to Murray, 6 June 1916, Elibank Papers.
[4] This was a misjudgement. Murray sometimes even drafted Cowdray's letters to Spender.
[5] Spender to Asquith, 4 October 1917, Asquith Papers.
[6] Unsigned, undated document, clearly written by Spender in October 1917, Asquith Papers.

trying to fry much larger journalistic fish than the *Westminster Gazette*, and had been pressing the greatest of all press magnates, Northcliffe, to join his government. In confidence he offered Northcliffe the Air Board, the very post which Cowdray occupied in the government. Cowdray first learned that his office was being hawked about when he read in *The Times* an open letter from Northcliffe refusing it. He promptly resigned from the ministry, and never forgave Lloyd George this affront. In consequence, his weight was thrown wholly against those shareholders trying to unseat Spender. In fact, he soon after became principal proprietor of the *Westminster Gazette* so as to preserve it as a journal hostile to Lloyd George. In September 1918 Spender wrote : " Cowdray has been the good Angel of the W.G. & I cannot be too grateful to him. We should almost certainly have been on the rocks without him."[1]

Thwarted in this direction, Lloyd George turned to the *Daily Chronicle*. Earlier in 1917, while still on reasonably friendly terms with Robert Donald, he had talked to him about buying the paper. But a sum of over £1½ millions was not easy to raise, and Frank Lloyd, the proprietor, was not certain he wanted to sell. By the middle of 1918 the paper seemed more likely to come on the market, but Donald was now quite hostile to Lloyd George and sought to prevent it from falling into his hands. He got together a group of Asquithian Liberals, including Cowdray, with a scheme for taking over the paper, but their proposal failed to satisfy Frank Lloyd, who anyway intimated that he had now decided against selling until after the war. Donald therefore let the matter drop. By the time he learned that Lloyd had decided differently, the paper had been secretly purchased by a Lloyd George syndicate and his days as editor were at an end. The faithful Dalziel was to direct the paper, but only as the agent of Lloyd George, who was to have full control of editorial policy.[2] Spender wrote in great perturbation :

The D.C. was bought by the Lloyd George syndicate & the secret so well kept that Donald heard of it for the first time on Friday afternoon. Ll. G. & Freddy Guest [Lloyd George's chief whip] both took part in the affair & saw Frank Lloyd whose surrender astonishes me. . . . No one

[1] Spender to Murray, 6 September 1918, Elibank Papers.
[2] *Lord Riddell's War Diary*, p. 365 ; Taylor, *Robert Donald*, pp. 175–83.

believed that Lloyd's price (£1,600,000) could possibly be found, & the names of the subscribers except Andrew Weir & James White are still in doubt. . . .[1]

Of course it is a very serious business for the " old gang " & David Davies whom I have seen is already seething with vague ideas about a morning W.G. I think we ought to have a meeting the moment Parliament assembles & see whether we can bring out a morning sheet at all events for the election, if there is to be one.[2]

Nothing came of this " seething ". The upshot was that Lloyd George had got his newspaper, and that both Donald and Maurice were obliged to seek other employment. This struggle for control of Liberal newspapers, together with the existence of rival headquarters and funds, suggests that even before the end of the war separate Liberal parties existed outside Parliament. But for the one party to become conclusively two, the conflict had to be carried to a further level : into the constituencies. In a sense, the Liberal constituency associations, the party's organs in the electorates, were its sovereign bodies, for they alone had the power to nominate official Liberal candidates, and their choice did not require headquarters' approval " The Liberal Party ", stated an official document of Asquith's headquarters, " adheres to the principle that the local Associations are the right authorities to determine Liberal candidatures."[3] It followed that the composition of the party in the House of Commons was decided, not by the rival headquarters of Asquith or Lloyd George, but by Liberal associations free from dictation by either central organisation.

Now in fact their autonomy was rarely this complete. The Liberal leaders were prepared, where possible, to dissuade

[1] It is surprising that, even this early, Spender did not think of Lloyd George's political fund as a likely subscriber. Weir, who became Lord Inverforth in 1919 and was Minister of Munitions from 1919 to 1921, was a wealthy Scottish shipowner. James White, apparently, was a " notorious Lancashire company promoter who committed suicide in 1927." In 1918 he was mentioned for a knighthood, but instead asked for permission to float a company, the Treasury having forbidden new issues, and permission was granted. (Taylor, *Robert Donald*, p. 181.)

[2] Spender to Maclean, 8 October 1918, Asquith Papers.

[3] " The Liberal Party " document, Asquith Papers.

Liberal associations from adopting " disagreeable "candidates,
either by urging them not to disturb the unity of the party, or
by threatening to withhold financial aid towards their election
expenses. Such methods were soon employed by Asquith and
his colleagues. In the Derby by-election of December 1916—
as it happened, the first by-election following the change of
government—they intervened to forestall the adoption of a
Lloyd George Liberal. The Derby Liberal association first tried
unsuccessfully to secure Cyril Asquith, the leader's son, as its
candidate. Then it acted on the suggestion of J. H. Thomas,
who was Labour member for the other Derby seat, that they
offer the candidature to Joseph Davies, a close associate of
Lloyd George. Davies was invited to the constituency and
was well received, and Thomas told him that his nomination
was assured. But at this point (according to Davies's account,
which he says was endorsed by Donald Maclean) Asquith's
headquarters learned of his sympathy for Lloyd George and
strongly opposed his adoption. Howard, one of the whips,
went to the constituency and prevailed on the executive of the
Liberal association to override a decision already taken by
their general council to adopt Davies. In consequence, a new
candidate was decided upon.[1] The local Conservatives were
indignant at this proceeding, and only with difficulty were
restrained from breaking the party truce by putting up a
candidate.

There were other instances where party headquarters pressed
associations or candidates to follow an Asquithian line. But
such pressure never went to the point of causing a formal breach
in the party in the constituencies. To do this, Asquith's headquarters would have had to take punitive action against associations aligning themselves with Lloyd George, by repudiating
their nominees and running " approved " candidates against
them. Of this there was no suggestion. Where a Liberal
association proved steadfast in adopting a Coalition Liberal
and could finance his campaign, the party leaders bowed to this
decision and accepted him, with however bad a grace, as the
official Liberal candidate. Once elected, he became automatically a member of the parliamentary party.

Lloyd George also accepted the decision of Liberal associations

[1] Davies, *The Prime Minister's Secretariat 1916–1920*, pp. 34–7.

regarding candidates. Whatever he had done to divide the Liberal ranks, he was not prepared at this stage to establish a separate party in the country. Admittedly he had his own headquarters. But in the electorates his only organisation consisted of existing associations and federations (like the Welsh National Liberal Council) which threw in their lot with him. The political agents he sent around the country were seeking to win over established Liberal bodies, not set up new bodies in rivalry to them. In fact, on the one occasion when an over-zealous supporter did threaten to create an open breach by standing against an Asquithian candidate, Lloyd George intervened to restrain him. In the South Aberdeen by-election of March 1917, the Liberal association chose as its candidate a known follower of Asquith, Sir John Fleming, in preference to a disciple of Lloyd George, Sir George Murray. (Murray had purchased and presented to the Aberdeen Art Gallery a famous portrait of Lloyd George by Augustus John). Murray thereupon announced that he would stand anyway as a government supporter. But Lloyd George prevailed on him to withdraw, explaining that he did not want it said that his friends were impairing national unity. He would have been less than human—or anyway less than Lloyd George—had he not gone on to say that should Murray have persisted in standing he would certainly have been elected.

IV

So for all its dissensions, there was still a single Liberal party both in Parliament and the country. The reason why the division went no further is clear. Each section hesitated to take the ultimate step of splitting the party asunder and so encompassing its destruction. Whatever their feelings about Lloyd George, the Liberals outside the government feared " organic division " in the party and would not institute such a division themselves. Asquith in fact made a tentative appeal for reunion during a speech at Glasgow on 1 November 1918. He had established the first coalition, he said, on the clear understanding that it was only for the duration of the war, and he urged that there should be no election until parties had freed themselves to pursue their own policies on their own lines.

The lines of Liberal policy had been laid down at meetings of the National Liberal Federation. Was there any Liberal who did not accept them or would be content with less ? " Where, then," he asked, " are the differences among us ? " In the past each great party had suffered division on matters of principle, but nothing of the sort was true of Liberals now. As for the " personal aspect ", he said that he knew of no disposition " in any quarter of the Liberal party [towards] exclusions and ostracisms of anybody who is prepared to accept with a whole heart and carry out with conviction the principles of Liberal policy."

Lloyd George's followers, also, though they had gone far to divide the party, hesitated to disrupt it. Addison, who was ready to do so, found himself considered " too pugilistic " by his Liberal colleagues, who showed a "strong disposition" against " precipitating divisions ". Churchill was one of those inclined to keep a foot in both camps, while Guest, the chief Coalition Liberal whip, " still seems to dream of a reunion with Asquith's people, which, in my [Addison's] judgment, is past praying for." Even Lloyd George sometimes shared Guest's feelings. He gave his approval to attempts by coalition supporters like Murray of Elibank, Lord Reading, and Gordon Hewart, to persuade Asquith to join the government. He hesitated to hold an election during the war because it would mean a final " break with Asquith." And although he was attracted by a scheme to merge Conservatives and Coalition Liberals into a formal party under his leadership, he saw a difficulty in that it would mean " an absolute and definite split " in the Liberal party.[1]

Yet if Liberals on both sides were reluctant to divide the party utterly, they seemed in no hurry to effect a reconciliation. Apart from Asquith's rather reserved plea on 1 November 1918 (" Where, then, are the differences among us ? "), he and his associates made few gestures towards reunion. Their main contribution was to avoid mentioning the division in the party.

[1] Addison, *Four and a Half Years*, vol. 2, pp. 387, 447, 459, 528, 588 ; *Lord Riddell's War Diary*, p. 337. Yet when in September 1918 a serious attempt was made to draw Asquith into the government as Lord Chancellor, Lloyd George laid down conditions which Asquith was bound to reject : an immediate general election, and a revival of Irish conscription.

When Asquith, for example, held a conference with party agents in February 1918 and was asked to discuss relations with Lloyd George, he refused to speak on the matter. And the first war-time conference of the National Liberal Federation, in September 1918, succeeded in covering nearly every aspect of current affairs except the division in the party. (Only Pringle managed to slip in a reference to it by speaking of Lloyd George as a leader " whom we loved long since but lost awhile "; and this begged the question as to whether Lloyd George was lost " awhile " or for good). Even more was it true of the Liberals in the government that, though wanting to avoid " an absolute and definite split ", they would contribute virtually nothing to the reunion of the party. They were happy to invite Asquith, with perhaps two or three of his followers, to join the existing regime. But they had no intention of achieving Liberal reunion by bringing that regime to an end. Their alliance with the Con-servatives was paramount in their considerations, and for some of them not just for the duration of the war. As early as 1915 Lloyd George had shocked orthodox Liberals by adumbrating a union with former opponents after the war ; and repeatedly during 1917 and 1918 he spoke of converting the coalition into a permanent " National " party.

Thus while the Liberal party was able to maintain a precarious unity during these years, this provided no guarantee that ultimate division would be avoided. The personal antipathy felt by Asquithians towards members of the government showed no sign of abating. When Addison encountered McKinnon Wood in July 1918 he found him " full of venom against L.G.",[1] a feeling shared by many of Wood's colleagues. Not least was this true of Asquith. When he was approached by Lloyd George in January 1918 to draw up a joint statement on war aims he accorded the Prime Minister a very cool reception. Margot Asquith wanted it known " that Ll. G. had to come to us " to draw up this statement, as her husband " wd. *not* go to Downing St.'[2] As for proposals that Asquith should enter Lloyd George's government, he treated them with the same contempt as he had shown in December 1916. In May 1917 Murray and Reading, the Lord Chief Justice, pressed such a scheme upon

[1] Addison, *Four and a Half Years*, vol. 2, p. 550.
[2] Margot Asquith to Gardiner, 7 January 1918, Gardiner Papers.

him. Asquith considered the matter sufficiently important to leave a record of his response. He wrote that one of his guests over the Whitsun week-end was Reading, who it soon transpired had come on a political mission. On the Saturday morning Reading approached the matter indirectly, by talking about possible changes in the war cabinet. This got him nowhere. Asquith told him that the war cabinet was a hopeless and un-workable experiment, and that : " Self-respecting statesmen cd. not be expected to take part in such a crazy adventure." Asquith's account continues :

This (Monday) morning the L.C.J. returned to the charge, with something more like a frontal attack. He said that he, & many others, regarded my active participation in the Govt as essential, & he hinted that this was the view of the Prime Minister. I gathered that I cd. have any post I chose, except that of head of the Govt.

I answered that I must use perfectly plain language since he had raised the subject. I was quite ready to go on giving the Govt full support, so long as they carried on the war in the proper spirit, & to use my influence with my party, & in the country, in the same sense. But he & others had better understand clearly, & at once, that under no conditions wd. I serve in a Govt of wh. Ll. G. was the head. I had learned by long & close association to mistrust him profoundly. I knew him to be incapable of loyalty or lasting gratitude. I had always acknowledged, & did still, to the full, his many brilliant & useful faculties, but he needed to have some one over him. In my judgment he had incurable defects, both of intellect and character, wh. totally unfitted him to be at the head.

The L.C.J. with rather a wry face acquiesced. To some further vaguely tentative overtures, I replied that I could not associate myself with what he called " the counsels" of any Govt unless I had supreme & ultimate authority.[1]

In his stand on this matter Asquith was immovable. When Murray approached him in September 1918 with an offer of the Lord Chancellorship, Asquith made it clear that, quite apart from unacceptable conditions which Lloyd George had

[1] Memorandum by Asquith, 28 May 1917, Asquith Papers.

attached, he would " in no circumstances whatever " serve under Lloyd George. " The inwardness of Mr. A's attitude ", Murray recounted, " is that he does not really trust either Lloyd George or Balfour, and could not therefore serve in the Government with them. He spoke strongly on these lines ".[1]

But even more ominous than these personal antagonisms was the party's inherent division over the question of future relations with the Conservatives. While some Liberals expected in time to resume their pre-war opposition to the Conservatives, others hoped to establish a permanent alliance between the two parties. This meant that the Liberal party was incipiently divided about whether, ultimately, it should belong politically on the right or the left—what seemed to many observers the fundamental issue of British politics. As a leading Liberal editor and economist, H. D. Henderson, wrote some years later:

> The broad question which the two-party system asks :
> " Do you incline, on the whole, towards the Right, or towards the Left ? " is the most sensible question which it is possible to ask of the electorate. It is a question which corresponds far more closely to the realities of human psychology than the more complicated questions which a multiple-party system inevitably raises. The issue is one which presents itself in every department of life. Wherever men take part in collective action, and questions of policy arise, there is a fundamental cleavage between the more adventurous and the more cautious, the more open-minded and the more prejudiced, the more progressive and the more conservative. Men fluctuate, of course, pass from the one camp to the other, find themselves ranged on particular issues against those with whom they are normally in sympathy ; and some are not quite sure to which camp they normally belong. But the two camps are there. Who does not recognise their existence ?

Furthermore, he went on, " this fundamental cleavage " between left and right was " the abiding reality that lay behind the old warfare of Liberal and Tory, and compared with this the political issues or the political philosophies of the moment

---

[1] Memorandum by Murray, 2 October 1918 ; and A. C. Murray to Sir William Wiseman, 8 October 1918, Elibank Papers.

were of secondary importance."[1] It was already apparent
before the war ended that Liberals like Lloyd George and
Churchill, irrespective of their feelings towards their former
colleagues, had moved from one side to the other of the " fundamental cleavage " which was " the abiding reality that lay
behind the old warfare of Liberal and Tory," and that most
leading Liberals outside the government had not.

The consequence of this situation was that, although a
measure of unity remained in the Liberal party, this did little
to raise the party's morale, for it appeared that the danger of
" organic division " was only being postponed and not removed.
And as the price of avoiding a severance between the two sections
of Liberals, Asquith doomed his party to impotence. The main
body of Liberals simply ceased to participate effectively in
politics during the later years of the war. At a time when
Lloyd George was arousing great enthusiasm as a national
leader in some quarters, and deep antipathy as an adventurer
and instrument of reaction in others, Asquith elected to occupy
a political no-man's-land, where he was neither quite attacking
nor quite supporting the Prime Minister. Apparently he did
not appreciate the damage which this was causing the party,
for he seems to have regarded these years as an abnormal and
transitory period in which it did not greatly matter if Liberals
adopted differing positions or no position at all. Here he seriously miscalculated, for the last years of the war were not a
hiatus between eras of normality, but a crucial formative period
in which lasting allegiances were being made and permanent
alignments established. By its attitude of non-commitment,
the Liberal party appeared fumbling and irrelevant.

The virtual abstention from affairs which this attempt to
maintain a semblance of unity imposed on Liberals went far
to create the despondency so evident in their ranks by the
end of the war—the uncomfortable feeling that Liberalism was
a spent force with its mission almost at an end. " My old
party, the Liberals, are not fertile at present ", Haldane
wrote in November 1917. " The feeling is that their work
is over for the present."[2] At the same time Acland was writing :

[1] *Nation*, 5 November 1927.
[2] Haldane to his mother, 28 November 1917, Haldane Papers.

I really think that the Liberal party is dead, & that one will simply have to think of men & policies after the war—not of parties. I think the ex Cabinet ministers might have done more than they have done in working out policies on social questions & that sort of thing (for instance Asquith should have made a very big protest against dropping the Edn. Bill) but it would have been difficult to do without being violently attacked. " You *say* let us all unite and get on with the war but really you're taking advantage of the Govt being hard at work to undermine them & distract the country & divert it from working at the war."[1]

Not all Liberals were as resigned as Acland to their party's misfortunes. In Parliament and the press they deplored its seeming impotence and demanded a call to action. Some M.P.s complained of leadership which " almost breaks our hearts ", and asserted that their leaders " have been losing ground in the House and outside."

There are only two sovereign words in politics [one of them said] when an issue is raised, and those words are " Yes " and " No." Our leaders are apt to avoid saying " Yes " or " No," and they are apt to try to reconcile the two. I venture to hope that after this Bill [the Corn Production Bill] has passed they will be able to take up a firmer attitude on other measures.[2]

Similar sentiments appeared in Liberal newspapers. " A Liberal M.P." wrote deploring " the serious position " of the party in Parliament and the state of " impotence " to which it had been reduced.[3] And " An Old Liberal " asked " Where is the Liberal Party ? ": " It is strangely quiet, it is gone quite dumb. . . . There is surely need of a call to arms and for some definite statement of party aims from those whose duty it is to lead." His conclusion was that Liberalism " is paralysed with the fear of seeming disloyal, and compounds by being disloyal to itself. The party is gone tame. It has no fight in it. We want definite, clear, and decided leadership which shall be bold, courageous, and aggressive. The people must be convinced

---

[1] Acland to his wife, n.d., Acland Papers.
[2] *H. C. Deb.*, 97,56 (6 August 1917) ; *Manchester Guardian*, 7 August 1917.
[3] *Nation*, 20 October 1917.

that Liberalism is capable of meeting and solving the problems of the immediate future."[1]

V

What made the ineffectualness of the semi-divided, semi-united Liberal party so apparent was the confidence, assertiveness, and even aggressiveness of the other major parties. This was stated, if with some exaggeration, by " An Old Liberal. " The Labour party, he said, had taken the field unrestrained by having nine Labour members in the government. Its programme was before the country and it was selecting candidates by the score, nominating them indiscriminately against Conservatives and Liberals. The Conservatives, too, were working through auxiliaries like the Tariff Reform League and the "Primrose Dames ", as well as from within the government, fostering protection and delaying Home Rule " at the point of the party pistol."

If these remarks were tinged with party bias, they were founded on solid facts. The Conservatives were now in an impregnable position, and their back-benchers showed it by their continual agitation for a general election. Bonar Law too was prepared to counter any serious challenge to the government by threatening a dissolution, a threat which caused evident dismay among the Asquithian Liberals and the parliamentary Labour party.

Yet the powerful position of the Conservatives was not new ; it had been apparent, if to a lesser degree, since the early months of the war. The really novel factor was the enhanced stature of the Labour party, most of all outside Parliament. During 1917 and 1918 developments occurred in the political Labour movement which were to have a lasting effect on British politics. There was the gradual dissociation of organised labour, if not from the war, at least from governmental direction of the war, as reflected in the growing separation from their party of the Labour members of the government. There was the swelling assertiveness of the Labour movement in the country, as demon-

[1] *Manchester Guardian*, 10 August 1918. A similar despondency had settled upon the Irish Nationalist party, once such an important ally of the Liberals and now not expected to hold more than ten seats at an election.

strated by the adoption of candidates even against Liberals who opposed the government, and by the vociferous demand, which was conceded at a party conference in June 1918, for abrogation of the party truce at by-elections. Again, there was the demonstration by Ben Tillett, standing as an unauthorised Labour candidate in a Salford by-election, that, whatever Labour's chances against government candidates, it had an excellent prospect of capturing working-class seats from orthodox Liberals. This culminated in the adoption of the new constitution of 1918, which established the modern Labour party as a nation-wide organisation determined to fight elections against both major parties. These developments reflected attitudes fraught with grave consequences for the Liberals : the conviction that Liberalism had nothing left to offer and should be swept aside, and that Labour constituted the only real alternative as a governing force to the Conservatives. Among the many manifestations of this was a " striking article " in the *Herald* in November 1917, called " Let Labour Try Its Hand." The three wartime ministries, it said, had failed to cope with the war, and should be succeeded by a Labour government. " Liberal, Coalition and Lloyd George Governments have failed —*then let Labour try its hand.*"

These developments were bound to affect the attitude of Liberals themselves, especially those on the left of the party. The " pacifists ", having been at odds with almost everything their leaders had done since August 1914, were usually the first to respond. In June 1917 R. C. Lambert, a Liberal M.P. and opponent of conscription, had written : " Liberalism is not dead. It will revive with renewed strength now that the world has seen what Militarism really means."[1] But little more than a year later he, with fellow M.P.s like King, E. T. John, and Joseph Martin, and candidates like C. R. Buxton and R. Dunstan, had ceased trying to " revive " Liberalism. They had transferred to Labour and become declared opponents of the Liberal party. Nor was Labour's appeal confined to this group. Any Liberal who hoped for a new international order and major social reforms after the war, and who resented equally the quiescence of Asquith and the apostasy of Lloyd George, found Labour a profoundly unsettling influence.

[1] *The Parliamentary History of Conscription in Great Britain*, preface by Lambert, p. v.

The Liberal press provided many instances of this unsettlement. The *Nation* called Labour " the one quarter from which a really fresh and hopeful development can come."[1]   And in December it said of the furore caused by government regulations on pamphlet censorship : " it was to the Labor Party that men turned as their shield from this oppression . . . . it is not to the existing Liberal Party that the younger and finer spirits look for the Risorgimento of British democracy. On the contrary, they are beginning to flock to the banners of Labor." A " non-pacifist " Liberal M.P. supported this contention :

> In the constituencies [he wrote] it is in many cases the most active Liberals whose party ties are being severed, by the want of any attitude upon the war which can be distinguished from that of Conservatism and thus can provide some positive material for party support. . . .
>
> The keenest Liberals in the constituencies . . . are losing their touch with party and yielding to the attraction of ideas which are at least definite, and which, while Liberalism effaces itself, make an appeal to reason.[2]

And on 18 December 1917 a *Manchester Guardian* correspondent said regarding Liberal defections to Labour : " The publication of the masterly statement of war aims and peace policy by the Labour party will accelerate the tendencies towards political reconstruction in several directions."   In addition to those who had already gone over to Labour, there was " a considerably larger group of young Radicals " whose intentions, while still under discussion, would probably take shape early in 1918 :

> I am assured that definite political action is contemplated, particularly as the inactivity of official Liberalism is increasingly resented.
>
> The notion that Liberal principles are inapplicable to legislation or administration during war-time is strongly rejected.

VI

On 5 March 1918 two gatherings took place in the House of Commons which illustrated some of the threats to the Liberal

---

[1] *Nation*, 13 October 1917 (" The Coming Democratic Party ").
[2] *ibid*, 24 November 1917.

party. The first was a private meeting addressed by Lloyd George. Having suffered universal criticism for his attempts to lure the press magnates Northcliffe, Rothermere, and Beaverbrook into his government, he decided to defend himself before a group whose support he considered important. This was the Unionist War Committee, the " ginger " group of the Conservative party, chaired on this occasion by the arch-Tory Lord Salisbury. Lloyd George succeeded in his immediate object : his eloquence did much to allay their hostility. But it was thought remarkable that he should have taken such trouble with these right-wing Conservatives, and have ignored Liberals equally critical of his relations with the press barons. " There were many comments in the lobby on the strangeness of the Prime Minister's action in attending a meeting of a small Unionist group to defend his Ministerial appointments."[1]

Elsewhere in the House of Commons a different gathering took place that day. W. C. Anderson, " a Labour man of the most advanced type ", was the speaker, his subject was the future of democratic politics, and his audience a body of left-wing Liberals—" advanced Liberals ", said one observer, " who are looking longingly at the Labour party to give them a new political hope. . . . The significance of the meeting is that a large number of advanced Liberals in and out of Parliament are turning from the party machine and are trying to find hope in the Labour party."[2] The immediate outcome was the formation of a " Radical Committee " so that Liberal M.P.s who yearned to adopt a more definite, idealistic, and above all combative position than their party was offering could work out their future course. Where their deliberations would lead, be it in the long run or in the short, might be guessed from the assertions of members like Lees-Smith and H. G. Chancellor that " the future usefulness of the Liberal party will depend on its understanding of and sympathy with the aspirations of Labour and its sincere co-operation with the Labour party."[3]

The Liberal leaders made no move to counter this seemingly inexorable decline. These years were not without opportunity for resourceful leaders—if only the opportunity to make a determined last stand against the forces assailing them. Asquith

---

[1] *Manchester Guardian*, 6 March 1918.   [2] *ibid.*
[3] *ibid*, 15 March and 16 April 1918.

could have inaugurated a crusade for bold, constructive post-war reform ; and (at whatever cost to " Liberal unity ") could have assailed the conservative, anti-reformist forces so powerful in the government. He did neither. Haldane, after lunching with him in April 1917, concluded that he " is not now an enthusiast for reform." " I think time has changed the outlook on life of the ex-P.M., & that he is no longer keenly interested."[1] Admittedly Asquith told the N.L.F. conference in September 1918 that his policy now embraced the Fabian doctrine of the " national minimum ", whereby every citizen should have " in possession or within reach a standard of existence, physical, intellectual, moral, social, which makes life worth living." But the observer who saw this as opening " a new epoch in political development "[2] was very wide of the mark. For nothing followed from the speech : no crusade, no fervour, no concrete proposals expressing Liberal devotion to the cause of wiping out poverty and combating privilege. In the end all Asquith could offer his beleaguered followers was, not a call to arms, but the repeated assurance that the Liberal party was not a spent force, that it was " not going to be cast aside upon the scrap heap ", and that in the post-war era " it would be a calamity to the country if the Liberal party were not there ".[3] It even suggested the imminence of this calamity that he felt called upon to issue these frequent rebuttals.

[1] Haldane to his mother, 25 and 27 April 1917, Haldane Papers.
[2] *Manchester Guardian*, 28 September 1918.　　[3] *ibid*, 25 February 1918.

PART TWO

The Coupon Election
November-December 1918

6. LLOYD GEORGE AND THE COUPON

What do you think of L.G. now. . . .
Do you remember anything more contemptible in your life experience of public affairs than Georges recent Election speeches.

John Dillon to Scott, December 1918[1]

IT seems that in mid-1918 Lloyd George decided to hold an election the following November, whatever the state of the war. By October he appeared to be wavering ; but the sudden collapse of Germany ended his hesitations. So twenty-four hours after the termination of hostilities he announced his intention of going to the polls immediately as leader of the coalition.

A dispute has continued ever since over the merits of this decision. It has been said that an election at this stage was a repetition of the lamentable Khaki election of 1900, a crude cashing-in by one group of politicians on a victory achieved by the whole nation, held in feverish circumstances which precluded the electors from making a considered judgement. Against this it has been argued that the existing Parliament was already three years beyond its allotted span and was the product of an obsolete franchise, so that it possessed no authority for the post-war period. Yet whatever the merits of these views it is unlikely that they greatly influenced the actions of the participants. What mattered to them was a simple calculation : that Lloyd George's government could not possibly lose an election at this moment, and the groups outside his government could not possibly win it.

In the present context, the really taxing problem is posed by Lloyd George's behaviour towards his old party. When embarking on this contest which was to wreak such havoc upon the Liberals, he did not avow an anti-Liberal purpose. On the contrary, he plainly affirmed his adherence to the

[1] C. P. Scott Papers.

135

Liberal cause. He first announced his decision to hold an election
to a meeting of some 150 to 200 Liberals, many of them M.P.s,
whom he specially invited to 10 Downing Street on 12 November
1918. The terms in which he addressed this gathering were
every bit as " liberal " as his audience, and inspired one
journalist to write :

> The oak-panelled dining room in 10 Downing-street has
> never seen a more remarkable gathering than that which
> assembled yesterday morning to hear the Prime Minister
> outline his post-war policy ; and never has it heard from
> the lips of any statesman more democratic sentiments or a
> speech more instinct with the spirit of true Liberalism.[1]

The " keynote " of the speech, according to this writer, was set
in the opening sentences, in which Lloyd George stated that he
had done nothing in the past two years to make him ashamed
to meet his fellow-Liberals, and added the ringing declaration :
" Please God, I am determined that I never shall ! "

From this beginning, he went on to deliver (according to
members of his audience) " a magnificent Liberal speech."[2] A
principal issue of the election, he said, would be the nature of
the peace, and he asked : were they to return to the system of
national rivalries and competitive armaments, or " to initiate
the reign on earth of the Prince of Peace ? " " It is the duty of
Liberalism ", he affirmed, " to use its influence to ensure that
it shall be the reign of peace." He asked what were the conditions of peace, and answered that they " must lead to a settlement which will be fundamentally just." He pointed to the
settlement between Germany and France in 1871 as a peace
which had outraged the principles of justice, and urged that in
the present instance no sense of revenge or greed should override

[1] Harry Jones in the *Daily Chronicle*, 13 November 1918. Jones, a leading
political correspondent, was of course writing in a newspaper under Lloyd
George's control. But he had agreed to remain on its staff only on condition
that he would be free to maintain an unfettered Liberal position, and this he
proceeded to do. Before long his attitude brought him into conflict with the
editorial policy of the paper : on 19 November he attributed responsibility for
the divided state of the Liberal party in the election to the machinations of the
Conservatives, while the leading article was blaming Asquith. Thereafter his
contributions to the paper became meagre, and he left its service a month later.

[2] *Manchester Guardian*, 13 November 1918. No verbatim report of the speech
was issued, but extensive summaries appeared in the press. See especially the
Daily Chronicle and *The Times*, 13 November 1918.

the doctrines of righteousness. Vigorous attempts, he warned, would be made to bully him from the strict principles of right, and they must set their faces relentlessly against such efforts (a declaration which evoked loud cheering from his audience). A mandate to his government, he went on, " will mean that the British delegation to the Peace Congress will be in favour of a just peace." " We shall go to the Peace Conference to guarantee that the League of Nations is a reality."

When he moved to internal affairs, his address proved just as satisfactory to a Liberal audience—and would, according to some of them, " screw up " Asquith.[1] Lloyd George warned against the example of 1815, when victory in war had been used to deny reform at home. He outlined a programme for raising standards of health and housing and bringing " light and beauty " into lives at present denied them. And he advocated reforms like minimum wages and shorter working hours, development of transportation, and improvements in the " acquisition and purchase of land to ensure reasonable access." There was, he said, a revolutionary spirit in the air (" Properly used, there is value in that spirit ") which required wise direction and should be met by the sense of national unity which had won the war. And he roused his audience to high enthusiasm with the strikingly radical declaration :

Revolution I am not afraid of.
Bolshevism I am not afraid of.
It is reaction I am afraid of.

It was necessary, he said, to preserve national unity : " I have done my very best, even recently, to prevent disunion, even in our own party . . . . I want a united Government, representing all parties." He reaffirmed his belief in liberal doctrines like free trade and Home Rule for Ireland (with provision for the exclusion of Ulster). And he concluded as he had begun, by reasserting his fidelity to the Liberal cause. The watchword of his government, he said, would be " progress, wise progress." " I was reared in Liberalism. . . . I am too old now to change. I cannot leave Liberalism. I would quit this place tomorrow if I could not obtain the support of Liberals."

From two sides of the Atlantic " Liberal " statesmen applauded this speech. President Wilson sent a message

[1] *Manchester Guardian*, 13 November 1918.

expressing his "sincere admiration" for it. And Asquith described it as a perfectly clear and satisfactory exposition of Liberal policy, in no way impairing the unity of the Liberal party which it was their desire to maintain.[1]

In this as in most other respects, Lloyd George's 12 November speech stands alone in the campaign. On no subsequent occasion did he secure the approval of the American President or the British Liberal leader. Nor did he again speak with passion of his concern for the Liberal cause. And even when his later speeches contained some of the policy items advocated on 12 November, he never recaptured the note of radicalism and idealism sounded at Downing Street. Indeed most of the high principles slipped completely out of sight, and the difference in tone and temper of his later speeches was startling. For example, by the end of November he was employing the peace settlement of 1871 not as a warning but as a guide to action : " When Germany defeated France she made France pay. . . . There is absolutely no doubt about the principle, and that is the principle we should proceed upon ".[2] And in the later part of the campaign, instead of wanting to initiate " the reign of the Prince of Peace " and to resist attempts to bully him from the paths of right, he talked recklessly about expelling every enemy alien from Britain, punishing the Kaiser, and demanding from Germany " the whole cost of the war "—" we shall search their pockets for it."[3] One of his last election manifestoes opened with the slogans : " Punish the Kaiser "; " Make Germany Pay."[4] And in his final election address on 13 December, only a month after he had said that he feared not bolshevism but reaction, he completed his change of front by denouncing the leaders of the Labour party as a " Bolshevik group " who had " pulled Labour out of the Government " because " what they really believed in was Bolshevism."

[1] *ibid*, 14 and 18 November 1918.

[2] The two statements about the peace of 1871 are effectively juxtaposed in the *Daily News*, 4 December 1918.

[3] see his notorious speeches at Bristol on 11 December 1918.

[4] *Manchester Guardian*, 11 December 1918 ; cf. its editorial, " Vulgarising the Issue ": " Thus are the nations to be regenerated. . . . Thus are our spirits to be uplifted with the sense of a high destiny ". " We venture to say that in no election within living memory have the issues . . . been so paltry, or the mode of their presentation been so reckless and vulgar."

But his swiftest reversal of position was in his attitude to the Liberal party. Within four days of the 12 November speech he was behaving with outright hostility to the main body of Liberals. Speaking in London on 16 November, he made not a token reference to his concern for the Liberal cause. This he claimed was no time for a strong opposition in Parliament (" Opposition is organised fault-finding "), and he denounced the parties which were absent from his all-party government : the Labour party, which had withdrawn two days earlier, and " a section of the party to which I belong."

> They decided, as far as I can see from recent speeches, that reconstruction should be the work of a party or a section of a party. . . . I know we are promised support and helpful criticism. We have had experience of both during the last few years, and I cannot see wherein it was helpful and wherein it promoted efficient conduct of the war.

Constituencies, he concluded, should investigate " ruthlessly " the claims of such individuals to be supporters of his government.

Perhaps even these remarks were mild when compared with his later tirades against his former colleagues. At Bristol on 11 December he actually likened Asquith and his followers, by clear implication, to German soldiers who first sniped at, gassed, poisoned, and machine-gunned British forces, and then cried " Kamerad "; and he identified himself, by contrast, with a group of wounded servicemen conveniently situated in the front row of his audience. But though the 16 November speech provided only a foretaste of the crudities to come, it showed plainly enough that he had now declared war on the principal body of Liberals. The line from there to Bristol was a direct one.

Moreover, when on 16 November he exhorted electors to investigate " ruthlessly " the credentials of Liberals claiming to be his supporters, he was not just indulging in rhetoric. Within a matter of days he had begun assisting electors in this " ruthless " appraisal by issuing lists of authorised coalition candidates. Furthermore these candidates were provided with a letter, signed jointly by Lloyd George and Bonar Law, stating that they were the recognised government candidates in their constituencies. It was this letter which Asquith, employing the rationing jargon of the day, dubbed a political " coupon ", so coining the expression by which the election has ever since been known.

The effect of the coupon was far-reaching. It not only bestowed the government's favour on the candidate named but placed a ban on all the other candidates in his constituency. And as the large majority of couponed candidates were Conservatives, Lloyd George by this act was explicitly repudiating most Liberals. In all, only 159 Liberals received the coupon as against 364 Conservatives, which meant that if Lloyd George's directions were followed the electors would return a clear majority of Conservatives, and not Liberals, to the next House of Commons.[1] How did Lloyd George reconcile such conduct with his claim that he could not " leave Liberalism ", that he would " quit this place tomorrow " if he could not secure Liberal support, and that (" Please God ") he would never do anything which would make him ashamed to meet his fellow-Liberals ?

II

The wild inconsistencies of the Premier's conduct have led to the speculation that his actions during the campaign were at odds with his original intentions. The argument goes that he plunged heedlessly into an election as soon as the war ended, and was swept along by the feverish emotions of the time into conduct at variance with his statesmanlike motives. In this state of disorder he was lured into making rash promises about the peace settlement which he soon regretted, and allowed himself to be committed to a bargain over candidates injurious to the Liberal party and contrary to his own interests. In short, the distribution of coupons did not reflect his intentions at all. The arrangement by which he endorsed so many Conservatives at the expense of Liberals occurred, to quote the *Nation* on an earlier occasion," while he was looking another way." [2]

This argument made its appearance early in the campaign. The Northcliffe press called the coupon arrangement " A Very Bad Bargain ", " a personal triumph " for the Conservative

[1] For the statistics of the coupon arrangement, see appendix I at the end of this chapter, pp. 157-9.

[2] *Nation*, 1 December 1917.

party manager Sir George Younger, as a result of which " the great Tory wirepuller . . . has thrown his lasso over Mr. Lloyd George ".[1] This view was readily adopted by Liberals in and out of Lloyd George's camp. According to *The Times* on 2 December, the " Liberal element in the Coalition " were saying " freely " that Younger had got the better of their whip over the allocation of coupons. And Runciman spoke for the Asquithians when he called Younger " the engineer of the election ".[2] The announcement of the results seemed to confirm this view. " Last Sunday morning ", wrote a correspondent of the *Manchester Guardian* on 31 December 1918, " Sir George Younger awoke, like Byron, to find himself famous. He was universally recognised as the astute organiser who had 'wangled' a big Unionist party majority out of Mr. Lloyd George's comparatively amateur efforts to arrange a Coalition majority." The difficulty of regarding Lloyd George as a " comparative amateur " in politics was overcome by attributing the coupon arrangement not to him but to his whip. The real victim of Younger's sleight of hand was supposedly F. E. Guest ; the " preoccupied Premier "[3] had learned too late of the deal in constituencies which Guest had made on his behalf but against his real interest.

To be blunt, this explanation is frankly incredible.[4] It does not rescue Lloyd George from the charge of " amateurishness ", for it credits him with extraordinary naivety in allowing himself to be committed to a vital arrangement without his knowledge. And what is more, it is contradicted by available evidence concerning his preparations for an election. Just because the dissolution of Parliament followed hard upon the Allied victory, it does not follow that his plans for an election were made at the last minute. In fact they had been under way since the middle of the year, and by the later part of 1918 he could hold an election whenever he liked.

Despite the misgivings felt in Lloyd George's camp about

[1] See the extracts from the *Daily Mail* and *Weekly Dispatch* quoted in the *Manchester Guardian*, 2 and 3 December 1918.

[2] *Manchester Guardian*, 9 December 1918.   [3] *ibid*, 1 May 1919.

[4] Yet a multitude of Lloyd George's sins have been covered by the explanation that he was " looking another way." Mr. Frank Owen told a student meeting at Oxford in 1955 that Lloyd George's culpability in the Black and Tan affair lay in his failure to know what was going on.

dissolving Parliament with the Liberal party divided, preparations for a contest had been proceeding since July 1918, when
Lloyd George appointed a committee of prominent Liberal
supporters, under Addison's chairmanship, to put forward
proposals.[1] Guest wrote to him on 13 July informing him of
their deliberations :

Dear Prime Minister,

    After very careful consideration the Committee arrived
at the following unanimous recommendations :

(1) That a form of agreement with the Conservatives as
to candidates should be prepared and signed without
delay.

(2) That immediate steps be taken to draw up an agreed
programme which should be jointly signed as a basis
of policy.

(3) That a general statement of policy should be made
public by the Prime Minister at a favourable opportunity, leaving the fuller and more explicit pronouncement until some appropriate moment after the decision
had been made as to the date of the General Election.

A Sub-Committee was formed, as follows :

> Dr. Addison (Chairman)
> Lord Cawley
> Dr. Shakespeare
> Sir Hamar Greenwood
> Mr. Munro
> The Chief Whip (ex officio)

in order to prepare the outlines of a Programme which would
be acceptable to your Liberal colleagues and supporters. . . .

    From the opinions expressed yesterday, I am fortified in
my view that your chief considerations now should be :

(1) How to safeguard your supporters in the House of
Commons ;

and

(2) To enable us to get candidates into the field.

    As far as the *electors* are concerned you may rest assured

---

[1] The members of the committee, according to Addison (*Four and a Half Years*,
vol. 2, p. 553), were himself, Guest, R. Munro (Secretary for Scotland), Dalziel,
Sir Hamar Greenwood, Lord St. Davids, Sir Charles Sykes, Rev. Dr. Shakespeare,
and Lord Cawley (Chancellor of the Duchy).

that a *big majority* will vote for your continued leadership during the War.

I therefore trust that you will, at any rate, take some preliminary steps to force the pace.

With reference to the ' *khaki* ' *voters*, especially abroad, could not something be done to ensure their vote being cast for the Government ?[1]

In the ensuing months each of the principal recommendations in Guest's first paragraph was put into effect. The " general statement of policy " preparatory to an election, which was the third recommendation, was made by the Prime Minister at Manchester in September. The " agreed programme " " jointly signed as a basis of policy ", which was the second recommendation, was in existence at least by the end of October, for Guest in a further letter to Lloyd George on 29 October referred to " the letter which forms the agreement between Bonar Law and yourself ". (This was presumably the letter published during the election under the seemingly fictitious date 2 November). And the crucially-important " form of agreement with the Conservatives as to candidates ", which was the first recommendation, also existed by the end of October, for Guest on 29 October informed Lloyd George of its completion :

I have come to an agreement with Mr. Bonar Law that we should receive their support, where necessary, for 150 Lloyd George Candidates, 100 of whom are our old Guard.

This request was generously acceeded [sic] to by Mr. Bonar Law and I should like you to convey appreciation to him on behalf of your Whips office.

These will be all Liberal seats, and all Labour candidates who support you will be to the good.[2]

It is unnecessary to go beyond this letter for an explanation of Lloyd George's treatment of Liberals in the election. He had obtained from the Conservatives a promise of support " for 150 Lloyd George Candidates ". In the outcome, 159 Liberals received the coupon.

Yet at the time this letter was written Lloyd George was not in the thick of an election and too " preoccupied " to understand what it meant. He had not even decided on the date of an

---

[1] Guest to Lloyd George, 13 July 1918, Lloyd George Papers.
[2] *ibid*, 29 October 1918.

election, and Guest was once again urging him to make up his mind.[1] In the same letter of 29 October he wrote to Lloyd George :

All is quiet in the House of Commons.

In the lobbies everyone seems to have made up their mind that an election is imminent and I hope very much that you will shortly see your way to let us know your decision on this matter.

Lloyd George, in short, knew what arrangements were being made and saw that they were made well in advance. There are no grounds for assuming that they were the product of haste and confusion, or that he acted in a fit of absence of mind. As should have been apparent all along, the coupon arrangement reflected his clear intention and purpose.

III

Lloyd George, of course, never argued otherwise. He admitted waging electoral war on the majority of Liberal candidates. But he claimed that the responsibility rested with them. Their hostility towards him, he argued, as revealed on a particular decisive occasion, had forced him to reject them. Speaking at Newcastle on 29 November, he said that he was opposing no Liberal who had made it clear that he would support the coalition and could be depended on to do so. " Those whom we cannot see our way to support are the men who were perfectly prepared at a critical moment to take advantage of temporary difficulties in order to overthrow the Government." This incident, he announced, was the Maurice debate of 9 May 1918.[2]

Lloyd George's claim has been widely accepted (sometimes even by those who argue that the coupon bargain did not reflect

[1] Guest was also telling Riddell about this time that Lloyd George ought to seek reconciliation with Asquith and reunite the Liberal party. It is strange that he could not see the incompatibility between this and his desire for an election while the coalition remained intact. *Lord Riddell's War Diary*, p. 373.

[2] Yet in his *War Memoirs* (vol. 5, p. 2986), Lloyd George makes the extraordinary claim that neither he nor Bonar Law " alluded to the [Maurice] incident during the whole contest "; but that " the electorate had not forgotten nor did they forgive those who engineered or took part in this conspiracy . . . and the Mauriceites were annihilated at the polls."

his intentions), and so the Maurice debate has been accorded a crucial place in the demise of the Liberal party. Thus Sir Harold Nicolson says : " The ' Maurice Debate ' is important in political history as marking the first stage in the disintegration of the Liberal Party ".[1] But what does this mean ? If it means that Lloyd George saw Asquith's behaviour as creating an irrevocable breach between them, then it is difficult to reconcile with the fact, to which the Prime Minister also alluded at Newcastle, that he had pressed Asquith to join his government after May 1918. And if it means, as Lloyd George certainly seemed to be saying, that he placed his ban only on Liberals who voted against him in the Maurice division, then it is simply not true. How could a division in the old Parliament decide Lloyd George's attitude to the whole range of Liberal candidates, when many of them would not have been present at the division or would not have been members of the old House at all ? Anyway, when the voting figures in the Maurice division are compared with the distribution of coupons, Lloyd George's claim collapses. In all, 229 Liberal candidates fell under the government's ban in this election—that is, they were denied the coupon and one of their opponents received it. By contrast, only 108 Members of Parliament, including tellers, voted against the government in the Maurice division. And of these 108, 25 did not stand for re-election and twelve more did not stand as Liberals. Consequently, the Maurice division could only have caused the proscription of 71 Liberals. And nearly one-quarter of these—seventeen in all—did not fall under the government's ban : six stood in constituencies where no coupons were issued, and the remaining eleven received the coupon (as did the solitary Conservative who had voted against the government). In sum, of the 229 Liberals against whom coupons were sent, only 54 failed to pass the test of the Maurice division —what the coalition leaders called the " acid test ".[2]

As it happens, the Maurice division is scarcely more satisfactory in explaining why some Liberals received the coupon. Of the 159 Liberals who did so, just over one-third—54 again—

[1] Harold Nicolson, *King George the Fifth*, p. 323.

[2] In addition, four Liberals who voted with the government had the coupon sent against them (including one, E. G. Hemmerde, who retired during the contest).

had voted for the government in the Maurice division. The rest had been absent, or had voted against the government, or had not been members of the old House.

Thus even if the government did penalise some members who had voted against it in this division, and reward others who had voted for it, it certainly did not proscribe only those Liberals who had transgressed on this issue and recognise all the others. Lloyd George could have opposed every Liberal who had voted with the minority, and still not have attempted to secure a Conservative majority in the new Parliament.

Nor is it true that Liberals denied the coupon had invariably shown themselves hostile to Lloyd George in other ways. Certainly, as has been argued, there was much antipathy to him in the party. But in the majority of cases there was no way of deciding which Liberal candidates felt like this, and it is plain that the coalition whips never sought to. Many Liberal candidates who proclaimed their support for Lloyd George found themselves condemned as soon as they were adopted. Nor were all of them insincere in making this claim; for among the pitiful group of eighteen Liberals to be elected against the coupon in December 1918 were three (George Lambert, James Gardiner, and S. G. Howard) who acted as supporters of the government throughout the ensuing Parliament. And in many other cases the refusal of the coupon clearly bore no relation to the attitude of the candidate. There was the instance of E. G. Hemmerde, who had been regarded as a supporter of Asquith until the Maurice debate but had then turned against the Liberal leader and voted with the government. As a reward, he was among the select group invited to 10 Downing Street on 12 November and, according to his own account, was promised the coupon. But for reasons which were never explained, the coupon was then sent to his Conservative opponent. As a consequence, Hemmerde turned completely against Lloyd George, withdrawing from the contest and actively supporting the Labour candidate. He was not the only Liberal whose hostility to Lloyd George was the consequence, and not the cause, of the coupon going against him. A year later an observer wrote of the presence at the N.L.F. annual conference of a group, " nearly all disappointed candidates, whose special bitterness against Mr. Lloyd George's Government, let it be said frankly, may be traced to the fact that their importunities for the Coalition ticket were rejected."[1]

Another Liberal who was repudiated without explanation was H. J. Craig. Like Hemmerde, his behaviour in the old House had secured him an invitation to the 12 November meeting,[2] and when he saw Guest later that day and said that he intended to stand as a coalition supporter, Guest was " good enough " (in Craig's words) " to advise me ' to get into the field quickly and hold a public meeting at once.' "[3] At the time of this conversation Craig had already been in touch with the Conservatives in his constituency, and had been led to believe that they would withdraw their nominee and allow him a free run as the coalition candidate. What appears to have decided them otherwise was the receipt of a message three days after Guest's conversation with Craig informing them that their candidate would receive the coupon. Craig immediately wrote to Guest demanding an explanation. Guest replied that he had found himself unable to regard Craig's statement of his position " as sufficiently definite to prove that you will be a whole-hearted supporter of the Coalition Government." " I regret ", he added, " that our conversation was based on insufficient information." Craig made short work of this explanation. He referred to his " actual record as a supporter of the Government in the House of Commons," and said that Guest had given him " no opportunity of conforming to any particular standard of official orthodoxy."

You " regret that our conversation was based on insufficient information." I would have gladly furnished you with any further information you might have required ; you asked for none, nor am I now aware of the information which you have been willing to accept unchallenged from other quarters, and upon which you have been content to act.

I . . . invite you publicly and explicitly to explain in what respect my pledge of support to the Government . . .

[1] *Manchester Guardian*, 29 November 1919.

[2] No complete list was published of the Liberals invited to this meeting, but the *Daily News*, 13 November 1918, gave the names of about fifty Liberal M.P.s who were present, including Craig's.

[3] This and the quotations that follow are from the correspondence between Craig and Guest published in the *Manchester Guardian*, 23 November 1918.

falls short of that which you have received from other candidates, both Liberal and Conservative, to whose candidature you have given your official approval.

Unfortunately this invitation was not accepted. Guest preferred to leave it unanswered.

Certainly Guest would have found it difficult to explain how Craig was a less satisfactory coalitionist than recipients of the coupon like Wedgwood, David Davies, Guy Wilson, D. V. Pirie, and F. C. Thornborough, all of whom denied that they wanted the coupon and baulked at committing themselves to support of the coalition. And what could be said about P. W. Raffan, who was first classified by coalition headquarters as unfit to receive the coupon, and then (although he continued to express his opposition to the government) had the coupon forced upon him ?[1] Nor was it likely that Wedgwood's performance in the Maurice debate helped to account for the favour shown him. Admittedly he had not voted for Asquith's motion ; but this was because, as he told the House, he did not approve of military interference in politics. When he heard Lloyd George describe the motion as a vote of censure then he was strongly inclined to support it, for he had " very little confidence, indeed, in the present Government, and I think that a change would be extremely desirable." " It seems to me the Ministry over which the Prime Minister presides is getting too strong for him, and it is becoming too strongly biassed in all those Conservative directions that I most seriously distrust." So he regretted that Asquith had taken up Maurice's charges but desired to see him in power again.[2] Here indeed was the acid test.

Even without these instances in which the coalition plainly did not grant or refuse coupons on the basis of the Maurice division or the opinions of Liberal candidates, it would be clear that the allocation of coupons was not determined by the candidates themselves. For we have seen that Lloyd George and Guest had made an agreement whereby only 150 Liberals were to receive the coupon at a time when the election was still hypothetical and there was no way of knowing how many of the Liberals adopted would be government supporters. All this agreement meant was that a section of Liberals, especially

[1] For the " little provincial comedy " at Leigh, as Raffan described the coalition's behaviour towards himself, see *ibid*, 19 to 27 November 1918.

[2] *H. C. Deb.*, 105, 2400–2 (9 May 1918).

members known to have supported the government in the old House, would be safeguarded against Lloyd George's impending assault on the Liberal party. It did not mean that his assault would fall only on opponents of his regime. All Liberal candidates in excess of 150, whatever their attitude to the government or role in a supposedly crucial division, would fall under his ban. It is not surprising that in implementing this bargain the government sometimes behaved erratically, bestowing coupons on unwilling recipients or rejecting Liberals who had supported it but without sufficient advertisement. (It is plain from Guest's letters that in fact he had no recollection of his conversation with H. J. Craig). These anomalies were inherent in an arrangement decreeing that the fate of Liberals would be decided ultimately not by their views but by the number 150.

IV

Before anything else, the coupon bargain constituted a decision by Lloyd George about his political future. He was breaking definitely from the Liberals and throwing in his lot with the Conservatives. From this moment, the political arrangement of December 1916 was not a temporary wartime improvisation but a parting of the ways. In coming to this decision he was no doubt influenced by personal considerations, especially his estrangement from Asquith and friendship with Bonar Law. But he was influenced also by the bleak future confronting his late party. The Liberal party in its old form, he told Riddell in January 1918 and repeated many times thereafter, was a thing of the past and could not be galvanised into life. Hardly anyone thought that of the Conservatives.

Thus the main purpose of the coupon arrangement was to make permanent the political *status quo* ; it changed Lloyd George's situation only by defining it more clearly. From the start his premiership had depended principally on the Conservatives, and his electoral bargain showed that he intended to remain in office by their support, even if this meant open hostility to the Liberal party. The same was true of his behaviour during the campaign. Having decided to commit himself to the Conservatives, he felt free to conduct the campaign on jingo, anti-German, anti-bolshevist lines calculated to produce a Conservative victory and a Liberal rout.

So the puzzle comes down to this : why in his first speech of the election did he espouse the Liberal cause ? The answer, seemingly, lies in political calculation, and in that alone. There were good reasons why in abandoning the Liberal party he should take a body of Liberals with him. It made his change of allegiance less blatant ; it rewarded Liberals who had stood by him since 1916 ; and it provided a useful bargaining force in future arrangements with the Conservatives. But it involved certain difficulties. Many of his Liberal supporters were uneasy about the course he intended to follow—as earlier he had been himself. They desired a fresh lease of office for the coalition, but they baulked at an election which threatened irreparable damage to the Liberal cause. When on 6 November he told the Liberals in the government of his decision to proceed with an election, Churchill made difficulties suggesting continued uneasiness, and on his way home with H. A. L. Fisher spoke ominously of what this meant for the Liberal party. Fisher noted in his diary : " Drive home with Winston, who sees [? says] that here is a great split." Fisher too had misgivings.[1] When Guest asked him to move a resolution at the 12 November meeting supporting Lloyd George's decision he demurred, saying that he preferred to wait and hear the Premier's statement. It seems that Lloyd George's " magnificent Liberal speech " was designed just to overcome the misgivings of Liberals like Churchill and Fisher. For not only did the Premier say nothing about arraigning the Kaiser or searching the pockets of the Germans ; even more, he uttered not a word about the deal in candidates, involving " ruthless " proscription of a majority of Liberals, which he had already concluded with the Conservatives. Rarely has a political utterance been so shamelessly angled towards overcoming the doubts of its hearers at the expense of revealing the intentions of the speaker. In this object it succeeded handsomely. " A thoroughly satisfactory speech from the Liberal p[oin]t of view ", Fisher recorded in his diary. " I rise & propose the resolution of support, followed by Leverhulme and Churchill."[2]

---

[1] He was soon called in to prepare the government's first election manifesto, but this was probably intended to allay his uneasiness.

[2] The terms of the resolution are instructive. It affirmed that, being convinced of the necessity for a coalition government during the period of reconstruction

Since that time it has been usual to censure Lloyd George's subsequent campaign speeches, and to contrast them unfavourably with the high tone of this address. Tom Jones writes in his biography of Lloyd George :

> To secure a temporary advantage he played upon the baser passions of the electorate. He cannot be condemned by the standards of contemporary statesmen but, judged by standards set by himself, he is condemned because he did not lead, nor seriously try to lead, the nation along the path illumined by his own inner light—that light which sometimes shone through his utterances, as at Downing Street on 12 November.[1]

And yet it is arguable that Lloyd George was more guilty of deception at the beginning of the campaign than at the end. Doubtless he did not believe that Germany would pay the uttermost farthing, or regard the Labour leaders as instruments of bolshevism, so that by stating the contrary in his later speeches he was trying to win votes fraudulently. But at least these statements were of a type to produce a Conservative victory, and thus represented his real object in the election. At the 12 November meeting his sentiments may have been admirable, but they concealed his ultimate purpose. They expressed a concern for the Liberal cause which was contrary not only to his intentions but to the electoral bargain he had already signed and sealed with the Conservatives. Indeed he was only able to make the 12 November speech by a staggering act of *suppressio veri*.

v

What of the Liberals who attended the meeting and endorsed the resolution to hold an election ? In a sense, they were shockingly deceived. Fisher when he moved the resolution of endorsement seems to have known nothing of the coupon

---

(i.e. not indefinitely), " and being satisfied that the programme and policy, as stated today by the Prime Minister, is of such a character as to command the wholehearted support of Liberals," those present pledged themselves to support or stand as Liberal Coalition candidates, with the Premier as their leader. Nothing was said about endorsing or voting for Conservative candidates.

[1] Thomas Jones, *Lloyd George*, p. 163.

bargain or the impending attack on Liberal candidates, and to have imagined that the speech was intended to facilitate Liberal reunion ; later that day he wrote to Lloyd George " to offer good offices to Asquith."[1]   Even some of Lloyd George's fiercest opponents were befogged by the speech. Massingham, for one, completely missed the point of the election. He expected a war against Labour, but not against the Liberals.

> Doubtless the general scheme is Liberal [he wrote]. One can hardly conceive Mr. George as a Tory, and his clear calculation is to displace the Asquithian Liberals with a Radical party of which he will be the head. . . . As for Toryism, it is plainly doomed. By degrees it will disappear from the Cabinet till the earlier Liberal predominance is more or less restored.[2]

If Massingham could not divine the Premier's intentions better than this, Liberals under his spell were not likely to. And some of them continued to express their belief in the Liberal cause after Lloyd George had ceased to do so, criticising the use of the coupon as did Joseph Johnstone, pleading for Liberal reunion as did Alex Shaw, or stressing the continuing need for the Liberal party in national affairs as did MacCallum Scott. Yet having said this it must be admitted that a good many Coalition Liberals were deceived by the Premier because, in one part of themselves, they wanted to be. They may have been ignorant of the coupon bargain, but they knew that an election in these circumstances was likely to injure the Liberal party. Had not Churchill told Fisher on 6 November that " here is a great split " ? Yet both of them supported the resolution at the meeting of six days later, and said explicitly that an election in such circumstances was compatible with their belief in liberalism. If Lloyd George had swept them off their feet, they were unduly easy game.

The Coalition Liberals were supporters of a highly successful administration which had brought the country to victory, and they enjoyed all the legitimate satisfaction which identification with such a government brings. Not surprisingly, they were

---

[1] Fisher's diary, 12 November 1918, Fisher Papers.

[2] *Nation*, 16 November 1918. In its next issue, by which time the coupon arrangement was known, the *Nation* had revised its views and did not doubt that " Mr. George " could act as a Tory.

reluctant to end this situation, especially as only uncertainty lay before them once the government was dissolved. For when that happened they would be faced with party warfare on two fronts, from the intangible menace of Labour and the familiar menace of the Conservatives; and they would be resuming relations with leaders who deeply resented their recent behaviour. Either way, their chances of again coming into office were remote. Even should Asquith return as Prime Minister, few Coalition Liberals would be automatic nominees for government positions. The Coalition Liberal ministers, with a few obvious exceptions, were not considered very able (McKinnon Wood called them " a weak wing of second-rate Liberals "[1]) and they did not belong in the ruling section of the party. Mond was a case in point. He had found Asquith's circle closed to him since becoming an M.P. in 1906, and had seemed no nearer to securing office on the last day of Asquith's premiership than on the first. Even Fisher was not quite the exception he appeared. Certainly as a distinguished product of Oxford University he did not find Asquith personally inaccessible. Yet he owed not simply his advancement up the political ladder, but his political career as such, to the fact that Lloyd George had unseated Asquith. He had not liked the change of government in 1916,[2] and even after taking office remained sympathetic to the ejected Liberals. On 9 December 1916 he wrote rather apologetically to the Asquithian Gilbert Murray :

I have been and joined this Government ! In one sense the step is difficult to excuse or to forgive. All my sympathies are with Asquith and Grey. The Press Campaign against them has been hateful. As for the real merits of the dispute which finally broke up the cabinet, I can say nothing. . . . But I had immense confidence in Asquith's massive commonsense and ability to keep us out of disaster and I have not the same confidence in his successor, though in some respects he will doubtless be better.[3]

[1] *Glasgow Herald*, 28 November 1918.
[2] " My belief is that Asquith will return "; Fisher to Gilbert Murray, 6 December 1916, Fisher Papers.
[3] Fisher went on to explain that he was joining the government as an educationalist, and had secured assurances that the ministry would carry through substantial measures of educational reform.

But these were the views of Fisher the liberal academic. Fisher the politician, who had stepped overnight into Parliament and the government and was deeply anxious to remain there, existed only because Lloyd George had summoned him from the university on to the stage of politics. And what applied to the Liberal ministers was also true of many of the rank and file. Often for the first time, they now " belonged " politically, moving in the circle of those at the centre of power and in control of the machinery of government.

Furthermore, their political attitudes sometimes tempted them to prolong the existing regime. Some Coalition Liberals, it is true, were social reformers. Fisher only agreed to join the government because of its potentiality for " achieving improvements which could well be permanent " and carrying through " a big piece of national work ".[1] " I told L.G. [Fisher wrote to Murray in the letter of 9 December just quoted] that I could only join on condition that the Government was prepared to take up education seriously and to spend money on it. He gave me assurances on these points." But other Coalition Liberals were not from the radical wing of the Liberal party. Wedgwood detected among them some of " my old enemies, the Whigs," who had participated " in the famous cave that destroyed the land value taxation proposals in the 1909 Budget."[2] They had been drawn to Liberalism in the past by issues like free trade (in the case of Mond) or the claims of Nonconformity (in the case of Dr. Shakespeare) or temperance reform (in the case of Sir Thomas Whittaker), issues which no longer loomed so large in their view of politics. At least for the moment, the war had changed them. It had made them more nationalistic, and had rendered them antipathetic to the pacifist, anti-conscriptionist, and pro-alien wings of their own party. They were ready to curtail traditional liberties as serving the purpose of " wreckers " and " pro-Germans ", and they suspected organised labour of being unpatriotic and tainted with bolshevism. On all these matters they were at one with the Conservatives, even though they still differed nominally on issues like temperance or Welsh disestablishment.

In a way, Churchill exemplified this element in the Coalition

[1] Fisher to Murray, 12 December 1916, Fisher Papers.
[2] *Manchester Guardian*, 7 February 1919.

Liberals. He was far abler than most and much less cautious, taking up and dropping railway nationalisation in December 1918 with a rashness few cared to emulate. But he was like a section of Coalition Liberals in that his attachment to the Liberal cause no longer seemed certain. True, he remained a rigid free trader, and unlike Lloyd George went out of his way during the election to offer gestures of goodwill to Asquith (for which he received, and perhaps deserved, no thanks). But he now seemed obsessed by a strain of nationalism, an urge towards big battalions, a horror of bolshevism, and a dislike of Labour agitators, which even where present in the past had been nowhere near as prominent. Doubtless he could argue that the affairs of the world, not he, had changed ; that he would have been an anti-bolshevik before 1914 if bolshevism had existed. Even so, it was the case that the issues engaging him then had usually brought him into conflict with the Conservatives, and that those engaging him now did not. In March 1914 he had sounded a call to arms with the famous expression, " Let us go forward and put these grave matters to the proof." He had meant going forward to suppress the promised rebellion of Ulster ; and the Conservatives had hated him for it. In 1918 his call to battle was against the Bolsheviks, and it won the approval of many Conservatives. Perhaps it was only a change of emphasis. But that may be all that is required to carry a politician, or a section of a party, from one allegiance to another. And in the case of Churchill and other Coalition Liberals, the issues which they were now emphasising brought them closer and closer to the Conservatives.

None of these remarks holds good for all of Lloyd George's followers. In their case nearly every generalisation runs into serious exceptions.[1] But one consideration does cover most of them. At this moment they were subject to severe pulls in two directions : towards preserving their liberalism on the one hand, and towards prolonging their alliance with the Conservatives under Lloyd George's leadership on the other. It is clear how well Lloyd George met their needs on 12 November. He offered them the best of both worlds. The coalition would be preserved by an election at the most favourable moment, but the election would not be avowedly anti-Liberal. Its purpose

---

[1] For a development of this point, see appendix 2 to this chapter, pp. 159-63.

would be to keep in office a man who both had " won the war " and could not " leave Liberalism ", and who to prove it was offering a visionary, radical programme of peace and reconstruction. The trouble was that Lloyd George ceased to show such consideration for their feelings once they had consented to an election. Thereupon he made it explicit that they were to have the best of only one world—the non-Liberal world. By then they were too committed to do much if they would, and too anxious to retain what he was still offering them to want to do much. Perhaps they had simply been less realistic, or more hypocritical, than their leader in imagining that the two worlds ever could continue into an election. But that they had hoped for it is a fair deduction from Lloyd George's elaborate efforts to deceive them.

These events had two important results. First, they produced a Coalition Liberal party in Parliament. Hitherto there had been Liberal M.P.s associated with Lloyd George, others associated with Asquith, and a good many who had sought (most of the time successfully) to keep a foot in both camps. But after the election there was a Lloyd George party with a clear-cut personnel, consisting of Liberal M.P.s who had been awarded, and had not vocally repudiated, the coupon.[1] The subsequent history of the Coalition Liberals can be explained by this simple fact : they were a Liberal party called into existence by an anti-Liberal fiat. They had no *raison d'être*—unless the volition of Lloyd George was to be considered reason enough.

The second result is painful to refer to, yet it explains much that happened thereafter. Lloyd George's reputation never recovered from his blatant, almost perverse, display of *realpolitik* in the last months of 1918. By polling day there seemed almost no facet of the art of political deception left for him to demonstrate. Tom Jones suggests that in his finer utterances we may perceive his real convictions. This may have been true prior to the election and after he got to the peace conference. But during the actual contest he seemed to possess no " inner light "; only a zest for manipulating audiences which was approaching the level of an obsession. Never the most trusted of politicians, he

---

[1] Plus a handful of other members: usually M.P.s from constituencies to which coupons had not been allocated, but including three Liberals opposed by the coupon who took Lloyd George's whip.

cquired from this performance a reputation for sharp practice
nd want of scruple which dogged him for the rest of his career.
As one result, the Conservatives whom he served so well at
his time were able, with shameless ingratitude, to cast him
side four years later, and to make it appear that such conduct
eflected not on their honour but on his. Perhaps he was not
ll that less scrupulous than the men who ruled in his stead
uring the 1920s and 30s. But he certainly made far less effort
o keep up the appearance of scrupulousness. It is remarkable
hat a man so adept at gauging reactions in the short run could
ail to appreciate the cumulative injury which he might render
is career when he pledged himself to one position to secure a
articular object and then, with the object achieved, behaved
s if the words had never been uttered.

APPENDIX 1: THE STATISTICS OF THE COUPON

. *The recipients of the coupon*

n all, 541 coupons were issued for the 602 constituencies in England, Scotland,
nd Wales. The recipients were as follows : 364 Conservatives, 159 Liberals,
nd eighteen candidates of the National Democratic party (N.D.P.), a right-wing,
 patriotic " working-class party, previously known as the British Workers
eague and very hostile to Labour.
 Geographically, the coupons were distributed as follows :

	Conservatives	Liberals	N.D.P.s
England	320	108	15
Scotland	34	28	2
Wales	2	20	1
Universities	8	3	—
	364	159	18

he following points may be noted regarding the above figures:
 i. They refer to " couponed " candidates, that is candidates who were awarded
ie coupon by coalition headquarters, not to candidates standing as supporters
 the coalition. Not all recipients of the coupon were coalition supporters, and
ce versa.
 ii. Owing to the erratic conduct of the coalition itself it is no easy matter to
ompile an accurate list of the recipients of the coupon, and all the handbooks
ontain inaccuracies. In some instances the whips changed their minds after
oupons had been issued : in S.E. St. Pancras and the three Cardiff divisions,
r example, they awarded coupons and then withdrew them. In the case of
reenock they included the name of the Conservative candidate in their final

official list (and he appears as a couponed candidate in every handbook), but the next day publicly stated that this was an error and that no candidate was to receive the coupon in that constituency. Again, at one stage of the contest the coalition described all candidates returned unopposed as recipients of the coupon, but later omitted Merionethshire from this category. However, despite such instances, it is believed that the above figures are accurate.

iii. To mention some disputed cases, it may be noted that in the above statistics the following constituencies were regarded as having received no coupons : Broxtowe, Chatham, Forfar, Greenock, Merionethshire, Rotherham, Tottenham South ; and that the following candidates, whose party affiliation has been a subject of disagreement, have been classified as follows : Miss Pankhurst (Smethwick) among the Conservatives ; James Parker (Cannock) and J. Taylor (Dumbarton) among the Liberals ; and Clem Edwards (East Ham South) among the N.D.P.s.

B. *Constituencies without coupons*

No coupons were issued to Irish constituencies, where the political situation differed markedly from elsewhere.

In addition, there were 61 constituencies in England, Scotland, and Wales which received no coupons. These fall into a number of categories :

i. Constituencies in which both Conservatives and Liberals were standing as supporters of the coalition, and the coalition whips either thought it politic to support neither (as in Stalybridge and Hyde, and in three divisions of Manchester) or could not agree which to support (as in Greenock).

ii. Constituencies in which only one candidate was standing as a coalition supporter but the whips, for what appear largely accidental reasons, did not send him the coupon, sometimes because he asked not to receive it (e.g. Hilton Young in Norwich), and sometimes because he was late in entering the contest (e.g. W. Cozens-Hardy in Norfolk South).

iii. Constituencies in which no coalition supporter was standing (e.g. Camborne, where the expected Conservative candidate failed to appear).

iv. Constituencies in which, owing to the presence of an " outstanding " candidate (though they were outstanding in a variety of ways), the coalition apparently thought it better not to intervene. These candidates were : T. P. O'Connor ; Asquith ; the notorious independent Pemberton Billing ; and the founders of the reactionary National party, Brigadier-General Page Croft and Sir Richard Cooper.

v. By far the largest group, and amounting to nearly half the total (29 out of 61) : constituencies which were being contested by working-class candidates (other than members of the N.D.P.) who had been noteworthy for their support of the government during the war and for their hostility to the " pacifist " wing of Labour. A few in this group, like G. N. Barnes and G. J. Wardle, had broken with the Labour party and remained members of the government, but did not, apparently at their own request, receive the coupon. The majority of this group, however, like J. Clynes and J. H. Thomas, had gone with the Labour party into opposition, but the government leaders preferred to reward their wartime services by not supporting candidates against them. Perhaps by doing this (and by bestowing coupons on candidates of the N.D.P.) the government hoped to preserve something of its supposed all-party character, at a time when this appearance was wearing thin.

APPENDIX 2 : THE DIVISION IN THE LIBERAL PARTY

The line of division in the Liberal ranks can be variously explained. To some it was a division of left (Asquithians) against right (Lloyd Georgians), of semi-socialists like Wedgwood Benn against anti-socialists like Mond. To others it was a division of whigs (Asquithians) against radicals (Lloyd Georgians), of believers in private enterprise and government retrenchment like Leif Jones against pragmatic social reformers, improvident of the public's money, like Addison. Again, some have seen it as a division of anti-militarists (Asquithians) against jingos (Lloyd Georgians) ; but it has also been explained as a division between slavish supporters of the military (Asquithians) and advocates of civilian control (Lloyd Georgians).

These explanations so cut across, and even contradict, each other that they defeat the attempt to provide a simple, clear-cut account of the division. Another type of explanation finds the key not in policy but in personalities. It suggests that the Asquithians were men of rigid political principle, and upright if sometimes narrow personal character, whereas Lloyd George's followers were more fluid in their principles, and not always too scrupulous in their private affairs. As regards the matter of political principle, it has been suggested to me by Mr. R. B. McCallum that " the Asquithians were the purest Liberals, people for whom politics was *being a Liberal,* all other matters such as war and peace, defeat or victory, prosperity or slump, being less material factors. . . . And the charm of Asquith was that he was so purely a Liberal, a Liberal *et praeterea nihil,* initiating no policies, finding no new causes, a Liberal of purest *essence.* All this quite obviously Lloyd George was not." This does not mean that Asquith was never guilty of deviations from, say, free trade. But at least he seemed to consider the issue of free trade-versus-protection important. Lloyd George sometimes conveyed the impression that he did not give a damn either way.

This approach to the division in the party would help to explain why the Asquithians failed to cope with the war : on matters involving principle they were just too inflexible. In May 1915 Scott sent Simon, the Attorney-General, a hideous passage from one of Horatio Bottomley's journals (quoted in part above, p. 49). In it Bottomley defied the censor to take action against him. He had no need to worry. Although Simon considered it " a disgraceful and poisonous production ", his liberal principles would not allow him to suppress it. " I think myself ", he wrote, " that we must let this access of misdirected zeal work itself out as it will do in a very few days."(!) And even this was written " more in sorrow than in anger " (Simon to Scott, 14 May 1915, C. P. Scott Papers). A government which was not prepared to counter such illegitimate attack was not likely long to survive it. By contrast, Lloyd George and Churchill suffered from no such misguided concern for the liberty of the press—only concern about its power. Their flexibility carried over into other

fields : fields in which vital decisions about the running of the war had to be
made.

There is another facet to this. Whereas the habitual charge against Asquith's
supporters was that they were stiff-necked and unbending, Lloyd George's
associates were sometimes considered a good deal too pliable. Early in 1916
John Dillon, the Irish Nationalist, spoke regretfully of " the sort of man with
whom [Lloyd George] hd. now surrounded himself & with whom he was to be
seen in frequent conference in the tea-room "—one of them " an adventurer on
the make ", another " a sort of lunatic " (Scott's diary, 10 January 1916, C. P.
Scott Papers). And Scott in 1921 described one of Lloyd George's principal
Liberal colleagues as " a dreadful person, vulgar & soapy like the worst type of
Methodist preacher only less sincere " (*ibid*, 5 December 1921). This difference
sometimes applied even in matters of finance. Asquith seemed naturally to
attract men like Donald Maclean and Vivian Phillipps who acted on the most
rigid and upright standards where money was concerned. Certainly some
Asquithians were very wealthy and others were not ; but either way they were
rarely " on the make ". This was hardly true of all of Lloyd George's supporters.
Handel Booth's career, for one, expired in financial scandal. And perhaps it was
not wholly accidental that when a well-known Liberal partnership split up after
1918, the member who was a strict Presbyterian, of upright life and bitter tongue,
went with Asquith, and the member who was fond of the bottle and the ladies,
and hence was sometimes short of cash, went with Lloyd George.

Yet having gone this far, it is necessary to add that it would be outrageous to
regard the Asquithians as possessing a monopoly of the Puritan virtues. Lloyd
George's supporters included men like Fisher, Montagu, Alex Shaw, and MacCallum
Scott, against whom no charges regarding political principle or financial morals
could be levelled. They had been drawn into his company by the conviction
that success in the war, or the promotion of liberal reforms, or both, could best
be furthered by supporting his regime.

Thus even the most enticing of explanations covers only a selection of cases.
It is easy to give a straightforward interpretation of who went with, and who
went against, Lloyd George as long as only extreme cases are considered. The
problem is always the large middle, which only with difficulty can be forced
into the required pattern. For example, it is clear that the majority of "ginger"
Liberals supported Lloyd George, and that the majority of " pacifists "—the
opponents of conscription *à outrance*—opposed him. But taken together they
did not constitute a majority of Liberal M.P.s. In between was a large body of
uncommitted, or only semi-committed, members who probably hoped that they
would never have to make a decision for or against Lloyd George. (And of course
many never did. He made it for them).

What this points to is that many Liberals became followers of Lloyd George
not through any " natural " or " inevitable " process, but simply by accident.
Here are some examples. Sir Ryland Adkins was an influential Lancashire M.P.
When Asquith wrote to Balfour on 18 September 1915 regarding Liberal and
Labour opposition to conscription (see above, p. 73) he was basing his views
partly on a letter from Adkins to the chief whip which had been passed on
to him. Adkins wrote that he had recently been in Lancashire, and had been
informed " by those on whom I can rely that there is great resentment against
the conscriptionist campaign & much alarm lest the Government should intro-

duce in any way the method of compulsion, either for military service or more still for industrial purposes. I have been in correspondence with the Local Trades Council & Labour Party who pass unanimous resolutions against compulsory service in any form. . . . I have never in my life (& I recollect well each political crisis since 1884) seen anything to equal the anxiety of responsible people now, & their definite conviction that compulsory service would involve the gravest social disturbances." Finally, Adkins spoke critically of the conscription campaign in the press and the House, singling out for disapproval Lloyd George's Liberal ally Chiozza Money. (Adkins to Gulland 17 September [1915], Asquith Papers.) The following April, when the second conscription crisis was at its height, Adkins was one of the hundred Liberal M.P.s who signed a memorial to Asquith stating that his continuance as Prime Minister was a national necessity. And in May 1918 he voted with Asquith over the Maurice issue. Now if the division in the Liberal party was clear-cut before November 1918, Adkins seemed to rate as a prime Asquithian. But this was not so. None of these actions separated him finally from Lloyd George. In November 1918 he received the coupon, and from then until he lost his seat in 1923 he acted in Parliament as a Lloyd George Liberal.

Another interesting case is Sir Archibald Williamson. In July 1915 he wrote to an M.P. at the front :

> If any of your friends speak of the reprehensibles in the House—the Hogges-Pringles-Dalziels etc [it is instructive to see the two extremes of pro- and anti-Lloyd George, Dalziel on the one hand, Pringle and Hogge on the other, here being lumped together]—you can assure them they are in number but a handful, and have no influence on the assembly in which the solid men say nothing but silently and steadily support whatever is proposed by the Government, feeling that we must trust the men in office and support them throughout even when we know mistakes are and must be made.
>
> The nastiest thing that has happened or nearly happened is L. G. trying to get rid of the P.M. But it did not and wont come off. [Williamson to A. C. Murray, 18 July 1915, Elibank Papers.]

The following April Williamson also signed the memorial to Asquith urging his continuance in office. But, despite his criticism of Lloyd George, he adhered throughout the war to the principle of " trust[ing] the men in office and support[ing] them throughout ", and so in the Maurice debate voted with the government. Thereafter he found himself being drawn into Lloyd George's camp : he was invited to 10 Downing Street on 12 November 1918 and was given the coupon. From then on he was numbered among the Lloyd George Liberals.

The ambivalent attitude of Liberals like these to the division in the party is well brought out by the comments of A. C. Murray on the fall of Asquith. On 5 December 1916 Murray wrote in his diary that the government, and particularly Asquith, had done magnificently. When the story of its work came to be written, and the difficulties it had overcome were revealed, history would be astounded. Time would show whether the change of government was justified. He did not like the way in which it had been brought about—especially the vile and scurrilous campaign in the Northcliffe press—but he did not agree with those who said that Lloyd George had deliberately compassed Asquith's fall just so as to step into his shoes. Lloyd George, he believed, had only one thing at heart, the vigorous prosecution of the war. Six weeks later Murray wrote :

> Asquith still continues to be the subject of criticism on the part of people who are not fit to black his boots. It may well be that, for one reason and another, the change of Prime Minister from Asquith to Lloyd George was not undesirable, but it was Asquith to whom the whole country turned when the bad time came in 1914. His brilliant successor has taken on a task of which the back has been broken by the less showy man. . . . To the balance and imperturbability of that astute calm man [Asquith] civilization owes a debt that it can never repay. [Murray's diary, 5 December 1916 and 20 January 1917, Elibank Papers.]

Clearly it was a toss-up in which direction such a Liberal would go. In 1918 the penny came down on Lloyd George's side, in that Murray adhered to Lloyd George and Lloyd George endorsed him. But a few years later he turned against the coalition government, and thereafter figured as one of Lloyd George's strongest critics.

Here were three cases of " Lloyd George Liberals " (as they had become by 1918) who in 1916 were not hostile to Asquith, and whose ultimate choice of camp was not fore-ordained. Nor were they isolated cases. As related earlier, in April 1916 one hundred Liberal M.P.s signed a memorial describing Asquith's retention of office as a national necessity, and this was interpreted by Addison as a demonstration against Lloyd George. (See above, p. 85.) It might be assumed that these one hundred, anyway, were committed for good against Lloyd George. But this was not so. Two of them, A. H. Illingworth and Edward Shortt, had become ministers by 1918. And altogether one-third of the signatories were subsequently associated with Lloyd George in one way or another : that is, they voted with him in the Maurice debate, or attended the Downing Street meeting on 12 November 1918, or received (and did not repudiate) the coupon, or acted as Coalition Liberals in the post-war Parliament. (Many of them, of course, did several of these things).

To say this is not to deny that, already by November 1918, there were solid cores of " Asquith Liberals " and " Lloyd George Liberals ". But it does mean that there was no " natural ", " inevitable " division in the party, existing since 1916 and involving the whole range of Liberal members. On the contrary, the number of M.P.s not irresistibly committed to one section and against the other was substantial. Hence it rested with the party leaders—which in this situation meant Lloyd George—to decide whether or not the fissure in the party would be converted into a definite rupture. No doubt some of Lloyd George's right-wing supporters would have joined the Conservatives in attacking the Liberal party at the end of the war whatever he did. But equally clearly a substantial section of couponed Liberals—probably a considerable majority—would have joined him in adhering to the main body of Liberals. This course was not impossible for him. Buckmaster, in the month before the dissolution, argued for it : Lloyd George, he said, should announce that he had ousted Asquith and parted company with his Liberal colleagues only because of the necessities of war, and would return to the party on the conclusion of peace (Scott's diary, 26 October 1918, C. P. Scott Papers). These remarks have a particular interest because of their source. Even though he had gone out of office with Asquith, Buckmaster in 1918 was not a wholly committed Asquithian—in fact he had tried to bring the two leaders together. What caused his subsequent hostility to Lloyd George was not

December 1916 but November 1918 ; not the ousting of Asquith and himself from office, but Lloyd George's assault on the Liberal party as the ally of the Conservatives.

Obviously there were hazards for Lloyd George in returning to the Liberals. There was much suspicion of him among the rank and file. And there was the profound antipathy of Asquith and his entourage. But the suspicion in the party was largely caused by the belief that, in fact, he had no intention of returning ; that he was planning to split the party for his own and the Conservatives' benefit. His return would have done much to mitigate this suspicion. As for Asquith's hostility, a man of Lloyd George's stature could afford to ignore it. He had succeeded where Asquith had failed. He was " the man who won the war ", whereas " the now general estimate of Asquith " was that he was " a spent force " (ibid, 7 August 1918). If Lloyd George wanted to return to the Liberals no one could keep him out. He would be an enormous asset to a party decidedly short on assets. And whatever his nominal position, he would stand head and shoulders above every other member.

The hazard in going back did not lie in the resentment he might encounter, but in the dangers besetting the Liberal party which, even with his aid, it might not be able to surmount. By remaining allied to the Conservatives he was certain of a fresh lease of office ; if he returned to the Liberals there was no such certainty. His ejection from office by the Conservatives in 1922 does not prove that he miscalculated. Had he gone back to the Liberals he might have been out in 1918 instead of 1922. On the other hand, without millstones round his neck like the coupon election, the Treaty of Versailles (or rather the popular mythology concerning the Treaty), the Centre party scheme, and the Black and Tan episode, he might ultimately have been able to forge a new radical alliance or to enter the Labour party, thus escaping the barren years after 1922.

These are speculations, although not quite idle speculations. But amidst them there is one certainty. In 1918 Lloyd George was master of the Liberal party's destiny in at least this sense : that Liberals, with all their divisions, were not rigidly separated into two hostile bodies. It rested with him either to opt for reconciliation and so give the party a last chance of recovery, or to impose a rigid separation upon Liberal members and so destroy the only hope of a Liberal restoration. Perhaps for post-war Britain there were merits in the choice he made. For the Liberal party there was none.

7. LIBERALS WITHOUT LABEL

Mine is a most troublesome contest. Everyone is sick or busy or both : nobody is thinking of politics : & those recovering from 'flu are afraid to go out, & those who haven't had it are afraid of meeting those who have. Result, the meetings aren't what they used to be & ought to be. My agent Lee says we are going to do well : but a Labour man will drain away some of my votes, & there is a danger the Tory will get in. He is of course blessed by the Coalition.

Leif Jones to Gilbert Murray, 28 November 1918 [1]

THE first question for Liberals in this election, Asquith told a meeting of the London Liberal Federation on 18 November, was : where ought they to stand ? It suggests the ambiguity of the Liberal position that he thought it necessary to ask this question. And when the nation polled a month later, on 14 December 1918, there were some who wondered whether the question had even then been answered.

For the Liberals who bore Lloyd George's badge of approval, the situation was plain. They were supporters of the government and allies of the Conservatives. And for another section, the pacifists and anti-conscriptionists, the matter was not in doubt. They were opponents of the government, which they condemned as a Tory regime led by an apostate from Liberalism. But for the main body of Liberals, who had supported the war and consented to conscription, and yet were outside the coalition's ranks, it was indeed necessary to ask where they stood.

What at least seemed clear was that they stood in opposition to the Conservatives, against whose candidates nearly all of them were fighting. But did this mean that they opposed the coalition as a whole ? To do so, they must be in conflict with its Liberal as well as its Conservative wing. And this position the Liberal party refused to adopt. Despite Lloyd George's attack, Liberal headquarters did not repudiate him and his

[1] Gilbert Murray Papers.

164

Liberal followers, or deprive them of the status of Liberal candidates. This applied even in matters of finance. According to Liberal headquarters, the party fund was administered during the election in the interests " of the Party as a whole "—even though outsiders might think that the party no longer existed as a whole.

Every legitimate effort [Asquith's headquarters admitted] has been made to secure the adoption by Liberal Associations of Liberal candidates sound on the question of Leadership, but where a Liberal Association adopted a candidate who was known to be an adherent of Mr. Lloyd George, the decision was loyally accepted by Headquarters. Before and during the Election, general communications from Headquarters, from the National Liberal Federation and from the Liberal Publication Department were sent to every Association without any attempt at discrimination. Some of the Candidates now calling themselves Coalition Liberals either received from Liberal Headquarters or were promised but did not claim, contributions towards their Election expenses. " The Liberal Party adheres to the principle that the local Associations are the right authorities to determine Liberal candidatures."[1]

Another document of Asquith's headquarters shows that grants towards election expenses were made to coalition supporters in West Leeds (£500), the Attercliffe division of Sheffield (£752), and Wellingborough (£500).[2] Further, when the Leeds Liberals asked headquarters for advice about a Conservative proposal that the two parties in Leeds should run candidates jointly as supporters of the coalition, the officers of the party, if with some misgivings, agreed to the arrangement.[3]

So apparently the Asquithians stood in opposition to the coalition's Conservative wing but not its Liberal wing, and thus were uncommitted in attitude towards the government as such. Probably Asquith was encouraged to adopt so indefinite a position by the belief that even now Liberalism might be saved from " organic division ". After all, Lloyd George was still calling himself a Liberal, and it was assumed that such a person

[1] " The Liberal Party " document, Asquith Papers.
[2] Documents on election finance, Asquith Papers.
[3] Minutes of the Leeds Liberal Federation, 21 November 1918.

would not assail the main body of Liberal candidates. At worst, Asquith expected him to allow Liberals to offer themselves as government supporters, leaving it to the electors to choose between them and Conservatives doing the same; and the 12 November speech confirmed him in this view. At an informal meeting the next day the Liberal leader referred with cordiality to the speech, speaking (said *The Times*) in the following sense :

> He subscribed with a full heart to all that the Prime Minister was reported to have said. . . . There were no divisions in the Liberal Party, and, had he been at the meeting [of 12 November], the Prime Minister would have had no more appreciative or enthusiastic auditor. . . . He could see no obstacle in the way of any member of the Liberal Party giving cordial support to the coalition Government, so long as the Government's policy continued to be consistent with Liberal principles.[1]

Many Liberal candidates took the view that " no obstacle " prevented them from " giving cordial support to the Coalition Government ". Near the end of the campaign, a correspondent of *The Times*, surveying the West Riding of Yorkshire, said : " I have yet to discover an Asquithian Liberal who does not vie with his official Coalition opponent, whether Liberal or Unionist, in proclaiming his acceptance of Mr. Lloyd George's programme." " No Government ", agreed the parliamentary correspondent of *The Times*, ". . . has probably ever been faced with so weak an Opposition as that of which Mr. Asquith is the leader." Many of his candidates were " only too anxious to be regarded as true friends of the Coalition."[2] We can see this in the election addresses of the two Liberal candidates for Birkenhead, both of whom described themselves as " Liberal Coalition " candidates. Graham White, the candidate for Birkenhead East, criticised the coalition for holding an election while the armed forces were " still away on service and cannot take part in it personally ", but in all other respects placed himself firmly on the side of the government.

> I believe [he said] that the present Government, which backed by the nation has rendered the supreme service of

---

[1] *The Times*, 14 November 1918.　　　　[2] *ibid*, 10 and 12 December 1918.

winning the war, should have the support of everyone in
settling the Peace, carrying out demobilisation, and starting
vigorously those vital schemes—such as housing the nation
—on which everyone is determined, and which must not be
delayed.

The remainder of his manifesto was devoted to policy matters :
the treatment of ex-servicemen and dependents of the fallen,
housing, Free Trade, a League of Nations, and the peace settlement. Nothing was said about the division in the Liberal party,
and Asquith's name was not mentioned.

Similarly H. Bickersteth, the candidate for Birkenhead
West, said that : " In response to the unanimous request of the
Liberal Party, I have consented to stand as the Liberal Coalition
Candidate at the forthcoming Election." " I am firmly convinced of the advisability of a Coalition Government continuing
in office until the actual signing of the Treaty of Peace, the
demobilisation of the forces, and the transference of our
industries from war service to conditions of peace." Thereafter
he too turned to policy matters, without referring to the division
in the Liberal party or the relations of the Liberal leaders to
the government.

Had circumstances allowed, probably the great majority of
Asquithians would have gone through the election like this,
offering support to the government on account of its " liberal "
programme and ignoring the Conservative predominance in its
ranks. But the appearance of the coupon, which incidentally
was employed against both Birkenhead Liberals, converted such
a position from nebulous to absurd, and forced the party leaders
to reconsider. A few of them, it is true, clung to this position
to the end. Herbert Samuel went on proclaiming his support
for the government even after it had become plain that Lloyd
George was bent on driving him from Parliament. In a manifesto Samuel warned against the existence of " too much party
spirit ", and said :

The present Government is a combination of parties.
Mr. Lloyd George, who is its head, wishes to continue for
the settlement following the war the union of parties which
happily prevailed during the war. He wishes to use that
union in order to pass, by common agreement, a number of
bills for the benefit of the people. In this I think he is right.

If I am returned to Parliament I should support him in
that policy.[1]

But other prominent Liberals became more combative in face
of the government's assault. They now stressed the Conservative predominance in the government, and argued that the
Tories would never enact Lloyd George's social programme.
(Unfortunately this criticism became rather irrelevant when
the issue of the campaign moved from " homes for heroes " to
hanging the Kaiser). Could they, asked Runciman, expect
land reform from Walter Long, free trade from Austen Chamberlain, temperance measures from Sir George Younger, a
democratic Upper House from Lords Curzon and Milner, or
nobility in a programme associated with F. E. Smith ? If,
said Simon, Lloyd George meant the reactionaries to swallow
a democratic programme, he would need a great many radical
and Labour members to hold them down. " Look Before You
Leap. Think Before You Vote ", exhorted a major Liberal
advertisement on the eve of polling. If the coalition whips
had their way the next Parliament would be a " Tory House."
" Will a Tory House of Commons . . . give the people any real
Land Reform, or can a Tory majority be trusted to apportion
fairly the financial burdens of the War ? " The government
whips " are doing all they can to keep out Liberalism and
Labour." What was needed was " a Free Parliament of Free
Men " to be obtained by " voting for the LIBERALS."

The most noteworthy example of a reappraisal of attitude
during the campaign was provided by Asquith. His response
to the 12 November speech had shown him ready to adopt a
fairly benevolent attitude to the government. Even when
Lloyd George commenced his assault he did not immediately
retaliate. He told his first major election meeting on 18 November that he stood as a Liberal " without prefix and suffix,
without label and hallmark of any sort and description." He
expressed doubts about Conservative intentions, but said that
he would give " hearty support and fullest co-operation to any
Government, by whatever name it is called, which grapples with
the problem of reconstruction on progressive and democratic
lines." And he summed up by advising Liberals to throw their
whole weight on the side of their patriotic and democratic

[1] *Manchester Guardian*, 28 November 1918.

programme, keeping their eyes open and their hands free. This left him uncommitted either as supporter or opponent of the government. " Now ", wrote one observer, " no Liberal candidate can make anything out of Mr. Asquith's own answer to the question which he himself put : ' Where are we to stand in this election ? ' Practical politics are not worked by such refinements, and some of Mr. Asquith's hearers were very conscious of that."[1] The *Western Morning News* reported that a number of his closest followers were disappointed by the speech, and that Liberals came away from the meeting saying " there was nothing in it." Their view was echoed by the *Westminster Gazette*, Asquith's nearest ally in the press, which commented on 27 November : " Mr. Asquith, let it be admitted, has been no match for the modern politicians who capture opinion and make and unmake Cabinets with the aid of their press auxiliaries, and in recent months he seems to some of his followers to have carried modesty and self-effacement to excess." And the *Nation* moved from criticism of Asquith's leadership to a positive desertion of the Liberal camp. " RALLY TO LABOR ", it exhorted its readers. Labour had become " the one powerful, integral force in our politics outside Mr. George's compact " and in the next Parliament would be in effect the official Opposition—" for Mr. Asquith does not propose such a part for himself or his followers."[2]

The force of Lloyd George's attack, and the mounting discontent among Asquith's followers at his lack of response, at last drove the Liberal leader into a more combative position. At Huddersfield on 28 November he became the outspoken critic of the government which he had refused to be during the past two years. He attacked the way in which a junta in London had made a deal round a table labelling seats, ticketing candidates, and distributing political coupons—the first use of the expression. And he argued that Liberals were being proscribed not because they opposed the government's social programme but because they would not bind themselves by a blind pledge. (Many Liberals, it is clear, never had the choice of binding themselves). As for the claim that Conservatives had been converted to progressive views, he said that Liberals must be free to stop them backsliding. And he warned :

[1] *ibid*, 19 November 1918.   [2] *Nation*, 23 and 30 November 1918.

The new House of Commons will start with a minimum of moral authority—just because of the absence, the compulsory abstention, of our soldiers and sailors ; and, next, because of the presence in its midst of a large number of men who are really only minority candidates. . . .

If you have a gagged and fettered House of Commons you have lost the only safeguard which our Constitution presents for the intelligent revision of the proposals of the Government of the day. We have been fighting for liberty abroad. Are we going to have it murdered or stifled here at home ?

We will support with a whole heart, and with no reservations, a progressive policy, but . . . we should return to the new Parliament a body of Independent Liberals, fettered by no pledges, to think free, to speak free, to act, we believe not in a party sense, but in a larger and higher sense.

Yet however critical Asquith became, his actions never lost the appearance of shadow-boxing. The prime issue facing Liberals was whether they saw themselves as supporters or opponents of the government. This they never decided, except in so far as Lloyd George decided it for them. Leif Jones, for example, did not discuss the government at all in his election address, let alone say whether he supported it or not. And Asquith at his most critical never claimed to be an opposition leader seeking to overthrow the government and seize power himself. On 11 December he said in East Fife : " There was no question, of course, of displacing, or of attempting or desiring to displace, the present Government." And the next day he stated, as he had done at the commencement of the campaign, that he would support any government which would preserve a truly liberal policy in domestic affairs. So decisive had been his expulsion from office in December 1916 that the only role he could now find for himself was that of aiding the government in implementing its programme and combating attempts by its followers to thwart it. What had been said of him at the start of the campaign was almost as true at the end, that " practical politics are not worked by such refinements ".

II

It was not only the Asquithians' attitude to the government that seemed so vague. This was equally true of their attitude to the Labour party.

There was no ambiguity of relations between the coalition parties and Labour. As the *Westminster Gazette* admitted on 15 November 1918 : " In the confusion and perplexity that have overtaken the old political parties, the Labour Party now stands out as the one party which boldly calls itself an Opposition to the Government party." Labour's defection from the coalition had long been expected, and with the election the breach was complete. Labour members who remained in the government were expelled from their party, and Lloyd George seemed positively zestful in waging war upon Labour. His attitude was emulated by many of his Liberal followers, as in Leicester and Blackburn, where formerly Liberal and Labour had contested elections by agreement.[1] And even those Coalition Liberals who were not avowedly hostile to Labour were committed to an anti-Labour position both by the actions of the Premier and by the fact that Labour candidates were usually their only serious opponents.

The uncouponed Liberals by contrast seemed neither the enemies nor the allies of Labour. Clearly many of them inclined to sympathy with it, harking back to the days when the two parties had been associated as supporters of the Liberal government. Thus the Manchester Liberals stood aside for Labour in working-class constituencies as they had done in 1910, and Sir John Brunner, a recent president of the National Liberal Federation, campaigned in the constituency where he lived for Labour against the Conservatives. Further, a number of Liberal spokesmen referred to Liberal and Labour as joint victims of the coalition's attack.[2]

But these were isolated manifestations of sympathy. There

[1] The strongly " pacifist " views of MacDonald and Snowden, the Labour candidates, certainly contributed to the enmity with which they were regarded by the Liberals in these constituencies, among whom was Gordon Hewart, the Solicitor-General.

[2] see above p. 168.

was no concerted attempt by the Liberals to align themselves with Labour. What prevented them from trying was the lack of response from Labour itself, and in particular its changed attitude on the vital matter of candidates. Asquith referred obliquely to this when he argued that the new Parliament would not be representative because of the number of minority candidates returned. That is, he was anticipating Conservative gains from the Liberals as a result of Labour's intervention. In the past Labour had not run more than seventy-eight candidates, most of them by agreement with the Liberals. Now it was putting forward a sufficient number—more indeed than the number of uncouponed Liberals—to contest the election on a national scale. This made it difficult for Liberals to view Labour with cordiality. Even Arthur Ponsonby, whose sympathy for Labour was well known, and who was standing as an Independent Democrat after losing the Liberal nomination, was forced to criticise the adoption of a miner's candidate against him. This, he complained, might enable the coalition to capture the seat on a minority vote, and anyway his own position was identical with that of Labour.

For the already distracted Liberal party, Labour's decision to contest the election as a national party—a decision which to the last Liberals had not believed it would implement—presented a new and ominous challenge. Yet they were so accustomed to looking on Labour as the offspring and ally of Liberalism that they hardly knew how to revise their attitude. A private letter which Gilbert Murray wrote to the editor of the *Daily News* during the election illustrates their dilemma. He was campaigning in Westbury for Geoffrey Howard, who was opposed by a couponed Conservative and a Labour candidate —the latter, significantly, a former Liberal. Quite apart from his dislike of the Labour candidate on personal grounds, Murray felt that " the position of a straightforward Radical is very hard with all the Georgite press against him and our own press not very definitely supporting him. I am all for the co-operation, or the union, of Liberalism and Labour, and have e.g. canvassed for [Sidney] Webb for London University. But in a case like this, a stranger who is not in any way a better democrat than the sitting member and in many cases a worse one, just intervening so as to let the Tory in ", he could not help thinking that the *Daily News*, " our one comfort in these evil days, might be rather less neutral and more definitely Liberal. . . . Could you not urge your readers, in cases like this, to concentrate on the Liberal ? I mean cases where (1) the Liberal is the sitting member, (2) he is a ' free ' Liberal and a genuine Liberal, and (3) he is the only progressive and democratic candidate who has any chance of winning the seat."[1] From this it appears, not only that the *Daily News* (" our one comfort in these evil days ") was not stressing the claims of Liberals as against Labour, but that Murray himself only wanted the distinction made in certain cases. The Liberal candidate must be " free " and " genuine ", and his claim to the seat must be pre-eminent, in that he was the sitting member and the only " progressive " with any chance of winning. And even though Labour had declared war on the Liberals equally with the Conservatives, Murray still looked forward to " the co-operation, or the union, of Liberalism and Labour ".

III

In view of their mixed feelings towards Labour, it is not surprising that most Liberals chose not to attack it, nor to speak of it as an ally, but simply to ignore it. Yet the result was that once again they were failing to make a clear response to a plain challenge. All along the line their position was equivocal. They might say that on issues of policy their attitude was clear : they stood for free trade, Irish Home Rule, a League of Nations, a " clean peace ", and the " national minimum ". But in this election only one issue of policy mattered : the treatment to be meted out to Germany. And on it the Liberal position was not clear-cut. Most Liberals believed that Germany had committed a crime against humanity for which it should be punished. This meant levying heavy reparations and arraigning war criminals—including the Kaiser. But as a body the Liberals were not prepared to turn these serious judicial matters into cheap election stunts, as were Lloyd George and the Conservatives, and so were able to say very little.

More than this, the election was not being fought primarily

[1] Murray to Gardiner, 6 December 1918, Gardiner Papers. Murray's words did not go unheeded : see *Daily News*, 11 and 12 December 1918.

on policy matters at all. It was being contested on the issue of Lloyd George's bid for a renewed lease of office and Labour's attempt to unseat him. The Asquithians belonged on neither side of this conflict. They would not sever their connections with Liberal adherents of the coalition, and said that there was " no question " of " attempting or desiring " to overthrow the government. Nor would they take issue with Labour or state their attitude to the Labour party. Indeed there was much truth, if little appreciation of their difficulties, in *The Times*'s account of their position two days before voting. Asquith had " over 250 candidates going to the poll," it said, " but they are little more than a stage army." Some wanted to be regarded as true friends of the coalition, while others hoped " to prove to working-class voters that there is no fundamental difference between them and their Labour opponents. They are all things to all men. Their bond of union is a feeling of resentment at the holding of a General Election when the omens for their cause are so unpropitious."

Thus by 1918 the Liberals had lost what before the war had been their greatest asset : the advantage of being one of the two potential governing parties (which Labour hitherto had never been). A British election is primarily a contest between possible alternative governments ; and a party incapable of bidding for office is subject to a crippling handicap. In 1918 the Liberals were non-participants in the struggle for power, having surrendered to Labour this most vital attribute. In the circumstances, it is little wonder that the ruling party of four years earlier not only failed in this contest, but passed through it virtually unnoticed.

8. THE RESULTS

[A]nti-Germanism and the desire for revenge were strong amongst large masses of the people. . . . The Liberals are not thought as a party to be sufficiently venomous. . . .

McKenna to Gardiner, 29 December 1918 [1]

THE results of the election proved an even more shattering defeat for the uncouponed Liberals than had been anticipated. Virtually all the leaders of the group disappeared from Parliament. Asquith, McKenna, Runciman, Simon, Samuel, McKinnon Wood, Sir Charles Hobhouse, H. J. Tennant, and H. T. Baker among office-holders in the last Liberal government, and Gulland, Howard, Walter Rea, and Sir Arthur Marshall among the whips, were all rejected. Moreover most of them, as *The Times* remarked, were not merely defeated but hopelessly outclassed. In fact two ex-ministers, Hobhouse and McKinnon Wood, suffered the indignity of forfeiting their deposits, a provision instituted by the Reform Act of 1918 to discourage " freak " candidates.

No group of uncouponed Liberals survived : the " old gang ", the " pacifists " (whether they retained the Liberal label or not), independent critics of the government like Pringle, erstwhile coalition supporters like H. J. Craig, temperance advocates like Leif Jones, upholders of *laissez-faire* like R. D. Holt, all suffered indiscriminate defeat. So general was their downfall that their fate had to be particularly catastrophic to attract attention. Sir John Barlow, it was thought worthy of note, having represented Frome since 1892 except for a break in 1895–6, not only came third to Conservative and Labour but failed to save his deposit, while the pacifist J. H. Whitehouse, a Liberal M.P. since 1910, received just 504 votes in a total poll of 16,000.

[1] Gardiner Papers.

In all, 29 uncouponed Liberals were elected. Eight were returned for constituencies where neither a Conservative nor any other recipient of the coupon stood, and were either coalition supporters who were couponed in all but name, or anti-coalitionists, like Acland and Maclean, whose election was rather a lucky accident.

> My return was rather a fluke [Acland wrote to Asquith] for though I beat a good Labour man in a straight fight [by 532 votes], I should not have won if the Tory candidate, who had not got back from India in time, had been put forward. . . . I wish the seat were safe for Liberalism against all comers, for of course then I should be delighted to stand down so that you could take it, but it is not.[1]

Of the remaining uncouponed Liberals who succeeded, eight were returned against couponed candidates who were not Conservatives, three against Conservatives who did not possess the coupon, and ten against couponed Conservatives.

These 29 successes possessed no uniformity, either in type of constituency or in type of Liberal elected. Admittedly the seats secured by uncouponed Liberals were, with one or two exceptions, in former Liberal strongholds : agricultural divisions in Devon, Scotland, and North Wales ; and working-class constituencies in Scotland and the environs of London, as well as in Hull, Portsmouth, Cardiff, Wolverhampton, and the mining region of Durham. But all told these constituted only isolated remnants in what had been solid Liberal districts. Thus only one uncouponed Liberal was returned in the Scottish highlands, and one in rural Wales ; the two seats retained in mining districts of Durham were lonely survivors of a once-powerful Liberal tradition ; and far more noteworthy than the handful of Asquithian successes in industrial Scotland was the utter rout in Glasgow, where six Liberals, including three former M.P.s, forfeited their deposits.

If no region remained solid for the uncouponed Liberals, neither was there unity of outlook among those elected. Of the three who had held minor posts in the last Liberal government, two (Acland and Wedgwood Benn) were radicals who regarded Asquith as too much of a " whig ", while the third, George Lambert, belonged on the right of the party but inclined

[1] Acland to Asquith, 29 December (1918), Asquith Papers.

towards the coalition. Similar differences over leadership and policy were evident throughout the group. Maclean and George Thorne were attached to Asquith, Hilton Young to Lloyd George, and Hogge and Wedgwood to neither. In terms of policy Maclean held firmly to Gladstonian principles of public thrift and private enterprise, whereas Benn and Sidney Arnold supported " socialist " proposals like a levy on capital and the nationalisation of mines and railways. It was said that the effect of the election on Labour was to eliminate the intellectuals and pacifists and to spare the " steady " trade unionists. But with the uncouponed Liberals there was no pattern or uniformity ; the party in the new Parliament was a collection of fragments.

II

While the Asquithians were going down to defeat, the Liberals who received the coupon were everywhere successful. This was equally true of other recipients of the coupon, so that the most striking feature of the results seemed to be the triumph of couponed candidates irrespective of party. 136 of the 159 Liberals who received the coupon were elected, together with 333 of the 364 couponed Conservatives, and nine of the eighteen couponed N.D.P.s. That is, 541 coupons went out and 478 M.P.s came back. It is not surprising that the coupon has ever since been regarded as a " passport to Parliament ", or that large numbers of rejected Liberals attributed their defeat to the whim of Lloyd George and believed that, had he seen fit to allocate the coupons differently, he could have accomplished a Liberal triumph instead.

Yet was the Liberal rout really as accidental as this ? That is, was the election simply a triumph for Lloyd George personally, and not for the Conservative party ? It has already been shown that the circumstances of the election suited the Conservatives ideally. The Liberals as well as being divided were discredited by their " failure " during the first years of the war, as Labour was fatally hampered by its association with "pacifist" and "unpatriotic" elements. The Conservative party had provided the foundation of the successful wartime government, and was bound to benefit from the mood of extreme nationalism which had been apparent throughout the war and which vigorously asserted itself during the election. It was not, after all, Lloyd George who first raised the issues of punishing the Kaiser and extracting vast reparations from Germany. It was candidates of the Conservative party. And they found an audience ready-made for this type of appeal. The clearest feature of the first week of the campaign, reported *The Glasgow Herald* on 2 December, was the almost universal support for " relentlessly just " peace terms ; no candidate had the faintest chance of being elected if he showed any weakness on this, the main issue of the contest, and candidates who failed to make themselves clear on the matter were being reminded of the fact by the vigilant heckler. It was certainly true, as the *Manchester Guardian* said three days before polling, that Lloyd George did nothing during the campaign to restrain " the cheap violence of his followers ; rather, it must be said, he has played up to it ". But this does not mean that he introduced the " cheap violence ". His least responsible utterances had been exceeded days and sometimes weeks before he made them by Tory candidates who encountered a ready response among the electors. Coalition Liberals like Fisher, Addison, and J. W. Greig reported after campaigning in working-class districts of London, Manchester, and Scotland that interest centred almost exclusively on issues like " the expulsion of all the Germans in the district " and the " trial and execution of the Kaiser ". " The meetings would hardly listen to me ", Greig recalled, because " I was not strong enough at the early meetings on the question of indemnity and reparation "; " the feeling in Scotland was that they were out for reparation and guarantees."[1] The point about Lloyd George's conduct is that, as a Prime Minister of no fixed political abode, he could shift his emphasis to whatever issues were arousing the attention of the electors. And these were issues ideally suited to produce a Conservative victory, irrespective of the distribution of coupons.

This is borne out by the fact that there were several noteworthy Conservative successes where the coupon played no part. It has been said so often that Asquith lost his seat in the coupon election that it appears almost to have been forgotten that he

[1] Fisher's diary, 3 December 1918, Fisher Papers ; *H. C. Deb.*, 113, 551 (5 March 1919).

did not lose it on account of the coupon, for none was issued against him. Lloyd George, with a nice regard for the letter if not the spirit of former comradeship, was reluctant to proscribe his late leader personally, and seems even to have prevailed on Conservative headquarters not to put up a candidate against him. At first Asquith was expected to have an unopposed return, but the Conservatives in his constituency rebelled against this decision and adopted a candidate without reference to their leaders. When they requested the coupon for their nominee they were firmly rebuffed. Yet even without the coalition's blessing the undistinguished Colonel Sprot had no difficulty in beating the Liberal leader.

Something similar occurred in the Manchester constituencies. Lloyd George was on friendly terms with the Manchester Liberals, and anxious to avoid going too far in alienating the *Manchester Guardian,* so he used the coupon sparingly in this district. Of the ten Manchester constituencies, only four received coupons; three going to Conservatives and one to a Liberal. This left six divisions uncouponed : in three because there were Liberals and Conservatives standing who were equally favourable to the coalition ; and in the remaining three because Lloyd George wished to secure unopposed returns for Labour candidates like J. R. Clynes who, though now outside the government, had supported it during the war. These arrangements left the Conservatives in Manchester less well favoured with coupons than elsewhere. Of their eight candidates, only three had the coupon ; and two of the remainder were not only uncouponed but were publicly discouraged by Conservative headquarters from standing—one because he was opposing the couponed Liberal, and the other because he was standing against a " patriotic " Labour candidate. Yet every one of these eight Conservatives was elected ; whereas no Liberal was returned (even though one of them had the coupon and only two were opposed by it), and only two Labour candidates were successful—the two whom the local Conservatives, under pressure from headquarters, had agreed not to oppose. That is, Conservatives actively denied the coupon were every bit as successful as those who received it. Clearly the Conservative party, and not the coupon, triumphed in the Manchester contests.

What has obscured the Conservative victory in this election

is the fact that, where Liberals received the coupon, they escaped the fate of the rest of their party, and it has been assumed that the coupon alone made the difference. Yet the statistics which seem to reveal the coupon as a " passport to Parliament ", irrespective of party, conceal the fact that nearly all the successful couponed candidates who were not Conservatives were standing in lieu of Conservatives. Lloyd George, it will be recalled, had reached an agreement with the Conservative leaders that the Liberal section of the coalition " should receive their [the Conservatives'] support, where necessary, for 150 Lloyd George Candidates ". This did not simply mean that these Liberals would receive the coupon. It meant that Bonar Law would prevail upon his followers not to oppose them. In constituencies where Liberals received the coupon, he called on Conservative associations to refrain from putting forward candidates, and where they proved unamenable he brought the full weight of party authority to bear on them. In the last resort, a public telegram under Bonar Law's signature was sent to them on the day before nominations calling on them to withdraw their candidates and allow the couponed Liberals a free run. This came very near to constituting a repudiation by the Conservative leader of authorised Conservative candidates.

As a result of this arrangement, 127 of the 136 couponed Liberals returned to Parliament, and eight of the nine couponed N.D.P.s, had no official Conservative opponents—an official Conservative being the nominee of a constituency association, whether party headquarters welcomed his adoption or not. This means that, out of a total of 478 couponed candidates elected, 333 were Conservatives, and 135 were Liberals or N.D.P.s standing in the absence of Conservatives; so that at least 468 of these 478 were the logical recipients of any "swing to the right ". And as has been shown, there is ample evidence that such a swing occurred in this election.

To say this is not to argue that the Conservatives gained nothing from being coalition candidates. But they were not coalition candidates simply because they received the coupon. As a Liberal journalist observed in an aside of considerable insight, in this election " every Unionist candidate is ex officio a Coalition candidate ".[1] The whole Conservative party, with

[1] *Manchester Guardian*, 20 November 1918.

negligible exceptions, supported Lloyd George's administration and had done so since its inception, and the most prominent Conservatives were members of it. It was not the coupon but the facts of the situation which designated the Conservatives as supporters of the coalition. For Liberals the situation was quite different. With their party divided towards the government, nearly all Liberals not actually in office could be tarred with the Asquithian brush—as happened even to some couponed Liberals when the local Conservatives persisted in running candidates against them. Given the Liberal party's equivocal position, Conservatives would nearly always appear better coalitionists than would Liberals unless the government employed a device to label the latter as its supporters. It was, after all, as part of an arrangement to spare some Liberals from the coalition attack on the Liberal party that the coupon was devised. Had Lloyd George wished to safeguard no Liberals he need never have employed the coupon at all. Admittedly, under this arrangement, if he did not bestow the coupon on Liberals coming within his bargain he usually granted it to Conservatives, which meant that many more Conservatives received it than Liberals. But for Conservatives it did not clearly serve a vital purpose, because they were already " ex officio Coalition candidates ". For Liberals precisely the reverse was true.

Far from Lloyd George having it in his power to implement a vastly different coupon arrangement, and so convert the election from a Conservative into a Liberal triumph, he probably secured as much for Liberals as he could, given that he had decided to preserve the coalition and remain the ally of the Conservatives.[1] There was no likelihood that the Conservatives would have agreed to stand aside in more than 150 seats ; as it was Bonar Law's authority was severely taxed in securing this number of abstentions, and broke down altogether in some constituencies.[2] Lloyd George was certainly open to severe

[1] What would have happened had Lloyd George broken with the Conservatives and returned to a re-united Liberal party is, of course, another matter, and one about which it is difficult to speculate. The most that may be suggested, in the light of the 1945 election, is that an enormously popular war leader would not *necessarily* have led a discredited party to victory in 1918.

[2] Fisher found Bonar Law during the campaign deeply disturbed by accusations of having thrown over his own party. That morning he had received ten abusive

criticism from Liberals for embarking on an election as the ally of the Conservatives. But it does not follow that, having decided on this fundamentally anti-Liberal course, he was in a position to secure a better bargain for Liberal candidates than he did. The Conservatives were too convinced that they were on the verge of a great victory to let it go by default at his behest. Perhaps he could, while keeping the coalition intact, have made no bargain at all over candidates, and allowed Liberals and Conservatives to fight it out all along the line. But would more Liberals have been returned as a consequence ? The Conservatives would still have been in an overwhelmingly strong position, as is suggested by the fate of Asquith and the Manchester results. The main difference would have been that they would have had further opportunities of capturing seats, because they would have been free to contest the seats of couponed Liberals—the only Liberals who enjoyed any measure of success.

III

It follows from these considerations that in one vital respect both couponed and uncouponed Liberals shared a uniform fate : they enjoyed little success when fighting on two fronts against Conservative and Labour candidates—what for Liberals were to become the normal circumstances of three-party warfare. The importance of the coupon was that in some seats it obviated these circumstances, by securing the abstention of Conservatives. Consequently this section of Liberals achieved what may have been a largely fictitious success.

In all, 165 Liberals were elected in 1918, 136 with and 29 without the coupon. Only 20 of these were elected in single-member constituencies in the presence of official Conservative candidates, and but twelve of the 20 in the presence of Labour candidates as well.[1] Doubtless some of the Liberals elected in

---

telegrams from Liverpool—where one Liberal had received the coupon as against nine Conservatives. In this instance, and a number of others, the local Conservatives simply refused to withdraw their candidates.

[1] Including in both figures North East Derbyshire, where the total vote of two rival Conservatives exceeded that of the victorious Liberal. Two-member

the absence of Conservative or Labour opponents would have triumphed in conditions of three-party warfare. But the fact remained that the overwhelming majority of successful Liberals did not win in these conditions. Moreover, when Liberals did stand against both Conservative and Labour candidates they usually fared badly. In all, there were 144 single-member constituencies where Liberals (couponed or uncouponed) stood in opposition to both Conservative and Labour.[1] As has just been said, they won in twelve of them. Even more significantly, they came second in only 40 instances, and third in 92. In many ways this was the most disturbing feature of the results. There were good reasons why in this election the Liberals might not come first in triangular contests. But for Labour, in its first bid for the status of a major party, to relegate them so often to third position was profoundly threatening.

Only in the circumstances of the contest might Liberals seek for consolation. They could not hope to prosper in a " Khaki " election, and they had suffered severely from the division in their ranks. There were many good Liberals who had voted for Lloyd George's candidates, because they still regarded him as one of themselves or felt that gratitude for his wartime services should override party allegiance. As the war became remote, there was some prospect that the difficulties of the Liberals and advantages of the Conservatives would diminish. Yet it was plain that the problems which had overwhelmed the Liberals were not wholly transitory. There was no guarantee that the return of peace would revive the issues which had once rallied support to their cause, would dispel the attitudes which had drawn former adherents to Labour or the Conservatives, or would even secure them a more coherent role in politics than they had occupied in this election. Putting aside their temporary difficulties, it was clear that their very existence as a political force was in jeopardy.

---

constituencies are not included in these figures, but it may be noted that two Liberals were returned for Southampton and one for Combined Universities (both two-member constituencies), in each instance defeating one Conservative, and in the former defeating two Labour candidates as well.

[1] Excluding Paddington North, where there were six candidates altogether.

PART THREE

The Liberal Party and the Coalition

1919-1922

9. THE PARTING OF THE WAYS

Coalitionists swarming in the [National Liberal] club with a view to insinuating themselves back to comradeship. Poor success quiet steady resentment at their treachery being shown.

John Burns's diary, 3 January 1919 [1]

AMONG the problems facing Liberals after the 1918 election, the question of internal relations loomed large : could there remain a single Liberal party ? Despite the bitter resentment which now divided Liberals, not all of them wanted the breach to become final. Even some who had fallen under the Premier's ban, like George Lambert, were anxious to avoid disruption. And this was very much the case with the Coalition Liberals. Acland reported in January 1919 that " most of the Coalish Libs are pretending to be entirely unpledged & talking about meetings of the whole party & keeping going the sacred principles of Liberalism. As if they haven't broken every one of them by taking the ticket ! "[2] The " Coalish Libs " denied that by accepting the coupon they had broken " the sacred principles of Liberalism." A coalition, they said, was needed during the period of peace-making and reconstruction. But by supporting it they were not tying themselves irrevocably to the Conservatives or deserting liberal ideals (although when the need for a coalition would end they were reluctant to say).

As against these advocates of unity, many Liberals, and especially the leaders on both sides, were prepared for a rupture between the two wings. Lloyd George was anxious to convert his alliance with the Conservatives into a " Centre " or " National " party, and so did not want even nominal relations with the official Liberal party. Otherwise, with Asquith out of

[1] Burns Papers.
[2] Acland to his wife, n.d. (probably 21 January 1919), Acland Papers.

Parliament and a majority of Liberal M.P.s his supporters, he was strongly placed to get himself elected Liberal leader by the parliamentary party ; but when this was suggested to him, he rejected it for fear it should unsettle the Conservatives.[1] Asquith also had lost interest in preserving the semblance of a single party. For one thing, he deeply resented Lloyd George's treachery. For another, now that his fears of what would happen to a divided party in an election had been realised, nothing was to be gained by keeping up relations with the Coalition Liberals. Moreover, he feared that Lloyd George might injure the party further by seizing the Liberal leadership. (He could hardly be expected to guess that Lloyd George would not want the position). To forestall this, he had to institute a clean break in the parliamentary party so that a " meeting of the whole party " would not have a chance to choose a new leader.[2]

Acting as if no vacancy existed in the party leadership, Asquith in January 1919 (i.e. before Parliament met) appointed Sir Donald Maclean chairman of the non-coalition Liberals in Parliament. He sought support for this action from the two most experienced Liberals elected without the coupon, Acland and George Lambert. Acland recounted :

Asquith wanted to ask Lambert & me whether we objected to D. Maclean. As M[aclean] & Asquith seemed both to be on right lines of running the group vigorously as a group in close cooperation with Labour I said a hearty " yes ". Lambert played the ass at great length—wanted us all to pretend we belonged to the Coalition & wait for some split[,] & Asquith argued with him [as did Maclean, Gulland, and Acland]. . . .

I told Lambert straight that if the group didn't get going & into close relations with Labour some of us would

---

[1] Fisher's diary, 21 and 22 February 1919, Fisher Papers ; *Daily Chronicle*, 11 March 1919.

[2] Whether Asquith could have been forced out of the leadership by a vote of the parliamentary party, or whether on the other hand he was entitled to remain leader once he had been excluded from Parliament, were nice questions for which no precedents existed and which, in the event, were not put to the test (because Lloyd George let them go by default). But these considerations were certainly exercising Asquith.

take that on ourselves unofficially, & Asquith warmly
approved.[1]

As soon as Parliament met the group was duly " got going ".
A meeting for the purpose was summoned on 3 February 1919
and was attended by twenty-three Liberal M.P.s. Most of them
had been elected without the coupon, but a few recipients of the
coupon known to oppose the coalition, like Wedgwood, were
present. Despite obstruction from a few coalition sympathisers,
and from a radical section seeking to end Asquith's control of
the party, the meeting finally agreed to form an Independent
or Free Liberal party (soon dubbed the " Wee Frees "), with
Maclean as chairman. Acland sent his wife a lively account of
proceedings :

. . . Then to the Free Liberal meeting. It was rather fun.
Lambert who was senior P[rivy] C[ouncillor] present moved
me into the chair as he wanted to keep free to oppose what
we wanted to do. We talked for over three hours & though
it seemed very black for forming a group at first the saner
ones finally got on top & we settled to form one by about
16 votes to 4. There were two sets against it from opposite
points of view. Lambert & Godfrey Collins who want to
pretend that we are still upon the same boat [as the
Coalition Liberals,] & Wedgwood[,] S. Arnold & Hogge
who hate the old Lib party & dont want to have any sort
of connection with it, & between the two of them (both
very vocal) it seemed that we should get nothing done.
There was a critical moment. Hogge had moved that we
elect a sessional chairman pro forma as a peg for questions
& discussion. Then when we'd all spoken I asked them
to divide on it. He said it wasnt his motion & wanted to
substitute " that this meeting of Liberals take immediate
steps to reorganise the Lib party & meanwhile appoints a
sessional chairman." That was dangerous for it wld have
been negatived. Then someone else wanted to move that
we form a group " in order to reunite with the Co.Libs ".
That was equally dangerous for it wouldn't have been
carried either. So I boldly ruled them both out of order &
said that we must vote on what we had been discussing
which was that we form a group & proceed to elect a

[1] Acland to his wife, n.d., Acland Papers.

sessional chairman & officers. I moved it. Sir J. McCallum a dear old Scot seconded promptly, a crafty motion to adjourn (we shd never have met again if we'd once adjourned) was defeated & my motion was put & carried.[1]

This decision caused dismay to the majority of Coalition Liberals. In an effort to restore a single party, they summoned a meeting two days later of all Liberal M.P.s, which most of the Asquithians (but not Maclean) attended. The Coalition Liberals were most conciliatory. They protested their fidelity to Liberalism and their independence of the Conservatives, and they proposed that a committee of eight Liberals, four from each section, be set up " to promote the unity of the Liberal Party in Parliament." But the Independent Liberals, having made the break, would not be lured back. Only with reluctance did they appoint members to the proposed committee, and at no stage tried to make it a success. Its first task was to decide what constituted membership of " the Liberal Party in Parliament ", and here the Asquithians proved intractable. The Coalition Liberals suggested : " That the Liberal Party in the House of Commons includes all members who were selected as candidates by their local Liberal Associations." This had been Asquith's definition at the time of the election, but it suited his supporters no longer. As Sir Archibald Williamson for the Coalition Liberals indignantly reported : " The four representatives of the Minority Liberals had declined to accept the definition therein set out of a ' Liberal member,' or to come to an understanding on any other form of words as to who were Liberals in Parliament."[2]

For their intransigence, the Independent Liberals felt they had good reason. To them, the essential position of the Liberals was as a party separate from and in opposition to the Conservatives ; and they preferred that two Liberal parties should exist in Parliament than that their party should be swamped by members who on this issue had sold the pass. As their delegates explained in recounting the committee's breakdown :

> The circumstances in which many Coalition Liberals were elected and the pledges at present binding them to co-operate with Conservative leaders have created a situation

[1] Acland to his wife, 4 February 1919, Acland Papers.
[2] *Daily Chronicle*, 12 March 1919.

in which the first resolution proposed by Coalition Liberals cannot be accepted, as it gives to Coalition Liberals returned by Conservative votes, and pledged to support a non-Liberal Government, the right to define Liberal policy.[1]

With the dissolution of the committee, the division in Parliament became final. The Independent Liberals went their own way, becoming under Maclean an effective opposition. Although a smaller group than Labour, they far outshone it in debating strength, and often in appreciation of current problems ; and it was not long before Maclean was being referred to as "Leader of the Opposition".

The Coalition Liberals also set themselves up as a separate party, choosing Lambert (who lost the Asquithian whip in consequence) as their chairman. This appointment was significant. Lambert possessed sound Liberal credentials and was an outspoken critic of the coupon. By choosing him, they were signifying that, where Maclean was upholding liberalism from outside the government, they would uphold it from within. So during the ensuing months they met periodically to pass resolutions supporting the liberal position on various matters ; they sent deputations to ministers protesting against threatened deviations from free trade ; some of them made speeches criticising excessive government expenditure, especially on military purposes like the " mad enterprise in Russia "[2]; and occasionally numbers of them failed to support the government in the division lobby. This happened in June 1919, over the extension into peacetime of the wartime McKenna duties. On an Independent Liberal amendment, 35 Coalition Liberals supported the government, seventeen voted against it, and some 60, although present in the House, did not vote. Their abstention occasioned much comment, particularly as Churchill, Hewart, Montagu, and C.A. McCurdy were among them. This showed that, in defending liberal principles, the Coalition Liberals possessed allies in the government. In May 1919 Fisher told one of his colleagues : " we Liberal members ought to make a stand on Free Trade "; and in the following November he, Montagu, McCurdy, and Tudor Walters were pressing on

[1] *Liberal Magazine*, April 1919.
[2] John Wallace, M.P., offering " Some Reflections of a Coalition Liberal "; *Manchester Guardian*, 13 November 1919.

Lloyd George the " Liberal objections " to the Anti-Dumping bill.[1]

Yet despite these activities, the Coalition Liberals were never a very effective force. They were overshadowed by the vast body of Conservatives who also sat on the government benches. They were uneasy about their leader's intentions. And in taking their stand on " liberal principles ", they were frequently driven back on earlier definitions which hardly applied to present problems. For example, pre-war Liberal views on Ireland scarcely applied to the existing situation, with the result that the Coalition Liberals could find nothing to say about the government's shameful proceedings there. Nevertheless, on at least some issues they were able to lay down limits beyond which Lloyd George might not trespass ; as he found out early in 1920, when he tried to terminate their formal association with the Liberal party.

II

The establishment of separate groups in Parliament had not completely divided the Liberal party. In the country it remained theoretically one : followers of Lloyd George who secured the nomination of Liberal associations were still recognised as Liberal candidates, and Liberal M.P.s from both sections were invited to party functions (e.g. meetings of the National Liberal Federation). But the final rupture was not long in coming. What brought it about was Lloyd George's abortive attempt to unite with the Conservatives.

Liberals were slow to believe, even after 1918, that Lloyd George intended to separate from them for good. But during 1919, to their mounting indignation, his intentions became increasingly evident. He kept up the attack on Liberals in by-elections, employing the coupon against them in constituencies which had gone to Conservatives in 1918. Then at the end of 1919 he adopted a new form of attack. When the Coalition Liberal M.P. for Spen Valley died, and the Liberal association adopted Simon, a staunch Asquithian, to replace him, Lloyd George brought forward a Liberal candidate of his own. As a result Labour captured the seat on a minority vote.

[1] Fisher's diary, 29 May and 26 November 1919, Fisher Papers.

Haldane

Platform oratory. Top: Lloyd George addressing a meeting at the Free Trade Hall, Manchester. Below: Asquith speaking at the Liberal Club in Paisley, January, 1920

Such conduct could have only one objective : a final severance from the Liberal party and the " fusion " of Coalition Liberals with Conservatives. Churchill gave warning of what was afoot when on 16 July 1919 he publicly advocated the formation of a Centre party, arguing that " no deep division of principle " now separated the two wings of the coalition. He was recognised as speaking for Lloyd George as well as himself, for he had spent the previous week-end with the Prime Minister, and in his speech he made the first public reference to Lloyd George's Centre party scheme of 1910, which he would scarcely have done without the Premier's consent. Shortly after, Lloyd George began sounding his Liberal colleagues on the subject of "forming a new progressive party " (" Liberalism ", he warned them, " has no future ").[1] And in the months between December 1919 and March 1920 he set about launching his new party.

His first move was a speech at Manchester on 6 December 1919. It contained no direct reference to the Centre party, but it consisted largely of a fierce attack on Labour and condemnation of " socialism "; and this anti-Labour, anti-socialist platform had been chosen by him, if only for want of a better, as his public justification for " fusing " Conservatives and Coalition Liberals. Even now he tried to keep up some sort of a Liberal front. The speech was delivered in that haven of north-of-England Liberalism, the Manchester Reform Club, and was freely garnished with " liberal " phraseology, as when he referred to the progressive measures his government had accomplished and the " immense terrain " where reform was still needed. He even spoke approvingly of the resolutions recently adopted by the National Liberal Federation, all of which (" to the best of my recollection ") the coalition government would be prepared to accept, and complained that he had not been invited to the N.L.F. conference because he would have supported the radical amendments put forward by the Manchester Liberals.

As an attempt to execute a departure to the right while disguised as a left-wing Liberal, this speech proved much less successful than the performance of 12 November 1918. He had in fact been invited to the N.L.F. conference, and the resolutions over which he enthused embodied some of the features of

[1] Fisher's diary, 23 September 1919, Fisher Papers.

" socialism " he was now denouncing.[1] Further, this sort of performance suffered acutely from the law of diminishing returns. The immediate response of Liberals outside the coalition—" He is going to leave us "—showed that this time his radical pose had deceived no one.

Lloyd George's next step was to get the consent of the two wings of the coalition to fusion. The Conservatives looked easy, for their leaders had signified their agreement, and the rank and file had given no warning of hostility. But the Coalition Liberals were plainly more difficult. They, as we have seen, had sought in the early part of 1919 to preserve their links with the Asquithian Liberals, and at one stage had offered a qualified repudiation of the coupon. Even after the Independent Liberals had finally rebuffed them, they proved determined to uphold a liberal position. They responded to Churchill's " Centre party " speech in July 1919 by passing a number of impeccably liberal resolutions on matters like free trade and Ireland, showing (said some observers) that they were " Liberals still " and were " zealously keeping up their independent political existence "[2] —independent, that is, of the Conservatives. And it was clear that many of them deplored Lloyd George's action in running an unauthorised Liberal candidate in Spen Valley.

Evidently Lloyd George would have no easy job in persuading these Liberals to " fuse " with a much larger body of Conservatives. He spent a good deal of January and February 1920 urging the scheme on Liberal members of the government, inviting several of them to his home at Cobham over the week-end of 4 and 5 February and putting the case for fusion in " his most racy and amusing style." [3] Apparently satisfied with their response, he turned to the Coalition Liberal rank and file. At a party meeting later in February their chairman suggested, obviously at Lloyd George's instigation, that they should invite the Premier to their meeting on 18 March to tell them just where they stood with regard to the Liberal party. Lloyd George laid his plans carefully for this gathering. So as to assure

[1] During the next few days Conservatives had to be assured that Lloyd George's " recollection " was at fault. He did not support the resolution favouring an inquiry into the practicability of a capital levy, let alone the Manchester amendment for a levy, without inquiry, on all personal capital over £2,000.

[2] *Manchester Guardian*, 2 and 7 August 1919.

[3] Fisher's diary, 4 and 5 February 1920, Fisher Papers.

himself of a solid body of supporters, he arranged to meet the Liberals in the government (some twenty-five in all) two days earlier and secure their formal assent to fusion, and then to take them along with him on the 18th. In this way he might well over-awe potential opponents among the rank and file.

But the scheme misfired at the first stage. When he met his colleagues on the 16th he encountered so much opposition to the proposal, especially from junior members of the government whom he may not have consulted earlier, that it became plain he would not win their unanimous consent. This greatly increased the chances of failure two days later. Rather than risk it, he told his colleagues that he would not even mention the Centre party when addressing the rank and file. Consequently the much-heralded meeting on 18 March was a distinct anti-climax (especially as *The Times* had published a full account of the Premier's change of plans the day before).[1] Lloyd George repeated his attack on Labour and called for unity in opposing it, but on the crucial question of organisation he put forward no concrete proposals and spoke only of " closer co-operation in the constituencies " between Conservatives and Coalition Liberals. This was to transfer the initiative in forming a Centre party to the rank and file—as he told them, " I want your counsel and your advice "—when it was already plain that they were reluctant to follow, let alone lead, in the matter. Consequently, the whole scheme expired. For Lloyd George, this surrender was to have far-reaching consequences. At this moment he was letting slip the only opportunity which was to present itself of crossing permanently to the Conservatives, seemingly one of his prime objectives since the early months of the war.

Even at the time, it was thought surprising that the Coalition Liberals should have thwarted Lloyd George. As Bonar Law observed, they had appeared the main beneficiaries of the proposed merger. This was certainly Lloyd George's view. Talking to his colleagues at the fateful gathering on 16 March, he argued that Liberals could no longer hope to play a part in governing the country except in association with another party—in effect

---

[1] How *The Times* got hold of a narrative of the supposedly private meeting on the 16th, including Lloyd George's outline of what he would say on the 18th, remains a mystery.

a repetition of his earlier claim that " Liberalism has no future."
There was now, he said, no chance of the Liberals securing a
majority of seats. They had won a great victory in 1906, and
yet, he argued, the swing of votes to them had been only $2\frac{1}{2}\%$.
Now they had lost 10% of their supporters to Labour. Where
then were they to look for allies ? There could be no alliance
with Labour, for Liberals had nothing in common with commun-
ism and were pledged against nationalisation. On the other
hand, no differences of principle separated them from the
Conservatives. Therefore they should strengthen their union
with the Conservatives and prevent Labour from winning a
majority of seats through vote-splitting amongst its opponents.

The great drawback to this argument was its unblushing
opportunism. Whatever its merits as a plan for rescuing
Liberals politically, it clearly meant abandoning any distinctive
liberal position. Lloyd George's attempt to demonstrate an
unbridgeable gulf between Liberalism and Labour, and an
identity of outlook between Liberals and Conservatives, was
altogether too glib, especially coming from him. The election
campaign had shown how differences might arise between the
Liberal and Conservative positions, as well as revealing his own
capacity for switching from one to the other—in which respect
he was unlucky to be advocating fusion so soon after the appearance of J. M. Keynes's scathing account of his conduct during
the election.[1] Moreover, Lloyd George and Churchill simply
did not carry conviction when they spoke of the incompatibility
between liberalism and socialism. Not everyone had forgotten
that Churchill a year before had enthused over railway nationalisation, and had proclaimed himself not " quite " but " very
nearly " convinced that " Socialism is possible "—" the achievements of the Ministry of Munitions constitute the greatest
argument for State Socialism that has ever been produced."[2]
As for Lloyd George, it was remembered that as recently as
1919 he had favoured nationalising the coal industry, and had
put forward a programme of reconstruction containing many

[1] *The Economic Consequences of the Peace* enjoyed an extraordinary vogue
from the moment of its publication in December 1919. Its account of the 1918
election, although not without criticisms of Asquith, was reprinted as a Liberal
pamphlet by Asquith's headquarters.

[2] *Liberal Magazine*, February 1919.

" socialist " features, including sweeping proposals for state control of transportation and electricity. (These proposals he had abandoned, not because they were incompatible with liberalism, but because the Tories in the House of Commons had rebelled against them). In short, his proposed Centre party was too conservative in policy and personnel to be presented in any sort of liberal garb.

The anti-liberalism of the scheme was fastened on by critics in and out of the coalition. The *Manchester Guardian* called the socialist menace " a political bogy by which we decline to be terrified "; Lloyd George had only shown " how essential it is to maintain in being a wholly unpledged body of Liberal opinion which will find in the aspirations and efforts of Labour far more to support than to oppose." Asquith too argued that, while he stood by his criticisms of extreme socialist doctrinaires, there was no " logical antithesis between Liberalism and Labour." And Violet Bonham Carter pointed out that the supposed Bolsheviks against whom Lloyd George was warning them were men like Henderson and Clynes who had served in his own government : " When I think of Mr. Clynes and Mr. Henderson, my flesh positively refuses to creep."[1] Similar criticisms came from the coalition side. Lambert, while not doubting the Premier's sincerity, said that socialism was not an imminent danger, and that he could never see Liberalism and Conservatism fusing. And F. W. Mallalieu, the Coalition Liberal member for Colne Valley, stated that he would not agree to an attempt to divide the country into two conflicting groups, Labour and anti-Labour.

Among members of the government, the crux of the opposition to fusion was this abandonment of a liberal position. Some of them on 16 March objected to joining a party without "Liberal" in the title. (Earlier, Lloyd George had dismissed " Liberal labels " as " lead[ing] nowhere ; we must be prepared to burn them "[2]). Fisher in February had attacked fusion because it would " break liberalism " which he said was waiting for Lloyd George.[3] Montagu too favoured Liberal reunion, urging even at this late hour that, should Asquith be returned to Parliament, he ought to be invited to join the government. It needs to be

---

[1] *Manchester Guardian*, 8 December 1919, 25 March and 1 April 1920.
[2] Fisher's diary, 4 February 1920, Fisher Papers.   [3] *ibid.*

recognised that throughout the life of the coalition some of these ministers struggled to preserve a liberal position, resisting concessions to the Conservatives on tariffs, seeking a peaceful settlement in Ireland, and firmly withstanding Tory attempts to rejuvenate the House of Lords. Fisher drafted a letter of resignation in 1922 when Conservative pressure and the "Geddes axe" threatened his education estimates ; and Montagu earned the hatred of back-bench Tories by his sympathy for Indian nationalist aspirations. Now these activities did not convert the Coalition Liberals into an effective Liberal body inside the government, but they did make plain the attitude which killed fusion in March 1920. Unlike their leader, the Coalition Liberals could not bring themselves to turn their backs completely on their Liberal past and submerge themselves in the Conservative ranks. Had they considered only their political welfare, as Lloyd George was urging them to do, they would have gone along with him. But the security he offered them was in conflict with the view they took of themselves, to employ words quoted earlier, as being " Liberals still."

III

Yet the attempt at fusion was not without consequences. At last Lloyd George had gone too far even for Asquithian endurance. Far from repenting his betrayal of the Liberal party in 1918, he had found fresh ways to outrage it, culminating in his attack on the Liberal candidate in Spen Valley (and the loss of the seat to Labour, an odd introduction to a supposedly anti-Labour campaign) and his attempted union with the Conservatives. " It is not too much to say ", wrote an Asquithian Liberal of these events, " that there swept through the Liberal Associations of Great Britain a wave of hatred for the men who had forsaken the cause. And, curiously enough, it settled more fiercely upon the Prime Minister's followers than upon the Prime Minister himself." For, this writer explained, Lloyd George was felt to be gambling for high, selfish stakes and to be taking all the risks of political outlawry. " But it was believed that the men who followed him were for the most part his tools."[1]

In March 1920 the official Liberal party declared war at

[1] Harold Storey, *The Case Against the Lloyd George Coalition*, pp. 87–8.

every level on the Coalition Liberals. It was prepared no longer, Asquith announced, to endorse candidates who supported the coalition—" camp followers of the Tory army " who had succumbed to " the allurements of demagogy ".[1] Maclean reinforced this. He stated that, where a Liberal association did adopt a coalitionist, party headquarters would encourage its supporters in the constituency to put up a rival candidate. This was a major departure. For the moment, the paramountcy of Liberal associations in matters of candidates was at an end. Their chosen candidates were subjected to a standard of orthodoxy, and where they failed to come up to it both candidates and associations might be repudiated. There was overwhelming support in the party for this departure. Up and down the country, Liberal organisations passed resolutions attacking the coalition and condemning " closer co-operation " between Liberals and Conservatives. In Scotland and the Midlands, the regional federations unseated presidents who sympathised with Lloyd George. And at the general meeting of the National Liberal Federation at Leamington in May 1920, delegates proved determined to expel the " unclean spirit "[2] of coalitionism from their midst.

The N.L.F. general meeting was among the most "popular" and representative of Liberal functions, and the events at Leamington set the seal on the party's rejection of the Coalition Liberals. Strangely enough, a body of Coalition Liberal M.P.s, including several members of the government, decided to put in an appearance at Leamington, apparently convinced that by resisting fusion they had reaffirmed their standing as Liberals. In this they seriously miscalculated. When they tried to argue their case from the platform there was mounting interruption. T. J. Macnamara, having participated against Simon in the Spen Valley by-election, was a particular victim of rowdiness, and his remarks were delivered against a swelling chant of " Spen Valley, Spen Valley, Spen Valley." The climax came when one of the lesser lights of the government, Kellaway, began by observing that Asquith had been unfaithful to Liberalism in Boer War days. Pandemonium broke out. After ten minutes of uproar, the chairman added a further insult by ruling that Kellaway's speaking time had expired. From the body of the

[1] *Manchester Guardian*, 25 March 1920.　　[2] *Nation*, 15 May 1920.

hall Hewart, the Attorney-General, rose to denounce these proceedings, and stated that as a protest the Coalition Liberals would withdraw. The mass of delegates, not a whit repentant, roared their approval, and sped the retreating coalitionists on their way with cheers and shouts of derision.

With these events the division in the party was complete. By his announcement in March 1920 that headquarters would oppose coalition candidates nominated by Liberal associations, Asquith at last made his " long-awaited declaration of war upon Coalition Liberalism."[1] The response of Liberals in the country, and especially at Leamington, constituted the party's emphatic endorsement of his action.

IV

Bereft of his Centre party and rejected by the Liberals, Lloyd George was now practically without a party to belong to. He chose therefore to establish a Liberal organisation of his own. As mentioned earlier, his organisation hitherto had consisted only of a headquarters in London and such established Liberal bodies in the constituencies as had chosen to follow him. The number of the latter had fallen steadily since 1918. Several Coalition Liberal M.P.s, including Churchill and Macnamara, had been repudiated by their constituency associations, and by late in 1920 all the regional federations except Wales were in Asquith's camp. " Why ", inquired Guest on one occasion, " is it [that] the Liberals of the Coalition cannot get on the executive of the local associations ? "[2]

From mid-1920, Lloyd George's political functionaries set about establishing a new Liberal organisation. What it amounted to was that Coalition Liberal Councils, each covering one or more counties, were set up on the lines of the Liberal party's regional federations. There was no lack of money for this undertaking : the Scottish Liberal Federation was soon complaining that " attempts have been made to detach from the Federation certain officials by offers of better financial terms. One of these attempts was successful." [3] Less easy to come by

[1] *Manchester Guardian*, 25 March 1920.
[2] Quoted by Asquith, *Liberal Magazine*, April 1921.
[3] *Liberal Magazine*, February 1921.

was the interest and enthusiasm on which to base an organisation : little effort was made to establish bodies in individual constituencies, and in 1920 even the formation of a council for Lancashire and Cheshire was suspended for want of support. But by the end of 1921 the whole of the country was covered by these councils, and a monthly periodical, the *Lloyd George Liberal Magazine*, was being produced.

In January 1922 this national organisation was officially launched at a conference in London, and the new title " National Liberal party " was adopted. (It was not, in the light of continental and British history before and since, a very auspicious choice.)[1] The conference did not arouse great interest, and apparently the organisers did not expect it to. C. A. McCurdy, who had succeeded Guest as chief Coalition Liberal whip, was most reserved in the claims he made for the new party. Theirs, he told the conference, was a party unlike any other in at least one respect : it was distinguished by qualities of " humility and modesty." They alone did not claim that they were preparing to sweep the country, and did not boast candidates " by the hundred, if not the thousand ". Indeed they had no wish " to flood the country with candidates and to obtain a position of superiority to all other parties combined." They were content to " play a part " in helping to solve the great problems before the country. As for their national organisation, it had been called into existence " for purposes of defence rather than defiance."[2]

This was hardly a striking beginning for Lloyd George's organisation. For what it was worth, a Coalition Liberal party now existed outside Parliament, and among other things— although this was not apparent from McCurdy's statements— possessed a large reserve of candidates. But the prime question was whether they would ever be used, and if so, against whom.

[1] It has not been thought advisable to substitute " National Liberal " for " Coalition Liberal " after this date. " Coalition Liberal " was still widely employed, even after the coalition itself had fallen. And " National Liberal " is confusing, first because there existed at that time bodies like the National Liberal Federation and National Liberal Club which were Asquithian in sentiment, and secondly because since the early 1930s there has been another " National Liberal party " of rather different composition from Lloyd George's.

[2] *Manchester Guardian*, 20 January 1922.

V

Even in these unpropitious circumstances, some Liberals strove to reunite the party. One of them was Hogge, formerly among Lloyd George's severest critics. Hogge had for long been antipathetic to Asquith, and his feelings against his leader became so intense (Burns referred on one occasion to " J. M. Hogges cruel and vulgar reference to H. H. A."[1]) that he now began looking to Lloyd George as Asquith's only possible replacement.[2] Other Liberals too, anxious for their party's revival or hoping, like Scott, to redeem the erring Lloyd George, tried to encourage Liberal reunion. In the country the Manchester Liberals were active in the matter. And in Parliament some Independent Liberals attempted in June 1921 to restore harmony by instituting a series of luncheons attended by M.P.s from both sections.

Nothing came of these efforts. Among Independent Liberals generally, hostility to Lloyd George and his " camp followers " increased during these years. They regarded his post-war government, with its wild alternations of policy and squalid episodes like the Black and Tan period in Ireland, as proof of his unfitness ever again to belong in their company. He had shown himself, they felt, not merely a bad Liberal but a bad Conservative—even a government of reactionaries, Asquith said in May 1922, would be preferable to Lloyd George's regime. One example of this mounting antagonism is provided by Grey. During the war he had been a good deal more sympathetic to Lloyd George than some of his colleagues. But the ministry's conduct after 1918 moved him to " indignation and despair such as I have never felt about any other British Government ".[3] Typical of his later view is this passage from a letter of August 1920 :

We have indeed lost the peace. And the cause of it is Ll.G. who has some great qualities without being a great man & who is constitutionally incapable of understanding that

[1] John Burns's diary, 6 February 1919, Burns Papers.

[2] So ended the partnership of Pringle and Hogge. Pringle's relations with Asquith grew cordial, and his antipathy to Lloyd George became unrelenting.

[3] Lord Grey of Fallodon, *Twenty-Five Years*, vol. 2, p. 249.

straightforwardness is essential and " cleverness " fatal to success in the long run, whether it be in politics, in business or friendship or any human relations.[1]

Some Liberal attacks on the Premier were remarkably outspoken in these years. Simon said of him that " he incurs Liberal criticism because he sometimes acts like an unprincipled and like an undependable person." And he went on :

Cleverness, ingenuity, adroitness ! There has been nothing like it in human history. But, after all, character is more than cleverness. Sticking to a principle is more than adroitly shifting from one position to another. And, in the view of Liberals, Mr. Lloyd George has shown himself a faithless trustee of their traditions and beliefs.[2]

Pringle's references to the Premier were no more flattering : he said of the Cannes resolutions, which embodied Lloyd George's last attempt to settle the affairs of Europe, that they " did not carry any more conviction with Liberals than would the Sermon on the Mount if it were put into a company prospectus by Mr. Bottomley."[3] Mr. Bottomley had recently been sentenced to seven years' penal servitude for his financial swindles.

But the principal stumbling block to a Liberal rapprochement was not Asquithian enmity towards Lloyd George. It was the attitude of the Coalition Liberals themselves. For all their efforts to preserve a Liberal identity, and to escape absorption in a re-named Conservative party, their attachment to Liberalism was restricted. Independent Liberals, whether hostile to Lloyd George or anxious to win him back, were agreed that to achieve reunion the Coalition Liberals must end their alliance with the Conservatives. This condition the Coalition Liberals would not meet. Their attitude brought to nothing the lunch meetings of June 1921 (which the Independent Liberals hastily abandoned after a speech by Lloyd George reasserting his anti-Labour position), and wrecked a bid for Liberal reunion by the Manchester Liberals in January 1922.

The conduct of the Coalition Liberals appears inconsistent. Why, after rejecting the Premier's scheme to fuse with the Conservatives, should they decline to part with them ? It was

[1] Grey to Spender, 6 August 1920, Spender Papers.
[2] *Liberal Magazine*, August 1921.
[3] Speech at the N.L.F. annual meeting, 18 May 1922.

true, of course, that they remained followers of Lloyd George, who was as determined as ever to preserve the coalition. But this was not the whole explanation. Even the principal opponents of fusion, like Fisher and Montagu, appeared almost as reluctant as their leader to break off relations with the Conservatives. Fisher, during the Centre party discussions in March 1920, had conjectured that normal party relations might be resumed in " three or five years ", which was clearly not this year or next year, and was not even certainly sometime. And Montagu, in the election which followed the dissolution of the coalition in 1922, was still trying to preserve an alliance with the Conservatives in his constituency. Yet already by March 1920 there seemed no further need for a coalition, if it was only a temporary expedient for peacemaking and reconstruction. The peace had been made and internal reconstruction, where it had not been abandoned, all but completed, as Lloyd George practically admitted to Fisher at the time.[1] Why then, if they did not want a permanent union with the Conservatives, prolong the coalition further ?

Yet the answer is not far to seek. It lies in the circumstances of the Liberal party at this time, and in the outcome of its attempted recovery from the blows which had befallen it since 1914.

[1] Lloyd George told Fisher in January 1920 that once the measures still in hand had been carried there would " have to be a period of administration ", i.e. of legislative tranquillity. Fisher's diary, 28 January 1920, Fisher Papers.

10. A SEASON OF DEPRESSION

There is nothing to be got by being a Liberal to-day. It is not a profitable or a remunerative career.

Asquith addressing the N.L.F., 26 November 1920

In strict confidence our stroke oar neither sets the time nor rows his weight. And the worst of it is he does not know it.

Gladstone (draft letter) to Lord Robert Cecil, 22 April 1922 [1]

THE Independent Liberals started well enough following the débâcle of December 1918. Not only did they make a considerable impression in Parliament, but between January and April 1919 they captured three seats from the Conservatives in by-elections, including Central Hull where the radical J. M. Kenworthy converted a Conservative majority of 10,371 into a Liberal majority of 917. These successes, said a correspondent of the *Manchester Guardian*, " ensure the revival of the Liberal party as one of the chief political forces. The extinction of the Liberal party in the House of Commons no longer matters."[2]

His confidence proved premature. The Liberals owed two of their by-election successes to the absence of Labour candidates, and hoped that this presaged a revival of Liberal-Labour co-operation. They were soon disillusioned. From the middle of 1919, Labour showed itself determined to wage war on the Liberals, whatever the cost in Conservative victories. This determination was often strongest amongst recent converts to the Labour party. Better a Tory government than a Liberal-Labour government, Ponsonby declared, for if Liberals were present in a Labour administration they would destroy all prospect of the social reconstruction and international reconciliation in which Labour believed.

The difficulties facing the Liberal party in this situation were

[1] Herbert Gladstone Papers.   [2] *Manchester Guardian*, 1 May 1919.

painfully exposed in the Rusholme by-election of September and October 1919. A few weeks before, the Liberals in another Lancashire division, Widnes, had sought to encourage Liberal-Labour co-operation by withholding their candidate and supporting Arthur Henderson, who captured the seat from the Conservatives by 987 votes. The Rusholme Liberals expected Labour to reciprocate, and it was known that some Labour leaders, including Henderson, sympathised with them. But Labour supporters in the district took a different view. The president of the Manchester and Salford Labour party called the Liberals' pleas " the wail of a despairing party ", and said that, as Liberals were equally a capitalist party with the Conservatives, Labour adherents would be false to their principles if they did not contest the seat.[1] In face of this determination, Labour headquarters agreed to the adoption of a Labour candidate (himself a former Liberal who had changed parties in 1917).

In the outcome this by-election, which took place in the shadow of the great railway strike of 1919, proved fatal to the Liberals' prospects of recovery. Even with Pringle as their candidate, their vote barely advanced beyond that of the disastrous general election. The Conservatives retained the seat with a decreased majority, and Labour more than doubled its vote to oust the Liberals from second place.[2] To Labour supporters, this appeared highly satisfactory. They failed to conclude that on this basis the Conservatives might go on winning seats—and elections—for a considerable time. Rather, they took it for granted that Liberalism would soon disappear altogether, and that thereafter the entire Liberal vote would come to them.

From this setback in September 1919 to the fall of the coalition three years later, the Liberals fared disastrously in by-elections. They captured only two more seats from the Conservatives, and lost the industrial constituency of Penistone to Labour, making a net gain of four seats between 1918 and 1922. Particularly

[1] *ibid*, 8 September 1919.
[2] The figures were :

	General Election		By-Election	
Cons.	12,477	Cons.	9,394
Lib.	3,699	Lab.	6,412
Lab.	2,985	Lib.	3,923

discouraging was their showing in triangular contests, i.e. contests with both Conservatives (or Coalition Liberals possessing Conservative support) and Labour. Altogether, they fought twenty-four by-elections of this type, and came third in fifteen. So poor was their performance in by-elections that they let an increasing number go by default. Whereas they fought over half in 1919 and 1920, during the next two years they ran candidates in less than a third. And their electoral position in general was summed up, after a survey of the whole country, by Herbert Gladstone in mid-1922 with the words : " Apart from Scotland . . . we are now making no progress."[1]

In these circumstances the Independent Liberals were easy victims for the jibes of their opponents. Lloyd George said in 1921 that they had railed against 1918 as a snap election, yet were any of them demanding a general election now ? Austen Chamberlain called them " that persevering but most unfortunate party ". And McCurdy remarked that their political strength was in inverse proportion to the amount of noise they made.[2] In their own ranks, a certain gloom settled over the party. Asquith admitted in 1920 that the party had " been during these last two years in the trough of the wave ".[3] " Just the moment when Liberals seem most depressed", said Simon, " was the moment when the revival of Liberalism was most needed."[4] " Lloyd George For Ever and Ever ? " glumly inquired the *Nation* on 14 May 1921, and concluded that in view of Labour's attitude of non co-operation there was no foreseeable end to his period of office. Even the combative Pringle gave an occasional hint of despondency : " the Independent or true Liberals", he said in August 1921, " had been passing through a season of depression ".[5]

II

This succession of by-election failures made it clear that the injuries suffered by the Liberal party since 1914 admitted of no easy recovery. Moreover, as some Liberals complained

---

[1] Sir Charles Mallet, *Herbert Gladstone A Memoir*, p. 281.
[2] *Manchester Guardian*, 22 June, 15 July, and 26 November 1921.
[3] *Liberal Magazine*, December 1920.
[4] *Manchester Guardian*, 18 July 1921.   [5] *ibid*, 22 August 1921.

repeatedly, their prospects of revival were seriously hampered by lack of effective leadership and uncertainty on issues of policy. At times these shortcomings seemed to deprive them even of a certain role in political affairs.

Most prominent among the questions agitating Liberals was the problem of leadership. The party remained under the direction of the " old gang ", which meant in effect of Asquith himself. Yet his deficiencies as leader, which had been evident enough during the war, became still more pronounced after it. His finer qualities caused the *New Statesman* to describe him in June 1919 as " pre-eminently a man who honours the best traditions of British politics ", and to say that one of his speeches " came as a sudden and vivid reminder of days not, after all, so long past, when personal loyalty and public decency had still a very important place in English political life." (The contrast with his successor, if implied, was pointed enough). Yet offsetting these qualities was an increasing remoteness from the rough-and-tumble of politics hard to reconcile with his determination to remain Liberal leader. A newspaper cutting of February 1928, preserved in the Asquith Papers, described him in the years since 1918 as but a shadow of the earlier, younger man. " The voice, the manner, the trenchant periods were there, humour was more in evidence, but the fire, the vitality, the air of the fighting commander had gone." His decline, this journal concluded, " was the culminating misfortune of the Liberal Party at a time when its salvation depended on a resolute, vigorous and inspiring leader."[1]

Some fascinating personal glimpses of Asquith at this time are provided by the letters of Harold Laski. After nine years in the United States, Laski had returned to England shortly after Asquith, in the dramatic Paisley by-election of February 1920, was re-elected to Parliament. To begin with, Laski regarded him as a spent force. Hearing him debate in Parliament, he called him " clearly *passé*—no warmth, no eagerness, no incisiveness ", " a wreck of former talent." But on meeting him, Laski became conscious of that great personal charm which so endeared Asquith to his small circle of intimates, causing them, it was often felt, to shield him from some of the grimmer realities of politics. After dining with the Asquith family in February

[1] *Truth*, 22 February 1928.

Winston Churchill and F. E. Guest, April 1921

Sir Francis Acland addressing a meeting at the Tiverton by-election
in 1923

1921 Laski wrote : " He gave me not an atom of suspicion of
that indecisiveness of which his enemies speak. He trounced
Lloyd George in forthright fashion, spoke of the terrible character
of the government, all with the easy certainty of a man who
knows his own mind." But further encounters with the Liberal
leader, although confirming his personal regard, revived his
misgivings. During the coal crisis of 1921 Laski contrasted
Haldane's command of the subject with Asquith's lack of
knowledge. " He had not taken the trouble to acquaint himself
with the facts with the result that our talk was not discussion
at all." Two months later he wrote of the Liberal leader :
" His faults are inertia and a tendency to dwell too much on the
virtues of the past and too little on the dreams of the future.
But he is entirely [un-] selfish, amazingly loyal and full of that
deep steadiness of character which is, in the end, worth more
than brains." Laski also came to criticise Asquith's wife—of
whom earlier he had written highly—for treating her husband's
difficulties as solely the result of " intrigue and newspaper
dishonesty."

> She doesn't see that he says nothing to the point in these
> days, and of course, helps one but little in bringing him up
> to fighting scratch. He is as sweet and charming as can be ;
> but he is very self-indulgent and it's the very devil to get
> him to [read] the documents he ought to know without
> guidance . . . . they seem very content to wait in the curious
> belief that weariness of L.G. will drive the country back
> to them. It's absurd doctrine ; but as they move mainly
> among people who never contradict them they too rarely
> meet the other side.

By mid-1922 Laski was just about back where he had started,
and was engaged in an attempt to secure a new leader for the
Liberal party, " Asquith being now generally recognised as
hopeless."[1]

The shortcomings of Asquith in these years are not principally
to be accounted for, although some radicals thought otherwise,
by the fact that he was a " whig ", unwilling to embark on
constructive and unorthodox courses. Certainly he often gave
evidence of whiggish attitudes, especially on economic questions.
But there were still matters on which he could adopt the role

[1] *Holmes—Laski Letters*, vol. 1, pp. 271, 276, 312–3, 333, 341, 343–4, 428.

of a reforming Liberal. He espoused the Fabian doctrine of the " national minimum ", attacked the reparation clauses of the Versailles Treaty in near-Keynesian terms, and criticised Allied intervention in Russia. (Were we, he wanted to know, seeking to restore Tsardom, a form of government even more pernicious than that which had replaced it ?). But he never seemed fully committed, or deeply involved, in these matters, and sometimes it required a close search of his speeches even to discover what his views were. Only when he turned to issues of the past, like free trade or the wartime controversy over shells (both of which engaged much of his attention in 1919), was he roused to fighting-pitch. The *Nation* described his speeches at Leeds in June 1919 as " depressing reading ", with not an iota of constructive statecraft and no word of guidance on the great issues of foreign policy. His attempt to present the peril of tariff protection " as the matter of chief moment at a time when war and revolution are seething in all quarters of the globe " seemed to this journal " simply ludicrous." " How can Liberalism be rallied by the cry ' Back to 1906 ' ? "[1] " The party itself," said the *Manchester Guardian* in an editorial criticising the Liberal leaders, ". . . is sound enough and would respond with enthusiasm to an appeal to its generous instincts, to its sense of justice, to its humanity, courage, initiative. But the appeal comes not ".[2]

Such was the lethargy which characterised Asquith's leadership after 1918 that for some time he could not be persuaded even to make a serious attack on the government, and persisted in what one observer called his " melancholy and altogether unworthy exhibition of Christian meekness."[3] Already his lack of fighting quality in the 1918 election had been much criticised, the *Manchester Guardian* saying that while his conduct " had been animated, of course, by the highest patriotism ", it had not been " fully appreciated or even understood by the Liberal rank and file, and the prolongation of his forbearance after the gage had been definitely thrown down by the Prime Minister had a depressing and even paralysing effect not only on the elector but on the candidate."[4] At the first meeting of the Independent Liberals in Parliament in February 1919, strong

[1] *Nation*, 28 June 1919.   [2] *Manchester Guardian*, 25 June 1919.
[3] *ibid*, 29 November 1919.   [4] *ibid*, 30 December 1918.

criticism was voiced of " leaders who refused to lead ", and something of a revolt occurred, the meeting deciding to appoint Hogge, one of Asquith's strongest critics, as co-equal whip with the leader's own nominee George Thorne.

But in face of these manifestations of discontent, Asquith was slow to adopt a more combative attitude to the government. His first post-election address, to a gathering of Liberal candidates in April 1919, was so tame that it stimulated Wedgwood to leave the party altogether, and caused even Herbert Gladstone to deplore Asquith's failure to rouse the " crowds of buoyant and defeated candidates ". " If Father had been there, my word, what a time we should have had ! "[1] A month later, on the eve of an important address by Asquith at Newcastle, his closest associates were in despair at the prospect of another display of " meekness." Margot Asquith wrote to Spender on 15 May 1919 :

Dear Mr. Spender
All depends on you today ! You are the *only* person my husband wishes to see today before his speech. . . . If his speech at Newcastle is not a punching *fighting* speech he will fail. *However fine*—(this it will be probably) However *wise*, however *perfect* it may be—if he shows no indignation no snap he is done.

This is his 1st speech since [the] Treaty wh. tho unsigned is after all as good as signed. *The war is over* but our war opens Saturday. Ll. George counts with certainty on H. not fighting. . . . Dear Mr. Spender, [Vivian] Phillipps, Runciman, Sir R Hudson all come to me & beg me to tell him this today.[2]

Yet the speech which Asquith delivered at Newcastle could hardly be accounted a declaration of war. At most it was a declaration of the end of peace. In an extraordinary passage he announced : " There is in my judgment no longer any occasion for what is called the Party truce, of which the belated offspring was the present House of Commons, born if anything ever was, out of due season." Nothing in his earlier displays of reticence

[1] Mallet, *Herbert Gladstone A Memoir*, p. 277.
[2] Margot Asquith to Spender, n.d. (dated from internal evidence), Spender Papers. The letter as preserved in the Spender Papers is incomplete.

is more remarkable than this statement. Almost his entire political following had been wiped out at an election six months earlier, yet here he was describing the Parliament produced by this act of warfare as " the belated offspring " of " what is called the Party truce," and saying that he could no longer see " any occasion " for this truce. Not until a speech to the N.L.F. in the following November, during which he was egged on by his audience to " Hit out " and " Rub it in ", did he castigate the government sufficiently to earn the caption "War Declared."[1] And the hopes of more energetic leadership aroused in February 1920 by his triumph at Paisley were soon dispelled. A. C. Murray noted ten months later that Asquith had " entirely failed to come up to expectations ".[2] Rothermere, who considered that he had supported Asquith at Paisley and was wondering why, wrote that " My editors and political writers are astounded at Mr. A's obvious inadequacy for the position he is expected to fill."[3] And Grey said of him : " Asquith cuts no ice. He is using the machine of a great political brain to re-arrange old ideas."[4] It is evident that the parliamentary party became a less effective body as a result of his return ; and the dissatisfaction felt by its members at his performance even became the subject of a *Punch* cartoon. It was called " The Reluctant Thruster ", and it showed a protesting Asquith, in a medieval setting, being used as a battering-ram against the coalition castle. He was complaining : " I confess that at my time of life I should have preferred a more sedentary if less honorific sphere of usefulness."[5] (The parody of his style was just about perfect).

Only once during these years did Asquith give a really effective lead to his party. In the later part of 1920 the situation in Ireland deteriorated to such an extent that British forces (the Black and Tans) began countering the murder policy of Sinn Fein with undisciplined violence against the civilian population. This was bad enough as far as Liberals were concerned, but what in particular moved Asquith to indignation was Lloyd George's condonation of " the hellish policy of reprisals." Replying to

[1] *Manchester Guardian*, 29 November 1919.
[2] A. C. Murray's diary, 23 December 1920, Elibank Papers.
[3] Rothermere to Lord Murray, 1 April (1920), Elibank Papers.
[4] A. C. Murray's diary, 12 May 1920, Elibank Papers.
[5] *Lloyd George by Mr. Punch*, p. 153.

a notorious speech by the Premier at Caernarvon, Asquith, with almost unwonted ferocity, stated on 14 October 1920 :

> On the tone and taste of this latest speech I do not think it worth while to dwell. But all its blandishments and all its vulgarities have not diverted, and cannot divert, attention from the outstanding fact that . . . it is a naked confession of political bankruptcy.

What, he asked, was the feature common to reprisals ? They are in no sense acts of self-defence. They are acts of blind and undiscriminating vengeance. No pains are taken even to attempt to connect the victims with previous attacks on the military or police. Quiet, respectable, law-abiding, non-political farmers and shopkeepers, often with no sympathy whatever with Sinn Fein, have their premises burned over their heads, and are lucky to escape with their lives. In not a few instances these so-called reprisals are deliberately aimed—this is one of their most hideous features—deliberately aimed at the destruction of local industries and the ruin of the countryside. Take, for instance, the widespread attack on the creameries, one of the best and most promising products of the Irish co-operative movement. . . . I see that the Prime Minister goes out of his way to sneer at Sir Horace Plunkett [one of the chief promoters of the co-operative movement]. He says he does not represent anyone, and with exquisite good taste he adds—" He cannot even speak for his creameries." No, he cannot, and why ? Because not a few of them have been turned into smoking ruins by incendiary bands of soldiers and police, for whose proceedings Mr. Lloyd George and his colleagues cannot escape responsibility.

In his outbursts against the Black and Tan outrages, Asquith provided a glimpse of the qualities which had once made him a great Liberal leader. But it was no accident that Ireland alone moved him to this demonstration. For it was one of the great issues from the Liberal past ; and as soon as it disappeared from the scene of controversy he relapsed into his former attitude of remoteness and non-participation, " turning up in the House once in a blue moon " and " leaving all the hard work as Leader of the Opposition to Donald Maclean."[1] Sir

[1] A. C. Murray to Reading, 2 August 1922, Elibank Papers.

213

William Barton, an ex-Coalition Liberal, observed sadly : " I am not keen on joining Asquith, who seems to me in misfortune".[1] At a rather heated meeting of Asquith's followers in June 1921, " the young Independents made it clear that they are dissatisfied with the want of leadership of a rather forlorn, if gallant, band, 30 strong ".[2] A year later Maclean gave Laski a " melancholy " account of the state of the party : " Asquith devoted to bridge and small talk, doing no real work, and leaving the party leaderless. I gathered [Laski wrote] that they all want him to go, and see no means of explaining to him how much he stands in the way."[3]

Yet where were the Liberals to look for another leader ? Of ex-ministers who remained active, like Runciman, Simon, and Masterman, none possessed the stature or experience to lead the party. Others like McKenna, Haldane, and Samuel had either abandoned politics or were moving to other parties. An effort was made to bring Grey back into political affairs, in the hope that he would serve as a replacement for Asquith. But Grey's " whiggish " views on foreign policy, and particularly his support for an alliance between Britain and France, were so unpalatable to many Liberals that they caused considerable dissension. The same Sir William Barton who in 1921 considered Asquith " in misfortune " was to be found a year later attacking Grey for his views on foreign policy and praising Asquith for having expressed the " true Liberal position ".[4] If he possessed few other merits, Asquith by his remoteness was sometimes the leader who divided Liberals least.

III

The abortive attempt to restore Grey as a prominent Liberal figure pointed to another dilemma of the party : its dissensions over matters of policy. Liberals were largely agreed on issues like free trade or taxation of land values, which attracted little attention at this time. On more pressing questions they were often divided. The radicals in the party made repeated efforts to provide it with a positive, reforming programme, embracing

---

[1] *Manchester Guardian*, 6 April 1921.   [2] *The Times*, 29 June 1921.
[3] *Holmes-Laski Letters*, vol. 1, pp. 449–50.
[4] *Manchester Guardian*, 21 February 1922.

proposals like nationalisation of the railways and coal mines, a levy on capital, minimum wages, and revision of the peace treaties. These activities came principally from two sections : a group of Independent Liberals in Parliament, including Kenworthy, Wedgwood Benn, and Harry Barnes ; and the Manchester Liberal Federation, which included prominent Liberals of the inter-war period like E. D. Simon and Philip Oliver. As Maclean later admitted, Manchester was " the only part of the country where there is any real drive & initiative."[1] It was responsible for the establishment of the Liberal Summer School, which became one of the liveliest events in the party's year, and for the publication in 1920 of *Liberalism and Industry*, which set the pattern for much Liberal " re-thinking ". Its author, the Professor of Modern History at Manchester University, soon gave up his post to devote his career to Liberal affairs ; and a few years later the Summer School sang of him :

> My pamphlets ring the souls of men,
> My lectures grip them sure ;
> My words are as the words of ten,
> Because I'm Ramsay Muir.

The parliamentary radicals and Manchester Liberals scored a limited triumph in 1921 when they persuaded the party, at a special meeting of the N.L.F., to adopt an industrial programme. It included the establishment of a National Industrial Council and a joint council in each industry, state supervision of trusts and combines, nationalisation of some monopolies, and the limitation of profits. But this policy made little impact. A section of the rank and file, particularly strong in Yorkshire, condemned it as camouflaged state socialism. But the main problem was the hostility or apathy of the party leaders. Only Masterman in the upper ranks showed any interest in it. The views of the other leaders on economic questions followed wellworn grooves ; and if the party decided on new courses, they simply took no notice. Their attitude brought the radicals near revolt on several occasions. As early as May 1919 Maclean was subject to a hostile demonstration from some of his supporters in Parliament because he refused to endorse their motion for a capital levy. At the N.L.F. conference later in the year, Harry

[1] Maclean to Gladstone, 16 August 1924, Herbert Gladstone Papers.

Barnes said on the same matter that some of them were tired of marking time and wanted to hear the command to go forward. " It was a rank and file amendment, and was meant to give a lead to their leaders."[1] Kenworthy remarked on the same occasion that the executive's resolution on the League of Nations would have been acceptable to the Primrose League. And E. D. Simon, supporting the Manchester Liberals' proposal for a redistribution of wealth by means of taxation, warned that on this matter " rested the question of whether the progressive wing of the Liberal party was to continue to co-operate with the Liberal party."

The party leaders were impervious to these complaints. Runciman deplored attempts by Liberals to outbid Labour, and advocated rigid adherence to the principles of economic individualism. John Simon, it is true, called on the party to adopt a fighting programme, but it was not like that of his Manchester namesake : the major item in it was " a crusade to reduce wasteful public expenditure."[2] Government retrenchment, he announced (with touching faith in *laissez-faire* doctrine), was the most urgent and fundamental need of the country, for it lay at the root of social progress, industrial prosperity, security of employment, a high standard of living, and domestic peace. Maclean's economic thinking was hardly more lively or unorthodox. He too devoted most of his energies to a crusade for " economy ", and told a meeting in July 1920 :

He was often asked the question " What is your policy ? " Personally he had nothing heroic to offer. He believed we should only get things adjusted nationally by the same lines of simple common-sense and homely wisdom that were applied to any private concern, and he was not going to compete with the Labour party in making promises which he knew could not be fulfilled. We had been through a war and a convulsion, and the only way to get back to national health was by way of economy. We could not settle the world simply by saying we would nationalise everything. But in and through the ideals and principles of Liberalism a great deal could be done.[3]

Far from wanting to " nationalise everything ", not even the

[1] *Manchester Guardian*, 28 November 1919.   [2] *ibid*, 12 July 1920.
[3] *ibid*, 5 July 1920.

nationalisation of the coal industry appealed to these leaders.
Maclean held that it would be " disastrous " to hand over an
industry as vital as the mines to " the strangulating tentacles
of a new government departmental bureaucracy ",[1] and Asquith
stated during his campaign in Paisley : " The coalowners—
a much abused class—have been, after all, the pioneers of a
great industry, and they contain in their ranks some of the
ablest, most far-sighted, most enterprising and most inventive
of the whole of our capitalist class."[2]

These dissensions over some of the most controversial issues
of the day not only hindered the party from putting forward a
consistent programme, but cast a serious doubt on its role in
politics. In a sense this ought to have been clear : the
Independent Liberals were a " left " party antagonistic to the
Conservatives and close in outlook to Labour. As Maclean
told the proprietor of the *Daily News* on one occasion, both
Asquith and himself believed that the next government would
be composed of Liberals and Labour ; the only reason Liberals
contested by-elections against the Labour party, especially
in industrial constituencies, was to convince Labour of the
necessity for co-operating with them.[3] Again, Asquith and his
associates were very chary about accepting overtures from
Conservatives, even if they were progressive in outlook and
shared their disgust with Lloyd George. In 1921 Lord Robert
Cecil, the country's leading advocate of the League of Nations,
proposed that a new combination should be formed under Grey's
leadership, consisting of the Independent Liberals and a group
of Conservatives who shared Cecil's viewpoint—a combination
which would be " above everything, honest and straightforward " and would "provide the alternative Govt. wh. the
country desires ". Asquith and his colleagues shied away from
the scheme. Maclean called it " wholly impracticable. It would
take the life & heart out of the Liberal rank & file, who would
protest that they were being asked to join another Coalition."
Lord Crewe " expressed a similar view." And Asquith " strongly

---

[1] *ibid*, 17 October 1919.   [2] H. H. Asquith, *The Paisley Policy*, p. 74.
[3] Account by Maclean of a conversation with Henry Cadbury, 16 January 1920,
Asquith Papers. The *Daily News* had argued that the Liberals should not
oppose Labour in Ashton-under-Lyne, an industrial constituency, and Maclean
was putting the case for doing so.

insisted that the whole thing would be a complete fiasco if (as D. Maclean had said) it was to start with disheartening and devitalising the Liberal party ".[1] In face of these objections the scheme came to nothing.

Yet for all Asquith's anxiety to combine with Labour and avoid entanglement with even the most like-minded Conservatives, his very orthodox views on economic questions seemed to cast doubt on the supposed affinity between Liberals and Labour and on their separation from the Conservatives. As the Conservatives made doubly clear in 1919 by their revolt against Lloyd George's schemes to nationalise transport, hostility to state interference in the economy was now one of their basic tenets. (It was not even certain that tariff protection constituted an exception). As for retrenchment in government spending, this was an ideal of Conservatives in general and of rabidly right-wing Conservatives in particular. In 1921 the coalition lost two by-elections to reactionary candidates fighting under the label " Anti-Waste ", and the cheering which greeted the second of these results in the Carlton Club was a danger-signal to which Lloyd George quickly responded : in order to appease Tory wrath, he set up the Geddes committee to propose heavy cuts in government expenditure.

Hence although the Liberal leaders claimed to be on the " left " of politics, they found themselves on matters like nationalisation and government spending aligned with the Conservatives against Labour. This point did not escape comment. After one of Maclean's early speeches as chairman of the Independent Liberals, a Conservative M.P. inquired why his own party should be dubbed reactionary when such views were emanating from the opposition benches. Wedgwood Benn said much the same thing when addressing the N.L.F. : arguing for a compulsory minimum wage, he asked whether the Liberal party by its attitude on economic matters was to appear more reactionary than the coalition. And Lloyd George employed Asquith's first speech in Parliament following his return for Paisley to support the case for a Centre party. The Liberal leader's speech, consisting yet again of a plea for government

[1] Account by Asquith of a private meeting of 5 July 1921 (attended by himself, Cecil, Grey, Crewe, Runciman, and Maclean) to consider Cecil's proposal, Asquith Papers.

economy, was enthusiastically received on the Conservative benches, and Lloyd George offered it as evidence for his claim that there were no longer any differences between Conservatives and Liberals.

In sum, the Liberals found themselves uncertainly placed between the forces of right and left, and afflicted by internal struggles over vital issues of policy which invariably ended in deadlock or ineffectual compromise. This situation did nothing to revive the enthusiasm, or the voting strength, of the Liberal party ; rather it stimulated the continuing defection to other parties of former adherents who saw in Labour or the Conservatives a more clear-cut, committed attitude to the problems of the day. It was indicative of these persistent losses that by the time of the 1922 election McKenna, who shared Asquith's views on policy, had as good as gone over to the Conservatives, while Haldane and Arnold, who were close in viewpoint to the Manchester Liberals, had practically transferred to Labour.

IV

The disheartening circumstances of the Independent Liberals were a major influence on the conduct of the Coalition Liberals. In the failure of the Asquithians to revive, the followers of Lloyd George saw good reason for prolonging the life of the coalition. Already their position was insecure. Many Coalition Liberals sat for industrial constituencies where Labour was making a severe challenge. In by-elections between 1918 and 1922, while gaining no seats, they lost ten of the twenty-five they were defending, eight to Labour and two to right-wing Independents ; and all of the fifteen seats they retained were held with Conservative assistance. How many they would have kept without this assistance no one could say. The Coalition Liberals preferred not to put the matter to the test.

Yet their determination, on grounds of survival, to cling to the Conservatives made nonsense of their earlier decision to reject fusion. The whole point about fusion had been that—as far as any act of organisation could do—it assured them of Conservative support in their constituencies. Without it, they possessed no assurance. The result was that, although they retained their Liberal nomenclature, they possessed less independence *vis-à-vis* the Conservatives than if they had sunk their identity in a Centre party. In the present circumstances they dared not become too assertive lest they cause the Conservatives to reject them. This inhibiting situation helps to explain the gradual attenuation of the Coalition Liberals as a political force : in Parliament they almost ceased to function as a party, and though, as we have seen, they established an organisation in the country, it was very tentative and half-hearted. Guest even explained that the purpose of their organisation was, in Conservative areas, to secure votes for Conservatives :

> Supposing [he said in February 1921] it was a near thing in a Conservative constituency, they wanted at least 10 or 20 per cent. of Liberals organised to assist the Conservative when the next Coalition fight came. Twenty per cent. would turn any constituency one way or another, and it was not asking too much to, in a Conservative seat, offer a 20 per cent. Liberal vote organised for the purpose of Coalition and national unity.[1]

This meant, although Guest did not say so, that their organisation would be engaged in securing votes for Conservatives in most parts of the country, for under the bargain of 1918 the Conservatives had prior claim to a large majority of constituencies. It was little wonder that McCurdy boasted to the conference in January 1922 that their party, unlike any other, did not wish " to flood the country with candidates ".[2] Without trespassing on Conservative preserves, he could not even place the candidates he had.

Increasingly, therefore, the problem for the leaders of the Coalition Liberals was to give their alliance with the Conservatives the permanence it lacked. They could hardly revive the ill-fated Centre party scheme after all the rude things that had been said about it. But an alternative course lay open : to hold another election on the lines of 1918. This would do more than simply prolong the coalition. Longevity in itself could make a temporary arrangement permanent ; and it was generally agreed that if the parties to the coalition went to the polls together a second time they would have taken a major step towards formal union.

[1] *Liberal Magazine*, March and April 1921.   [2] see above p. 201.

But the Conservative rank and file had other ideas. From about the middle of 1921 it was becoming apparent that they were growing tired of their Liberal allies. To begin with their impatience took the form of vendettas against particular Liberal ministers, especially those ministers associated with reforming policies : Addison (whom Lloyd George jettisoned at their insistence in June 1921—an ill-reward for loyal service), Fisher, Montagu, and Edward Shortt. Montagu they hated most of all, as a Jew who in July 1920 had presumed to condemn the British perpetrators of the Amritsar massacre. On his own side of the House, Montagu-baiting became a regular sport of reactionaries like Joynson-Hicks and Rupert Gwynne, who applied to him expressions like : " Thick-skinned as a hippopotamus ", " A grave peril to the country ", " Anything to save his own skin ", and " There he sits unmoved and it is impossible to drive home to him that it was time he went." According to an observer of these displays, their " bitterest and most crudely personal taunts " were accompanied by " deep-throated and dramatically sustained outbursts of cheering " from the Conservative benches, and by derisive shouts of " Resign ", " Move him out ", and " Shame to him."[1] When in March 1922 Montagu fell from office almost by accident, the Conservative back-benchers went delirious with joy. Now, some of them were heard to say, it was time to get rid of Fisher and Shortt.[2]

But by March 1922 it was less a question of getting rid of individual ministers than of disposing of the Coalition Liberals as a whole. While Lloyd George and his followers looked helplessly on, the Conservatives made ready to cast aside their too-willing allies.

Basically, the reason for the fall of the coalition in 1922 is not to be found, as has often been stated, in the government's difficulties over matters like the honours scandal, the Irish settlement, the failures at Cannes and Genoa, or the Turkish imbroglio. It must be sought farther back, in the nature of the alliance originally formed between Lloyd George and the Conservatives. For all the personal magnetism which he exercised, right to the end, over most of the prominent Con-

[1] *Manchester Guardian,* 15 February 1922.
[2] Fisher's diary, dating doubtful (actually 9 March 1922), Fisher Papers.

servatives in his government, Lloyd George's relations with the mass of Conservatives were, and always had been, remote. They had rallied to him after 1914 because he promised to be a more vigorous war leader and because he shared their prime political objective : to expel Asquith from office and destroy the Liberal party at a Khaki election. But, with the few exceptions mentioned in the higher ranks, the Conservatives had never viewed him with trust or affection ; and, what was most important, they had never suggested that they meant to remain his allies once he had served his immediate purpose. Lord Eustace Percy has admitted that, three months after the 1918 election, he fought a by-election posing as an ardent supporter of Lloyd George when he possessed almost no respect for him.[1] His attitude distinctly resembles that of many Conservatives returned in 1918 ; for only a few months after being elected as supposed admirers of the Prime Minister, several hundred of them signed the famous telegram to Paris warning him, almost in so many words, that he had better not go back on his election promises.

In short, there had been all along a fundamental impermanence, and even insincerity, about the Conservative party's attachment to Lloyd George. Further, there were good reasons why this should become apparent in 1922. It was not that by then he had become a liability; he had simply ceased to fulfil any essential purpose. The circumstances which had made him a particular asset in 1918 (" the man who won the war ") had passed away. And by-elections were showing that the Conservatives could hold their own without the " 10 or 20 per cent." of Liberal votes which Guest was trying to organise on their behalf—as well as creating doubts as to whether such votes existed. Moreover, by this date the life of the Parliament elected in 1918 could not be prolonged much farther. An election must occur in 1922 or 1923 ; and, as has been said already, if it took place with the coalition intact, it would do much to render the alliance of Conservatives and Coalition Liberals permanent. This in itself was sufficient reason for the Conservatives to turn against the coalition in 1922. In the last resort it was simply the passage of time, and not issues like the honours scandal or the failure at Genoa, which sealed the doom of Lloyd George's premiership.

In the light of these considerations, it does not seem remark-

[1] Lord Eustace Percy, *Some Memories*, p. 74.

able that what caused the Conservative revolt to begin in earnest
was Lloyd George's decision at the beginning of 1922 to hold an
election. His success in negotiating an Irish settlement had
apparently set the stage for a triumphant appeal to the country,
and he began making preparations accordingly. The only
result was to set in motion the events which transformed the
Conservative campaign against Liberal ministers into an assault
on the coalition as a whole. In January 1922 Sir George
Younger, the Conservative party manager, publicly denounced
the holding of an election at that time, and sent all Conservative
associations a statement opposing it. A month later, following
a speech by Austen Chamberlain, now Conservative leader, in
favour of another coalition election, Younger retaliated by
advocating a " bill of divorcement " to end the " matrimonial
alliance " of Conservatives and Coalition Liberals.

Younger's actions shook the coalition to its foundations. From
that point, its demise was only a matter of time. Lloyd George
was " furious " at his conduct, and told his colleagues on
23 February that he was " not going to be bullied by a second-
rate brewer " ;[1] he would rather resign than continue in office
under such conditions. Shortly after, he wrote to Chamberlain
complaining of indiscipline in the Conservative ranks and
offering his resignation. Chamberlain responded loyally. In
public, he and several other leading Conservatives spoke out
in defence of the coalition. One of the most noteworthy speeches
came from Balfour, whom the right-wing *Morning Post* had
hoped would lead the revolt : he could, Balfour said, " see no
end " to the coalition, a " great national party " whose two
wings ought to draw " closer and closer ". In private, Chamberlain used these words as a text for calling Younger to order.
Writing on 8 March 1922, he drew Younger's attention to
Balfour's utterance and said :

This speech, which referred to the Coalition as two wings of
a National Party, was delivered by my request with the full
authority of my Conservative colleagues, and should therefore be taken as representing the definite and official policy
of the Conservative and Unionist Party. I shall be glad
if you will take all the steps which are necessary to secure
the energetic furtherance of this policy throughout all

[1] Fisher's diary, 23 February 1922, Fisher Papers.

branches of our party organisation. I feel confident that I can count upon you to take effective action in this sense. I may add that similar directions are being given by the Prime Minister to the organisations at the disposal of the Liberal wing of the National Party.[1]

Yet nothing could repair the damage which Younger had done. He had brought into the open the swelling revolt in the Conservative ranks against Lloyd George, and it did not matter that thereafter he kept silent. An attempt was made in March to recover some of the lost ground by securing a resolution of support for the coalition from Conservative M.P.s, but the manoeuvre failed dismally. The meeting arranged for this purpose broke up in confusion. The government leaders then fell back on the unhappy device of presenting to Parliament a resolution of confidence in themselves. Their first intention was to word it so strongly that it would bring into the open the extent of Conservative disaffection. But their nerve failed them, and they fell back on " a colourless document "[2] signifying support for the Genoa Conference. This was received with derision in parts of the House, and its passage signified nothing.

Anyway, on the crucial issue Lloyd George had been utterly defeated. He had needed an election to ensure the life of the coalition, and he had been forced to abandon it. (In public he even denied having decided on one). Yet he was loath to recognise the meaning of this crisis. Late in March he discoursed to his Liberal colleagues on the " unity " of the coalition, stressing the " value of Balfour's support ", and he " seem[ed] to indicate an early election and a fresh lease of Coalition power."[3] But could the government accomplish an election without a recurrence of these unhappy events ? For six months it sought to steel itself for a decision, searching all the while for the success in international affairs which might restore its shaken morale. Finally in October 1922 the Chanak crisis threatened it with a new rebellion anyway, and ministers decided to take the plunge. They resolved on an immediate election, and Cham-

[1] This is from a copy of the letter in the papers of Sir Edward Grigg. It is unsigned, but it seems certain that no one but the Conservative leader could have written to Younger in such a way. Chamberlain had become Conservative leader in March 1921, following Bonar Law's (temporary) withdrawal from politics on the grounds of ill-health.

[2] Fisher's diary, 28 March 1922, Fisher Papers.   [3] *ibid.*

berlain summoned a meeting of Conservative M.P.s to the Carlton Club on 19 October in an effort to secure their consent. (Members of the Upper House, most of whom would not have been sympathetic, were forcibly excluded). This desperate manoeuvre failed, as it seemed bound to do in view of events at the beginning of the year. The Carlton Club meeting resolved that at the next election they would not be the allies of the Coalition Liberals. Chamberlain promptly abandoned the Conservative leadership, in which he was replaced by Bonar Law. On the same day Lloyd George sent in his resignation as Prime Minister. So ended—as it was to prove, forever—his remarkable career as a minister of the crown.

In strictly party terms, these events were not of great significance. The Coalition Liberals had surrendered so much of their identity and independence to the Conservatives that Lloyd George's supersession as Premier by Bonar Law constituted little more than a palace revolution. The Coalition Liberals, however, could not be expected to see things in this light. The events of 19 October 1922 confronted them with the prospect they had feared more than any other : the prospect of standing alone in a political world which no longer appeared to hold any place for them.

11. THE LIBERAL RECOVERY?

Breakfast with Ll. G. . . . He plunged at once with " Well, what do you think of the results of the general election [?] " I said I thought it was a disaster for the Libl party worse if possible than that of 1918 because there was less excuse for it. He agreed.

Scott's diary, 6 December 1922 [1]

1922 was an election of few surprises. For months it had been apparent how the parties would behave, what programmes they would offer, and how, broadly, they would fare at the polls. The one element of uncertainty was provided by the Liberals. Would the two Liberal parties come together now that the Coalition section had been rejected by the Conservatives ?

Without waiting for the Independent Liberals, the followers of Lloyd George answered in the negative. Back in February, when Lloyd George had offered to resign following Younger's " bill of divorcement " speech, he had told Chamberlain that he would support a Conservative government. And on the afternoon of the Carlton Club meeting, a gathering of Liberal ministers (" being dependent on Tory votes ", as Fisher had described them three days earlier) decided to act with those Conservatives who had stood by the coalition, and adopt a programme suitable to them. Only Mond argued that they should separate from their " distinguished Tory allies ", whom he considered an " encumbrance ", and take a stand as Liberals desiring reunion. [2]

By his decision to act with Chamberlain, Balfour, and Birkenhead, Lloyd George abandoned all prospect of playing a major role in the election. When he set out to address a meeting at Leeds two days after resigning, he promised to become a central figure in the contest by sheer force of personality. He left London with the rousing declaration : " The burden is off my

[1] C. P. Scott Papers.
[2] Fisher's diary, 23 February, 16 and 19 October 1922, Fisher Papers.

THE LIBERAL RECOVERY?

shoulders, but my sword is in my hands." And his journey
north seemed more akin to the procession of a conquering hero
than the retreat of a political cast-off. At the larger centres along
the line, he was received with remarkable demonstrations of
spontaneous enthusiasm.

But his speech that evening finished him as a force in the
election. " Somewhere between St. Pancras and Leeds ",
maliciously observed a correspondent of *The Times*, " there must
be lying a sword. It may be that upon reflection it has been
restored to its scabbard and forgotten amidst the luggage upon
the special train. At any rate, the three thousand Coalition
Liberals who crowded the palatial Majestic Picture House here
today were disappointed."[1] Lloyd George, admitted a more
friendly observer, " came as near to boring an audience as it is
possible for so interesting a being to do." " What Leeds really
gave us was ' the old actor ' in the least expected role of Fabius,
demonstrably playing for time, delaying decision."[2] He spent
nearly the whole of the speech ranging back over the achievements of the coalition, laying particular stress on the contribution
of loyal Conservatives like Balfour and Chamberlain. He offered
no programme, failed to elucidate his relations with other parties,
and said nothing of the future. One other omission aroused
comment : he did not apply to himself the word " Liberal ".

This omission was scarcely accidental. Lloyd George did not
mean to commit himself, either by damning the Conservatives
or wooing the Liberals. He had pronounced the Liberal party
dead many times in the past six years, and was not anxious to
tie himself to a corpse. Yet what other course was open to him ?
He had closed all avenues to Labour, by recklessly denouncing
it during his attempt at a Centre party. And after suffering
abrupt rejection by the Conservatives, he could not for the
moment make overtures to them. Yet his hopes still lay in
their direction. So he chose to do nothing, trusting that in time
he might revive the alliance on which he had gambled his
political career.

In consequence, he occupied throughout the campaign the
same innocuous position as during his first address. Although
a party leader, he failed to issue a manifesto. This was
appropriate enough, for he was a leader with nothing to say.

[1] *The Times*, 23 October 1922.   [2] *Manchester Guardian*, 23 October 1922.

As he told a meeting on 25 October, he had no " great slogan " to offer, and stood as hitherto for the union of " all men who believe in the existing fabric of society, who believe in the principles on which our prosperity has been built, free private enterprise—of men who are opposed to revolutionary proposals, and who are equally opposed to reactionary proposals." Bonar Law's policy of " tranquillity ", he said, did not differ in any way from his own. His followers should " disregard the origin of this break in the combination " ; " whatever government is in power, we must not offer it any factious opposition." And at Newcastle on 7 November, he explained that it was desirable to elect Coalition Liberals so as to provide a " bodyguard " for Bonar Law, acting in a way " not to embarrass the government, but to save them from some of their worst friends."

The Coalition Liberals, in short, made no attempt to resume relations with the Asquithians. What obsessed them throughout the election was relations with the Conservatives. They were frankly attempting to buy Conservative aid, and to get it were prepared, like their leader, to offer Bonar Law a pledge of " general support ". But in some of their constituencies not even this pledge would dissuade the Conservatives from running candidates, and Lloyd George on 25 October issued a severe warning : " If Diehard candidates are put up, either directly or indirectly, to attack Coalition Liberals throughout the country then we shall have no alternative but to spread the war." He was still a believer in " national unity " (i.e. unity between Conservatives and Coalition Liberals), but if Coalition Liberals were attacked : " We shall not confine our fighting to our seats. If they mean to smash up national unity all round, we shall defend it all round."

Three days later Younger—appropriately enough—gave Lloyd George his reply, in the form of a blunt rebuff. He wrote to Conservative associations telling them that no arrangement existed at headquarters between the parties to the late coalition, and that Conservatives were free, in constituencies held by Coalition Liberals, to run candidates or not as they pleased. At most times this might have been unremarkable, but in the circumstances of this election it was an incitement to Conservatives to attack Coalition Liberals. In a number of constituencies the Conservative associations were quick to respond.

By the beginning of November, thirty-five of Lloyd George's followers had come under their attack, many of them since the appearance of Younger's letter. It seemed that Lloyd George must go through with his threat to " spread the war ", and from Mond in Wales he received a powerful plea to do so. Mond wrote :

I wish again to beg you to put yourself unreservedly at the head of Liberalism when you speak next. Wales cannot understand its leader not leading but waiting to see what George Younger is going to do. It is so unlike you that even I am troubled. I am fighting for Unity in the Liberal Ranks, it is now my [? our] chance against annihilation or being dragged at the victorious chariot wheels of Bonar as a small rump. Asquith has missed his chance, but you have yours if you take it. It is not the counting of a seat here or there that matters, it is the much bigger question of retaining the confidence of Liberalism and especially Welsh Liberalism. You have sufficiently shown your loyalty and appreciation of our late Tory colleagues. Now come out and give support to the Liberals who have followed you and thrown in their lot with you since 1916. Day by day, from all over the country I get support from Liberals for Reunion. The rank and file will accomplish what the Leaders are fearing to do. But I want you to lead, you the greatest democrat of the age. Break the fetters, undo the chains, remember how you have assured me of your Liberal faith and how hampered you have been in the Tory straight waistcoat. Come down here where Liberalism is still strong and alive and in your native air lead us to victory.[1]

Rothermere, the press magnate, also wanted Lloyd George to stand up to the Conservatives. He urged him to employ some of the 150 candidates whom McCurdy had in reserve, thirty of them hand-picked candidates who could be sent to constituencies adjoining those of Coalition Liberals under attack. Fisher spent much of 2 November at party headquarters discussing the pros and cons of retaliation, and a list was drawn up of twenty-eight constituencies to be assailed.[2] But when nominations were

[1] Mond to Lloyd George, n.d. (but clearly late October or early November 1922), Lloyd George Papers.
[2] Fisher's diary 1 and 2 November 1922, Fisher Papers.

received on 4 November, there was no sign of " Mr. McCurdy's phantom host ". As Lloyd George had no intention of putting himself " unreservedly at the head of Liberalism ", as Mond wanted him to do, there was little point in provoking further conflicts with the Conservatives by a policy of tit-for-tat. His followers would not benefit from it, however much the Conservatives might suffer. Even though a third of their seats were under attack from their former allies, the Coalition Liberals still had 112 candidates with no Conservative opponents (and four others with only Independent Conservative opponents) ; and most of them had troubles enough without provoking " Tory retaliation ". As Churchill summed up the situation on 2 November : " we have much to lose and nothing to gain by spreading the war ".[1]

So the Coalition Liberals spent the election not attempting to further a cause or present a point of view, but trying to arrange their political survival ; and to this end they were prepared to pose as " general supporters " of a party which had first bundled them out of office and then assailed a number of their seats. This situation caused Lloyd George to adopt an astonishing variety of postures in the last days of the campaign, while making a desperate tour in support of hard-pressed followers. (He even spoke in Bedford on election day in a vain attempt to save Kellaway). In one place he attacked the Conservatives for opposing his candidate and so enhancing Labour's chances, in another he criticised the Independent Liberals for contesting one of his seats and so improving the Conservatives' prospects, in a third, a two-member constituency where Conservative and Coalition Liberal were running in double harness, he commended not only his own candidate but the Conservative as well. If anything emerged from this performance it was his refusal to accept the finality of the blow which had befallen him a month before, or to look beyond the now defunct combination of parties which had been the basis of his power. As one observer put it : " Mr. Lloyd George is still Coalition, whether the Conservatives will have him or not ".[2]

---

[1] *ibid.*   [2] *Manchester Guardian*, 4 November 1922.

II

The one thing to be said for the Coalition Liberals' behaviour was that it left the followers of Asquith in no doubt about Liberal reunion. While Lloyd George continued going cap in hand to the Conservatives, the Independent Liberals would not touch him.

This however was one of the few things that was certain about the Asquithians' position. The fall of the coalition had placed them in a difficulty. They had expended so much energy denouncing Lloyd George's regime, and especially its leader (had not Asquith said that a government of reactionaries would be preferable ?), that it was not clear how they felt about the Conservative ministry which had displaced him.

Some Liberals hardly resolved this problem. They were so bound up in castigating Lloyd George's record that they appeared to condone his successor. This was certainly true of Grey. Oblivious to the fact that the coalition had vanished as if it had never been, he argued that " the great dividing political issue must be between those who think it was a crime against the nation to destroy that Coalition Government, and those who think it would be a crime against the nation to re-establish it."[1] Invited, rather inappropriately, to address a meeting intended to celebrate Liberal reunion in Manchester,[2] Grey devoted his speech to an unsparing condemnation of the coalition and avoided criticising the Conservatives. When this omission was pointed out to him, he explained a few days later : " In the serious state of affairs, especially abroad, he was not prepared to go in for any factious opposition."[3] (Lloyd George also, it will be recalled, deplored " factious opposition " to the government).

Most Independent Liberals sought to avoid this seeming indulgence to the Conservatives, and made their condemnation of the late ministry cover its successor also. " It must be remembered ", said the party manifesto, " that both wings of the Coalition are responsible for its misdeeds, and neither can

[1] *Liberal Magazine*, November 1922.

[2] Manchester was one of the few districts in which Liberal reunion was achieved. But this did not mean much. The Coalition Liberals there had all along been a weak group, holding no seats, and even while the coalition existed had suffered many indignities from the Conservatives.

[3] *The Times*, 10 November 1922.

escape its share of public condemnation." The new government, Asquith stated on 31 October, was " a revised Coalition under an alias." It was no different from its predecessor, said Simon ; there would still be extravagant commitments in the Near East and vast expenditure on armaments. While Lloyd George and Bonar Law were crossing (blunt) swords in the limelight, argued Violet Bonham Carter, they were uniting in the dark and passing coupons under the table. Yet although they tried to make their attacks on the coalition do service also as criticisms of Bonar Law, the Independent Liberals seemed not to possess the same venom towards the new government as the old, and more than once suggested a sneaking admiration for the men who had turned Lloyd George out.

While trying to elucidate their relations with the Conservatives, they had to cope with the perennial problem of their attitude to Labour. The Labour party was not only the main barrier to their revival, but it presented a direct menace to the re-election of leaders like Asquith and Maclean. Yet the Liberals dared not combat it so fiercely as to commit the sin of Lloyd George, who, Spender wrote, had been planning just before his fall to " lead both wings of the Coalition in a grand crusade against the ' Red peril ' "—" an il-Liberal proceeding which is best calculated to create the Red peril."[1] They sought to handle this difficulty by making criticisms of Labour which did not amount to outright denunciations. Simon, seeking to capture Spen Valley from Labour, said that he had never joined in vulgar abusive clamour against the Labour party, and agreed with many things in its manifesto. But he could not subscribe to its proposals for nationalisation and a capital levy, and held that the latter should be resisted in the interests of the working class itself. Asquith too said of Labour that " in some matters of great importance they speak with almost the same voice as ourselves. It might almost seem, to use an old expression, as if they had stolen our thunder." But, he warned, the ultimate purpose of Labour, " to be accomplished, it is true, by stages and not at a single go ", was " the organised control of enterprise by the State over the greater part, if not the whole, of the industrial field."[2] It might seem that more positive speaking

[1] *Westminster Gazette*, 28 October 1922.   [2] *Liberal Magazine*, November 1922.

than this was required if Labour was to be prevented from stealing the Liberals' thunder.

Uncertainly placed between the major contestants for office, the Independent Liberals were in no position to capture attention by the forcefulness or novelty of their programme. Despite the efforts of radicals like Graham White in Birkenhead, Geoffrey Mander in Herefordshire, and the untiring Manchester Liberals, the party did not present the appearance of an active force for social reform. Its " image " was better reflected by the candidate in Cornwall who, when asked for its policy on " education, housing, and the general matters that concerned the workers ", replied that it was " not going to offer any baskets of ' rare refreshing fruit '." He, certainly, had few delicacies on display. His solution to the problem of unemployment was the restoration of complete free trade and " the very strictest economy "— " sweeping away the army of officials which the Government had made, and leaving the money in the pockets of the people to fructify." When questioned about a legalised 48-hour week, he replied that hours of work should be left to negotiations between master and man.[1]

The official party programme leaned heavily towards this Gladstonian orthodoxy. " It would be easy ", said the party manifesto, " to follow the example of others and attempt to purchase electoral support by displaying a long series of glittering promises." The Liberals would not succumb to this temptation : " the simple truth is that great and necessary schemes of social reform, involving large outlay of public money, cannot be realised unless and until real Peace has been established by a foreign policy, based upon and conceived in the spirit of the League of Nations, and national finance is placed upon sure foundations by a course of rigorous economy." The negative nature of Liberal policy is illustrated by an election pamphlet called " When the Liberals Come In." This was its account of what a Liberal government would do :

It will spend less money on fighting and preparations for fighting. It will stop the waste that is still going on in Government offices. It will reduce the taxes. It will reduce the debt. It will bring back Free Trade. It will set trade

[1] These were the views of Sir Courtenay Mansel; *West Briton and Cornwall Advertiser*, 19, 23, and 30 October 1922.

with foreign countries going again. This means that when the Liberals are in living will be cheaper, business will revive, and there will be plenty of work.[1]

Once more, the Liberals had adopted a policy devoid of the " reforming " or " disturbing " (according to viewpoint) features of the Labour programme, and closely akin to the Conservative slogan of " tranquillity ". In fact, as a result of Bonar Law's careful avoidance of issues like tariffs and the powers of the House of Lords, the Conservative and Liberal programmes were practically identical. Both argued that " great and necessary schemes of social reform " were impractical at the moment, that rigid retrenchment was " the first essential " in tackling unemployment, and that support for the League of Nations should be the basis of foreign policy (neither was very specific about what this meant). In consequence, *The Times* could fairly say that candidates of both parties " make declarations for peace and retrenchment which of themselves do not provide the electorate with much material for selection " ; and the *Western Times* of Exeter, whose sympathies inclined to the Liberals, admitted that apart from Labour " any candidate . . . might make the speech of any other candidate."[2] This meant that the Liberals were hopelessly placed to make an impact on the electorate when they had no prospect of securing a majority— for Asquith again conceded defeat without waiting for the electors to vote, saying that he hoped in the next Parliament they would see the government " confronted and controlled by such a formidable and living Opposition as would keep them and the country out of mischief and danger ".[3]

The uncomfortable fact which emerged from the 1922 campaign was that the Independent Liberals were becoming a forgotten party on the sidelines of politics. Lloyd George played no effective part because, in the circumstances of his followers, he chose not to ; Asquith because, seemingly, he had no choice. Laski in discussing election prospects wrote that he expected the Conservatives to win, Labour to make great advances, and the Coalition Liberals virtually to disappear. What would happen to the followers of Asquith he did not bother to con-

[1] *Glasgow Herald*, 26 October 1922.
[2] *The Times*, 11 November 1922 ; *Western Times*, 3 November 1922.
[3] *The Times*, 10 November 1922.

jecture. And the Tory F. S. Oliver, explaining why he had voted for a Conservative he personally disliked, wrote to Lord Milner : " I was between the devil & the deep sea ; for the alternative was a follower of that all but forgotten shadow your old college friend H. H. A."[1] This came from an unfriendly witness, yet it expressed the position of the Independent Liberals in this election. For no one, however hostile, would have dismissed Ramsay MacDonald—or even Lloyd George—as an " all but forgotten shadow ".

III

The object of the two Liberal groups in contesting seats was essentially different. The Coalition Liberals were seeking to retain what they had secured in 1918. The Independent Liberals were attempting to recover at least part of what they had lost. Neither was conspicuously successful.

The role of the Coalition Liberals in 1922 was purely defensive. They contested only 163 seats, which meant that they were not pretending to run for office. And their choice of constituencies followed closely the pattern of 1918. 139 of the 163 seats they contested had been allocated to Liberal or N.D.P. candidates (who now stood as Coalition Liberals) under the coupon bargain of 1918, or had been won by uncouponed Liberals who supported the coalition. That meant that in only 24 constituencies were they trying to break new ground, and in seventeen of these it was at the expense of Labour or the Independent Liberals, not the Conservatives. Thus in only seven constituencies throughout the country did local Coalition Liberals (not their leaders) decide to challenge the Conservatives.

In the outcome, this defensive performance was only half successful. 60 Coalition Liberals were elected (including a few sometimes classified as Independent Liberals), as against 138 in 1918. Compared with the last election, they held 57 seats, gained three (two from Independent Liberals and one from Labour), and lost 81, including 21 which they did not even contest—because, usually, their situation was already past redemption. The heaviest of their losses (39 seats out of 81)

[1] Oliver to Milner, 15 November 1922, Milner Papers.

were to Labour. Here lay the major difficulty of the Coalition Liberals : a large proportion of their holdings were in industrial districts like the Clyde, South Wales, and the West Riding of Yorkshire which had once been centres of working-class Liberalism. They had not fallen to Labour in 1918 because of the patriotic fervour of that election, but in 1922 many of them could not be held even with Conservative aid. Scotland, for example, was the p incipal area in which, in response to what the *Glasgow Herald* called " the realities of industrialism ",[1] the Conservatives were prepared to " co-operate " with their former allies. As Sir Halford Mackinder, a Conservative member of the old House, put it : " Either we hang together, or we hang separately."[2] But it transpired that a good many of them " hanged " anyway, the Coalition Liberals losing eight of their twelve seats in industrial Scotland, including Churchill's at Dundee. A similar misfortune befell them in South Wales and the West Riding of Yorkshire. Their experience in Sheffield was instructive. In 1918 Conservatives and Coalition Liberals had divided Sheffield between them, the former taking three seats and the latter four. But the Conservatives had secured middle-class constituencies which Labour did not even bother to contest in 1922, while the Coalition Liberals occupied working-class seats for which Labour made a dead set. The rowdyism suffered by the Coalition Liberals caused one of them to state in an advertisement that he would " attempt to address the electors."[3] Despite the absence of Conservative opponents, three of their four seats fell to Labour.

Most of the remaining Coalition Liberal losses were to Conservatives (31 in all). Some of these, also, were urban constituencies : for example four working-class divisions in or near London, both Southampton constituencies, and two seats in Leeds. But the majority of Conservative gains were in rural areas, particularly southern England. Cambridge county rejected Montagu, Bedford rejected Kellaway, the Isle of Ely rejected Colin Coote, St. Ives rejected Sir Clifford Cory ; and the mixed constituency of Dorset East fell to an Independent Conservative, even though Guest had the support of the Con-

---

[1] *Glasgow Herald*, 18 October 1922.   [2] *The Times*, 1 November 1922.
[3] *Manchester Guardian*, 10 November 1922.

servative association, and his committee-rooms sported portraits of both Lloyd George and Bonar Law.

For all this, 60 Coalition Liberals survived. This was considerably better than the virtual elimination of the party which Laski had anticipated, but it was bad enough, especially considering the way they held their seats. They survived as an anachronism : a coalition party in a post-coalition world. Except in Wales, no Coalition Liberal was elected against a Conservative opponent. They won in an overwhelming majority of cases because the Conservatives thought it better to support them than to risk the capture of their seats by Labour (or, in northern Scotland, by Independent Liberals). The fourteen seats they won in Scotland, and the 34 in England,[1] were none of them contested by Conservatives. Most of the former were rural seats which the Independent Liberals might have captured, and most of the latter (with exceptions like South Molton and Northern Cornwall) were industrial constituencies which Labour could well have won, had the Conservatives put up candidates. Only in Wales was Coalition Liberalism capable of standing on its own feet. Here it secured four of its eight seats in face of Conservative opposition ; and the other four were not contested by Conservatives because they had no prospect of success. But nearly everywhere else the Coalition Liberals were bound hand-and-foot to the Conservatives. They survived, where they survived at all, as a kept party.

IV

Equally discouraging—although for different reasons—was the fate of the Independent Liberals. If they had not figured as contenders for office, they had made a determined effort to re-establish themselves as a major party. Liberal headquarters alone spent nearly £127,000 on the campaign, most of it (roughly £121,000) on assisting candidates.[2] Of the 325 Independent Liberals who stood, nearly 200 received financial assistance from headquarters. Considerable sums were devoted to bringing forward candidates in less hopeful regions like London and the

[1] University constituencies and the Speaker's seat, Halifax, are excluded from these considerations.

[2] Documents on election finance, Asquith Papers.

Home Counties, so as to keep the party fighting along a national front.

Yet even the *Liberal Magazine*, taking the most hopeful view of the results (and calling them " The Liberal Recovery " !), could only say that they revealed " a slight but unmistakable increase of vigour and liveliness " and showed the party to be " on the threshold of complete recovery." *The Times* was not saying anything different, but saying it from a different viewpoint, when it stated that it could not " speak with confidence " of the future of Liberalism.[1]

The number of seats won by Independent Liberals, compared with 1918, just about doubled : from 27 to 56. Actually their gains were greater than this, for altogether they captured 43 seats (again comparing with 1918) : 32 from Conservatives and right-wing Independents, ten from Coalition Liberals, and one from Labour. But they lost fourteen of the 27 seats they had won in 1918, nine to Labour and five to Conservatives or Coalition Liberals. Their main advances were in rural areas, like the Scottish Highlands, Yorkshire, and odd seats in southern England. In addition they captured some dozen-and-a-half working-class constituencies from Conservatives and Coalition Liberals, but these successes were largely offset by losses to Labour : for example, the three mining divisions of Durham which they had saved in 1918 fell to Labour, and Maclean came third to Labour and Conservative in Peebles.

The meaning of these results was plain. At every point, their chances of recovery were being crabbed by the Labour party. In straight fights with Conservatives or Coalition Liberals they did well enough,[2] but as soon as Labour intervened their prospects slumped. Thus in constituencies which Labour did not contest, their percentage of votes advanced considerably : in 31 constituencies where in 1918 and 1922 there were only Independent Liberal and Conservative candidates, the Liberal share of the poll increased by 10% (from 38.2% in 1918 to 48.4% in 1922). But when Labour entered the field, as it did in most constituencies, the Liberals were less fortunate. In 54

---

[1] *Liberal Magazine*, December 1922 ; *The Times*, 17 November 1922.

[2] 31 of their 56 seats were secured in this way, and five others in straight fights with Labour. Two Independent Liberals were returned unopposed, and the rest in triangular contests.

constituencies which were contested by Independent Liberal, Conservative, and Labour candidates in 1918 and 1922, the Independent Liberal vote increased by only 4½% (from 22.7% of the total to 27.2%). Not surprisingly, the Liberals won few seats in triangular contests, and those usually by desperately narrow margins. Of the eighteen seats won by Independent Liberals in conditions approximating three-party warfare,[1] only two yielded majorities in excess of two thousand votes. As many as fourteen were won by majorities of under a thousand.

Worst of all, such advances as they made provided no evidence that the Independent Liberals were regaining a secure base of support, or were appealing to a coherent body of voters likely to be dependable in the future. They made a number of freak gains (as by the ebullient Frank Gray in Oxford City) in areas with little or no Liberal tradition. They regained some lost ground in rural Scotland, but none in North Wales, Devon, or Cornwall. Their advances in rural England, including some districts which had rarely returned a Liberal, could be attributed to temporary disgust among agriculturists with the treatment they had received from the coalition : thus the Tory Griffith-Boscawen, who had been Lloyd George's Minister of Agriculture, fell to an Asquithian in a part of Somerset which had last returned a Liberal in 1885. And although on balance the Liberals gained more working-class seats than they lost, their advances were puny compared with the great sweep forward of Labour.

In the broad outcome, the Conservatives secured 345 seats, so retaining office, and Labour secured 142. As a result, Labour moved unchallengeably into the position of official opposition party. In doing so, it showed itself determined to appropriate the role of the Liberals in their days of power. Labour head-quarters interpreted the results as showing that they were now gaining followers amongst all classes of the community, and had become the inheritor of the old radical tradition—witness their gains in former Liberal strongholds like Scotland and Wales. In the past, it argued, the radicals had secured victories for the Liberals but the whigs had taken office. Now the progressive

[1] Fifteen of these were in contests with Conservative and Labour ; one with Conservative and Communist ; and two with Coalition Liberal and Labour.

sections of the community, such as the Free Churches, were gathering round the Labour party.[1]

However much Liberals might want to challenge this attempted appropriation of their former position, one thing was certain. They were far from recovering that position for themselves.

---

[1] This claim regarding the Free Churches was not without substance. At a conference of Liberals representing several Lancashire constituencies in 1924, the point was made " That Nonconformity in places had been drifting towards Labour and that in more than one Constituency Nonconformist Ministers were reluctant to take sides—one case was mentioned where only one Minister took the platform for Liberalism." (Minutes of the Lancashire, Cheshire, and North Western Liberal Federation, 17 May 1924.)

PART FOUR

Revival and Relapse

1923-1924

12. LIBERAL REUNION

I told Ll. G. of the conquest he appeared to hv made of the Asquiths & rashly told him that Mrs. A. had told me in a letter to me that " he had behaved very well." He fired up at once at the implied suggest'n that he hd ever behaved otherwise. . . .

Scott's diary, 5 January 1924 [1]

FOR most of 1923 the Liberals grappled with the problem of reunion. It was not their only problem, but it was the one about which they might do something. And to members in both wings it seemed important. Many Coalition Liberals saw reunion as giving them a more definite place in politics; and Independent Liberals like Acland, Hogge, and Scott hoped that it would reclaim a leader possessing the vision and vigour their party lacked.

Yet did the conditions for reunion exist ? The fall of the coalition had not revealed them. Apart from a few districts like Manchester and Leeds, the two parties had spent the 1922 election fighting each other, Asquithians attacking a third of Coalition Liberal seats. The party manifesto called the coalition an " abandonment of principle and the substitution of auto-cratic for parliamentary government ", and said that it had " broken up in general confusion and discredit, leaving behind it an unexampled record of extravagance and failure." " Some-thing which was not wholesome ", said Grey, " has gone out of the political atmosphere." To Wedgwood Benn the " some-thing " was specifically Lloyd George : it was good to be clever, Benn said, but better to be honest.[2] And for most Independent Liberals, including Asquith, the only satisfaction to be derived from the election results was in " gloat[ing] over the corpses

[1] C. P. Scott Papers. Some words in shorthand have been expanded.
[2] *Glasgow Herald*, 21 October 1922 ; *Liberal Magazine*, November 1922.

which have been left on the battlefield " : the corpses of Coalition Liberals like Churchill, Guest, Hamar Greenwood, Kellaway, and Montagu, " all of them renegades ".[1] In London's principal Liberal club on election night, it appeared to one observer that members viewed the Coalition Liberals as the chief enemy. Their defeats were cheered uproariously, whoever the victor ; thus when Kellaway was beaten by a Conservative, an official of the club wrote alongside the result " magnificat, jubilate." And the gloom engendered by Maclean's defeat at Peebles was only relieved by the news that Churchill had gone down in Dundee.[2]

After the election these feelings remained a formidable obstacle to reunion. As against those radicals who saw Lloyd George as a potential saviour of Liberalism, others like Masterman, Gardiner, and Massingham resolved to defect to Labour if he returned to it. Massingham wrote that if Liberals allowed Lloyd George back, " their career as a party of ideas and of influence in their day and generation will be over." He pictured the ex-Premier during a debate on the Ruhr " tak[ing] the floor in quite his old form, delighting the Liberals, confounding the Tories, and putting inadequate idealists like Lord Robert Cecil to open shame. There was a slip or two in the performance, such as that in which Mr. George reduced by some thousands of millions the burden that he proposed to lay on Germany's back." But " in these days who asks a statesman to observe more than a twenty-four hours' truce with his opinions of yesterday ? " For Lloyd George, " mobility in morals, opinions, and party attachments is all in the day's work."[3]

But more than personal resentment blocked the way to reunion. The election had revealed not only Asquithian bitterness but Lloyd George's determination to cling to the Conservatives. And after the contest most Coalition Liberals persisted in this attitude. There were a few like John Murray who did not, arguing that the " true place for Liberalism is the Left," and that Labour and the Liberals had better " relearn the old lesson of British politics that parties are two, the ' for '

[1] *H.H.A. Letters of the Earl of Oxford and Asquith to a Friend*, Second Series, p. 37.
[2] *Manchester Guardian*, 17 November 1922.
[3] *Nation*, 17 and 24 February 1923.

and the ' against,' and that the nation has little use for either so long as it is divided against itself."[1] But others like Churchill and Guest stood unrepentantly for an anti-Labour Centre party, in which liberalism would be " no more than a political expression, and an attitude of mind." And a substantial number of Coalition Liberal M.P.s voted regularly with the government, or did not vote at all. (Lloyd George was one of the latter). Asquith said on 7 March 1923 :

> There are, I believe, fifty-three " National Liberal " members, all told, in the House. An analysis of their votes up to March 1st shows the following results : Twenty-six have voted more often with the Government than with the Opposition ; seven have voted an equal number of times with and against the Government ; and fourteen have voted more often with the Liberals than with the Government.

He and his colleagues, he went on, were regarded as a fossilized whig coterie needing a radical infusion from the Coalition Liberals. Yet when the Independent Liberals put forward a proposal empowering local authorities to levy rates on land values, only twelve Coalition Liberals voted at all, six for and six against.

One who came within Asquith's category of voting " more often with the Government than with the Opposition " was Sir Courtenay Warner. He was horrified to learn in August 1923 that the Conservatives intended to oppose him at the next election. This, he said, made it " difficult for me and others like myself to give greater support to the Government and bars the way to uniting with the Conservative party."[2]

In this situation reunion could not even begin until Lloyd George had declared himself an opponent of the Conservatives. But this was more than he would do. In March 1923 he said that he favoured Liberal reunion and was prepared to consult with Asquith (he also said that he did not seek the Liberal leadership) ; and twice in by-elections he prevented his party from coming into conflict with the Asquithians. But this was not going very far. It did not make him an opponent of the government, which he at no point attacked directly, and it did not obviate for the future a new alliance with the Conservatives.

---

[1] *The Times*, 23 August 1923.   [2] *Manchester Guardian*, 11 August 1923.

On these matters Independent Liberals anxious for reunion pressed him hard, recognising that here was the prime obstacle to their plans. But though he repented of concessions to tariff protection made during the coalition, and urged Liberals to adopt a social programme of " fair play for the underdog ", he would not declare against the government or rule out a new coalition with the Conservatives.

As a consequence reunion made no headway. The majority of Independent Liberals would not countenance it while Lloyd George's intentions remained so vague. Both the N.L.F. annual conference and the parliamentary party supported Asquith when he said that, though reunion was desirable, it could only be achieved by " co-operation in debate and in the division lobby ", and that he would not consult with Lloyd George until the latter could " guarantee the support of [his] party " in Parliament. (" If he and Mr. Lloyd George met what were they to discuss—the state of the weather or the winner of the Grand National ? "). He suspected Coalition Liberals of viewing reunion as the first step towards a crusade with the Conservatives against Labour. (Sir Edward Grigg, Lloyd George's former private secretary and an M.P. for Oldham, certainly did). Asquith quoted a post-election manifesto of Lloyd George's which urged " moderate men of progressive outlook in all parties to see the wisdom of acting together " and which said that " progressive minds are by no means confined to the Liberal Party. I have met and worked with them in the Conservative Party, and the election will have taught many men and women in the Labour Party that violent and extravagant proposals impede progress." Asquith asked :

What did it mean ? It meant . . . that the illusory phantom of a Centre or Middle Party—in fact, a Coalition under an *alias*—was still regarded, if not as the ideal, at any rate as the only practicable solution of the problem presented by the results of the election. I am entitled to ask those who are now urging the paramount and immediate necessity of some dramatic move to hasten Liberal reunion whether they look upon it as a stepping-stone towards a Centre Party, or whether the idea of a Centre Party has been definitely abandoned.

And he inquired what was to be the slogan for the new Liberal programme which Lloyd George was demanding. " Is it to be the slogan of a combined campaign by a united Liberal Party against Labour—pilloried as the ' common enemy ' ? " If so he would have nothing to do with it. Liberals had no quarrel with Labour as such.[1]

So despite all the talk about reunion, nothing was achieved in the year following the coalition's fall. Probably neither leader was altogether sorry. Lloyd George was content to bide his time and not commit himself irrevocably to the Liberals. And Asquith retained some of the personal feeling which showed in the speeches of Grey, Simon, Pringle, and others. Addressing the Scottish Liberal Federation on 12 October 1923, he was critical of the Conservative government but deemed it an improvement on the coalition. The Conservatives had not displayed much initiative or even policy, " but it is something gained that . . . we have finally arrayed against one another men and women on the lines of honest political conviction." When he had addressed them a year earlier, he said, they had been in hot pursuit of the coalition, and he had rarely been engaged in more promising sport. " I hope ", he added in a moment of informality, " I don't indecently transgress the sanctities of domestic life when I tell you that my daughter said to me, when we were coming here, with a sigh ' How I miss the Coalition.' "

II

Within a month of this speech, Liberal reunion was accomplished. The transformation was largely the work of Stanley Baldwin, who had succeeded the ailing Bonar Law as Prime Minister in May 1923. At Plymouth in November he suddenly announced his belief in tariff protection, and dissolved Parliament to secure a mandate for it.

There is a mystery here (apart, that is, from the mystery of what had come over Baldwin), and as usual it concerns Lloyd George. He had gone off on a triumphal tour of the United States in September, and was still away when Baldwin made his announcement. While he was in America it was rumoured that

---

[1] Speech by Asquith at Cambridge on 7 March 1923. Lloyd George had certainly used the expression the " common enemy ", but claimed that his critics were distorting his meaning by saying it referred to Labour.

he had been converted to tariffs on a grand scale—that he meant to propose a sweeping policy of empire protection involving tariffs on foreign food-stuffs. These rumours were afterwards seized on by Baldwin to excuse his own conduct : he claimed that he had dissolved Parliament, win or lose, so as to stop Lloyd George from capturing the Conservatives on the tariff issue. (He also offered other explanations incompatible with this).

Now Lloyd George certainly did hold views on empire development, as shown by a letter of 12 October 1923 which McCurdy wrote him in America referring to their schemes.[1] But as far as is known these schemes included only a minor provision regarding tariffs : the remitting of duties which existed for revenue purposes in the case of empire goods. This was far removed from a plan to construct a tariff wall round Britain just so as to lower it on imperial products. And evidence of Lloyd George's support for the latter scheme is entirely lacking. If he and his colleagues were not staunch Liberals, most of them were fairly good free traders. Churchill in June 1923, replying to a charge of political inconsistency, described the defence of free trade, and in particular opposition to food tariffs, as the first principle of his political endeavours. And during 1923 Lloyd George, although failing to declare against the Conservatives, did declare against tariffs. At Manchester in April he said that the next election would be fought on the issue of protection, and that as free traders they should clear the decks for it by repudiating measures like his own Safeguarding of Industries Act. Nor did he forget this speech in the following months. Asked soon after the 1923 election about this story that, on his return from America, he had intended " to wave suddenly the flag of Protection ", he replied : " There is not a shred of truth in it. I reiterated my views on the question of Free Trade in a couple of speeches which I delivered this year before I went to America. I have not wavered in the least from that position." [2]

Even the view that McCurdy believed him to favour empire protection is open to challenge. McCurdy was chairman of directors of Lloyd George's *Daily Chronicle,* and without waiting for Lloyd George to return to England this paper declared for

[1] Owen, *Tempestuous Journey,* p. 672.
[2] *Manchester Guardian,* 20 December 1923.

free trade. In a leading article clearly written by McCurdy,[1] it said that Baldwin's Plymouth speech on the tariff issue raised the prospect of an election dividing the country into free traders and protectionists. " [A]ll Liberal politicians ", it claimed, " will be on the Free Trade side " of this " great divide ", and it was unfortunate that the free trade forces would be less united than between 1902 and 1905. Labour then had not been cut off from the Liberals by schemes like a capital levy, and Liberal unity had not been hampered by " personal victimisation and proscription, such as is blocking it today."[2] McCurdy was just then playing a great part in developing Lloyd George's programme, and as we have seen was at this time corresponding with him on the matter. Yet he seems to have regarded his chief as a convinced free trader.

Of course an element of doubt remains, and probably always will. Perhaps in one part of himself Lloyd George toyed with the idea of recapturing the Conservatives by embracing protection. But the obstacles to this course must have been evident to him. Apart from anything else, he could hardly expect to recover a party which had accused him of want of principle by recklessly changing his principles. And it would mean losing most of his Liberal followers, who during the coalition had been quicker to defend free trade than any other aspect of the liberal faith. Certainly this was not, as Mr. Owen believes, " The Chance He Missed". At most the question is whether he was so desperate to regain the Conservatives that, even momentarily, he thought a chance might lie this way. And that is not very probable.

III

Anyway, when on 9 November 1923 friends, inquirers, and journalists rushed aboard his ship at Southampton (Mond leading the race so as to secure a " Free Trade pronouncement " from him " for fear Beaverbrook should capture him "[3]), Lloyd George's mind was made up. He declared for free trade. This opened the way to Liberal reunion. Whatever the Asquithians

---

[1] He spoke in almost identical words to a Coalition Liberal conference a few days later.

[2] *Daily Chronicle*, 29 October 1923.

[3] Fisher's diary, 9 November 1923, Fisher Papers.

might feel about him, they did not want another 1922 election. Baldwin had given them a chance to redeem their failure, and disunion was a luxury they could not afford. In any case, their conditions for reunion had been met. Lloyd George was now at one with them in opposing the government. Even Churchill had declared against the Conservatives, and Guest was prepared to accept Labour assistance in capturing a Conservative seat ; and by now probably no other issue would have caused this pair to take such a stand. Moreover, Asquith's headquarters literally could not afford to prolong disunion. Lloyd George had come out of the coalition with a party fund exceeding one million pounds. (Gladstone had earlier called him a prodigal coming home with a full purse and no sign of repentance for his riotous past). By contrast the Asquithians were in parlous condition to fight another campaign. As Mond bluntly put it : " The ' Wee Frees ' have no money."[1]

Even before Lloyd George's return, Mond was preparing the way for reunion. He saw Asquith and his wife " and found them both favourable to Liberal reunion." Lloyd George was informed of this at a gathering of prominent Coalition Liberals on the day of his return. Fisher recorded : " L G asks us all ' Shall he meet Asquith ?['] Opinions unanimous for it."[2] They agreed that the meeting should take place the following Tuesday, with Mond visiting the Asquiths over the week-end to finalise arrangements. Four days later Fisher noted : " Mond says that L G & Asquith have met & arranged a joint campaign. The meeting very easy and cordial." But there was one sour note introduced by Lloyd George.[3] Though appealed to by Mond, he declined to attend the meeting which Asquith was addressing at the Queen's Hall two days later. He offered the unconvincing explanation that he was not tuned up for the campaign, having just landed from America, and had not been keeping up with contemporary political discussion in Britain.

The upshot of this reunion was that the two leaders issued a joint manifesto, Lloyd George contributed £90,000 to headquarters election expenses, and a committee of four (two

---

[1] *ibid*, 13 November 1923. Fisher may have summarised what Mond said.

[2] *ibid*, 9 November 1923.

[3] According to a memorandum by Vivian Phillipps, 13 November 1923, Herbert Gladstone Papers.

nominated by each leader) was set up to deal with problems of candidates. This last was, for purposes of the election, the thorniest issue. In a good many constituencies rival candidates and organisations still existed, particularly where Asquithians were trying to unseat Coalition Liberals. So it was agreed that these rival bodies should unite to choose candidates, except that where a constituency was already represented by a Liberal of either persuasion then both groups should support him. This merger did not prove too difficult, because Lloyd George's organisation in the constituencies was usually so meagre. But where his followers held seats and possessed a substantial organisation, difficulties sometimes arose. Independent Liberals were on occasion reluctant to support coalitionists they had fiercely opposed, especially where, as in some two-member constituencies, the coalitionists were trying to maintain a tacit understanding with the Conservatives. In a few instances reconciliation was not attained : in two constituencies, Central Hackney and the Western Isles, sitting Coalition Liberals abandoned their seats because the Asquithians would not stand down; and in two others, Camborne and Cardigan, Independent Liberals actually went to the polls against Coalition Liberals. But elsewhere reunion was accomplished on the basis of the leaders' agreement.

The only other hitch in election arrangements occurred in the details of the manifesto. Lloyd George had a number of items, stressing the " positive " side of the Liberal programme, which he wanted included, and the manifesto was held up a few days while these were hammered out. (There was also a passage attacking the government's Turkish settlement which probably reflected his views rather than Asquith's). Yet on the whole election matters proceeded amicably. What was to prove the real trouble with this rapprochement was that it did not look beyond the election, and simply ignored long-term questions. What after all had caused Lloyd George to return to Asquith's company ? Up to that moment he had not been over-anxious for Liberal reunion, and had let it lie for a year hoping that something better would turn up. Only the extraordinary conduct of his arch-enemy Baldwin had caused him to rejoin the Liberals now. Baldwin had led the opposition to Lloyd George at the Carlton Club, and was dealing him a further blow by raising the issue most likely to draw Chamberlain and his associates back into the Conservative fold. But he was risking his political neck in the process. A united Liberal party fighting for free trade might eliminate Baldwin's majority in Parliament and shake his hold on Conservative allegiance. This meant that there were quite diverse reasons why Lloyd George might be deciding for Liberal reunion. Perhaps he was just happy to be back with the Liberals. But perhaps he was chiefly attracted by the chance of revenging himself on Baldwin and throwing politics into a ferment from which a new coalition might emerge. Or, for that matter, he might not have decided what reunion meant to him : given his past statements and present followers, he could hardly do anything but declare for free trade, irrespective of his ultimate intentions or wishes.

But for Asquith, it was urgently important to find out what reunion meant to Lloyd George. After all, Lloyd George in 1923 was a powerful independent figure with a vast party fund and a well-staffed political headquarters. Did he now become Asquith's subordinate and place his fund and machinery at the leader's disposal ? Or did he remain free to issue manifestoes of his own and do what he liked with his money? Doubtless Asquith felt that to press him on these matters would spoil their reconciliation, and that any proper reunion must involve trust and confidence. But his reticence caused these crucial questions to be left unanswered—except in the sense, as Gladstone lamely remarked soon after, that Lloyd George did " in a sort of a way agree " to contribute more money.[1] But a sort of agreement with Lloyd George was no agreement at all. And so there developed the anomaly of a united Liberal party in which an individual who was not the leader issued his own policy statements, maintained his own headquarters, and preserved a mighty fund unavailable to the main Liberal forces as they staggered towards bankruptcy. At the time Asquith met Lloyd George to arrange reunion it was seven years since their last negotiations. Had the Liberal leader forgotten, or was it that after everything he had never really understood, the sort of man he was dealing with ?

[1] see below, p. 293.

13. VOTE AND SEE

It is the greatest joke that the Liberal has got in here [Hemel Hempstead]. . . .
Of all constituencies this was regarded as the most hopeless. . . . I hope Labour
won't fight it again.

Barbara Hammond to Gilbert Murray, 16 December 1923 [1]

THE Liberal appeal in the 1923 election was two-fold. One side
of it was positive and radical, proposing innovations to meet the
economic recession. The other was negative and cautious, resisting deviation from the *status quo*.

The Liberal manifesto, which probably owed more to Lloyd
George and McCurdy than to Asquith, stressed the reforming
side of liberalism and upheld the view (which McCurdy had been
pressing in the *Daily Chronicle*) that Liberals while exposing the
fallacies of protection must offer a cure for the nation's ills. It
struck at the government's principal failures : to restrain the
French action in the Ruhr, and to remedy, or even hitherto show
concern about, unemployment. It said that during the French
occupation of the Ruhr Britain seemed to have no " voice or
mind or conscience of her own ", and so had " ceased to exercise
any guiding influence upon European affairs." It deemed the
" economic restoration of Europe " essential to " the revival of
our industries and the establishment of peace ", urged a reopen-
ing of full relations with Russia, and advocated the admission of
" all nations " (i.e. Germany and Russia) to the League of
Nations. But it also insisted that Britain's unemployed could
not be left waiting upon a European settlement " with no
prospect but unemployment benefit and Poor Law relief." And
it said that neither protection nor socialism would help them.
" The last thing which taxation on imports can achieve is to
provide more work for those engaged in manufacture for
export " ; and equally undesirable would be " the destruc-

[1] Gilbert Murray Papers.

253

tion of enterprise " and " the frightening away of Capital ".

What was required, affirmed the manifesto, was " a bold and courageous use " of national credit in support of " enterprises that would permanently improve and develop the home country and the Empire "—enterprises such as internal transportation, afforestation, " the supply of cheap power by the co-ordinated use of our resources of coal and water ", and the development of the empire (e.g. " railway building in the Dominions and India "). These proposals are clearly similar to the schemes for economic revival put forward by Lloyd George in the years that followed ; and during part of the 1923 campaign he could be found advocating them in his warmest radical tones. After a speech in which he attacked social problems and offered Liberal schemes to overcome them, one observer wrote : " It was very much like listening to the Lloyd George of 1910 to hear him on the ' hope and the promise ' which Liberal policy held out to the poor and the broken." [1]

Yet this positive note did not dominate the Liberal campaign— or even Lloyd George's part of it. The party had been challenged on a specific proposal which was anathema to it. Its first task, and for some Liberals its only task, was to assail protection and defend the established fiscal order. This caused it to adopt a primarily negative role, warning that protection would mean higher prices—what one candidate called " the inevitable increase in the cost of living "—and portraying through cartoons the activities of " Baldwin and Co. High Price Tailors " whose shop windows displayed signs like " All prices raised 20 per cent " and " You pay—we prosper." Asquith's daughter issued a " Message to Women " which argued that " upon Free Trade every home depends for cheap food " and that Conservative policy represented " an attack on the standard of life of the poorest homes in the country." Sometimes the free trade case was decked out with a sort of faded, backward-looking patriotism. A handbill issued by Liberal headquarters bore the caption " 1914-1918 " and pictured two soldiers in the trenches. " Free Trade ", it claimed, " financed the fighter. . . . Free Trade has *proved* itself for Great Britain. Protection is the makeshift of *lesser* nations than ourselves." Lloyd George sometimes sounded this note also :

[1] *Manchester Guardian*, 27 November 1923.

When trouble came, look at this country—we spent ten thousand millions upon the war. I never knew we had ten thousand millions. I had been listening for twelve years to Protectionist orators who said we were done and ruined, that we hadn't a sixpence in the stocking . . . .

Ours is a seafaring land, and Free Trade is the natural element for a seafaring nation. . . . Stand by the glory of this island, the free flag of commerce and trade and industry— the land that won the battles of freedom.[1]

On the familiar ground of defending free trade Asquith was at his most effective, demolishing with enthusiasm Baldwin's lame presentation of his case.

We are supposed [he said on 30 November] to have the advantage of being governed by honest and simple men. Their policy, if policy it can be called, is still at this moment wrapt in a cloud of mystification and equivocation such as might have excited the wonder and admiration of Machiavelli himself. There are, in fact, three quite distinct and even irreconcilable versions of what it is that the electors are being invited by the Government to support.

It was not merely a case of " Wait and See ", he said ten days earlier, but of " Vote and See." This was pretty vigorous leadership from the Asquith of these years, but essentially negative in approach and based on a defence of the *status quo*. In similar vein, Edward Grigg was to be found " declaring that the attempt to rush the country into Protection . . . is as dangerous to our true interests as the capital levy and Socialism ", and appealing to people " with traditional British common sense to put country above party once more and vote for steadiness, sanity, and the safe middle course."[2] Simon claimed that both Conservative and Labour were proposing risky experiments, and that only a Liberal government would not shift its financial policy from month to month. And Lloyd George denounced the " wild men " who had taken over the government and asked his audience " to assist in this election in guiding the destinies of the country upon safe and sound lines in the future." He called protection and socialism " two

[1] *Liberal Magazine*, December 1923.
[2] This is Grigg's account of the approach he was taking in his speeches, in a letter to Grey, 1 December 1923, Grigg Papers.

forms of suicide " and equated liberalism with " safety " and " security ".[1] " It is rather interesting ", commented a *Manchester Guardian* correspondent on polling day, " to find so wide a disposition to regard the Liberals as in this election the conservatives with a small ' C '. On the one side there is the fear of higher prices from the Conservative party and on the other side fear of the capital levy ".[2]

II

The outcome of this campaign was a marked improvement in the Liberal position. It is necessary to stress this because some authorities have denied it, and have reached the strange conclusion that Liberal support declined in 1923 compared with 1922.[3] This view suggests a weakness in the psephologist's approach to election results : it is equipped to deal with major parties in conflict with each other, but not with quirks like unopposed returns or splinter parties. The Coalition Liberals in 1922 provide such a problem : where should their vote belong in a contest neatly divided into Conservatives, Labour, and Liberals ? Usually it has been lumped in with the Independent Liberals, and their combined vote called the Liberal total for 1922. If this total is then compared with the Liberal poll in 1923, it may reveal a decline in the latter year. But such figures are meaningless. A study of the Coalition Liberals in 1922 shows that theirs was not a purely Liberal vote. Nearly all Coalition Liberals who polled well possessed a substantial measure of Conservative support. If not all of their vote belongs to the Conservatives, more does probably than belongs to the Liberals. So in assessing the Liberal showing in these elections it is necessary to exclude constituencies where Coalition Liberals stood in 1922. This has disadvantages too, because it leaves a smallish and not quite representative sample which may exaggerate the Liberal advance in 1923. But it is less misleading than any calculation which includes the Coalition Liberal vote.

[1] *Liberal Magazine*, December 1923 ; *Manchester Guardian*, 19 and 24 November 1923.

[2] *Manchester Guardian*, 6 December 1923.

[3] D. E. Butler, *The Electoral System in Britain 1918–1951*, pp. 173–7.

On this basis, we discover the following : there were 62 constituencies contested only by Independent Liberals and Conservatives in 1922 and 1923, and in these the Liberal share of the poll increased by 6%—from 45·2 in 1922 to 51·3 in 1923. And there were 97 constituencies contested by Independent Liberal, Conservative, and Labour candidates in 1922 and 1923, and here the Liberal poll increased by over 4%—from 27·2 to 31·4. This advance resulted in a substantial number of seats gained. With the aid of an expenditure of £150,000 by Liberal headquarters, 158 Liberals were elected in the 456 constituencies they contested.[1] This constituted a net advance of 42 seats on the 1922 election, when 116 Liberals of both wings were returned. But the real advance was considerably greater, for the reunited party was bound to lose a good many Coalition Liberal seats secured only with Conservative aid in 1922. In the nicely chosen words of the *Liberal Magazine* for December 1923 : " in the last Parliament a considerable number of seats were held by Liberals on a temporary and insecure basis, having been won in circumstances which have now passed away." In some constituencies these circumstances had " passed away " even before the election—witness the sad case of Sir Courtenay Warner quoted earlier[2]—and Lloyd George's declaration against the government brought them to an end in most others. Only seventeen of the 60 constituencies which returned Coalition Liberals in 1922 were not contested by Conservatives in 1923. Consequently nearly half the Coalition Liberal seats were lost (29 all told), and many of the others only saved because of the " swing to the Liberals ".

By contrast, the main Liberal forces made substantial gains. They failed to hold twelve out of the 56 seats won by Independent Liberals in 1922 (and Asquith only retained Paisley through a divided Labour vote). But 83 seats were captured by Liberals, most of whom were Asquithians ; thirteen from Labour, one from an Independent, and the great majority—69 in all—from Conservatives. It was these inroads into Conservative holdings which formed the basis of the Liberal revival in 1923.

---

[1] In two of these constituencies there were rival Liberals, and in each the Asquithian challenger unseated the sitting Coalition Liberal—in itself a sort of swing to the Liberals.

[2] see above p. 245.

What sort of seats did Liberals capture ? The first thing evident on election night was that the cotton industry had turned against the government. Baldwin's proposals had thrown Lancashire Conservatism into disarray. The provincial leader, Lord Derby, was plainly unhappy on the matter, and some of his followers became downright incoherent. Dr. T. Watts, the former Conservative member for Withington, announced that he had been a free trader at the last election and was still a free trader. But he realised that unless they did something to grant their colonies preference they might lose them, and that unless they acted on unemployment " we should have an upheaval." Baldwin, he concluded, had decided on tariffs but not general or permanent tariffs, and he supported Baldwin's policy " all the way ".[1]

As against this gentleman who remained a free trader but accepted protection, there were many Lancashire Conservatives who just remained free traders. " I may be a Conservative, but that's not to say I'm a fool ", Lucy Masterman heard some of them remark while she was campaigning for her husband in Manchester.[2] And J. A. Hutton, a prominent figure in the cotton industry, said that he was a free trader first and a Conservative second, and would support a Liberal or Labour free trader before a Conservative protectionist. So Liberal gains here were not un-expected. The former Conservative member for Rusholme gave up hope early on, saying that if he did not win this time he would do so next, and would know he had gone down fighting for what he believed was right (a common conviction among candidates expecting or experiencing defeat). But the number of Liberal successes here exceeded all expectations. The party won five of the ten Manchester constituencies where it had won none since the war, including an " unbelievable victory "[3] in the Exchange division, reputedly the barometer of commercial Manchester, and another in Withington, a residential suburb of Manchester business men. Similarly a Liberal won Altrincham in Cheshire, " a kind of superior suburb of the cotton capital ". Among the Liberals returned in these contests was Masterman, who had lost his seat in a by-election of 1914 following his elevation to the government, and had seemed doomed to fail in every attempt

[1] *Manchester Guardian*, 20 November 1923.
[2] Lucy Masterman, *C. F. G. Masterman*, p. 333.   [3] *ibid.*

to re-enter Parliament. " We've won, my dear," he said to his
wife as they heard of his return for Rusholme, " and I thought
we were never going to again."

But there was more to the Liberal revival than this. Fisher,
hearing the results in London, noted : " The Liberal victory at
Bath is the first indication that it is not merely a revolt of the
cotton industry."[1] Bath certainly did not bring to mind cotton,
or industry of any other sort. A select watering place with a
considerable retired population, it had been described by
Spender a year earlier as " in its permanent character a Tory
constituency. . . . there are more old tory tabbies in the place
than—I should think—in any other single town in the country
outside London."[2] Bath was one of the seats which caused the
Manchester Guardian to say : " It is indeed curious how many
Liberal successes there have been in places which have cathedrals,
racecourses, and esplanades."[3] Salisbury, Wells, Ely, and
Chichester were also places with cathedrals ; and Blackpool,
Southport, Weston-super-Mare, and Torquay possessed esplanades. The Liberals won them all, and others equally improbable :
places like Devizes, Hemel Hempstead, Rugby, Chelmsford,
and Aylesbury which (said the *Manchester Guardian*) " may
suggest Liberal desires, but hardly Liberal hopes ".

Some of these seats showed the Liberals making advances,
not only in towns with large numbers of landladies and retired
people, but in rural districts as well. This was especially noticeable in the west of England (but not only there), where they
won constituencies like St. Ives in Cornwall, Totnes in Devon,
Thornbury in Gloucestershire, and Bridgwater, the Minister of
Agriculture's seat, in Somerset. They also captured middle-
class seats in the large cities : for example, two better-off
divisions in Liverpool (" an area which ", said Asquith, " Conservatism has been accustomed to regard as its own preserve"),[4]
dormitory suburbs of London like Finchley and Willesden East,
and the reputed Conservative stronghold of Edinburgh North.
In addition they made some gains from Conservatives in working-
class areas, as in Cardiff, Plymouth, Portsmouth, the mining
district of Nuneaton, and the hat-making constituency of

---

[1] Fisher's diary, 6 December 1923, Fisher Papers.
[2] Spender to Gladstone, 3 March 1922, Herbert Gladstone Papers.
[3] *Manchester Guardian*, 8 December 1923.   [4] *The Mersey Liberal*, May 1924.

Luton ; but the main Liberal advance was not in this type of district.

Two things stand out about these results. The Liberals did not recover lost ground in some former strongholds, like the industrial regions of Scotland, South Wales, and the Yorkshire West Riding. And they did make startling gains in districts with little or no Liberal tradition. For example Aylesbury, Blackpool, Chelmsford, Chichester, Sevenoaks, and Tiverton had not gone Liberal even in the *annus mirabilis* of 1906. And scarcely any Liberals expected to win two of the three county divisions of Berkshire, which the *Daily Chronicle* thought very unfavourable soil for them, being but little touched by the march of modernity. If King Alfred returned to Wantage, the *Chronicle* remarked during the campaign, he would find it little altered.[1] Yet had he visited it after the election he would have found it represented in Parliament by E. A. Lessing, a Liberal expert on Soviet Russia. " What ", Asquith asked of some of these results, " is the explanation of these unexpected, and in some cases un-hoped-for, victories ? "[2] The organisers of the Liberal cause in Chichester could not help him ; they " only knew 12 Liberals ", and had secured a candidate (their first since 1910) only at the eleventh hour. Like Lloyd George, they found the result " most surprising ".[3]

III

To answer Asquith's question we must look back to the circumstances of the contest. The Liberals as a " left " party benefited from the swing against the government caused by unemployment and foreign affairs, especially in constituencies where Labour did not intervene (and they won 68 seats in straight fights with Conservatives). But equally they gained from being " the conservatives with a small ' C ' "—that is from the reaction of normally Conservative voters against the government's fiscal proposals. " This ", said a correspondent of *The Glasgow Herald*, " is a cost-of-living election. More and more candidates are being pressed to talk about the effect of Protection on the cost of living. It is a subject of absorbing interest to all the electors, and especially to the womenfolk whose domestic concern it is

[1] *Daily Chronicle*, 21 November 1923. [2] *Manchester Guardian*, 25 February 1924.
[3] Fisher's diary, 9 December 1923, Fisher Papers.

to make ends meet." Prophetically, he referred to fear of a rise in the cost of living as influencing " fixed-salary " dwellers in the middle-class suburbs of London and in the holiday resorts on the south coast of England.[1] And a *Times* correspondent said of the results : " The general opinion in Unionist circles yesterday was that Mr. Baldwin's policy had been defeated mainly on the ' dear food ' cry ".[2] This was certainly the view of the Conservative candidate for Stroud, who had lost his seat : " Those of them who had voted for the Conservative party had used their brains, and were not led away by the parrot cry of ' Your food will cost you more.' "[3]

But it was in more respects than the cost of living that the Liberals seemed momentarily a " safer " party than the Conservatives. Much of British politics between the wars might be summed up in the expression " the failure of nerve ". The First World War had inflicted crippling blows on the youth, vitality, and creativeness of the nation, and had left much of it yearning for a pre-war order which in retrospect seemed secure and stable. The Conservatives, employing slogans like " Tranquillity ", " Safety First ", and " A Doctor's Mandate ", made a direct appeal to this unnerved, backward-looking side of the nation— in every inter-war election except this one. But in 1923 they abandoned their " safe " role and proposed to institute a sharp break in the economic order. This approach was favoured by Conservatives like Leopold Amery who regarded conservatism as a positive, crusading, innovating force. But the Ameryite view was clearly at odds with the main Conservative appeal of these years. And Baldwin, the living embodiment of " Safety First ", was not the man to put across such a brand of conservatism. For the moment he had been convinced that it was a winning ticket—this is the real explanation of his decision to fight an election on it, and it was a mistake he never repeated. But he advocated it in such a vacillating, half-hearted way, not really understanding what it was all about, that he robbed it of even the faint chance of success it might have possessed. And while Baldwin floundered, Asquith was on hand to offer Conservatives (with small or large " C ") a " safe middle course " between " two forms of suicide ". *The Glasgow Herald* showed

[1] *Glasgow Herald*, 1 and 3 December 1923. [2] *The Times*, 8 December 1923.
[3] *Gloucestershire Echo*, 7 December 1923.

clearly that this appeal met the needs of many Conservatives. Protection, it lamented, " will deal a staggering blow to the economic and financial stability of the nation ", and was being supported by people with no real appreciation " of the fundamental difficulties involved in a fiscal revolution ". " We protest against the Unionist party being launched upon an enterprise in which it cannot succeed without disaster to the country and cannot fail without disaster to itself." And it used words which summed up a large part of the Liberal appeal in this election :

> ... Free trade is not a theory. It is a fact—the one supreme fact in our economic polity, eighty years old, still going strong, and capable of summoning defenders, if the truth were told, from the inner consciousness of multitudes of those who are proposing—surely in something like a fit of absence of mind—to destroy it. How few people there are who can say, after a searching inquisition, that they owe nothing but enmity to the system on which our trade rests and our unexcelled prestige has been erected.[1]

With the Conservatives planning " a staggering blow to the economic and financial stability of the nation ", not even the Labour party seemed as dangerous as before (" The Capital Levy is not a present danger. Protection is "[2]); and the Liberals, reunited in defence of " the one supreme fact in our economic polity," seemed no danger at all. *The Glasgow Herald* felt that there was " not much, if any, reason to regret that there is once more a reunited Liberalism to interpose between the extremes of reaction and the flighty adventures of Socialism."[3] And the *Daily Mail* concluded that " If The Liberals Win " " there would be *some chance of the tranquillity which the late Mr. Bonar Law with admirable insight declared that the country so urgently needed.*"[4] When even the *Daily Mail* could talk like this, it is not surprising that the Liberals enjoyed a substantial revival at the expense of the Conservatives. They were the beneficiaries of a swing against the government on both radical and conservative grounds. And for probably the only time since the war, a non-Liberal newspaper was to be found entertaining the notion of a Liberal government.

[1] *Glasgow Herald*, 9 November 1923.   [2] *ibid*, 19 November 1923.
[3] *ibid*, 14 November 1923.   [4] *Daily Mail*, 4 December 1923.

Yet how substantial was the Liberal revival ? Some of its features were decidedly unsettling. The party had won a quarter of the seats in the House, but many of them were desperately insecure. Of their 158 successes, 68 were gained in straight fights with Conservatives and 23 in straight fights with Labour, and many of these would be endangered simply by the abstaining party deciding to intervene. Again, of the 139 seats won in straight fights or triangular contests, 91 were secured by a margin of under two thousand votes, 46 of them by majorities of less than a thousand : Tiverton was won by three votes, Hemel Hempstead by seventeen, Newbury by 41, Burslem by 63, Stirling and Falkirk by 156, Battersea by 186, Abingdon by 254, and Basingstoke and Torquay by under 400. Admittedly Liberals were lucky to win some of these at all. But what would happen when Baldwin " returned to normal ", and the Liberals helped Labour into office ?

Here was another unsatisfactory feature of the results : they offered Liberals no solution to the problem of relations with Labour. The Labour party's gains had more than kept pace with the Liberals'. It remained the second party in the land and the alternative government to the Conservatives. Now that office was so near, and an absolute majority (seemingly) not far away, Labour supporters were reinforced in their determination to drive the Liberal party from the field. They believed more than ever that it was a corpse encumbering the ground, and that it only needed to be swept aside for the power and authority it had once exercised to be theirs.

14. LIBERALS AND LABOUR

Give Labour its chance.

Gladstone to Maclean, 12 January 1924 [1]

He [Ramsay MacDonald] reverted again & again to this dislike & distrust of the Liberals. He could get on with the Tories. They differed at times openly then forgot all about it & shook hands. They were gentlemen, but the Liberals were cads.

Scott's diary, 15 July 1924 [2]

THE 1923 election gave no party a majority in Parliament, and left the Liberals, with 158 seats, holding the balance between the Conservatives with 258 and Labour with 191. Asquith on 18 December left no doubt about his intentions. He would not, he said, lift a finger to keep Baldwin in office. If a Labour government was ever to be tried, as it was bound to be, it could not be tried under safer conditions. As for the Liberals, they would retain their " unfettered freedom " and " unconditional independence. " So when Labour on 21 January 1924 moved a vote of no confidence in the Conservative government, Asquith led his party into the opposition lobby.

His conduct at this juncture has been criticised. It has been said that he should have used his control of the situation to lay down clear conditions on which Labour might take office, including regular consultations with the Liberals. This misinterprets his position. He was not free to make and unmake governments on his own terms, and whatever he said in public he had some inkling of the fact. Writing to Pringle eleven days before Baldwin's defeat in Parliament, he said that the future now seemed settled : Baldwin would resign and " Ramsay " come in.

I doubt whether either of them is right. Baldwin could

[1] Herbert Gladstone Papers.   [2] C. P. Scott Papers.

easily have snapped his fingers at a no-confidence amendment and announced that, as leader of much the largest section of the House, he had better moral authority than anyone else to carry on the King's Government until he was absolutely blocked. And Ramsay might well have declined to start the 1st Labour Government under impossible Parliamentary conditions.

But we have to look at the actual situation as it has been created, not by us but for us. I agree of course that we must give the Labour Government a reasonable chance, at the same time being careful not to arouse the suspicion that we are acting in collusion, and with a new coalition.[1]

Some of these judgements are very odd, not least his view that Baldwin might have " snapped his fingers " at a no-confidence defeat. But the letter does show that he recognised himself as an observer, and not a master, of a situation which had been created " not by us but for us." Even in wanting to avoid the appearance of " acting in collusion " he was probably making a virtue of necessity, for neither MacDonald nor Baldwin would negotiate with him. All that his choice amounted to was that he could keep Baldwin in office or throw him out. If he chose the latter, then MacDonald would be asked to form a government, and he would certainly not consult Asquith about it.

And was Asquith free to make the former choice ? All along he had refused to ally with the Conservatives against Labour, and for the past year had rejected Liberal reunion because the Coalition Liberals would not vote against the Conservatives. The *Liberal Magazine* was only stating the established Independent Liberal position when it said, immediately after the 1923 election :

there are no conceivable circumstances in which the Liberal Party could enter into a coalition, alliance, partnership, understanding, or other collusive arrangement . . . with the Conservative Party. Liberals are not separated from Conservatives merely by a difference in the way of doing things . . . . They are separated in their fundamental aims, in thought, in idea, in principle ; and there is neither any event nor any formula that can ever bridge this gulf.[2]

[1] Asquith to Pringle, 10 January 1924, Asquith Papers.
[2] *Liberal Magazine*, December 1923.

The only Liberals who with any consistency might have voted with Baldwin were the former Coalition Liberals, and their losses had been so great that they were not in a position to save the government : Churchill and Hamar Greenwood, who furiously opposed putting Labour into office, had just been defeated for the second election running. There were a few left in Parliament to uphold their position : Sir Ellis Griffith considered it against " the decision of the country " to turn out a government in a minority of ninety-nine so as to bring in one in a minority of 233.[1] But even many ex-Coalition Liberals did not agree. At least momentarily, they were so angered by Baldwin's conduct that they were prepared to give Labour a chance. This was true of recent Centre party advocates like Grigg ; most of all it was true of Lloyd George. Fisher had a " long talk " with him three days after the election and found him " all against a Coalition "—" Never again ", he declared. Later that month he wrote to Scott saying " I am entirely in accord with the line you have taken in the ' Manchester Guardian ' " (strongly advocating a Labour government). And in a *Daily Chronicle* article he argued that even if the Conservatives dropped protection they should not be kept in office. He scoffed at those who a year before had regarded an alliance of Conservatives and Liberals as immoral, but now hysterically demanded one ; the country did not want socialism but it did want reform and reconstruction, and if MacDonald grasped his opportunity the Liberals would see him through.[2]

In the division which brought Baldwin down, only ten Liberals voted with the government and half-a-dozen others were absent unpaired—all of them being former Coalition Liberals or the successors to Coalition Liberals. 138 Liberals, by contrast, voted for Labour's motion, and three others paired for it. (The Speaker, a Liberal, is not included here). The relative solidarity of the party suggested how far it was committed in advance to this course of action.

[1] *H. C. Deb.*, 169, 621 (21 January 1924).
[2] For Lloyd George's attitude see Fisher's diary, 9 December 1923, Fisher Papers ; Lloyd George to Scott, 26 December 1923, Lloyd George Papers ; *Daily Chronicle*, 5 January 1924.

II

On the face of it the experiment of a Labour government holding office with Liberal support was full of promise. As Lloyd George wrote, on all the pressing questions of the day, such as housing, the settlement of Europe, and the utilisation of credit so as to provide productive work for the unemployed, the Liberals were prepared to go just as far as Labour.

There were difficulties on the Liberal side, of course. Some Liberals, intent on proving themselves better radicals than Labour, tended to pin-prick the government for not getting ahead with reforming measures. Pringle excelled in such conduct, and even Ramsay Muir spent his maiden speech criticising the government for its lack of reforming zeal. Further, there remained a Liberal right wing which was appalled to see the " Socialists " in office, even under Liberal restraint. Some of the wealthier Asquithians outside Parliament took this view ; and the number of former Coalition Liberal M.P.s who opposed the Labour government soon increased. Grigg and Guest repented quickly of their votes to put Labour into office, Grigg writing only three days afterwards that he wanted not to assist Labour but " to organise against them and fight them to the death. I think there are many young men of this opinion in both the Liberal and Conservative Parties who must come together, whatever the leaders say or think."[1] And in April Guest announced that he would not again stand for Stroud because he had won it with Labour support, and called on Liberals to co-operate with Conservatives in ejecting Labour from office.

But against the twenty or so Liberals who habitually voted in opposition to the government, and others like Pringle who were over-fond of criticising it, the overwhelming majority of Liberal M.P.s were prepared to give it regular support. Their attitude was exemplified by the party's decision to sit on the government side of the House, and by the action of party head-quarters in persuading the Liberals of Burnley not to contest the by-election which Henderson, the Labour Home Secretary, was fighting to get back into Parliament. The attitude of the great majority of Liberal M.P.s was stated by Vivian Phillipps,

[1] Grigg to Sir Abe Bailey, 24 January 1924, Grigg Papers.

the chief Liberal whip, in a speech of 9 February 1924 :
For the first time for ten years the forces of progress in this
country were able to command a majority in the House of
Commons. The field of opportunity presented to them was
so wide that if they could keep in step it was scarcely possible
to set a limit to the extent to which they might transform
conditions. . . . With goodwill and consideration, not only
in Parliament but in the constituencies, they could march
together a long way before their paths need diverge. . . .

By the result of the recent Election it had fallen to a
Labour Government to try to do many things which
Liberals desired to see done. They as Liberals were ready to
put the public need before any mere party interest and to
help a Labour Government to do these things.

Yet within nine months the hopeful experiment of a minority
Labour government had collapsed in ruin. For this the overwhelming responsibility lay with Labour. Requiring active
Liberal support to retain office, Labour responded not by con-
ciliating or even ignoring the Liberals, but by seeking to pul-
verise them. MacDonald gave fair warning of what was to come
by delivering a tirade against the Liberals barely a week after
the election. " Liberal papers like the ' Daily News ' ", he
wrote, " have never been more dishonest nor more gleeful in their
gloating over the prospects of a Labour defeat " ; the Liberals
" fought so generally with a petty nastiness that the common
report from our candidates is that the dirtiest hitting came from
Liberal opponents."[1] This hysterical nonsense typified his
attitude to the Liberals during his first premiership. At no time
did he make a practice of informing the Liberal leaders about
government business, and his studied offensiveness towards
them made their task of keeping him in office peculiarly difficult.
Masterman in October 1924 attributed the collapse of Liberal-
Labour co-operation to " the work of one man alone"—" the
present Prime Minister."[2] And Lloyd George was scarcely
exaggerating when he asked in November : " How could
[Asquith] have conjectured that the leader of a great party
would have behaved like a jealous, vain, suspicious, ill-tempered
actress of the second rank ? "[3]

[1] Quoted in *Manchester Guardian*, 14 December 1923.
[2] *Nation*, 11 October 1924.　　　　[3] *Daily Chronicle*, 1 November 1924.

Even some Labour supporters asked the same question. The *New Statesman* on 11 October 1924 roundly criticised Mac-Donald's lack of courtesy to the Liberals, and his tremendous vanity and easily-wounded pride.

> If he had treated his Liberal allies with even common courtesy he might have remained in power not merely until 1925, but for some years to come, possibly even for a decade.

> But instead he has missed no opportunity of insulting and deriding those who placed him in power. . . . Why should he cherish such intense personal feeling against Mr. Asquith, who, after all, . . . is probably the greatest and certainly the most disinterested of living statesmen.

Yet except for the *New Statesman* and a few Labour members, principally Snowden, the attitude of the Labour party was faithfully reflected by its leader. The same petulant rage against the Liberals for continuing to exist was apparent among Labour back-benchers, and in the country Liberal M.P.s were subject to a spontaneous assault by Labour organisations, especially in constituencies which Liberals had narrowly captured from Conservatives in the absence of Labour candidates. The Manchester radical Philip Oliver described how, after tramping all night through the division lobbies to keep the government in office, he was informed that Labour had adopted a candidate against him; and John Harris, another " left " Liberal, complained that while he was busy supporting the government Labour was carrying on intensive propaganda in his constituency—" a seat regarded as a safe Tory preserve " which Labour had not hitherto contested.[1] Both Liberal leaders felt the force of this attack. Lloyd George for the first time encountered Labour opposition in Caernarvon Boroughs, and Asquith, who had only held Paisley owing to a divided Labour vote, was now faced with a united Labour force and a particularly strong Labour opponent. On occasion Labour's campaign went so far as to deprive Liberals of their right of free speech, Maclean being shouted down by rowdies during a meeting at St. Pancras. And in June 1924 Labour's intervention cost the Liberals one of their seats. The member for Oxford City (a most precarious Liberal holding) was unseated on petition, and the Liberal party's chance of retaining the constituency was destroyed by the

[1] *Manchester Guardian*, 8 and 25 April 1924.

decision of the local Labour party to put up a candidate. The Conservative was elected on a minority vote.

III

Thus the formation of a Labour government, far from enabling Liberals and Labour " to march together a long way ", promptly placed the Liberals in an appalling dilemma. By acceding peacefully to office, and introducing " sound " and orthodox legislation like Snowden's budget, Labour seemed confirmed as the " radical alternative " to the Conservatives. This threatened the Liberals with redundancy. Grigg wrote as early as February 1924 : " Ramsay MacDonald is definitely established as the national leader of the Left. . . . I have very little doubt that if his health stands him in good stead, he will take with him a very large section of the Liberal Party when next he goes to the country."[1]

What made this situation particularly desperate for the Liberals was their inability even to claim credit for the government's successes ; they could hardly identify themselves with the achievements of a ministry which, while dependent on their votes, abused them as an " exploded fiction " and " a corpse encumbering the ground ". To counter this attack and escape the impression of redundancy, they had to show that they contributed something distinctive and essential to the situation : that Labour possessed extreme socialist tendencies which they alone were holding in check. But were such tendencies apparent in men like MacDonald, Snowden, Clynes, Thomas, or Webb ? And if they did exist, were the Liberals really equipped to restrain them ? The fragility of their claim became evident the first time they sought to call the government to order. Immediately on coming into office John Wheatley, the Minister of Health and a member of Labour's left wing, rescinded the order of an earlier government preventing the Poplar guardians from exceeding a prescribed scale of outdoor relief. (Poplar was a London district afflicted with crushing poverty, and the too-generous guardians were Labour representatives like George Lansbury). Wheatley's action smacked of " socialist despoliation of property ", which the Liberals had insisted they would

[1] Grigg to Bailey, 28 February 1924, Grigg Papers.

prevent. Accordingly Asquith, in what Grigg called a " masterly performance ", announced in the " plainest and most unequivocal terms " that unless the government reconsidered the matter—" as I hope they will "—their action stood no chance of receiving " the countenance or approval of the House of Commons."[1] His strong lead did much to rouse the spirits of his followers, who were already growing panic-stricken at Labour's assault in their constituencies.

But where did Asquith's challenge lead ? If the government refused to climb down in face of his warnings—and it was showing no disposition to be conciliatory—then his conduct pointed straight to a government defeat and a general election. This was a prospect which dismayed most Liberals. The day after delivering his challenge Asquith wrote privately that the last thing he wanted was to force a political crisis.[2] This remained true in the following months. ". . . Labour knows only too well that the Liberals do not want an election at the present time ", Grigg wrote in April.[3] And on 21 October the *Daily Chronicle* said that the Liberals' " disinclination to enter upon an early struggle was well-known to all politicians." Hence having delivered his challenge to Wheatley, Asquith was obliged to execute a partial retreat. He acknowledged himself satisfied with a statement from Wheatley and MacDonald that they had no intention of countenancing " Poplarism " among local authorities. The Liberals thereupon voted with the government against the closure so as to prevent their own motion from coming to a vote, giving rise to the impression that they had run away from their challenge for fear of the consequences. " When next the Liberal Party proposes to stage a formal protest against a Government irregularity," caustically observed *The Glasgow Herald*, " let us hope its backbone will prove equal to the occasion." [4] And Grigg, who was not at all satisfied with the government's explanation, wrote : " Since they knew quite well that Mr. Asquith had decided not to vote against them anyhow, they could afford to be very valiant and unapologetic.

[1] *ibid*, 14 February 1924 ; H. C. Deb., 169, 863 (13 February 1924).
[2] H. H. A. *Letters of the Earl of Oxford and Asquith to a Friend*, Second Series, p. 95.
[3] Grigg to Bailey, 24 April 1924, Grigg Papers.
[4] *Glasgow Herald*, 27 February 1924.

I protested against the course which we took, but unavailingly."[1]

Between February and October 1924 the Liberals made desperate efforts to discover a way out of the trap which had enclosed them, forcing them to keep in office a government over which they could exercise only limited control and which subjected them to unremitting attack.[2] In March and April the parliamentary party held anguished meetings to consider its course, and fierce resentment was expressed at Labour's behaviour. One who spoke strongly at the second meeting was Lloyd George. He was not, like Guest, returning to his Centre party position, but he was utterly disillusioned with the course he had advocated in January. Grigg recounted " a long and very interesting private talk with L.G." at the end of March :

In the last few weeks Labour has put up a candidate against him in his own constituency in Wales and is making a dead set there to cause him difficulty. There is nothing like action of this kind for giving leaders a stimulus in the way they should go, and L.G. is now beginning to realise, I think, that co-operation with Labour is absolutely illusory as a goal for sensible Liberals. For the moment this makes his position even more difficult than before since the hostility against him by a number—probably a large number—of the Conservatives is unabated.[3]

At the party meeting on 15 April Lloyd George spoke out against Labour's behaviour " in a speech which was frequently cheered and which undoubtedly expressed the feeling of the meeting ".[4] He deplored Labour's contemptuous attitude to the Liberals, who were expected to " fetch and carry " for the government without being consulted about parliamentary business, and said that unless there was a change the party must " assert itself." They had no desire to turn the government out, but their situation was becoming impossible.

Only one proposal emerged from these party recriminations : a suggestion by Lloyd George, which Asquith supported and the

[1] Grigg to Bailey, 28 February 1924, Grigg Papers.
[2] The only times that Liberals could safely take a stand against the government were when, as on the Rent Restrictions Bill, ministers had made it clear they would not resign if defeated, or, as on the question of laying down five new cruisers, it was certain the Conservatives would vote with the government.
[3] Grigg to Bailey, 27 March 1924, Grigg Papers.　　[4] *The Times*, 16 April 1924.

meeting readily accepted, that during the Easter recess members should consult their supporters and report back regarding their feelings. Exactly what they hoped to find out was not clear, but this more positive speaking inspired Liberals to make a last attempt at establishing working relations with the government. Their leaders made direct appeals to Labour to adopt a more reasonable attitude. Lloyd George said during the recess that they wanted the government to be a success and had tried to make it so; why then could they not co-operate on terms of dignity to them both ? Labour could not have it both ways, Maclean argued, taking the Liberals' support and yet attacking them. Both of these leaders referred to a concrete proposal which would ease the situation, and which members came back from their constituencies announcing as the prerequisite for their continued support of the government—a measure of electoral reform. At last Liberals were coming to appreciate the handicap from which they suffered as a third party under the " first-past-the-post " system. In general they polled votes out of proportion to the few seats they captured. And in particular they faced in 1924 the loss of seats to Conservatives owing to Labour's intervention. The most thoroughgoing solution to this problem would be proportional representation, but even the alternative vote would help. Here then might lie a way of easing relations between Liberals and Labour. John Harris reported that, in the view of his supporters, further Liberal co-operation with the government should be dependent on an agreement that no election would take place until a measure of electoral reform had been enacted. The same conclusion was arrived at by a party meeting immediately after the Easter recess, on 30 April. As it happened, a P.R. bill introduced by a Liberal as a private measure was due for its second reading later that week. The meeting decided to back it as a party measure, and requested the government both to support it and to provide facilities for its passage into law during the session. The Liberals, it was said, were seeking a way out of their difficulties by requesting P.R. as a " fair price " for their support.

Labour's reply was unequivocal : it would give the Liberals nothing for their support. And it was the reply, primarily, of the Labour rank and file. The cabinet, apparently acting before the Liberal meeting, decided to advise its followers to support the P.R. bill. But the Labour back-benchers were so incensed by the Liberals' supposed " ultimatum " that the cabinet agreed to leave the matter to a free vote. Thereupon Labour members joined with the Conservatives to reject the measure, ninety-one Labour M.P.s voting against it and only twenty-eight for it. The view of the majority was expressed by James Maxton soon after, while addressing a May Day rally in Glasgow. The Liberals, he said, had tried to drive them into a particular lobby, but they had decided to tell Asquith, Lloyd George, and the rest to go to hell. Now, he added, the Liberals were threatening to hold a series of week-end meetings throughout the country. God help Asquith and Lloyd George if they tried to address a meeting at Bridgeton Cross on a Saturday night.

From this moment the Liberals had nowhere to turn. There was now not the faintest prospect of co-operating with Labour on dignified terms. They must either continue to support the government in conditions they had already condemned, or bring on themselves the election they plainly feared.

In the upper ranks of the party the conviction was growing that, at whatever cost, they must meet Labour's attack. At the end of May the Conservatives assailed the government over its failure to reduce unemployment, an issue on which Liberals felt strongly, especially considering Labour's grandiose election promises. At a meeting of the Liberal shadow cabinet on 27 May, Lloyd George, Pringle, Simon, Phillipps, and Howard urged that they should vote against the government on this question.[1] But Asquith was still wishing to postpone a crisis which might jeopardise his and the party's survival, and he evaded his colleagues' pressure by deciding to put the matter to a party meeting. Here the feeling was much less bellicose. The " general opinion ", " frankly expressed ", was that it was not in the Liberals' interest to precipitate an election, one member saying that a contest at this time would be disastrous for them.[2] Here is Grigg's account of the gathering :

The Liberal party meeting last week, which had to decide

---

[1] Fisher's diary, 27 May 1924, Fisher Papers. Fisher and Masterman took the opposite view.

[2] *Glasgow Herald* and *Manchester Guardian*, 30 May 1924. Asquith gauged the feeling as being seven to three against defeating the government ; Fisher's diary, 29 May 1924, Fisher Papers.

whether to turn the Government out or not, was a desperate farce. I made the strongest appeal I could for taking our lives in our hands and fighting, but it was no good. I never had a harder audience to speak to in my life. I asked L.G. after the discussion what he thought of it, and he said : " If, during the war, the Divisional Commander had summoned a meeting of the rank and file to decide whether they should go over the top to-morrow morning or to-morrow six weeks, how do you suppose the rank and file would have voted ? "

If you put the question of facing a general election at any time to a party meeting of precariously placed and highly impoverished Members of Parliament, there is really no question about their answer. We are therefore pottering on, supporting the Government and yet criticising it. The time must, however, come soon for taking our lives in our hands, and I am quite certain that L.G. means to give a lead when he sees an opportunity.[1]

So strongly did Lloyd George oppose the party's decision, which meant going into the government lobby, that he stated he would abstain.[2] The Liberals, Asquith announced in Parliament, had no reason to love the Labour party.

This crisis in May showed that, for a while at least, the Liberals would continue to overlook the government's sins of omission. But in the inflamed state of feeling between the two parties, they could not go further and endorse sins of com-mission—actions by the government which transgressed "liberal principles ". This in itself doomed the government to a short life. Ministers had only to follow the prompting of their left wing on a single important issue to precipitate a rupture. Such a development took place early in August, just as Parliament was dispersing for the summer recess. Representatives of the government, after prolonged negotiations with Russian delegates, assented to a draft treaty with the Soviet Union. Two things about it deeply offended Liberals. It had been completed under

[1] Grigg to Bailey, 5 June 1924, Grigg Papers.

[2] If the Liberal party as a whole abstained, this would lead to the fall of the government, because there were more Conservatives than Labour members in Parliament. The Liberals in effect had only the choice of supporting or opposing any measure which MacDonald was prepared to treat as an issue of confidence.

pressure from the Labour left wing, who had resisted the abandonment of negotiations. And it contained a provision whereby, to induce the Soviet government to settle the claims of British bondholders, Britain would guarantee a loan raised by Russia on the British money-market. Nothing would persuade a majority of Liberal M.P.s to vote for this scheme, which meant loaning the Russians money so as to persuade them to pay back some of what they owed. In the absence of Asquith, who was ill, Liberal leaders like Lloyd George, Simon, Runciman, Grey, Maclean, and Masterman denounced the treaty, particularly the provision for a guaranteed loan. And the official Liberal Publication Department was unsparing in its criticism of what it called *A Sham Treaty*. In this matter the leaders clearly spoke for their rank and file. A small radical section, including Kenworthy and Hogge, supported the treaty, but the main body, including many " left " Liberals, were firmly against it. E. A. Lessing, who was an expert on Russia and by no means a bitter antagonist of the Soviet regime, issued a pamphlet severely criticising the treaty, and the Manchester Liberals united in condemning it. The party, wrote Masterman, was practically solid against it.[1]

All that was required to complete the party's rejection of the proposal, and so to bring down the government, was a firm lead from Asquith. Lloyd George visited the ailing leader in September and found him " quite firm " in opposing the treaty.[2] The Liberals, Asquith wrote soon after, were not attracted to a crusade against bolshevism, and wanted " our relations with Russia [to] be put upon business-like lines and secured by adequate safeguards ". But this " cannot be attained by crude experiments in nursery diplomacy." Parliament should not give even " an anticipatory and contingent sanction " to " a loan of undefined amount, upon unspecified conditions ".[3]

So when Parliament re-assembled on the first day of October 1924, the life of the first Labour government was practically run. The ministry had sealed its fate by heaping such humilia-

---

[1] *Nation*, 4 October 1924. This was less true of the Liberal press ; but it seems, as was argued by the *Nation*, that on this matter Liberal opinion was not faithfully represented by its newspapers.

[2] Fisher's diary, 16 September 1924, Fisher Papers.

[3] *Manchester Guardian*, 22 September 1924.

tions on the Liberals that they could not support repugnant measures, and then committing itself to such a measure. MacDonald had stated on 27 September that rejection by the House of the main lines of the Russian treaty would constitute a vote of censure on the government.[1] Asquith met the parliamentary party four days later and invited them to support a motion repudiating the guaranteed loan. This invitation the Liberals, with only a handful of exceptions, accepted with enthusiasm. Their decision gave the government " definitive notice to quit."[2] Upon receiving it MacDonald decided to quit earlier. He treated as a motion of censure a Liberal proposal for an inquiry into what is known as the Campbell case, which also had " Communist " connotations ; and when the motion was carried by a combination of Liberal and Conservative votes he dissolved Parliament. There were good reasons for holding an election before so dubious a proposal as the Russian treaty, on which anyway the government was divided, became the chief political issue.

It is possible to doubt the wisdom of Asquith's decision to force the government out on a " Russian " matter. As the *Manchester Guardian*, five days before the government was defeated, warned :

No doubt there is plenty of anti-Russian feeling in the country which could be exploited against the pro-Russian feeling of a section of Labour, but . . . in this line of attack Liberals would be easily outdistanced by the Tory party under the ardent inspiration of Mr. Churchill and their own Die-hards. It is unlikely that the Labour party would gain anything out of a conflict on this ground, but then neither would the Liberal party. The Tory party might.[3]

Kenworthy too warned the party meeting on 1 October that an election on the Russian issue could prove disastrous. Yet what else were the Liberals to do ? They could not seek a compromise with the government, because it would not negotiate with them. And they had all along justified their support

---

[1] Oddly enough Viscount Snowden states in his *Autobiography* (vol. 2, pp. 685–6, 698) that defeat on the Russian treaty would not have been treated as a matter of confidence. He ignores this speech by MacDonald, and similar utterances by Ponsonby and others, and refers only to an earlier statement by MacDonald whose meaning is ambiguous.

[2] *Glasgow Herald*, 9 October 1924.   [3] *Manchester Guardian*, 3 October 1924.

of a Labour government on the ground that they would prevent it from following extreme courses. Were they now to endorse a reckless and objectionable proposal just to save themselves from an election ? However valid the *Manchester Guardian's* prophecies, the Liberals really had no choice. In the last stages of the Labour government, as in the first, they were the victims of circumstances which had been created " not by us but for us."

IV

The Liberals emerged from this Parliament in a profound state of shock. They had never anticipated that Labour in office would behave like this. In one way their surprise was inappropriate. Labour's conduct was consistent with its determination since 1918 to wage electoral war upon them at whatever cost in Conservative victories. Yet the Liberals had never imagined that Labour would carry its vendetta to the point of accomplishing its own ejection from office. They failed to appreciate that the missionary zeal of Labour would not allow of compromise for so sordid an objective as power ; that the Marxist fundamentalists in Labour's ranks were so obsessed by rage against " bourgeois " parties that they preferred to abandon a chance of internal reform and international conciliation than to accomplish it with Liberal aid ; and that a section of Labour " idealists ", if only subconsciously, found office itself repugnant because it menaced their ideals with the test of practical application, and so were eager to force their leaders into " extreme " courses which would obviate this danger. Moreover large numbers of Labour supporters believed so firmly in the operation of " the swing of the pendulum " that they were prepared to abandon office so as finally to eliminate the Liberals, convinced that this would ensure a majority Labour government, if not at the next election, then at the next election but one. To hardly any of them did it occur that the destruction of the Liberal party might initiate, not an alternation of Conservative and Labour governments, but a succession of Conservative governments with Labour as a semi-permanent opposition. Such perhaps is the fate of parties, especially parties heavily weighted with historians, which draw too freely on " the lessons of history ".

Anyway, in their assumption that Labour, however it might

behave at elections, would work with them to keep a Labour government in office, the Liberals proved utterly deluded. For them this was of far-reaching importance : in effect it brought their career as a party involved in governing to a close. Once they had fallen to third position, they could only occupy a place as a party of government if Labour would accept their co-operation whenever the " progressive " forces captured a majority. The events of 1924, by showing this not to be the case, doomed the Liberals to an unrelieved prospect of opposition, with all the problems of retaining support which this involved. And even if their support did hold up sufficiently to give them once more the balance in parliament, all that lay before them was a prospect of recurrent general elections which they possessed neither the confidence nor the resources to contest.

15. THE RAPTURE OF THE SECOND HONEYMOON

On 20 March 1924, four months after Liberal reunion, Sir Edward Grigg wrote privately :

There is no sign at present of any real understanding between Asquith and L.G. Asquith has been ill lately and has hardly been in the House of Commons at all. L.G. also has been away and seems to be keeping himself to himself to a very large extent. On the whole this is much the best line and I am glad that he is following it. He ought not to mortgage himself and his funds in any way to the Wee Free organisation. They have no desire except to strangle him at the earliest possible opportunity. [2]

What went wrong with the Liberal rapprochement so smoothly accomplished in November 1923 ? Lloyd George at least had no doubt : the official Liberal party wanted " to strangle him at the earliest possible opportunity." Faction within the party, he wrote immediately after the 1924 election, " had much to do with the putting off until the battle was upon us " of the reorganisation he had deemed to be necessary. And he told some of his intimates that he had never had any difficulty about arrangements with Asquith if allowed to see him alone, but that the bodyguard who had refused to let Asquith meet him in the crisis of December 1916 had done the same continuously during 1924. [3]

[1] Herbert Gladstone Papers.   [2] Grigg to Bailey, 20 March 1924, Grigg Papers.

[3] *Daily Chronicle*, 15 November 1924 ; Grigg to Sir Archibald Sinclair, 6 November 1924, Grigg Papers.

Clearly some leading Asquithians did harbour resentment against Lloyd George. Gladstone took the view that the Liberal success at the 1923 election was purely a triumph for Asquith, and that Lloyd George had contributed nothing but funds. And Maclean made it plain during the 1923 contest that he did not want Lloyd George (who had advocated his defeat in 1922) appearing for him. But not all Asquithians wanted to maintain the feud. This was true of Asquith : to some of his associates, he seemed a good deal too amenable to Lloyd George. What caused his hostility to revive was not their intervention, as Lloyd George liked to think, but Lloyd George's own conduct.

A week after the letter quoted above, Grigg wrote to Bailey :

I had a long and very interesting private talk with L.G. a couple of days ago. He is, as you can imagine, thoroughly dissatisfied with the conduct of the leadership of the Liberal Party, and is quite convinced that absolutely no good can be done with the Party while Mr. A's end of Abingdon Street controls the machine. He has, however, been very careful not to allow Mr. A's side of the organisation to get hold of any of the National Liberal funds. L.G. keeps his money in the hands of his own trustees and is free to take his own course.

The point about the reference to " Mr. A's end of Abingdon Street " was that both Liberal leaders had headquarters there. Soon after the fall of the coalition Lloyd George had taken offices at 18 Abingdon Street, three doors away on the same side of the road from Liberal headquarters at 21 Abingdon Street. During 1923 this had caused many mix-ups : on one occasion an aged and rather doting Conservative peer had called at No. 21, in mistake for No. 18, to discuss the apportionment of coalition funds, had demanded to see " Davies " (which happened to be the surname of the secretary at both places), and on being confronted with the secretary of Asquith's body had denounced him in fruity language as an imposter. It was assumed that reunion would end such mishaps. Yet the cause of them persisted. Lloyd George did not close his headquarters, but preserved it as a well-staffed and well-financed institution, symbolising his disregard for the existing Liberal leadership and refusal to let it get hold of any of his money.

Here was cause enough for Asquithian hostility, irrespective of past quarrels. Gladstone may have betrayed personal bitterness when he wrote : " L. G. wishes to get most of us out of this office & there will be no difficulty so far as I am concerned ! "[1] But, as Grigg's letter shows, this was precisely what Lloyd George wanted.

II

Lloyd George in 1924 was embarking on a new course. At least for the moment, he harboured no illusions that the Conservatives would take him back. Grigg wrote regretfully in March that his " general tendency is to move towards the Left," and in May that he was " suffering from a very unhappy trend to the Left, owing largely to the personal animus against him, which still is very strong in Conservative quarters " ; and it is clear that Lloyd George was not participating in the cave of right-wing Liberal M.P.s which Grigg was trying to form (" we may take L.G. with us ultimately, whatever he thinks of our efforts now ").[2] At the same time, he soon abandoned hope of amicable relations with Labour. To this extent he was back with the Liberals. But it was very much for want of a better. He had pronounced the party doomed too often since 1914 to rejoice at being back, and he was not at all satisfied with its present circumstances. If it was to facilitate his political comeback, it must be much strengthened. This gave him, irrespective of his ultimate course, an immediate objective : to restore the Liberals as a respected and powerful force. But he was convinced that this could never happen under its present leaders—the " fossilized whig coterie " who had led it through all its misfortunes. It was not in his nature to ask whether he had contributed to the party's disasters. The present, not the past, concerned him ; and he believed that he could rally the party where they never would. One day in June 1924 he and Fisher were walking in the countryside near Churt when they came upon a tree covered with moss and dying because of it. " Like the Liberal party ", remarked Lloyd George.[3]

It would be idle to deny that there were grounds for his

---

[1] See below, p. 294.
[2] Grigg to Bailey, 6 March and 22 May 1924, Grigg Papers.
[3] Fisher's diary, 22 June 1924, Fisher Papers.

criticisms. Not only had the party leaders failed to take up current issues like industrial policy, as they had been urged to do. Even more, they seemed to have placed themselves above the political struggle, regarding a lack of the common touch less as a deficiency than as a sign of grace. Gilbert Murray, perhaps the most respected member of Asquith's inner circle, held it to be a virtue of liberalism that it appealed to the " thinkers " and not the masses, between whom there could be only a superficial sympathy. " Liberalism stood for Freedom of Speech and Thought. Thinking men, rich and poor, were with them ; but the uneducated masses liked neither, any more than the Tory did." If the masses still supported free trade, he wrote, it was primarily because they identified it with cheap food. (In the colonies, " where they are less respectful of intellect ", they " went straight for thumping Protection "). Liberals, on the other hand, desired free trade " on broad scientific grounds ". Again, the " unthinking mob " opposed Liberal foreign policy, which tried to see the viewpoint of the foreigner, and Liberal policy on liquor. As for Labour, it had become in part a Tory party, attracting the jingo mob, the sporting mob, and the vast masses who loved drink and betting and hated " idealists ".[1] One might contrast these rather priggish sentiments of Gilbert Murray with the views which Lloyd George put before the Liberal Summer School in August 1924, while urging it to take the bold view that the great days of office were still to come. He would like, he said, to suggest a new topic for the agenda of the Summer School : it should consider the best method of reaching the people with its programme.

It is no use talking about soap-boxes and laughing at the open-air propaganda of the Labour party. We, the Liberal party, for any weaknesses we have need the open-air order. . . .

Liberalism has got to consider not merely its message— it must see it knocks at every door with it.

If these views seemed to highlight the shortcomings of the established leaders, it was no accident. " Some digs at Gilbert Murray ", Lloyd George told Fisher (" with a twinkle ") after the meeting.[2]

[1] *Nation*, 15 March 1924.   [2] Fisher's diary, 7 August 1924, Fisher Papers.

So Lloyd George determined to save the party in his own way, and in spite of its leaders. At times, indeed, he seemed prepared to save it in spite of itself. His attitude on imperial and foreign policy often differed from that of the bulk of the party. In a debate on reparations in March 1924 he took a quite different line from that of most Liberals, which Simon had already presented. British interests, he said, should not be treated as " secondary in all these negotiations." " I protest against the new spirit, which seems to proceed on the assumption that England is to pay, but, when it comes to receiving, it must be some other country. It is always some other country. . . . I think it is about time that someone should stand up for the rights of Great Britain."[1] This speech was uproariously cheered by the Conservatives, but received in stony silence by the Liberals. Lloyd George thereupon publicly rebuked his party. Liberalism, he wrote in the *Daily Chronicle*, must not allow the Tories to monopolise the appeal to patriotism.

> As long as it is possible for the Tory Press and even Liberal papers to draw attention to the fact that an appeal from a Liberal member in the House of Commons to stand up for British interests in Europe is " received in grim silence on the Liberal benches," Englishmen will continue to suspect Liberalism of an anti-patriotic bias.[2]

Grigg wrote of this incident :

> ... L.G. has given a very amusing punch in the ribs to the Wee Frees by last Saturday's article in the *Daily Chronicle*. . . . It was badly received, of course, by the Left Wing of the Liberal Party, and has led to protests both public and private, but L.G. sticks to his guns and there was no-one brave enough to tackle him at the Liberal Party meeting last Tuesday.[3]

The rapture of the second Liberal honeymoon, observed the Conservative Sir Robert Horne, had soon gone ; Lloyd George had set Liberalism's teeth on edge by stressing Britain's contribution to the war effort and by demanding consideration for British interests.

One of the Liberals who delivered a public rebuke to Lloyd George over this incident was his pre-war aide and subsequent

---

[1] *H. C. Deb.*, 170, 1716–7 (6 March 1924).   [2] *Daily Chronicle*, 22 March 1924.
[3] Grigg to Bailey, 27 March 1924, Grigg Papers.

antagonist Masterman. But while Lloyd George's line on foreign policy was confirming Masterman's antagonism, his attitude on internal affairs was undermining it. This attitude was expressed in an address to the London Liberal Federation in May. Liberals, Lloyd George said, must recognise the enmity of both Tories and Labour. The struggle between Liberalism and Toryism was unending, and now Labour had become just as deadly a threat. The solution for Liberals was to raise the banner of a new crusade : a crusade for the creation of greater wealth, from the land, the mines, and electricity ; and a crusade against the vested interests which were hampering the nation's development, like land monopoly, trusts, the building unions, and the drink monopoly. If Liberalism launched out on a nation-wide campaign it would win a victory amazing to its friends and enemies. In the next two months, largely at his instigation, the party launched a " Great Liberal Campaign " throughout the country during which hundreds of meetings were held and which culminated in a demonstration at Belle Vue, Manchester, where Lloyd George addressed an audience of 25 to 30 thousand. At the same time he set up, on his own initiative and at his fund's expense, a number of " expert " committees to draw up programmes on the coal mines, electrical production, and the land system. The manner in which he went about it is indicative of his utter disregard for the party's leaders—and for anyone else who differed from him. The first production of his experts, a book called *Coal and Power*, took many M.P.s by surprise, and led them to ask why they had not been consulted ; and although Asquith approved of its contents, his endorsement did not appear in the early copies because it was only obtained after the book had gone into print. And when Mond, having been invited by Lloyd George to serve on the committee on land, disagreed with Lloyd George's ideas, he received a sharp rebuff which was to prove the first stage in their estrangement.

Lloyd George's ideas for reforming agriculture included a form of land nationalisation : agricultural land (other than that owned by the person who farmed it) was to be taken over by the state and leased on " cultivating tenure ". This tenure would give security of occupation and even some right of bequest, but only if the tenant's standard of farming satisfied the supervision of a local committee. If it did not, he could be displaced.

Mond, who had figured in 1923 as the principal exponent of private enterprise in a parliamentary debate on socialism, resisted this scheme. At the end of September his opposition drew this rebuke from Lloyd George :

As to land, I very much regret that you cannot see your way to accepting the proposals which I put forward, even as a basis for discussion. As you and I will have to take a special responsibility for the Welsh Land Programme it is rather serious that there should be a divergence of opinion between us. But had I not better have a look at your constructive proposals ? Up to the present—you will forgive me for saying so—your sole contribution has been to criticise mine. Let me see what you propose, and then we can put our heads together with a view to arriving at a solution that we can both urge upon the Welsh Liberal Federation.

As we have no time to spare—for we might very well be in an election within the next few weeks—I hope you will let me have your ideas as soon as possible. There is no question of Keeble and yourself resigning, as there is no Committee in existence. I simply invited a few friends for an informal interchange of views, and if we find that it is impossible to secure co-operation, then each of us will have to take his own course.[1]

Mond's reply was conciliatory: if his attitude had been unconstructive, " this is not unnatural when you had drafted a scheme so attractive in so many directions." But he emphasised the need to " get something of an agreed character " (as against Lloyd George's assertion that if they could not agree, " then each of us will have to take his own course "). And the suggestions he put forward placed prime emphasis on the " vital importance " of disclosing " the fundamental difference between Liberalism and Socialism ".[2] This was hardly the purpose of Lloyd George's scheme.

What is noteworthy about Lloyd George's side of this correspondence is his determination to press ahead with his ideas irrespective of the attitude either of the party leaders or of a close associate like Mond. He held that " the Welsh Land Programme ", to appear for an election " within the next few

[1] Lloyd George to Mond, 29 September 1924, Mond Papers.
[2] Mond to Lloyd George, 30 September 1924, Lloyd George Papers.

weeks ", was the responsibility of himself and his colleagues in Wales without reference to party headquarters. (As it happened, he did get his land ideas incorporated in the 1924 election manifesto, though how is a mystery ; the other leaders pointedly ignored the subject in their speeches). And in his statement that " there is no Committee ", and that what Mond had attended was a gathering of " a few friends ", there was the clear implication that Mond need not be invited to future friendly gatherings—which, according to Mond's later account, was precisely what happened.

But if Lloyd George's search for a programme smacked of indiscipline to some Liberals, and of " socialism " to others (both Coalition and Independent in origin), it was profoundly attractive to a third group : the radicals who had striven to revive their party as a positive, innovating force. They contrasted his " evergreen optimism "[1] and fervour for a nation-wide campaign with the lethargy of their leaders since 1918, and his readiness to propagate fresh and disturbing ideas with Asquith's orthodoxy and inflexibility. Hence pre-war radicals like Masterman and Acland, who had come to detest him after 1914 (" What a really jumpy unstable unreliable devil L G is ", Acland wrote in 1917[2]), and post-war radicals like Ramsay Muir and E. D. Simon, found themselves being drawn into his camp. " I've fought him as hard as anyone ", Masterman told his wife, " but I have to confess, when Lloyd George came back to the party, ideas came back to the party."[3] And Acland in 1925 was to announce that, having sworn by Lloyd George before the war and sworn at him during it, he had now returned to his former attitude. Muir, looking back on this period, described the same response among a later generation. Rank and file Liberals, he wrote in 1927, " nearly all opposed to Mr. Lloyd George during the days of the Coalition," had worn themselves out between 1918 and 1923 trying " to persuade the official Liberal Party to study, propound, and advocate measures of social and political reform. Their efforts were in vain. The N.L.F. passed resolutions, but the official party never took up any of these questions." Then Lloyd George came back,

[1] *Glasgow Herald*, 27 May 1924.
[2] Acland to his wife,—August 1917, Acland Papers.
[3] Masterman, *C. F. G. Masterman*, pp. 345–6.

and the social reformers found him, unlike his colleagues, ready and eager to work with them, to discuss live topics, set inquiries afoot, hammer out projects of reform, and submit them to free criticism. So first by ones and twos and then by battalions, those who wanted a live progressive policy were drawn into association with him.[1]

In 1924 this shifting of allegiance was an ill-defined, subterranean movement. But the presence of Muir and Masterman on the body which produced *Coal and Power*, and of Acland on the land committee, were suggestive of changes to come.

III

Lloyd George's decision to ignore the official Liberal machine, leaving it to get along as best it could, caused uneasiness throughout the party and dismay at its centre. His independent attitude on policy matters, and the continued existence of his own headquarters, made mock of the second Liberal honeymoon. And his determination " not to allow Mr. A's side of the organisation to get hold of any of the National Liberal funds "[2] publicly exposed the party's financial difficulties.

The situation regarding finance was simple. " The 'Wee Frees' ", as Mond had said in November 1923, " have no money " and Lloyd George had a lot. He had begun accumulating a political fund as soon as he became Prime Minister, drawing it from wealthy individuals who thought him essential for winning the war, or who looked to his government to resist " bolshevism " and " socialism ", or who wanted peerages and found that they could be obtained by a simple cash transaction. Whichever motive prompted them to give, they gave. The share of coalition funds which he took with him in 1922 ran into millions of pounds, though the precise number of millions was not revealed. Gladstone in 1924 referred to him as having " power to raise a million in cash ",[3] and some calculations put the total of cash and assets (like the shares in the *Daily Chronicle*) at three times that amount. This fund belonged to no party. It had been donated to Lloyd George for unspecified, though presumably political, purposes, and when he ceased to be Prime Minister it remained in his control. (Theoretically it was controlled by a

[1] *Nation*, 29 January 1927.   [2] see above, p. 281.   [3] see below, p. 283.

group of " trustees " ; but they were his nominees and he took
their assent for granted). This situation was less unusual than
it seems. Although the Liberal fund was a party and not a
personal fund, its disposal was at the sole discretion of the chief
whip appointed by the party leader. What by 1924 was
anomalous was that Lloyd George while not leader of a party
retained a large fund, and that the party to which he belonged
was almost without one.

It should be stressed that the poverty of the Liberal party in
the 1920s was a separate matter from the disposal of Lloyd
George's fund. That fund was a capital sum accumulated by a
defunct, non-Liberal government largely in a discredited manner,
and so offered no constructive solution to the problem of
financing the Liberal party. But the party had lost its known
source of income, and with another election so close at hand
could not despise Lloyd George's tainted money. In the past the
party had been largely financed by gifts from the wealthy.
Sometimes these contributors were candidates or the patrons of
candidates, and undertook to finance local associations and
election contests. Sometimes their gifts went direct to the
Liberal whip and so to the central chest ; and no more than with
Lloyd George were such gifts always disinterested. The sale
of honours had been a feature of pre-war politics under both
Liberal and Conservative regimes, and reputedly had done much
to keep the Liberal party solvent. After 1918 these sources of
income dried up. Constituency associations could no longer
employ the party's favourable electoral prospects to attract
wealthy individuals with parliamentary aspirations. As the
secretary of the Midland Liberal Federation, writing on behalf
of headquarters, told an impoverished association in 1925, it
had become " a very formidable thing " since the war to secure
candidates " because in dark times like these when there are so
few decent chances to offer a candidate it has become exceedingly
difficult to find men and women who are prepared to face a
contest and provide all the money."[1]   Nor could the Liberals
retail contingent honours, as the Conservatives had been doing
in 1914, in the expectation of their imminent return to power,
because the traffic in honours was discredited and the party
was too far from office. And events since 1914 had taken some

[1] W. Finnemore to A. Andrews, 5 September 1925, Asquith Papers.

of the wealthiest Liberals out of the party. They had gone into alliance with the Conservatives during the war and had stayed with them after it, thanks to the " failure of nerve " and the emergence of a Labour party disrespectful of the traditional leaders of " progressive " parties. Others had turned away owing to party dissensions after the war. A finance committee of one Liberal Federation reported in 1920 that " it was impossible at this special time to get new subscribers ", while another Federation referred in 1922 to " the loss of big subscriptions through death and by reason of the Coalition split ". Something of the problem of keeping a divided party solvent is revealed by a report of the former committee two months after the coalition's fall : " several good friends who had rendered valuable financial assistance were unwilling to subscribe any considerable sums as their contributions would depend on how the Federation faced the question of re-union. Some were strongly in favour of reunion others were not." That is, whatever the party did it was bound to lose financially.

Defections from the Liberals since 1914 had increased the number of wealthy people to whom the Conservatives could look for finance, and Labour was finding a hitherto untapped source of income in the trade union levy, that is in the small but numerous contributions of a mass of organised wage-earners. But the Liberals were losing their old source without finding a new one ; and a succession of three elections in five years had placed a considerable strain on the subscribers who remained. One wealthy Liberal pointed out during 1924 that he had contributed £22,000 over the past year, and did not feel he should be asked for more ; but to Liberal headquarters, the election which might be upon them at any moment was not going to cost less just because it came so soon after the last two. Meanwhile such reserves as headquarters possessed were being drained away. In 1922, after four years of preparation, it had raised in donations only £48,413 of the £126,948 it spent on the election. The remaining £78,535 was provided by the realisation of capital.[1] This meant that even by 1923 the party was hard-pressed. As it happened, the circumstances of the 1923 contest unloosed many purse-strings. Baldwin's threat to the established fiscal system brought in donations of £74,187 to Liberal head-

[1] Documents on election finance, Asquith Papers.

quarters. But even so it was Lloyd George's £90,000 which enabled the party to get through the election fairly comfortably.

By 1924 neither source of extra finance—i.e. contributors frightened by Baldwin, or the Lloyd George fund—was available. Baldwin had renounced protection and become again the leader of the " safe " party, and the Liberals had proved unsafe by putting Labour into office. Not only occasional contributors but some party stalwarts were outraged by this decision. Lloyd George wrote privately regarding Liberal support for Labour : " Quite a number of the ' important and influential ' emphatically dislike it".[1] And the *Manchester Guardian* reported on 8 January 1924 : " I have been told that eight prominent Liberals who are rather important as supporters of party finance have made a protest to the Liberal leaders against any action to support a Labour Government in office." These defections caused the Liberal leaders to turn with increased anxiety to Lloyd George. It was with consternation that they discovered that his fund was not available to the party.

IV

The Liberal leaders were soon regretting their failure to settle the fund question before the election. Gladstone late in December 1923 laid down the basis for a settlement : the funds of both sides should be pooled, but Lloyd George should keep a reserve from his fund for his own purposes.[2] Maclean went to Lloyd George in January 1924 with this proposal, and was turned down flat. Lloyd George would not pool his fund under any circumstances. At most he would make a periodic contribution to Asquith's headquarters, and this only if two of his associates were included among the administrators of the Liberal fund. The two whom he named, Guest and Sir William Edge, happened to be especially repugnant to orthodox Liberals. Maclean agreed that some of Lloyd George's associates—but not this pair—should join in administering the Liberal fund, but only if Lloyd George agreed to the pooling of resources. This produced

[1] Lloyd George to Scott, 26 December 1923, Lloyd George Papers.

[2] Much of the narrative that follows is based on documents in the Herbert Gladstone Papers. Gladstone was the director of Liberal headquarters from early 1922 to the end of 1924.

deadlock. Probably Maclean was not too sorry. His somewhat austere attitude on money matters extended to party funds. He had never been involved in selling honours, and in fact had three years earlier turned down an offer of £50,000 from someone anxious for an honour and prepared to take a long shot on the Liberals getting back into office. Consequently he viewed Lloyd George's fund with distaste. In his opinion, it would be much better if the party could get along without it.

Gladstone shared his view of the fund, but he knew that the party could not get along without it. In the circumstances of the 1924 Parliament, an election might occur at any moment and preparations should be proceeding apace. Yet without assistance from Lloyd George he could see no way of financing candidates. So he decided to drop the demand for pooling resources, and ask Lloyd George for a one-year contribution to Liberal headquarters and a lump sum for an election (of £20,000 and £100,000 respectively). This virtually conceded Lloyd George's position and as Lloyd George had now gone cool on Guest and Edge there seemed no obstacle to an arrangement. But when Maclean reopened negotiations on this basis in March, he learned differently. To begin with Lloyd George returned no answer to the new proposal. Then, when pressed, in April he intimated through one of his staff that he did not feel he was being sufficiently consulted about the affairs of the party. Until this was remedied, he declined to contribute. This complaint was difficult to pin down, seeing that he was invited to all meetings of the shadow cabinet and of the parliamentary party. However headquarters set about securing a greater measure of reconciliation between the Liberal wings in Wales and Scotland. Hoping that this would satisfy him, in July Maclean tried again.

But by mid-1924 the ground of Lloyd George's complaint had changed once more. Now he refused to contribute because of the alleged inefficiency of Liberal organisation. Until it was improved, he would not waste his money on it. Pressed at least to give something towards an election, he agreed to contribute £100,000 when an election came. But nothing would persuade him to put this in writing, or to make it so definite that the party could use it to obtain a bank credit. This reduced Gladstone to despair. He now calculated that, given the difficulty of obtaining funds elsewhere, he would need at least £130,000 from Lloyd George for an election. In the meantime, no further candidates requiring assistance from headquarters could be adopted.

Gladstone therefore decided to call in Asquith. He wrote him two letters : one setting out in formal terms the financial situation, which was designed to be sent on to Lloyd George, and the other urging him to intervene and suggesting ways he might go about it. In the course of the second letter he wrote :

I am telling people who ask for money for the purposes of candidatures that I can do nothing at present. Only one thing is possible—to get a business guarantee of sufficient help from L.G.

If we take a firm stand he cannot refuse to give what we reasonably ask. With power to raise a million in cash— given him presumably for political purposes—it is impossible for him to justify refusal in the open. He does refuse so far as we at Abingdon St. are concerned. He cannot refuse you & the party. I suggest to you 2 possible courses. You could send my official letter (enclosed) to L.G. & see him on the subject. I have drawn the letter with that in view. It is just a statement of facts.

Donald [Maclean] finally asked if he would guarantee £100,000. Now that figure is too limited & will make finance anxious. We might get through but it would leave us penniless & still at L.G.'s feet. I dont say that I would not accept it. This is the less difficult because my responsibility ends in any case with the Gen. El. But I dont like it to end under such conditions. Therefore I put the figure at £130,000 & we ought to get that. . . .

The alternative [course] would be to summon a meeting of the " pundits " including of course L.G. & to have it out in discussion. I dont believe he would face this. He could hardly face Donald & Hudson but he managed that. They could not exercise pressure.

If after my letter & at an interview he remains obdurate you could indicate the second course.

After all we are not asking for much of an advance for he did in a sort of a way agree to contribute. He can afford £130,000 easily. . . .

This is my fifth occasion of responsibility for Gen. El.

finance. I know exactly the position & do not exaggerate its difficulties.

I detest bothering you but it is sheer necessity.[1]

Stirred to action by this missive, Asquith sent Gladstone's formal letter to Lloyd George with a strong plea for assistance. Lloyd George replied on 20 August. He argued that : " When you and I settled the question of reunion . . . there was not a word about ' pooling resources.' " Nevertheless : " I could help, and am anxious to do so." But in his view the urgent problem was not funds, but organisation. Labour alone " has a machine fitted for the times " ; those of the Liberal and Conservative parties were quite unsuited to the new conditions. He went on :

I have deliberately made no enquiries as to the position of our fund. But I understand that the trustees are in a position to make an adequate contribution to the fighting funds of the party in the event of a fight. I do not however feel disposed to recommend them to do so till you & I have gone thoroughly into the question of reorganisation, with a view to bringing the machine up to date. Until that is done, I cannot feel confident that the money will be used to the best advantage.[2]

Gladstone commented on this :

I have just seen L.G's Memo. The position is as clear & no clearer than it was when I wrote.

He is quite wrong in thinking I am only on the defensive. We have been brought to a standstill for lack of funds. . . .

By all means let the question of organisation be gone into as fully as possible. I am not afraid of it. . . .

So far as I am concerned you know that I am in your hands. L.G. wishes to get most of us out of this office & there will be no difficulty so far as I am concerned![3]

But further considering the matter next day, Gladstone decided that Lloyd George might be weakening in his refusal to assist, and advised Asquith to act on a suggestion put forward by Lloyd George for a meeting of the two party leaders together with Mond and Maclean. This took place early in September.

[1] Gladstone to Asquith, 1 August 1924, Asquith Papers.
[2] Lloyd George to Asquith, 20 August 1924, Asquith Papers.
[3] Gladstone to Asquith, 27 August 1924, Asquith Papers.

Lloyd George discoursed once more on the inefficiency of the Liberal machine, and proposed that Mond should make an investigation into it. His choice of investigator was odd. Mond had striven for Liberal unity, and recognised that Lloyd George was impairing it by his attitude over funds. Further, he frankly did not think that Lloyd George knew anything about organisation. Consequently when he made his investigation and reported to Lloyd George, it was to stress the need for candidates in view of the imminence of an election. Lloyd George thereupon decided that he had not wanted an investigation by Mond alone, but by a committee under Mond. So Mond went ahead and set up a committee. On 25 September he wrote to tell Lloyd George of its appointment :

Organisation

I saw Donald Maclean yesterday, and had a long talk with him. We have arranged a Committee to deal with this subject, composed as follows :

Maclean, Stott [a prominent Manchester Liberal], Walter Runciman, Godfrey Collins and myself. I think that is a good Committee, after considering many names. . . . I have been going into the whole question, and I think I can see where the difficulties of the present lie. Those of organisation are not so difficult to deal with, but in all these matters personal questions may arise which are more difficult. We have arranged to meet next Tuesday, and to proceed vigorously to work, and I do not see why it should take long to make proposals or to put forward a sound scheme which can be immediately proceeded with.[1]

This letter was not calculated to please Lloyd George. Three of the five members of the committee were pronounced Asquithians.[2] And Mond did not appear to think the problems of reorganisation very imposing (" not so difficult "). Lloyd George's reply four days later doomed the committee from the start : " As to organisation, frankly, I do not think much of your Committee. You seem to have rigidly excluded every independent person

[1] Mond to Lloyd George, 25 September 1924, Lloyd George Papers.

[2] Collins had been elected as a coalition supporter in 1918, but in 1921 he had turned against Lloyd George and was thereafter a confirmed Asquithian.

who knows anything about our task in the country, with the exception of Stott. However, you can tell me later on what conclusions you have come to, and I shall judge accordingly whether I can recommend the Trustees to assist."[1] The last sentence of this letter deserves attention. The question at issue was whether Liberal headquarters was deserving of a contribution from Lloyd George's fund, which was theoretically controlled by trustees. Yet as dictated, this sentence read : "However, you can tell me later on what conclusions you have come to, and I shall judge accordingly." The concluding clause " whether I can recommend the Trustees to assist " was added as an afterthought by Lloyd George in his own hand.

Mond replied the following day, " hop[ing] the Committee will work out better than you expect " but not really meeting Lloyd George's objections : " We shall, of course, call in our experts in different directions, but I am anxious to get out a general scheme and deal with the personnel quickly, so that we can get ahead especially with fixing candidates. Elaborate details of re-organisation can be left to be dealt with when the principles are fixed."[2] This meant that Mond had gone over completely to the headquarters view that long-term questions of reorganisation must take second place to the desperate problem of preparing for an election. Lloyd George, on the other hand, was prepared to wait until " later on " before deciding to help towards an election. This was not because he doubted that a contest was at hand—" we might very well be in an election within the next few weeks ", he wrote to Mond at this time.[3] It was because he was prepared that the poverty of headquarters should be revealed in its starkest form : through the party's inability to finance an election.

This correspondence had taken events to the beginning of October. That is, negotiations had been proceeding throughout the entire life of the Labour government without any progress being made. Now the defeat of the government in Parliament was only days away. On 3 October Asquith wrote again to Lloyd George informing him that, in view of the imminence

[1] Lloyd George to Mond, 29 September 1924, Mond Papers.
[2] Mond to Lloyd George, 30 September 1924, Lloyd George Papers.
[3] see above p. 286. Mond was the recipient of two rather severe letters from Lloyd George on the same day.

of this event, the committee on organisation had decided unanimously that the party must immediately equip itself for an election, and appealing to him to assist. He suggested that if Lloyd George had any questions, Maclean should visit him the next day. This Maclean did, but it was all to no avail. What he received was not an offer of assistance but a violent attack on the committee investigating organisation, and a refusal to contribute under present conditions. When Maclean pointed out that the party needed £130,000 from him to run even 400 candidates, Lloyd George dismissed this number as unnecessary. 280 to 300 candidates would be enough. There the matter rested. Four days later the government was defeated in Parliament. Still Lloyd George did nothing. Howard later recounted that for two days " we sat at Abingdon St unable to promise a single new candidate financial help."[1] Then on 11 October, apparently as a result of an ultimatum from Mond, Lloyd George informed headquarters that he would contribute £50,000, but that was all. This was a long way from the £130,000 which Gladstone had considered the lowest satisfactory amount, and only half of the £100,000 which " would leave us penniless & still at L.G.'s feet."

What were Lloyd George's motives ? Maclean and his colleagues did not doubt that he possessed some deep and subtle purpose. To them his views about the number of candidates the party need run could mean only one thing : that he did not want the Liberals to aspire for office, and was laying plans for a new coalition resulting from a stalemate election. Yet all of Lloyd George's reasons for withholding his money, including that about candidates, look like rationalisations. He probably had no deep purpose : he just liked having the money. Someone described him in this respect as a typical Welsh peasant, who had got hold of some cash and did not want to part with it. He suffered from the delusion that as long as it was there, he remained free to go where he pleased—to seize any opportunity of changing parties that came along, or to launch the land campaign which he firmly believed would revolutionise British politics. That by clinging to his fund he might simply be injuring the Liberal party and bringing himself into disrepute probably did not occur to him. It was one of those simple

[1] Howard to Gladstone, 10 August 1925, Gladstone Papers.

calculations of cause and effect of which, in political matters, he rarely seemed capable.

V

The party's financial paralysis and patent disunity did much to destroy what little confidence it had left. The poverty of headquarters was seriously affecting the machine in the country : one federation, which was in financial difficulties after having its grant from Abingdon Street halved in 1923, was shaken to learn in July that headquarters could do nothing to assist. And the stultifying effect on election preparations was reflected in the experience of the Bolton Liberal association, which was informed by Howard on the eve of the dissolution " that no financial support could be given for the next Election."[1] Yet the existence of Lloyd George's vast resources was common knowledge. It was clear that money was there, but was not being made available : that reunion, in words Asquith was to employ two years later, was " a fiction, if not a farce." So even when at the last minute Lloyd George did make some money available, it helped little. " The discouragement," recalled Gladstone, " was general. Liberal associations which had vainly sought for candidates declined to fight. Candidates, who a few months before had been eager to stand, held aloof and gave excuses."[2]

[1] Minutes of the Bolton Liberal association, 7 October 1924.
[2] Communication to the press, 11 June 1926.

16. FIGHTING TO LOSE [1]

The Party decision of yesterday definitely makes an early Gen. El. probable.
As I am chiefly responsible for organisation I must put the exact position on
record.

Neither in candidates funds or organisation are we prepared at this moment
for an election.

Draft of a letter (marked " Not sent. I didnt wish to bother him ") from
Gladstone to Asquith, 5 October 1924 [2]

' If the Liberals are to fight this election as they should ",
warned the *Daily Chronicle* on 24 October 1924, " they should
clear right out of their own heads and everybody else's the idea
that theirs is in any sense a moribund party ". The Liberals
proved unable to do this. The evidence of moribundity faced
them on every side. They were unable to contest more than
346 seats, 110 less than the previous election and too few to
support the pretence that they were contending for office. They
suffered from what a prominent Manchester Liberal called (in
April 1925) " certain evidence of a disturbing nature which
suggested that Liberal unity was more apparent than real "[3]—
although what was most disturbing was that it seemed neither
real nor apparent. And most of all, after their experience of
Labour in office they simply did not know what role they
occupied in politics.

If anything was certain in their situation, it was the reverse
of their certainty of a year before : they would not keep Labour
in power after this election. As the *Manchester Guardian* said
on polling morning (29 October), the result of the contest was
clear. The experiment of a minority Labour government was
at an end, destroyed by Labour's own hand ; MacDonald had
made its continuation or immediate revival impossible. Accord-

---

[1] A. G. Gardiner in the *Nation*, 8 November 1924.
[2] Herbert Gladstone Papers.
[3] Minutes of the Manchester Liberal Federation, 3 April 1925.

ing to the *Nation* on 25 October, everyone was agreed that the
Liberals would have to turn the government out after the
election, and if necessary support a Conservative administration
And the Manchester radical Philip Oliver said that the Liberals
were obliged to defeat Labour on the Russian Treaty, but that
if the Conservatives took office and introduced protection, then
" out they go "[1]—that is, the Liberals would now maintain a
Conservative government on the same terms as earlier they had
supported a Labour. Yet it was less than a year since the
Liberal Magazine had claimed that " there are no conceivable
circumstances in which the Liberal Party could enter into a
coalition, alliance, partnership, understanding, or other collusive
arrangement of any kind or for any purpose, with the Conserva
tive Party."

In trying to explain this apparent change of front, the
Liberals spent the election condemning Labour. Their manifesto
blamed the election on the government's unwillingness to face
an inquiry into the Campbell case or a discussion of the " reck
less proposal " for a loan to Russia. It deplored Labour's
" halting, ineffective and unimaginative " efforts to deal with
social reform, and attacked the government's record in para
graphs headed " The Russian Blunder ", " The Government and
Unemployment ", and " Housing ". Pamphlets issued by
Liberal headquarters included " What is the Labour Party
Afraid Of ? ", " We Don't Want Socialism ", " The Labour
Party's Great Failure ", and " The Russians Want Your
Money." And even a radical like Geoffrey Mander, seeking to
capture Stourbridge from the Conservatives, spent most of his
election address attacking Labour. By contrast the Con
servatives were barely mentioned in Liberal propaganda. The
party manifesto never used the words " Conservative party "
at all, and failed to stress the free trade issue which had gained
Liberals so many Conservative seats ; and the speeches of the
party leaders were largely indulgent to the Conservatives. A
week before polling, the *Manchester Guardian* complained : " in
spite of Mr. Baldwin's nominal disclaimer, Protection is just
as much an issue at this election as it was at the last, and one
can only marvel at the totally inadequate importance assigned
to it in the manifestos and speeches of some of the shining light

[1] *Manchester Guardian*, 24 October 1924.

of Liberalism."[1] It may be doubted whether the best efforts of the Liberal leaders could have made free trade " just as much an issue at this election " as in 1923. When Noton Barclay, a Manchester Liberal, tried to raise it he was told by an interjector to " keep to the issue before the country." But it showed how their new-found antagonism to Labour had driven them towards the Conservatives that the Liberal leaders should just ignore the great question dividing them from the Tories. Liberals of the more impatient sort, said the *Manchester Guardian*, " might even detect in this misplaced reticence the beginnings of the blight of electoral compromises."

There were better grounds than this for detecting such a blight : for various reasons Liberals were suspected of electoral bargaining with the Conservatives. In fact, there was no nation-wide pact between the " anti-socialist " parties, despite persistent rumours to this effect. Liberal headquarters would have found it difficult to impose such a pact on their supporters, and the Conservatives were too eager to recapture seats lost to the Liberals to make a bargain with them. (Even a former Coalition Liberal like General Seely, who during 1924 had been relied on in Parliament more by the Conservatives than the Liberals, was subject to Conservative attack). But two things created the impression of an electoral bargain between Liberals and Conservatives : the absence of Liberal candidates in many Labour-held constituencies, and the electoral circumstances of the Liberal leaders. Regarding the first, the failure of Liberals to contest over 250 seats, including 36 which Labour had won in 1923 on minority votes, was principally caused by " a want of the sinews of war ". As some Liberals, like the London Liberal Federation, frankly admitted, financial stringency was preventing them from fighting several constituencies. An appeal by the Federation for an election fund of £15,000 had only brought in £3,214 by 23 October, five days after nominations had closed. But whereas some constituency associations lacking candidates announced that there was " no coalition ", others, as in Leigh, Wallsend, Frome, Chorley, Hamilton, and Rutherglen, publicly supported the Conservatives. In Leigh, which had been held by an Asquithian in 1918 but had since gone to Labour, the Liberals stated that they were standing aside " for patriotic

[1] *ibid*, 22 October 1924.

reasons " ; in Barrow and Hamilton (the latter " A Model Pact ") Liberals even signed the Conservatives' nomination papers.[1]

In these circumstances, it rested with the party leaders to confirm or dispel the notion that Liberals and Conservatives were acting in collusion. Maclean said at the beginning of the campaign that to defeat Labour's challenge to the Liberal party there should be as few three-cornered contests as possible—an obvious bid for electoral agreements with the Conservatives. And four of the party's most prominent figures—Asquith, Lloyd George, Simon, and Mond—were free from Conservative opposition in their constituencies. Simon alone said that he had made no agreement with the local Conservatives. Asquith, Lloyd George, and Mond all applauded the Conservatives' self-lessness in standing aside. (Lloyd George in his first election speech on 14 October had spoken scathingly of Labour's conduct and said : " That is the way they have treated our support, and, so far as I am concerned, they shall have no more of it.") For Lloyd George this behaviour was not remarkable : though he had abandoned the Centre party position, it was always possible that he would return to it. But what is to be said of Asquith ? His conduct looked like a renunciation of everything he had uttered about party relations since the war.

The first thing to be said is that the events of the past year had left him with no firm ground of party relations on which to stand ; the second thing, that given his desperate personal position he scarcely had time to worry about the niceties of political consistency. For the moment he was hardly Liberal leader at all. He was the candidate for Paisley, rendered panic-stricken by the imminence of defeat. The Paisley Labour party, divided in 1923, was now united, and its candidate, Rosslyn Mitchell, had earned in his Liberal days the title of " the pocket Rosebery ". Only if Asquith polled the full Conservative vote of the previous election was he likely to survive this challenge.

At the opening of the campaign Conservative headquarters in Scotland decided not to oppose him and persuaded his prospective opponent, Colonel Shaw, to stand elsewhere. But the Paisley Conservatives resented this action, and many seemed

[1] *Glasgow Herald,* 23 October 1924 ; *Manchester Guardian,* 13 and 14 October 1924.

likely to abstain. To bring them to the polls, Asquith needed
to court them assiduously. Hence he was to be found welcoming
prominent Conservatives to his platform, including his Tory
opponent in the famous by-election of 1920, and endorsing
electoral pacts against Labour. In a speech of 20 October, he
said that personally he had had nothing to do with arrangements
in his or other constituencies for the withdrawal of candidates,
Liberal or Conservative, " whose competition with one another
might have confused the issue, given to the Socialists a wholly
delusory advantage, and in some cases enabled them through
a minority of the electors to capture a seat to which, on democratic principles, they had no title." He made this appeal to the
Paisley Conservatives :

> Such an arrangement was made here in Paisley, and I
> gratefully acknowledge the wholehearted loyalty with which
> it was entered into by Colonel McInnes Shaw, whom I have
> found a doughty as well as a fair-minded antagonist, and
> whose withdrawal—I am sure we can enter entirely into
> their feelings, because we can put ourselves in their places—
> must have been a cause of deep disappointment both to the
> leaders and the enthusiastic rank and file of his own party.

He went on to make his most quoted statement of the election :
" Both the old political parties in this election have found
themselves, as they believe, confronted with a common danger,
which without any loss of identity or compromises of principle
on one side or upon the other, they are making reciprocal
sacrifices to avert."

Asquith's choice of phrase was unfortunate. The expression
" common danger " was quickly transmuted into " common
enemy ". This was an expression which Lloyd George had
employed in 1923 (allegedly in regard to Labour), and according
to Asquith it had proved him unfit to return to the Liberal fold.
How long, asked Snowden, was it since Asquith had told them
that Liberal and Labour were agreed on nine-tenths of their
programme ? He was sorry to find the Liberal leader calling
Labour " the common enemy ". One expected such things of
Lloyd George, but Asquith ! And from within the Liberal camp
Asquith's conduct aroused considerable criticism. The Manchester Liberals offered as their last campaign slogan : " Toryism Still the Enemy." MacCallum Scott sent a message of

support to all Scottish Labour candidates not opposed by Liberals, stating that " in order to save his own seat in Paisley Mr. Asquith has entered into a compact with the Tories to facilitate a Tory majority in this election ".[1] And the *Manchester Guardian* reported on the morrow of defeat that numbers of the keenest Liberals felt strongly about their leaders' failure to stand up to Conservatism. " Many of the best of Liberal fighters are bitterly asking themselves whether Liberal leaders whose own hopes of election rest upon charitable contributions of Tory votes can ever be anything but dumb dogs in the day of trial."[2]

Yet if Asquith made the worst of a bad situation, and revealed a leaning towards the Conservatives which had sometimes been suspected but which he had always denied, it was still true that political incoherence was the only course open to him. The Manchester Liberals might argue that " Toryism " was " Still the Enemy ", but they admitted that, if left holding the balance, they would put the Tories into office. In these circumstances there was simply no logical position left to the party, as MacCallum Scott admitted by defecting to Labour. It was not only " conservative " Liberals who felt they must direct their fire against Labour. The *Nation*, four days before polling, asked " Should Liberals vote Tory ? ", and decided that it could not condemn electoral pacts : the alignment of Conservatives and Liberals against Labour was a logical reaction against proposals like the Russian loan and the tactics which Labour had pursued. The whole course of the Labour government, it claimed, had been directed towards destroying the Liberal party. Nothing could be more healthy for British politics than that these tactics should bring disaster, and while it was not desirable that the Conservatives should gain an absolute majority it was to be hoped that they would capture as many seats as possible from Labour. The reconciliation of Liberals and Labour could only come when it had been shown that Labour's attempt to destroy the Liberal party was doomed to failure.

This then was the condition to which events since 1923 had reduced the Liberals. The *Nation* was driven to welcome pacts between Conservatives and Liberals, and the loss of Labour seats to the Tories, as opening the way to a Liberal-Labour rapproche-

[1] *Glasgow Herald*, 24 October 1924.　[2] *Manchester Guardian*, 31 October 1924.

ment—for as it said a fortnight later: " If there is to be any future for the Liberal party, it can only be as a party of the Left ".[1] Perhaps there was no inconsistency in such a position, but it certainly seemed inconsistent. To all appearances the Liberals had executed a right-about-turn since the last election, when the Conservatives had been their principal target and Asquith would not lift a finger to keep Baldwin in office.

II

The 1924 election wiped out the Liberal gains of a year before. The Conservatives won the contest by a landslide, securing 415 seats as against 258 in 1923. Labour fell from 191 to 152. But the real sufferers were the Liberals. In 1923 they had won 158 seats. This time they secured only 43, holding 34, gaining nine, and losing 124. Their proportion of the total vote fell heavily. In 39 constituencies fought by just Liberals and Conservatives in 1923 and 1924, their share of the poll fell by nearly 9%— from 51·0 to 42·3. In triangular contests they did even worse. In 126 constituencies fought by Liberal, Conservative, and Labour candidates in 1923 and 1924, their share of votes fell by over 10%—from 34·7 to 24·0. These figures probably exaggerate the actual defection of Liberal voters, for one feature of the election was the large increase in the number of people going to the polls. The circumstances which caused these previous abstainers to vote militated against their voting for the Liberals.

What had happened ? Had the Liberals suffered an irreversible disaster, or been overwhelmed by temporary difficulties ? There were reasons for believing the latter, and for saying that they had been downright unlucky : that they were victims of a transitory wave of anti-Bolshevik hysteria engendered by the Russian loan and the Zinoviev letter. In addition, they had been harmed by temporary domestic difficulties : lack of funds and candidates, internal dissensions, inept leadership (" Both our leaders talked Russia all the time "[2]), and the want of a bold

---

[1] *Nation*, 8 November 1924. The *Nation* at this time was edited by H. D. Henderson, with J. M. Keynes a frequent contributor. It had passed out of Massingham's hands in May 1923.

[2] *Manchester Guardian*, 5 November 1924.

and distinctive programme. Many candidates felt that the Zinoviev letter, appearing just four days before polling, had itself made the difference between success and failure, by bringing out the " frightened vote ". In London it was noticed on polling day that people were hastening to vote at an early hour, including some who had never voted before and others for whom it was a physical hardship to get to the polls, and this was recognised as foreshadowing a Conservative victory. Other Liberals saw the dismal state of their organisation and programme as contributing to the party's setback. One who did so was Lloyd George. The 1924 election, he wrote soon afterwards, could not have been theirs in any circumstances. They had been obliged to resist pernicious proposals menacing Britain's security, and the electorate had chosen the traditional party of resistance. The turn of Liberalism would come when the country felt the need for a move forward. But the party would have to prepare itself by renewing its organisation (which was " heart-breaking to those who were privileged to have a glimpse at its working ") and putting forward a clear programme. " Let Liberalism clarify its message and renovate its broadcasting machinery, and the future is with it."[1]

No doubt the Liberals did lose some seats, as in Devon and Cornwall, because of transitory factors like the Zinoviev letter. But it is unlikely that these accounted for more than a dozen, or perhaps a score, of their losses. The really heavy setback resulted from more deep-seated causes. Lloyd George in writing as he did assumed that the 150-odd seats won by Liberals in 1923 represented normality, and that what needed to be explained were the abnormal losses of 1924. There was, he had argued after the 1923 election, a distinct radical majority in the country. Bonar Law's success in 1922 on a programme of tranquillity had been fortuitous, secured by minority members on a minority of votes. The nation had " intended " to give a clear majority for progressive measures, and in 1923 it had given this verdict " in more unmistakable terms ", condemning protection and socialism but demanding

---

[1] *Daily Chronicle*, 1 November 1924. Before the election Lloyd George had considered both the Conservative and Liberal machines archaic. He could not revive this point as regards the Conservatives in view of the results of the election.

reform and reconstruction.[1] Was this really the case ? It has
been shown that many former Conservative supporters went
Liberal in 1923 so as to defend the *status quo*, and that Liberal
gains in the commercial districts of Lancashire, the agricultural
regions of southern England, and a variety of watering-places
and holiday resorts, did not necessarily constitute a demand
for " reform and reconstruction " at all. Consequently the
bizarre circumstances of the 1924 contest were not needed to
deprive the Liberals of many of these seats. The fact that the
Liberals had put Labour into office was bound to injure them.
The Liberal who in 1923 had won Altrincham, " a well-to-do
Manchester suburb in Cheshire ", had soon found himself
receiving indignant letters from constituents, saying that had
they known they were assisting in the formation of a Labour
government they would never have voted for him.[2] And even
had there been no Labour government, the fact that the Conservatives had " returned to normal " was probably sufficient
to rob the Liberals of many of these constituencies.

Moreover, many Liberal gains in 1923 had occurred in the
absence of Labour candidates. In that it was settled Labour
policy to contest every constituency as soon as possible, even
at the cost of Conservative victories, the Liberals held some
of these seats after 1923 in transitory circumstances. In
1924 Labour contested 51 Liberal seats which it had not fought
in 1923, and the Liberals lost 46 of them (all but one to Conservatives). In the circumstances of this election the Conservatives secured 24 of these on majority votes. Yet in less
favourable conditions they would probably have captured just
as many, only they would have done so more often owing to
Labour's intervention.

Thus the Liberals stood to suffer heavily in any election after
1923 : first from the loss of constituencies which they had
acquired fortuitously from the Conservatives, and secondly from
the intervention of Labour candidates. Moreover, they stood
to lose also from the continuing movement of Liberal voters to
Labour. The peculiar circumstances of the 1924 contest, in
letting loose a wave of anti-bolshevism, were as harmful to
Labour as to the Liberals. Yet in spite of this, Labour improved

[1] *ibid*, 5 January 1924.
[2] *Manchester Guardian*, 8 December 1923 and 15 January 1924.

its situation in many constituencies, particularly working-class constituencies. Often it did so at the expense of Liberals. Labour captured sixteen seats from the Liberals, and the Communists one seat, and only in five of these was Conservative intervention a contributory factor. The pact in Paisley, which had cost Asquith so dear in reputation, did not even keep him in Parliament: the Labour vote was up five thousand on the combined Labour polls of 1923. Another only slightly less distinguished victim of this attack was Hogge, who lost Edinburgh East to the first Labour candidate to contest it. And it was noteworthy that in nine of the twelve constituencies lost to Labour in three-cornered contests, the Liberals came bottom of the poll.

Even in seats lost to Conservatives, the Liberals sometimes suffered from defections to Labour. In constituencies like Bootle, North West Camberwell, Cardiff East, Hackney Central, Portsmouth Central, and Stalybridge and Hyde, Liberals from being sitting members found themselves not even challengers; and altogether in 23 seats lost to Conservatives they came third on the poll. This defection of voters to Labour in circumstances supposedly injurious to " progressive " parties, coupled with the withdrawal of former Liberal M.P.s like R. D. Denman and MacCallum Scott, was not the result of accidental events. It was part of a profound movement of allegiance which had been in progress since 1914, and which the Liberals were proving unable to stem.

III

This election showed the Liberal party incapable, at least for the moment, of winning English constituencies unaided. Of the 43 Liberals elected, one was the Speaker and three were university members, and these may be set aside. Of the remaining 39, nearly half (eighteen all told) were returned for Scotland and Wales, mostly in agricultural districts. At least in the Scottish highlands and non-industrial Wales, Liberalism was still capable of winning seats by itself. (By contrast, of the five seats won in industrial Wales and Scotland, four were gained with Conservative assistance). But in England there was no district where Liberalism remained dominant. The party won 21 English constituencies. Not one of these was agricultural in nature, which meant that in all of them Labour was a potential threat; and in fifteen of the 21, Liberals won in the absence of Conservative candidates. That left six constituencies in England where an outstanding candidate, or a combination of candidate and Liberal tradition, enabled the party to survive without Conservative aid. One of them was Central Hull, where Kenworthy's personal position was so strong that he possessed Labour support. (When in 1926 he transferred to Labour and fought a by-election, he won by a handsome majority and the Liberal lost his deposit). The others were Devonport, Middlesbrough West, and Wolverhampton East, where Leslie Hore-Belisha, Trevelyan Thomson, and George Thorne respectively had established considerable personal followings; and two divisions of working-class London (Lambeth and Bethnal Green) where Percy Harris and Frank Briant retained much working-class support. These half-dozen holdings, three of them won by majorities of under 600, were too scattered to provide any basis for a Liberal recovery.

These results had a marked effect on the personnel of the parliamentary party. Whereas the 1923 election had reduced the former Coalition Liberal section and increased the number of Independent Liberals, 1924 told against the followers of Asquith far more than against those of Lloyd George. Of the 83 seats captured in 1923, most of them by Asquithians, 79 were lost in 1924. And of the 44 seats which had returned Independent Liberals in 1922 and had remained Liberal in 1923, 31 were lost in 1924. Coalition Liberal losses were less severe. Of the 31 seats which had returned Coalition Liberals in 1922 and had remained Liberal in 1923, only fourteen were lost in 1924. And of the nine seats captured by Liberals, eight were gained from Labour (the other was from an Independent), and these victors over Labour were usually not Asquithian in sympathy.[1] This meant that a majority of the survivors were Lloyd George's personal followers. 21 of the 43 were former Coalition Liberal

[1] Major H. E. Crawfurd, who captured West Walthamstow from Labour in a straight fight, and Runciman, who captured Swansea West from Labour in a triangular contest, were exceptions. This was Runciman's first success since his defeat in 1918.

M.P.s or candidates, and some half-dozen others, like Hore-Belisha and John Duckworth, were closely connected with Lloyd George. The election, in short, had destroyed the parliamentary Liberal party as an effective force, had removed Asquith from its ranks, and had placed what remained of it at Lloyd George's feet.

PART FIVE

The Search for a Solution

1925 - 1935

17. ASQUITH AND LLOYD GEORGE: THE LAST PHASE

Who would have believed that in a controversy between these two statesmen Mr. Lloyd George would be triumphantly and unmistakably in the right?

'*Nation*', *29 May 1926*

THE years 1925 and 1926 witnessed the last stage in the struggle between Asquith (removed to the Upper House as Lord Oxford) and Lloyd George. In the end, Lloyd George triumphed utterly. Asquith relinquished the party leadership and his supporters were driven from control of the Liberal machine. Lloyd George became the party's outstanding figure, laying down its policy, paying its bills, and reviving its fighting spirit.

Perhaps this would not have happened but for the dismal state of the party. Asquith's attempts to restore Liberalism during his last years as leader seemed to show that, at least under his direction, it was past restoration. His first action was to appoint a committee under Maclean to find out what was wrong and suggest ways of putting it right. This committee met Liberal organisations throughout the country, hearing complaints and gathering suggestions. (Its efforts to penetrate into Wales, however, were rebuffed by Lloyd George. Maclean was told that matters of Welsh organisation could best be discussed by those acquainted with the country " among themselves "). The committee found Liberals outspoken in demanding " real reunion ", by which they meant removing " the impression that there still exist two offices in Abingdon Street and two separate funds ",[1] and in calling for a full complement of candidates at the next election. How unity and candidates were to be achieved was not made clear. But two concrete proposals did

---

[1] Press cuttings in the Minutes of the Lancashire, Cheshire, and North Western Liberal Federation, 21 November 1924.

emerge. First, the chief administrative body of the party ceased to be the autocratic Liberal Central Association, under the control of the chief whip. It became a new Administrative Committee, representative in nature because consisting largely of the N.L.F. executive which was elected by the rank and file. Secondly, an appeal was launched for a million pounds (the Million Fund), to be raised mainly in the constituencies through small contributions. This was to provide finance for both the local associations and headquarters ; and the central part of the fund was to be controlled, not by the Liberal Central Association, but by a committee appointed by the new administrative body.

Precisely how these new directing committees were related to the party leader was not made clear. In the past the leader had clearly controlled headquarters because he appointed the chief whip. Now, it seemed, Asquith was agreeing to a reduction in the leader's authority and a measure of democracy in party administration. This was the product of sheer necessity. For one thing, the old headquarters had no money and little prospect of raising any under the old system. So it was not too much of a sacrifice to hand over fund-raising to a more representative body. Further, Asquith's position as leader had become quite anomalous. Even though there was no move to displace him, a majority of Liberal M.P.s were not his supporters. They were adherents of Lloyd George. So for once the authority of the Liberal leader did not derive from the parliamentary party. To make good this deficiency, Asquith had to look to Liberals in the country to provide the support he no longer possessed in Parliament.

The change in party organisation, and the appeal for a million pounds, were launched at a great Liberal convention in January 1925, attended by delegates from throughout the country. Yet this scheme to rejuvenate Liberalism by calling forth the energies of the rank and file only showed in the long run how feeble the party was becoming in the constituencies. In May 1925 a finance committee of the Scottish Liberal Federation, referring to the difficulty in getting new subscribers, attributed this to " the want of interest in Liberal Organisation in about two-thirds of the constituencies in Scotland."[1] At the same time

[1] Minutes of the Eastern Finance Committee, Scottish Liberal Federation, 7 May 1925.

the secretary of the Midland Liberal Federation was telling headquarters that the problem of maintaining agents in the constituencies was " becoming very acute in this area. Our agents are going & by & bye we shall be left pretty naked for anything like concerted work."[1] And Lloyd George, after eighteen months of conducting his land campaign, had some telling things to say about the state of Liberal organisation in rural areas : " Whatever the decay of agriculture might have been, it was nothing to that which had fallen upon the Liberal organisations in a very large number of constituencies throughout the country. In many cases there was no organisation. In some the organisation was purely nominal, and in only too few cases was there a live vigorous association . . . . the propaganda conducted by the Land and Nation League represented in the great majority of county constituencies the only effort put forward to educate the electorate in Liberal principles."[2]

One sign of the atrophy which had overtaken constituency organisations was inability to secure candidates. This was of great symbolic importance to Liberals. The belief was widespread that failure to contest seats had gravely injured their cause in 1924, and the convention of January 1925 resolved that 500 candidates must be put forward next time. Yet in its annual report for May 1926 the Yorkshire Liberal Federation had to state : " A circular letter has been issued to our Constituency Associations urging the importance of an early choice of a prospective candidate. So far the response to this appeal has been small . . . .with regard to 54 Constituencies we have sitting members in 5 and adopted Candidates in 11. This is a matter which calls for prompt and serious consideration." A year later the matter had become " even more urgent." The number of prospective candidates had fallen to seven, and one sitting member (Kenworthy) had defected to Labour.[3] Nor was Yorkshire alone in its difficulties. Late in 1925 the Lancashire and Cheshire Federation was trying to raise a Fighting Fund of £10,000 in three years, for fear that otherwise many constituencies would be without candidates for the next election. And in September 1927 the best that the Scottish Federation

---

[1] W. Finnemore to R. H. Davies, 30 July 1925, Asquith Papers.

[2] Speech at the National Liberal Club on 5 April 1927.

[3] Annual reports in the Minutes of the Yorkshire Liberal Federation.

could say about candidates was " that while they were not being adopted as fast as we would like we were slowly adding."[1]

But the most evident failure of these years lay in the field of finance. In the past, headquarters had received sufficient income to run itself and aid needy constituencies—quite apart from assisting candidates at elections. But the purpose of the Million Fund was to shift the burden of both local and central expenses on to the constituency associations : it was hoped that they would not only become self-sufficient but would keep headquarters solvent. (According to the *Liberal Magazine*, it would rest on their " honour " and " party comradeship " " to bear their fair share of the cost of central activities "[2]). Yet only in its local aspect was there a partial success. H. F. Oldman, the N.L.F. secretary, wrote from Liberal headquarters in September 1925 :

> The Million Fund is progressing very well indeed in so far as the local efforts are concerned, Associations are raising more money than ever they have done before, and the psychological effect of obtaining a large number of local subscribers is as valuable as the financial, if not more so, and in this way the Million Fund will do a great deal to lift the Liberal Party into its proper place in national politics. Necessity has thrown the financial burden on to the local Associations, but I think events will prove that nothing has been more useful in the work of reviving the Party.[3]

But it is likely that this letter, which was written to explain why headquarters had no money, gives too rosy a picture for some constituencies. In 1927 the financial situation of the active Manchester Liberal Federation was " extremely serious. For the last three years there had been an annual deficit of £1200." [4] And when Phillipps, chairman of the body which was raising the Million Fund, sent Sir Charles Hobhouse a cheque for £75 as a loan (" through you ") to the Chippenham Liberal association, he issued this warning :

As I explained to you in a previous talk which we had on

[1] Minutes of the Eastern Organising Committee, Scottish Liberal Federation, 30 September 1927.

[2] *Liberal Magazine*, February 1925.

[3] Oldman to W. Finnemore, 30 September 1925, Asquith Papers.

[4] Minutes of the Manchester Liberal Federation, 2 November 1927.

the matter, we have had to make a rigid rule against giving grants of any kind [i.e. to constituency associations], and it is very important that there should be no sign of any deviation from this rule. The present case is put to me by you as one for exceptional treatment, and I understand that the loan will be repaid by the end of the year, and that if the Association fails to raise sufficient money for this purpose, you will make yourself personally responsible for repayment.

You will appreciate that care must be taken to avoid any impression that H.Q. is ready to make loans to constituencies. We shall have an avalanche of borrowers if this idea gets about.[1]

If the Million Fund appeal had not made all constituencies self-supporting (" We shall have an avalanche of borrowers ") it had failed even more in its second aspect, to provide money for headquarters. According to Oldman in the letter quoted above, it had made matters rather worse : " The success of the local part of the Fund and the concentrating of the energies of the local Associations on their own finances has had the inevitable result of diminishing the flow of contributions to Headquarters Funds ". One consequence was that " it really is impossible to make any financial contribution to local Associations for organisation purposes, even where exceptional circumstances exist." This was written with respect to an impoverished association whose agent, on whom organised Liberalism in the district depended, had received no salary for eight months. " It is constituencies such as this that we must look to in the future," wrote Oldman, " and this makes it all the harder to have to refuse their very reasonable request." Another letter from headquarters regarding this association admitted that " they have a real claim, but, apart from the grave unwisdom of breaking our rule, we really have no money from which we could give them any help."[2] Eventually, after five months of negotiations, headquarters decided to contribute £75 of the £200 owing to the agent, but to send it to the secretary of the Midland Liberal Federation " on the understanding " that he " devises some plan by which the constituency shall not know

[1] Phillipps to Hobhouse, 28 July 1926, Asquith Papers.
[2] Phillipps to Maclean, 1 October 1925, Asquith Papers.

the source from which the money comes."[1] It was not only needy associations which felt the pinch of headquarters poverty. The district federations, which were supposed " to act as the agent and intermediary between Liberal headquarters and the Liberal Associations ", and so expected " substantial financial grants from Abingdon Street "[2], saw these grants dwindle to nothing. The Lancashire and Cheshire Federation, which had been dismayed when its grant was halved (to £550) in 1923, learned two years later that thereafter it would receive nothing at all.

By the end of 1925 the attempt to restore Liberal finances through an appeal to the ordinary supporter had foundered. Headquarters by then was so hard-pressed that in December it resorted to the historic course of approaching directly the rich men in the party. But now, to Asquith's great distaste, it was he and not the chief whip who had to make the appeal. His effort was not in vain. Some £25,000 was raised, enough to enable headquarters to carry on for a while longer. But the long-term problem had not been solved. Ten months later, in a statement which brings out plainly the party's desperate financial situation, Asquith recounted :

I was driven myself last December to the humiliating task of making a personal appeal to the better-to-do among our followers to come to the rescue, and provide us with a wholly independent fund of adequate amount. Many generous contributions were made, but the fact remains that at this moment our Central Office is faced in the near future with the certainty of serious and perhaps fatal financial stress, in relief of which it is idle, in the present condition of the Party, to expect that a repetition of last year's appeal or any other expedient, would meet with a substantial response.[3]

[1] Unsigned letter, probably from Phillipps, to Howard, 12 October 1925, Asquith Papers.

[2] Minutes of the Lancashire, Cheshire, and North-Western Liberal Federation (report of a special committee on finance), 3 October 1924.

[3] Memorandum by Asquith, 6 October 1926, Spender Papers.

II

Yet the stricken party was not without resources, of men or enthusiasm. In the hopeless situation of 1924, with only 346 candidates, it had polled three million votes. It retained a number of constituency organisations which were active and dedicated. And it suffered from no lack of able, sometimes outstanding, thinkers on social and economic questions : pre-war radicals like Acland, the post-war Manchester group, economists of the first rank like J. M. Keynes, H. D. Henderson, and Walter Layton, and devoted young Liberals like Elliott Dodds and Kingsley Griffith. The annual gatherings of the Liberal Summer School left no doubt of the party's intellectual resources.

But the Summer School was a sounding-board for ideas, not a means of channelling them into political action. Here was the party's deficiency at every point : what resources it possessed— in the constituencies, the press, and bodies like the Young Liberals and the Summer School—were disorganised and fragmented. Its prospects of revival were hamstrung by its deficiency at the top : the lack of a driving, consolidating central force to make the most of such life and vitality as existed. The Liberal decline did not make the problem of leadership less urgent, but more. Perhaps there was no way out. But certainly there was none as long as the party continued to be oppressed by the inadequacy of its leader, and by the fierce struggle which Lloyd George was waging to replace him.

III

Lloyd George's first step towards dominance in the Liberal ranks was taken in December 1924, when he secured election as chairman of the parliamentary party. The post of chairman had been created by Asquith in 1919, following his first defeat, and in effect he had chosen Maclean to fill it (although the Independent Liberal M.P.s had endorsed his choice). Maclean had continued as chairman even after Asquith's re-election in 1920, and Simon had occupied the post during 1923. But after the 1923 election it had lapsed. With Asquith again defeated in

1924, it was necessary to revive it. This time, however, he was in no position to appoint its occupant. Admittedly he did, " in his capacity as Leader of the Party ",[1] nominate the whips, but even here he exercised caution. Whereas the chief whip, Godfrey Collins, was manifestly his nominee, the assistant whip, Sir Robert Hutchison, was clearly selected (if not appointed) by Lloyd George. Further than this Asquith could not go. Had he tried to appoint the chairman, the parliamentary party might have repudiated his action. Anyway, without causing an open breach, how could he select anyone but Lloyd George ?

Lloyd George was determined to have this post, and summoned support from as far away as America. Fisher, engaged in a lecture tour of the United States, received an urgent appeal to attend. " Just before lunch ", he recounted, ". . . there descended a bomb shell in the shape of a wire from L G demanding or asking [sic] my immediate return in order to be present at the Liberal Party meeting on Dec 1 when the question of the Chairmanship of the Liberal party will come up. This supported by another wire from Hilton [Young] & McCurdy. I suppose they want me to support L G against Simon."[2] Fisher had no wish to cut short a tour which was financially important to him, and sought to delay his return. But two days later he received an " urgent cable from L G urging return in time for the Liberal party meeting on Dec 2 ",[3] and accordingly he cancelled his programme and set sail for England.

Meanwhile a number of Asquithians were seeking to block Lloyd George's election. Pringle, who had lost his seat, summoned the numerous defeated Liberals in London to a meeting, at which was founded the " Liberal and Radical Candidates, Association " consisting of candidates in the 1923 and 1924 elections and any who should be adopted thereafter. Pringle demanded for this body a say in choosing the parliamentary chairman. But no precedent could be found for such a body participating in the affairs of Liberal M.P.s, and Asquith would not support him. This left the last line of resistance to the Asquithian remnant in Parliament. Wedgwood Benn announced publicly that he could not acknowledge Lloyd George as his

[1] *Liberal Magazine*, January 1925.
[2] Draft letter from Fisher to his wife, 17 November 1924, Fisher Papers.
[3] Fisher's diary, 19 November 1924, Fisher Papers.

parliamentary leader, and attributed to him the party's defeat.
" The people have no confidence, and rightly so, in Mr. Lloyd
George."[1] And when the parliamentary party met on 2 December, Runciman (whom Fisher earlier in the day had found
" rather icy "[2]) argued that no chairman should be appointed
and that Collins, as whip, should summon their meetings.

This resistance was overborne by weight of numbers. The
outcome of what Fisher called " a prickly little party meeting "
was that Lloyd George was elected chairman by twenty-six
votes to seven, with seven abstentions. But nine of the M.P.s
who had not supported him promptly formed themselves into a
" Radical Group " under Runciman. Although remaining within
the parliamentary party, they intended to have as little to do
with Lloyd George as possible. When on 8 December he summoned a party meeting to consider the King's Speech, only
eight M.P.s turned up, with Collins " the only Wee Free "
among them.[3] (Collins as whip had not joined the Radical
Group). And on subsequent occasions when the chairmanship
came up for election the " Radicals " persisted in voting against
Lloyd George.

These events restored the evident division among Liberal
M.P.s which had existed in the first post-war parliament. The
" Radicals " deserved their name not so much because of their
" advanced " views on social policy (most of them did hold such
views, but some, like Runciman and H. E. Crawfurd, did not)
but because they were prepared to oppose Baldwin's regime.
According to Runciman, their " distinctive characteristic "
was that " they were not embarrassed by compromise in any
direction, either right or left. . . . They had gone into the
House of Commons in spite of their opponents, not by their
goodwill, and that gave them a degree of freedom which was
not enjoyed by some other people. In the House of Commons
they would take a pronouncedly Radical line, regarding Tories
equally with Socialists as their political foes."[4] Kenworthy,
another member of the group, said that they must show " that
true Liberals have finished with all ideas of pacts, Coalitions and
Centre Parties. Also that we are not a party for the sole purpose

[1] *Manchester Guardian*, 15 November 1924.
[2] Fisher's diary, 2 December 1924, Fisher Papers.
[3] *ibid*, 8 December 1924.   [4] *Liberal Magazine*, January 1925.

of fighting ' Labour '." They should " work for the overthrow of the Conservative Government at the earliest possible moment."[1] These views placed the group in direct descent from the Wee Frees of five years before ; and in fact all its members had been Independent Liberal M.P.s or candidates between 1918 and 1922.

The existence of the group detracted from Lloyd George's success in securing the party chairmanship. Particularly was this so because, apart from himself, the " Radicals " provided most of the fighting spirit in the parliamentary party. As Runciman's jibe implied, most of Lloyd George's supporters had been elected with Conservative aid and would not offer regular opposition to the government. Even their attachment to Lloyd George was shaky. They were drawn to him by past allegiance. " It is he that has made us," Masterman pictured them as saying, " and not we ourselves."[2] But they were quite out of sympathy with his " flaming and tearing propaganda " in favour of land reform, and his " incorrigible predilection for wild-cat, half-baked measures."[3] So to avoid embarrassment they generally stayed away from Parliament altogether ; " this kind ", observed Masterman, " cometh not forth but by prayer and fasting." Their conduct caused Liberals much discomfort during the next four years. In 1928 one newspaper, in an editorial entitled " Unworthy Liberals ", confessed that : " Whenever the Labour and Conservative parties desire to foul the Liberal reputation they can do so most effectively by bringing out the story of how the forty Liberal M.P.s have behaved during the last four years—' a few vote one way ; a few vote another way ; most of them don't vote at all.' " This journal endorsed some bitter criticisms made by Muir : " they have laid us open to charges it is difficult to meet."[4]

For Lloyd George this situation created a particular difficulty. Not only was he embarrassed by the actions of his followers, but he usually found himself speaking in Parliament with the Liberal benches all but deserted, and with the Liberals who

[1] *ibid.*

[2] *Nation*, 26 December 1925. Masterman was at this time the *Nation's* parliamentary correspondent.

[3] *ibid*, 28 November and 5 December 1925.

[4] *Bolton Evening News*, 1 November 1928.

were in their places generally those least sympathetic to him.

IV

Lloyd George had achieved little by becoming chairman of the parliamentary party. He still had to win recognition by the party in the country.

His prescription for doing so was the same as in 1924, with his position enhanced by Asquith's relegation to the Upper House and the failure of the Million Fund. He would allow the official party machine to collapse in poverty, and attain the chief position by force of personality allied to a daring programme. That he succeeded was evidence of the party's hopeless position and Asquith's mismanagement as much as of his own qualities. Granted that he remained " without question the greatest ' draw ' among politicians ",[1] his political instinct was not infallible. He could not appreciate the distaste caused by his decision to hold on to a large political fund when the party he belonged to was frantic for money—conduct particularly injudicious for a man already tarnished by the Marconi and honours scandals. And though he proposed to give the party an up-to-date, forward-looking programme, what he offered seemed rather old-fashioned and irrelevant. His action in appointing a committee to produce a daring policy on land, and his determination to propagate this policy whatever his colleagues might think, were not really novel. He had been doing the same thing in 1912. Then he had appointed a committee of ardent land reformers to draw up a programme, and Grey had reported that " Lloyd George is prepared to leave the Cabinet and go out and preach the gospel of land reform on his own." As a consequence a manifesto " deprecat[ing] a strenuous land campaign at the present moment " was drawn up by a number of Liberal M.P.s who said that they did not intend to follow blindfold the proposals which might suddenly be announced by any particular member of the government.[2] His conduct in the mid-'20s simply repeated this pattern. And its effect on the party was even more disturbing. Predictably

[1] *Manchester Guardian*, 27 July 1927.

[2] A. C. Murray's diary, 19 July, 3 September, and 21 November 1912, Elibank Papers.

he aroused the opposition of orthodox thinkers, like Mond
and Hilton Young among his own followers, and Runciman and
R. D. Holt among Asquith's. But they were not his only critics
Radical economists like Keynes and H. D. Henderson simply
could not take seriously his belief that reform of the land system
held the key to a national economic revival.

Indeed during 1925 Lloyd George got into very deep water
through his decision both to launch a land campaign and to
make no contribution to party funds. The land scheme was
not published until October, but a first draft had been sprung
on the party during the general election. Both its contents
and the manner of its appearance had aroused much criticism
So when the report of the " Land Inquiry Committee " finally
appeared (in the form of a book called *Land and the Nation*,
known from its cover as the Green Book) there was immediate
opposition, especially to the proposal for ending private
ownership of agricultural land and converting farmers into
" cultivating tenants " supervised by county committees.
This increased to a storm of protest when it was announced
in October that Lloyd George had founded a new body, the
Land and Nation League, with himself as president, to carry
on a nation-wide campaign in support of the Green Book. Many
Liberal associations and candidates voiced their opposition
But the strongest protest came from headquarters, in the person
of Phillipps.

Phillipps was director of the Million Fund appeal, and he
attributed its failure to Lloyd George. Money, he believed,
was not forthcoming because Liberals thought headquarters
could draw on Lloyd George's fund. Repeatedly he had urged
Lloyd George to contribute. In mid-1925 Lloyd George did say
that he would give £20,000 a year for the next three years, but
only if the party formally adopted his land policy. Phillipps
could not accept such terms, and urged him to modify them
Eventually Lloyd George agreed that as long as the party leaders
were willing to summon a convention of Liberals to decide on
the policy, he would hand over the first £20,000. This the
shadow cabinet agreed to do, and arrangements for the convention were put in train. Phillipps therefore asked Lloyd

[1] *Land and the Nation* dealt with rural land. There was also an urban report
Towns and the Land, but this excited little controversy.

George for the initial £20,000. He received a flat refusal. Lloyd George repudiated all knowledge of the agreement in this form, and declined to contribute anything unless and until the convention accepted his land policy. Simultaneously he launched the Land and Nation League, devoting to it, reputedly, £80,000 from his fund, and arranging to hold five thousand meetings before the date of the convention. (He had earlier agreed, under pressure, not to conduct public propaganda until after the convention had met). This was too much for Phillipps. In a speech at Hull on 20 November he told all.

There was an impression in some minds, Phillipps said, that Liberal headquarters could have recourse to Lloyd George's fund. This was not so. Admittedly Lloyd George had contributed to the cost of the last two elections, " but there had been no unity of funds and no pooling of resources." It was a private fund, and Liberal headquarters had no sort of control over it. Quite recently, he continued, Lloyd George had intimated to him " that he did not feel that he could make a contribution from his fund to the work of Liberal headquarters until he knew what would be the result of the forthcoming conference on the proposals of the Land Inquiry Committee." Phillipps hoped that the decision of that conference " would be wholly uninfluenced by any considerations of pecuniary advantage to the Liberal Party. Liberalism must be free and independent or it was not worth working for." He believed that there were hundreds of thousands of Liberals " who would deny themselves for that ideal."

Even Asquith, while continuing to strive for party peace, felt bound to back Phillipps up. When he appealed for money to a group of rich Liberals, as related earlier, it was specifically to free the party from dependence on Lloyd George. He also wrote to the chairmen of the district federations expressing the " considered view that it should be made clear and public that the Liberal Million Fighting Fund is the only one available for the Liberal party, and that, whatever may be the financial needs of the party, it cannot receive help from any fund, contributions from which might be conditional on the limitation or restriction of its complete independence in matters of public policy."[1] And in private he wrote what must have been one of his sternest

[1] *Manchester Guardian*, 27 January 1926.

letters to Lloyd George, deploring the launching of the Land and
Nation League. He had, he said, just received a deputation
from the executive of the N.L.F.

As you know, the Executive had accepted the invitation
which, with your cordial concurrence, I addressed to them
more than a month ago to arrange for the summoning of a
representative Liberal Conference, at which the Land
Policy of the Party was to be the subject of full and
free discussion. They have been much concerned to learn
that a new organisation has, in the meantime, been started
under your auspices for the public propaganda on a large
scale of the proposals set out in the Report of the Land
Committee.

I have not shown myself unsympathetic to the work of
that Committee. In the only public reference which I have
made to the subject, I expressed warm admiration for the
thoroughness and ability with which they had conducted
their inquiry. . . .

I raised no objection to your suggestion that, in the
meantime, the Committee should be free to carry on the
work of explaining their specific proposals to the Executives
and members of Liberal Associations throughout the
country. This was to be done, as I understood, in friendly
conferences and at meetings between Liberals where there
would be a free interchange of views. . . .

There can be no doubt that at present there are wide
divisions of opinion among Liberals on the proposals of the
Committee. I receive myself frequent, almost daily, communications from stalwart and hard-working members both
of our local Executives and of our rank and file, many of
them men of advanced Progressive views, expressing
their own doubts and difficulties, and deprecating, at this
stage anything in the nature of propaganda, either on the
one side or the other. . . .

As the Leader of the Party, I feel it my duty, with all
good will, to deprecate anything that would damp down
or dissipate, still more anything that would divide, our
united energies.

It would in my opinion be a very serious matter if at this
stage there were any conflict, or appearance of conflict,

between the National Liberal Federation and the new organisation proposed for promoting the views of the Land Enquiry Committee.[1]

To all appearances Lloyd George remained unmoved. On 2 December 1925 the N.L.F. executive took advantage of negotiations between himself and the Candidates' Association over land policy to state that advocacy of his original land proposals " will necessarily be suspended." The Land and Nation League promptly issued a fierce rejoinder calling this statement " premature, inaccurate, and wholly misleading." Yet the fact that negotiations were going on suggested that Lloyd George realised he had gone too far. The strong opposition from Liberal organisations in the country, the hostility shown by his own supporters in Parliament, and the decision of Liberal headquarters to bring the conflict over funds and policy into the open, caused him to back-pedal. The months from December 1925 to February 1926 found him at his most conciliatory. In the course of discussions with the Candidates' Association in December he agreed to a major alteration in his policy : cultivating tenure, instead of being introduced for all agricultural land simultaneously, was to be established gradually, as land came on to the market or was proved to be badly administered. At the Land Convention in February 1926 he gave away even more (" Mr. Lloyd George has conceded much, very much, in the interest of party unity "[2]). Cultivating tenure, instead of becoming the normal form of agricultural land-holding, was to be only one of several forms. With these alterations the most disturbing feature of his proposals, which had caused them to be dubbed " land nationalisation ", largely disappeared, and the controversy in the party came to a close. Whether he lost much by these changes is doubtful, because it is unlikely that any land policy at this time would have proved an electoral winner. Certainly his campaign for the revised proposals, although supported by a high-powered organisation and thousands of meetings, never aroused much interest.

Where had this controversy got Lloyd George ? He had lost

[1] Asquith to Lloyd George, 21 November 1925, Asquith Papers.

[2] *Manchester Guardian*, 20 February 1926. All was not amity at the convention, however. Pringle made a sharp remark to Hore-Belisha, whereupon Hore-Belisha (in full view of the convention) slapped Pringle's face.

colleagues like Mond and Hilton Young, who marched off to the Conservatives in protest at his socialist tendencies. And he had aroused adverse comment from Liberals at many levels. Yet from his point of view it was not all loss. During negotiations over his policy, his " broadminded and reasonable spirit "[1] had gained him much respect in the Candidates' Association, " the most representative of all organised Liberal bodies outside the N.L.F."[2], and at the convention. Some who had come to the latter, like Sir Charles Hobhouse, to oppose his policy declared themselves " vastly satisfied " by the outcome. Further, Lloyd George had shown that, alone among Liberal leaders, he was concerned about party policy and could secure action on the matter. From February 1926, the Liberal land policy was the amended version of the policy he had instigated ; and it fell to Phillipps, rather inappropriately, to request Liberal federations to form committees which would co-operate with the Land and Nation League in propagating it.

Apparently, then, if the party was ever to have a vigorous, adventurous programme, he was the person who would get it adopted. This point was not lost, for example, on leading members of the Summer School. When they decided to institute a thorough-going inquiry into British industry, as the basis for an industrial programme, they turned to Lloyd George for support. Nor did they turn in vain. He promptly offered to finance the inquiry from his fund, and to serve on it himself as an ordinary member. The question of an industrial policy was one on which many Liberals felt strongly. They deplored Asquith's failure to advocate the industrial programme adopted by the party after much agitation in 1921. At the annual meeting of the N.L.F. in 1925, an amendment calling for the propagation of this policy was carried unanimously, after its mover had condemned their leaders' failure to show any interest in the question. So by his display of energy on policy matters, Lloyd George was establishing new ties with the active forces in the party. He was doing so, as it happened, just when he needed support most—at the moment when his struggle with Asquith erupted into an open conflict.

[1] *Liberal Magazine*, March 1926.
[2] *Manchester Guardian Weekly*, 11 December 1925.

V

In October 1926, with his leadership of the Liberal party almost run, Asquith gave this account of Liberal reunion :

We have now for nearly three years been trying the experiment of " Liberal Reunion ". There is not one of us that does not know that in practice it has turned out to be a fiction, if not a farce. The control of the Party has throughout been divided between two separate authorities : the Liberal Central Office and Mr. Lloyd George's rival machine—the former very scantily, and the latter very richly, endowed. Things came very nearly to a crisis a year ago when the " Land Policy " as embodied in the Green Book was let loose, and followed up by an intensive and expensive propaganda. I insisted upon its being submitted to a representative Conference before it was incorporated in the Party programme. Prolonged negotiations between Sir Donald Maclean and Mr. Phillipps on the one side, and Mr. Lloyd George on the other, showed that he regarded his accumulated fund as at his own disposal, to be given to, or withheld from, the Central Office of the Party, as a dole, upon such conditions as he thought fit to impose. . . .

Under such conditions, to talk of Liberal Unity as a thing which either has been, or has any fair prospect of being, achieved, seems to me to be an abuse of language.[1]

Had Asquith chosen to break with Lloyd George over these questions of policy and money, he might have taken a large section of Liberals with him. But when the breach came in May 1926, it was not over these matters. It concerned a difference of policy regarding the general strike. Asquith, Grey, and others supported the government in demanding uncon-ditional abandonment of the strike, whereas Lloyd George (like several church leaders) favoured negotiations. He also demanded criticism of the government, which he considered " equally, if not more, responsible " for the outbreak of the struggle.[2] This caused him to take umbrage at some of Asquith's

[1] Memorandum by Asquith, 6 October 1926, Spender Papers.
[2] *Liberal Magazine*, July 1926, contains all the principal documents in this quarrel between Asquith and Lloyd George.

statements, and on 10 May he wrote to the chief whip declining to attend a meeting of the shadow cabinet but stating the grounds of his difference.[1] Asquith wrote the next day that Lloyd George " was in the sulks, and had cast in his lot for the moment with the clericals—Archbishops and Deans and the whole company of the various Churches (a hopeless lot)— in the hope of getting a foot-hold for himself in the Labour camp. He is already, being a creature of uncertain temperament, suffering from cold feet. So much so, that I have a message this morning from Miss Stevenson [Lloyd George's private secretary] asking me to arrange for a joint meeting in July at Carnarvon, which he and I are to address ! "[2]

In the next few days Asquith's attitude hardened. When he met some of his closest colleagues on the 18th he proved to be, according to Hudson, " *far more* indignant at L G's behaviour than I have ever seen him. . . . The note of the gathering was H H A's indignation."[3] As for the other members present, from the start they had seen Lloyd George's action as constituting a breach. They argued that Asquith should write to him stating that his patience was exhausted. Asquith did this on the 20th. " I never thought he would come right up to it," Maclean commented, " but he has."[4]   In his letter Asquith sharply rebuked Lloyd George for absenting himself from the shadow cabinet on " wholly inadequate " grounds. Such conduct " I find impossible to reconcile with my conception of the obligations of political comradeship." Asquith did not stop there. Without awaiting a reply, he sent the letter to the press, thus converting a private difference into a public breach. " I don't suppose ", commented Laski, " that since the Russell-Palmerston row over Louis Napoleon, one distinguished statesman has ever so written to another."[5]

What were Asquith's grounds for taking such a step ? Clearly he was horrified by the general strike, and considered it outrageous that Lloyd George should stop short of full condemna-

[1] The Liberal shadow cabinet was chosen by the Liberal leader. It consisted of prominent Liberals whom he invited to join it.
[2] *H.II.A. Letters of the Earl of Oxford and Asquith to a Friend*, Second Series, p. 171.
[3] Hudson to Gladstone, 18 May 1926, Herbert Gladstone Papers.
[4] Maclean to Gladstone, 20 May 1926, Herbert Gladstone Papers.
[5] *Holmes-Laski Letters*, vol. 2, p. 843.

tion. But equally clearly he regarded Lloyd George's conduct as only one in a series of outrageous actions. Nearly all the Liberals who urged him on 18 May to break with Lloyd George had pressed him to do so six months before, when Lloyd George was trying to railroad the party into accepting his land programme and was even prepared to use his fund for the purpose. Asquith had come very near to rejecting him then. Now Lloyd George had defied him once too often. But, from Asquith's point of view, it was to prove a considerable misfortune that the general strike should have acted as the last straw. For it raised quite different issues from the earlier causes of dispute, and proved a much less effective ground for rallying support.

Asquith's precipitate action sent a shock of dismay through the party. In the upper levels he possessed many allies, including, as he wrote, " all my respectable and capable colleagues ", " all the people I care for ".[1] Gladstone published a fierce attack on Lloyd George for his behaviour over funds. And twelve members of the shadow cabinet (including Grey, Simon, Runciman, Maclean, Phillipps, Pringle, and Collins) weighed in with a condemnation of Lloyd George which concluded that " confidential relations are impossible with one whose instability destroys confidence." But this was not enough. The excommunication of Lloyd George required the support of the party in the country. There was no likelihood that it would be endorsed by the parliamentary party. However unhappy some supporters of Lloyd George might be about his recent actions, they would always back him in a personal confrontation with Asquith. If Asquith had any right to remain Liberal leader, it was because he possessed the allegiance of the party outside parliament. And at this moment the rank and file would not go along with him. They were prepared to express their confidence in him as leader—sometimes, as at the Women's National Liberal Federation, in moving fashion. But they would not take the necessary step of anathematising Lloyd George. Bodies like the Yorkshire Federation and the Lancashire and Cheshire Federation, which possessed much sympathy for Asquith, held anguished meetings about the " difficulties in the party " but decided to pass no resolution. The Scottish executive did express their unabated

[1] *H.H.A. Letters of the Earl of Oxford and Asquith to a Friend*, Second Series, pp. 173 and 176.

confidence in him and their opposition to separate organisations and funds. But this resolution also expressed their desire to co-operate with all Liberals in pressing forward a vigorous social and industrial policy (which was rather a hit at Asquith). And their chairman said that the resolution " contained nothing that could hurt or offend anyone "[1]—not the attitude Asquith was demanding towards Lloyd George. Some organisations went so far as to criticise their leader. The London Liberal Candidates Association sent him (privately) a resolution " view[ing] with profound dismay any intention to exclude Mr. Lloyd George from the Councils of the Liberal Party."[2]

But the real rebuff came with Asquith's failure to persuade either the N.L.F. annual meeting or the Candidates' Association to condemn Lloyd George. The former represented the rank and file. The latter, in addition to being " the liveliest body in the party ",[3] was a semi-parliamentary institution, and this gave it great prestige. Many of its members were ex-M.P.s ; and Liberals looked to it as the parliamentary party of the future possessing all the qualities which were lacking in the present group of " unworthy " M.P.s. Neither of these bodies was prepared to endorse their leader's action. The N.L.F. meeting did pass a strong resolution of confidence in Asquith, who was absent owing to illness. But it also expressed an earnest desire " to retain the co-operation of all Liberals in pressing forward a vigorous and constructive policy of social and industrial reform." This was no rejection of Lloyd George (to whom, delegates were told, the resolution had been shown beforehand). Further when he appeared at the conference he received a rousing reception, many delegates rising and singing " For he's a jolly good fellow." The more prominent Asquithians, who " were not among the vocalists ", left the conference soon after in disgust.[4]

Worse still for Asquith was the decision of the Candidates Association. The chairman and secretary of this body, Pringle and Harcourt Johnstone, both detested Lloyd George. They had

[1] Minutes of the executive of the Scottish Liberal Federation, 29 June 1926.
[2] H. L. Nathan and H. Heathcote Williams to Asquith, 3 June 1926 Asquith Papers.
[3] *Manchester Guardian*, 23 September 1926.
[4] *Manchester Guardian* and *The Times*, 18 and 19 June 1926.

publicly endorsed a tale which was going the rounds that during the general strike Lloyd George had met three Labour leaders at Snowden's house and had offered to transfer himself and his fund to their party. With this story in currency, the meeting of the Candidates' Association was an event of high drama. Lloyd George was not present at the outset, but he sent a message offering to attend if it was necessary to rebut accusations against himself. His presence being requested, he appeared and demolished in fine style the story of his overtures to Labour. He produced both a watertight alibi for the day in question and a letter of support from Snowden, whose word was accepted on such occasions. The Association thereupon resolved to send a delegation to Asquith asking him to restore complete unity in the party under his leadership. Asquith, of course, could do nothing of the sort. He had said that he would not " continue to hold the leadership for a day " unless the party upheld his rejection of Lloyd George, and this the party had refused to do. A serious breakdown in health kept him off the political scene from June to September. But when he returned in October 1926, it was to announce his resignation as Liberal leader.

VI

There were many reasons why in this crisis the party failed to support Asquith. It must be said that his shortcomings as leader were never better exemplified than when he chose this occasion for a breach with Lloyd George. To all appearances it was the latter, for once, who was being badly treated. He had been given no warning that an attack was coming, and no opportunity, by explanation, conciliation, or apology, to keep the peace. The party too, it seemed, was being badly treated. Without warning or consultation, it was being asked to condemn a prominent individual for differing from his leader on a policy matter and for staying away from the shadow cabinet. Such condemnation lay quite outside the party's traditions. Liberals had always shown the greatest latitude to members who differed from official policy, even when it had been laid down by a party conference ; and on this matter no conference had spoken. As Laski wrote, " I never thought I should live to sympathise with the latter [Lloyd George], but here I think that Asquith has made a profound mistake by trying to set up standards of party orthodoxy to which no man can possibly be asked to conform."[1]

These considerations would have applied even if, on the issue between them, Asquith clearly had occupied a liberal position and Lloyd George a non-liberal. But no such clarity existed. It was possible to take two views of their differences : either that no real issue of principle separated them ; or that a real issue did separate them because Asquith stood for unconditional surrender and Lloyd George for negotiation. Lloyd George adopted both views. In his temperate, measured reply to Asquith (largely written by C. P. Scott[2]) on 24 May, he said that he did not know what they were quarrelling about: " if there is to be another schism in the party, one would like to know what it is about. Is it on a question of policy ? If so what ? " But he did stress that he had taken a stand for conciliation : " In both the Boer War and the Great War the Liberal Party disavowed the policy of refusing to announce terms or to engage in parleys for peace until there had first been an unconditional surrender. On both occasions that attitude was regarded as a Die-Hard policy."

Now from either standpoint, Asquith's position was insecure. If there was no serious divergence, why his denunciation of Lloyd George ? And if there was such a divergence, by what standard was he the better Liberal ? Before the publication of Asquith's letter, the *Nation* had committed itself to Lloyd George's side. His behaviour during the general strike, it said, was " the clearest proof that he has given that he is actuated once again by the generous impulses of Liberalism." He had not, it admitted, got his emphasis right. " But he said the things which it was especially the duty of Liberals to say ". And the Liberal journalist S. K. Ratcliffe (Kappa in the *Nation*) compared Lloyd George's " courageous wisdom " during the strike with the behaviour of Simon ; Lloyd George had " withstood more than some others the infection of the passion of war."[3] So if Lloyd George was to be ostracised for his attitude during the

[1] *Holmes-Laski Letters*, vol. 2, p. 843.

[2] Lloyd George had drafted a fierce rejoinder to Asquith, but he showed it to Scott who made short work of it and produced the dignified reply which was in fact dispatched.

[3] *Nation*, 22 May 1926.

strike, what was to happen to these other Liberals who had taken up the same position ?

Asquith had not only attacked Lloyd George on bad grounds. He had attacked on what for him was the most dangerous ground of all : the ground of right versus left, of whig against radical. Since Lloyd George had returned to the party he had justified his unco-operative attitude by arguing that Asquith and his associates were hidebound and unadventurous ; and this charge Asquith had greatly resented. Yet his action now seemed to confirm it. During the 1924 election he had injured his reputation immeasurably by flying panic-stricken into the arms of the Conservatives. Yet at this very next crisis he had done the same thing. He called the general strike " a war against society ", " the gravest domestic danger which has threatened the country in our time." (Had he really forgotten the behaviour of the Conservative leaders in the pre-war Irish crisis ?) So to him Baldwin's government became " for the moment the embodiment and organ of the national self-defence ". Such statements seemed to confirm, despite all his denials, Lloyd George's charge that in his heart he was at one with the Conservatives.

Certainly many radicals took this view. What, asked Muir, was the ultimate cause of antipathy to Lloyd George ? It was a genuine fear of his radicalism among negative-minded men, who were well known for the things they disliked—Lloyd George, land reform, Toryism, protection, the Labour party, and socialism—but not known for the things they loved. Was one of them connected with any contribution to constructive Liberal thought ? He admitted to certain misgivings about Lloyd George, and did not intend to be bound to his chariot-wheels. But if forced to choose between Lloyd George, who was alive and eager and really bent on working for a better Britain, and a group of men who had shown no interest in constructive work, his choice could not be in doubt.[1]

Had Asquith been able to appeal to a record of vigorous leadership, or offer his party any prospect of revival, he might have surmounted this crisis. But the party was weak, penniless, defeated, and without prospect of restoration ; and he was asking it to condemn the only leader who possessed ideas,

[1] *ibid*, 29 January 1927.

vigour, and money, and who was not afraid in the hour of danger to say unorthodox and unpopular things. Not only to the active spirits who fretted under his " splendid negations ", but to many who revered him as a representative of the great Liberal age, such action seemed unwarranted.

So, sixteen months before his death in February 1928, Asquith withdrew from the political scene. Some words of Laski's provide a suitable summing-up : " Asquith has had terrible faults, and very limited horizons ; but I know no man in our public life more loyal or more generous. He has been lazy and self-indulgent and indecisive, but no one has ever lost anything by trusting him and he has never been charged with deception."[1]

---

[1] *Holmes-Laski Letters*, vol. 2, p. 885.

18. FIGHTING TO WIN

[A]t the general election, whenever it may come, a Liberal majority is not impossible, and a formidable Liberal party in Parliament is almost assured.

'*Manchester Guardian*', *2 June 1927*

THE retirement of Asquith did not end Liberal quarrels. A painful struggle ensued for control of the party machine. Yet in time there emerged a sort of peace, and even a sort of hope. A conciliator, in the person of Sir Herbert Samuel, became head of the party machine. An arresting programme was derived from the report of the industrial inquiry. And Lloyd George contributed his finance, his eloquence, and his wealth of experience. Thus equipped, the party girded up its loins to slay the beast of unemployment and ascend once more the throne of office.

First of all, however, it was necessary to unravel the tangle left by Asquith's resignation. The evident division in the party had not been closed. On the one side Lloyd George was still chairman of the parliamentary party. And in November 1926 one of his supporters, Sir Robert Hutchison, was elected chief whip by Liberal M.P.s. (Godfrey Collins, whom Asquith had appointed whip, resigned his post soon after Asquith gave up the leadership). Automatically Hutchison became chairman of one section of the party organisation : the Liberal Central Association. But the other section, controlling the Million Fund, was directed by one of Lloyd George's enemies. In January 1925 the party machine had been reorganised : an Administrative Committee (largely the N.L.F. executive) had been set up to manage party funds, and this committee had appointed a small Organisation Committee to direct day-to-day affairs. The chairman of the latter body was Phillipps—one of the twelve who had signed the letter forswearing further relations with Lloyd George. What then was the relationship between the section of the party under Lloyd George's control and that which Phillipps directed ?

Lloyd George decided to find out. He used his fund for the purpose. He offered a substantial sum of money to the hard-pressed Administrative Committee. To begin with he proposed that he should meet the cost of running candidates in rural constituencies, while leaving Liberal associations free to choose whichever candidates they pleased. Then, during negotiations, he went further. He agreed to finance all 500 candidates for the next election, and also to help towards the cost of running headquarters. For this purpose he began by offering the income from his fund, but this proved insufficient. So he sold his holdings in the *Daily Chronicle* (for, it was rumoured, at least two million pounds) and agreed to hand over a lump sum of £300,000 for the next election, as well as granting headquarters £35,000 per annum for the next three years.[1] But his offer was not unconditional. He stipulated that the Organisation Committee, which would actually control the money, should have a " neutral " chairman (i.e. someone other than Phillipps) and a personnel " acceptable to all interests ". It was difficult for the Administrative Committee to concede these terms as the price of getting his money. Lloyd George, realising this, withdrew his stipulations during negotiations. But it was recognised that the withdrawal was only formal. No one doubted that if he gave the party his money, he would not allow his avowed enemies to have the spending of it.[2]

It took the Administrative Committee three months, from 20 October 1926 to 19 January 1927, to decide whether to accept this offer. First it appointed a sub-committee, headed by Sir Charles Hobhouse, to negotiate with Colonel Tweed, the chief of Lloyd George's organisation. Then it asked the sub-committee to negotiate directly with Lloyd George. Then finally it decided to meet Lloyd George itself. (All this took place in a blaze of publicity : a report by Hobhouse's committee, which was submitted on 17 November and marked " Secret ", appeared

[1] Part of the £35,000 came from interest on the £300,000, which was invested until the election.

[2] Lloyd George in fact blundered in ever laying down conditions. Phillipps from the start realised that if the party accepted a grant from the Lloyd George fund his own position as head of the party organisation would be impossible. (Memorandum by Phillipps, 28 September 1926, Herbert Gladstone Papers).

in the press the following day). The party's dilemma was indeed painful. If it accepted Lloyd George's money, it laid itself open to the charge of having been" bought ". Yet it needed cash badly. The already-serious financial situation had deteriorated alarmingly since Asquith's " famous letter of June ", and " large subscribers " in particular were holding back.[1] How could the party machine carry on, let alone secure 500 candidates for the next election ? Phillipps certainly did not know ; in September 1926 he was writing that before long it might be necessary to close down Liberal headquarters.[2] Anyway, had not the party really made its choice already ? It had refused to support Asquith against Lloyd George, for reasons not primarily financial. Having done so, why refuse assistance from Lloyd George's fund ? And if this meant removing Phillipps, did not the responsibility lie with him for signing a denunciation of Lloyd George which the Administrative Committee did not endorse ? So on 19 January 1927, after a protracted meeting and a " pretty sharp debate "[3], the Administrative Committee decided by seventeen votes to eight (with several abstentions) to accept Lloyd George's offer. It also decided, although by a smaller majority, to make a change in the Organisation Committee. Phillipps had withstood strong pressure to resign voluntarily, so he and the rest of his committee were asked to surrender their posts. (Theoretically they remained eligible for re-appointment by the new Administrative Committee about to be elected).

This decision caused a crop of resignations. Sir Robert Hudson and R. H. Davies withdrew from the Liberal Central Association, which each of them had served for over thirty years ; and Grey and Violet Bonham Carter ceased to act as directors of the Million Fund. This did not end their protest. They founded a new body called the Liberal Council, headed by Grey and supported by distinguished Liberals like Phillipps, Runciman, Maclean, Pringle, Collins, Gladstone, Spender, A. G. Gardiner, and Gilbert Murray. The Council was not a new

[1] Minutes of the executive, Scottish Liberal Federation, 24 February 1927. Asquith's letter of denunciation to Lloyd George was written in May 1926, but he followed it in June with a letter to Collins further condemning Lloyd George.

[2] Memorandum by Phillipps, 22 September 1926, Herbert Gladstone Papers.

[3] *Manchester Guardian*, 20 January 1927.

" party ". It did not challenge the authority of the N.L.F., or oppose official Liberal candidates who followed Lloyd George. But it sought to rally Liberals who opposed both him and the decision to take his money. And it provided constituency associations of like viewpoint with a supply of speakers, literature, and candidates.

The history of this Council was not to prove very distinguished. It helped to give colour to Lloyd George's claim that what had kept the party divided since 1923 was not just personalities or rivalry for the leadership, but a difference in ideology. However right-wing his followers in Parliament, in the country his main support came from Liberals who wanted the party to turn left. The Liberal Council did not share this wish. It spoke for Gladstonian orthodoxy—as befitted a body including R. D. Holt, J. M. Robertson, and Leif Jones. In home affairs it devoted its energies to only two causes : free trade, and retrenchment in government spending. These it defended against all comers. It condemned Baldwin for deviating (ever so slightly) from free trade, and it denounced with equal vigour Lloyd George's ally H. D. Henderson for questioning the efficacy of retrenchment. As a *Manchester Guardian* correspondent put it :

In a way this [economy] campaign is critical of the campaign of social reform with which Mr. Lloyd George's name is associated. It is as if the Liberal Council had taken the individualist line, if one may use that old word, as against the quasi-Socialist line of Mr. Lloyd George's expert advisers.[1]

Could these old shades of the Gladstone era, to which the Council adhered so rigidly, really breathe new life into the decrepit body of Liberalism ? There were a good many Liberals hostile to Lloyd George who doubted it. (Baldwin, after all, was neither attacking free trade directly nor flinging the public's money about). To these Liberals, only two courses lay open. Either, like Wedgwood Benn, they could break with the Liberal party and go over to Labour—Benn's defection in February 1927 was a severe blow to the radicals in parliament. Or, like Elliott Dodds, they could allow distrust of Lloyd George to be outweighed by sympathy for the new thought and daring programme he was offering. However distasteful they might

[1] *ibid*, 11 October 1927.

find him personally, it seemed better to follow him along radical paths than to attach themselves to the staid leadership and stale doctrine of the Liberal Council.

II

This course was made easier for Liberals by the appointment, in February 1927, of Samuel as head of the party organisation. When Lloyd George, in trying to unseat Phillipps, had urged the appointment of a "neutral" chairman, it had seemed that no such person existed. But Samuel filled the bill. He had been absent from Liberal quarrels since 1918, serving with distinction as High Commissioner to the new mandate of Palestine. After leaving that post in 1925 he had gone to Italy to study philosophy. But Baldwin had persuaded him to return to England to grapple with the problems of the coal industry. (He had produced an excellent scheme for coal, but no scheme for stirring Baldwin into action). Soon afterwards he had helped to persuade the T.U.C. to call off the general strike. Hence he was on hand, unoccupied, and highly regarded as a conciliator, just when the Liberal party needed him most. He could hardly refuse its plea to assist.

Samuel's appointment as Phillipps's successor was the first gleam of hope that Liberal troubles might be abating. As a happy augury, he was offered the post unanimously by the Administrative Committee, which retained a considerable Asquithian minority. And he made it clear that in directing the party machine, spending its recently-acquired funds, and helping to select candidates, he would be answerable to no one but this committee—which meant not to Lloyd George. (Samuel's writ, however, did not run in Wales, where the local organisation remained under Lloyd George's control and would brook no interference from headquarters). Typical of the party's enthusiastic response to the new management is this comment from the Yorkshire Liberal Federation's annual report :

The year that has seen [Asquith's] loss has seen the return to active Liberalism of a great administrator. The new Organisation Committee, under Sir Herbert Samuel, was not formed without difficulties. Under his chairmanship it has created a rallying centre round which all men and women who desired to serve Liberalism could form.[1]

Nor did Samuel act only as a peace-maker. As a " great administrator ", he was able to carry through the reorganisation in the country which Lloyd George's money had made possible. By this time many constituency associations were derelict or impoverished. In the past headquarters had come to their rescue with grants of money, but now the need was too great. If Lloyd George, in the words of critics, had put the party back on the gold standard, there had been a limit to his largesse. So it was decided to strengthen the district federations, equipping them for the task of rejuvenating constituency organisations. Since 1925 the federations had received no help from head-quarters. Their only assistance, ironically, had come from Lloyd George's Land and Nation League : a grant of between £50 and £200 and the use of a campaign van. Under the new dispensation they each received about £1800 per annum to cover the salaries and travelling expenses of a full-time staff of four. Three of these employees were to work mainly in the constituencies, touring the federation area, spending " weeks or even months " in electorates where organisation was moribund, and if need be acting as election agents until associations were put on their feet.

This reorganisation enjoyed a considerable, if not unqualified, success. In Scotland it produced only meagre improvement. Despite the prospect of financial aid, candidates were not forthcoming. At the end of 1928 the secretary of the Scottish Federation reported that only thirty-two candidates had been adopted for seventy-one constituencies, an actual drop of four on a year earlier. (The meeting which received this information could only hope " that quicker progress would be made "). But Scotland seems to have been exceptional. In February 1929 Samuel was even moved to criticise the competence of the Scottish Federation and to tell it that its performance was less satisfactory than anywhere in England. Certainly the situation of the Yorkshire Federation was quite different. Since 1924 its annual reports had grown increasingly gloomy, especially regarding candidates. But the report for May 1928 announced : " It is with pleasure that we are able to report a year of progress." There

[1] Annual report in the Minutes of the Yorkshire Liberal Federation.

had, it said, been active propaganda in most constituencies, with effective use of the campaign van in rural areas. Literature had been widely distributed, and attendances at meetings had been " very encouraging ". Particularly welcome was the situation regarding candidates. Twenty-six prospective candidates had now been adopted " and it is confidently anticipated that the number will be considerably increased shortly." Even finance was not the problem it had been. According to the treasurer, " the federation was in a better financial position to-day than ever before ". " The Yorkshire organisation ", concluded the annual report, " is in a state of efficiency in excess of anything which has been known for a considerable time."[1]

III

Yet despite Samuel's invaluable contribution as peace-maker and administrator, he did not meet all the party's needs. The *Manchester Guardian,* in welcoming his first speech in the north after taking up his new appointment, remarked *inter alia* that his address contained " a curious element of detachment ", was characterised by " judicial calm ", and treated the Conservative and Labour parties with " scrupulous fairness ", " giving to each such credit as it might fairly claim, and a good deal more than some ardent spirits might be inclined to allow."[2] Although made in no spirit of criticism, these remarks suggested a deficiency in Samuel : he did not come across as an " ardent spirit ". He could dissect social evils, but not arouse indignation against them. He could propose ways of meeting the nation's problems, but not sound the call to a crusade. At least in public, he seemed to lack fire in his belly.

One Liberal only could make good this deficiency. As S. K. Ratcliffe wrote in December 1926 : " The man who can touch liberal doctrine with fire and make the simple commonplace cruelty of mean streets look and feel like a new thing—that man must lead by the plain right of endowment."[3] Here was Lloyd George's essential function ; and someone perceptively likened

---

[1] Minutes of the Central Organising Committee, Scottish Liberal Federation, 7 December 1928; annual report and press cutting in the Minutes of the Yorkshire Liberal Federation.

[2] *Manchester Guardian,* 24 March 1927.   [3] *Nation,* 4 December 1926.

his present partnership with Samuel to his pre-war partnership with Asquith. If, as he believed, Liberalism could be revived by a crusade, it must be under his direction.

First he needed a platform. The basis was provided by the committee of experts which investigated British industry : economists like Walter Layton, Philip Kerr, Keynes, Henderson, and Seebohm Rowntree, with parliamentary strategists and candidates like Muir, E. D. Simon, H. L. Nathan, Masterman (until his premature death), and Lloyd George himself. There was even an Asquithian on the committee, Sir John Simon, although he played little part in its deliberations, and only at the last moment agreed to sign its report. The conclusions of the committee were published as *Britain's Industrial Future*, known also from its cover as the Yellow Book. It was a weighty and valuable economic treatise, marked by " severity of argument ", " scientific detachment of analysis ", and a lack of " crude appeals to self-interest ".[1] Its adoption by the party, said Samuel, " would make Liberalism even more worth fighting for than it had been before."[2]

Yet when it appeared early in 1928 it caused no great stir politically. It contained a mass of proposals, but not a handful of clear-cut, arresting proposals—even Samuel admitted that it would not startle by its originality. It swept aside the argument regarding private versus state enterprise as largely irrelevant, which may have been good economics but was, for the time, poor politics. And it failed to translate its guiding principles—the rationalisation of industry under an Economic General Staff, and the supervision of industrial relations by a Ministry of Industry—into a party programme. One Liberal journal summed it up by saying that as a treatise on economics it was a work of genius, but that its value as propaganda was doubtful : the Liberal party was revealing itself as the most intellectually brilliant group in modern politics, but was in danger of becoming a research department to other parties.[3]

This was not Lloyd George's intention at all. For him the prime function of the Yellow Book was to facilitate the Liberal

---

[1] *Manchester Guardian*, 3 February 1928.

[2] Address to the annual meeting of the Lancashire, Cheshire, and North Western Liberal Federation on 11 February 1928.

[3] *Bolton Evening News*, 3 February 1928.

party's return to power. Hence he and some of the other authors set about deriving from it an election programme : a set of " categorical, definite, detailed, practical proposals " (to quote Lloyd George on 1 March 1929) for overcoming one specific problem—unemployment. The level of unemployment had been abnormally high throughout the 1920s. By putting forward a concrete scheme to combat it, in contrast both with the inaction of the Conservatives and the woolly proposals of Labour, the Liberals might succeed in capturing the attention of the electorate.

So was born the great Liberal appeal of 1929. Lloyd George launched it on 1 March, at a dinner for Liberal candidates. The keynote of his address, which the *Liberal Magazine* believed would " rank as one of the historic utterances in British politics ", was this " momentous declaration " :

> If the nation entrusts the Liberal Party at the next General Election with the responsibilities of government, we are ready with schemes of work which we can put immediately into operation : work of a kind which is not merely useful in itself but essential to the wellbeing of the nation.
>
> The work put in hand will reduce the terrible figures of the workless in the course of a single year to normal proportions, and will, when completed, enrich the nation and equip it for successfully competing with all its rivals in the business of the world. These plans will not add one penny to the national or local taxation.

This address was followed by the publication of the pamphlet *We Can Conquer Unemployment* (" the little Yellow Book "), in which were set out the schemes to be undertaken, the amount of employment they would create, their cost, and how they would be financed : for example 350,000 men were to be employed in constructing roads and bridges (maps were included showing where these would be), 60,000 men employed on housing, 60,000 on telephone development, and 62,000 on electrical development. It is unlikely that the British electorate has ever been paid the compliment of a more far-sighted and responsible party programme.

Lloyd George had not waited for the dissolution to launch this great effort. With the Liberal party starting so far behind scratch, it clearly required an exceptional campaign to get its programme across. He followed up his initial address with public meetings in great centres, some of them relayed to audiences in surrounding districts : his speech at the Albert Hall on 26 March was heard by a combined audience of 50,000 in places as far away as Derby, Norwich, and Bournemouth. Samuel, meanwhile, went off on a twenty-three day speaking tour involving eighty-four meetings, which began at Land's End and was only prevented from reaching John O'Groats by the needs of his own constituency. In May came the final spurt to the polls, during which the Liberals put forward an unprecedented number—for the post-war period—of posters, handbills, pamphlets (Keynes and Henderson weighing in with *Can Lloyd George Do It ?*), and candidates. This was the Indian Summer of the old Liberal party. Soon after the programme was launched two Liberal candidates triumphed at by-elections, and J. L. Garvin wrote that the Liberals " have enjoyed their very best week since the war."[1] It would be fair to say that between 1 March, when Lloyd George launched his policy, and 30 May, when the nation polled, the Liberals enjoyed their very best three months.

For Lloyd George, this campaign was a mighty personal triumph. Hostility to him in the party was almost silent. Of the men who had repudiated him three years before, only Phillipps publicly rejected his unemployment programme. Runciman appeared on his platform on 1 March and endorsed his schemes. Grey, on behalf of the Liberal Council, said that the unemployment programme was " absolutely right " (even if the promise to fulfil it in a year was not). As for the Liberal leadership, Grey said it was not in question : " It is settled, as it always has been settled, by the decision of the Liberal members of the House of Commons."[2] And Simon was almost fulsome (too much so for Runciman and Maclean) in expressing support for the policy and person of " the remarkable man who now leads the Liberal party."[3] Nor was Lloyd George's success confined to the Liberal ranks. For the first time since 1914, the policy offered by the Liberals became the main topic of an election campaign. Certainly it was much criticised : the government

[1] *Observer*, 24 March 1929.   [2] Speeches of 10 April and 17 May 1929.
[3] *Manchester Guardian*, 16 May 1929. Lloyd George had not been elected leader of the party. But with Asquith's resignation in 1926, the leadership reverted to the person favoured by a majority of Liberal M.P.s i.e. Lloyd George.

even issued a White Paper, at public expense, attacking it. But it received much support from the press, as well as from a group of prominent businessmen on the eve of polling. And from the Liberal viewpoint, attack was almost as valuable as praise. The first necessity for a Liberal revival was that their proposals should become the battleground of an election contest.

But would revival go to the second stage ? After the politicians had done with wrangling, would the electors cast their votes on the basis of the Liberal programme, supporting or opposing the party which had put it forward ? Or would they pass judgement rather on the performance of the Conservative regime over the last five years—a performance which the Liberals had proved impotent either to assist or hinder ?

19. A LOST BATTLE

We seem to be a split party once more.

Ramsay Muir at Scarborough, 11 November 1931

By midnight on election night, the outcome of the fateful contest of 1929 was already apparent. The Conservatives were not being routed. But, especially in industrial districts, they were losing ground heavily. Labour was increasing its already considerable holdings in Yorkshire and north-eastern England ; and in London, Lancashire, and the Midlands (even including Birmingham) it was making substantial headway. Yet in all this there was nothing for the Liberal party. At 12.30, Samuel's narrow victory at Darwen in Lancashire brought the net Liberal gains to one seat ; five constituencies had been captured and four lost. On the following day, when results came in from rural areas, the situation improved but slightly. Altogether the Liberals won only sixteen more seats than in the disaster year of 1924. As the N.L.F. executive admitted, this was " a severe disappointment ". " We made plans for a sweeping advance, and . . . we have only held our own." Even though there was " no literal loss of ground ", it was " a lost battle in view of our hopes and aims."[1]

The final results brought Labour once more into office, although still without a majority. Labour won 288 seats, the Conservatives 260, and the Liberals 59. Compared with 1924, Liberals held 24 seats, lost nineteen, and captured 35. They made no progress in industrial districts. Indeed they held fewer urban seats after the election than before, seventeen of their nineteen losses being to Labour. In Yorkshire and north-eastern England, for example, they gained one seat and lost four ; in Lancashire they gained four and lost four ; in working-class London they gained one and lost three.

[1] *Liberal Magazine*, September 1929.

The 35 seats which they captured (all but two from Conservatives) were largely in rural areas. They made one or two freak gains : Frank Owen triumphed at Hereford, " one of those uncovenanted victories which chequer election campaigns " ;[1] and a Nonconformist minister captured Ashford in Kent, which even in 1906 had been stony ground for the Liberals. But most of their advances were in anticipated regions : rural Scotland and Wales, where they captured seven seats, and non-industrial England south of the Trent. Even here things did not go as well as expected. Liberals had announced that they would capture at least fifteen seats in East Anglia and the neighbouring counties, but gained only nine. And they had anticipated a general advance in the West Country, whereas they captured only seven seats there, five of them in Cornwall.[2] Had the revulsion against the Conservatives been as strong in rural as in urban districts, the Liberals might have achieved something of their hoped-for revival. But it was not.

These results, admittedly, concealed a real Liberal advance in popular support. The Liberals had fought the election in nation-wide opposition to the other major parties : they had even run a candidate against Guest, who although hand-in-glove with the Conservatives retained the nomination of his Liberal executive. Hence although the Liberal advance was limited, it was achieved in the party's own strength and not through electoral bargains. And certainly in terms of the popular vote Liberals improved their position. There were 203 constituencies where in both 1924 and 1929 the three major parties ran candidates, and in these the Liberal share of the poll advanced by over 4% : from 24·8 in 1924 to 29·0 in 1929.

But this improvement still only gave them, overall, about a quarter of the votes cast—enough to run up a sizeable total, but not enough to put them at the head of the poll in many constituencies. With reason they might claim that an electoral system which gave them one-fourth of the votes and only one-tenth of the seats was grossly unfair ; yet few outside their own

---

[1] *Manchester Guardian*, 1 June 1929.

[2] For Lloyd George even this advance must have seemed a mixed blessing. His adversaries in the party had established rather a stronghold in Cornwall, and the Liberals elected there included Maclean—returning to Parliament for the first time since 1922—, Runciman, Isaac Foot, and Leif Jones, all of them hostile to him.

ranks felt the injustice. Anyway, in terms of either seats or
votes they had lost the election. No change in the electoral
system would have put them into office, or have extricated them
from the position in which they now found themselves : the
position of being a third party, uncomfortably holding the
balance between Labour and the Conservatives.

Why, despite their great effort and outstanding programme,
had the Liberals failed ? There were several probable causes.
In the first place, there was a deep-seated lack of trust in pledges
offered by Lloyd George. By general agreement, he had made
lavish promises at an election ten years before and had failed
to keep them : the slogans of 1918 were thrown up at him with
telling effect in 1929. But this was not his only handicap.
Through no fault of his own, he had become rather *passé*. He
might be offering the country effective leadership, but it was
leadership of a sort that had gone out of fashion. His blend
of reforming zeal and a hard-headed approach to national
problems (representing a union of the pre-war Chancellor of the
Exchequer and the wartime Minister of Munitions) seemed
almost anachronistic. The nation possessed little regard for the
men, or the methods, which had inaugurated the welfare state
and won the war. Its varying inclinations were better expressed
by the nebulous goodwill of Stanley Baldwin and the frothy
aspirations of Ramsay MacDonald.

But there was more to the Liberal party's failure even than
the past record and present capacity of its leader. The opening
words of Lloyd George's pledge were : " If the nation entrusts
the Liberal Party at the next election with the responsibilities of
government . . . ." Unfortunately for the party, only Liberal
devotees regarded this as remotely possible. The prevailing
disbelief in such an outcome was reflected in the question which
dogged Liberals (and them alone) throughout the contest :
what would they do if they again held the balance in Parliament?
This was the most they were expected to achieve. It was assumed
that the roles of government and opposition belonged to their
opponents. The Liberals might emerge as a third party strong
enough to decide which of their rivals would govern, but they
would not do more than this. That is, they would not be anything except a third party.

This conviction was fatal to their whole endeavour at a comeback. The programme which they offered was the programme of a party of government, or it was nothing. If they had no prospect of carrying it out, its value as a vote-winner departed. Once the Liberal party had ceased to be thought of as a contender for office it was trapped. No policy, however relevant or attractive, could save it.

The failure of 1929 was the end of the line for the old Liberal party. At this moment, the last vestige of hope disappeared. As George Lambert, who had recovered his seat in Devon, wrote four days after polling : " The future of the old party hardly bears thinking about."[1] Runciman, another successful candidate, wrote on the matter : " I feel nearly hopeless."[2] Others expressed this feeling by abandoning the party. A week after the election, one of the fifty-nine Liberal M.P.s, W. A. Jowitt, broke with the Liberals and joined the Labour government. He was followed into the Labour fold by recent M.P.s and candidates like G. Garro-Jones, A. Mackenzie Livingstone, and F. Martin. Others went in the opposite direction, including two of Lloyd George's former whips. Guest at last joined the Conservatives, and McCurdy became a leading light in Beaverbrook's United Empire Crusade.

It was not just that the Liberals had lost. More than this, they had run out of excuses. Previously they had consoled themselves with the belief that, for all its progress, Labour would never secure an absolute majority, and so must eventually make terms with them. Now Labour had come within twenty seats of absolute victory. A Labour majority in the future, admitted the *Nation*, was a " serious possibility ".[3] Further, Liberals had argued that their previous setbacks were largely accidental : in earlier elections they had been disunited, badly led, deficient in policy, and short of funds and candidates. In 1929 no such explanations were possible. The party had been substantially united, superbly led, and amply endowed in matters of programme, money, and candidates. Yet it had failed. After this, it was difficult to imagine the circumstances in which it would ever succeed.

---

[1] Lambert to Gladstone, 3 June 1929, Herbert Gladstone Papers.
[2] Runciman to Gladstone, 4 July 1929, Herbert Gladstone Papers.
[3] *Nation*, 8 June 1929.

II

During the next two years the party paid the price of its failure. The organisation in the country came to a standstill, personal dissensions revived, and the parliamentary party split into warring factions.

Two factors had restored the fighting spirit of the Liberal organisation : the hope of revival, and Lloyd George's subsidies. Now hope was gone, and the subsidies ceased. The special election fund was all used up, and as Lloyd George would not renew it the extra staff employed by headquarters and in the constituencies had to be dismissed—much to Samuel's regret. This process caused great bitterness. Phillipps met a party employee, hitherto sympathetic to Lloyd George, who had just lost his post and was " very bitter about everybody being thrown out on to the scrap-heap ". The federation which had employed him was " broke ", and there was no money even for the secretary's salary or office rent. The Liberals in the district were " up in arms ". When Phillipps suggested that, in that case, the local Liberals " would surely turn to and raise their own money ", he received an answer which he himself had offered to explain the failure of the Million Fund : " How can you get people to subscribe when they think that Ll.G has got all that money—and that it really belongs to the Party ? "[1]

Not only had the election fund gone but Lloyd George's annual grants to headquarters, and through it to the federations, soon ceased. The financial agreement of 1927 terminated automatically three months after the election. In an effort to secure its renewal, the Administrative Committee resumed the humiliating process of haggling with its leader over money. This also produced much ill feeling. Lloyd George came in for strong criticism, and gave as good as he got. (Phillipps refrained from committing to paper some of the remarks Lloyd George was reported to have made to Ramsay Muir). But it was all to no avail. Lloyd George would finance the party no longer. Under pressure he agreed to tide it over a few months more, but

[1] Phillipps to Gladstone, 26 July 1929, Herbert Gladstone Papers. The dismissed employee was to appear in Parliament in 1931 as a Simonite (anti-Lloyd George) M.P.

in June 1930 all financial assistance from him ceased. Thereafter the party, as a party, never secured another penny from
the Lloyd George fund.

This left the Liberal organisation in dire straits. It was back
in the circumstances of 1925, with the experience of the Million
Fund to show that, apart from Lloyd George, no substantial
source of finance existed. Muir, who succeeded Samuel as
chairman of the organisation in January 1930, wrote : " The
situation seems to me to be really critical, both for the country
& for the party. There is a real danger that we may be wiped
out . . . . I have to try to make the party self-supporting. The
chest is practically empty."[1] Headquarters grants to the district
federations ceased entirely, leaving many organisations in
parlous condition. One result was that candidates could not be
secured. In October 1930 the N.L.F. passed a resolution at its
annual meeting " regretting that it has not been possible to
contest many of the recent by-elections " and declaring " that
the financial deficiency in this and other respects must be made
good forthwith ".[2] Yet by mid-1931 there were, in part owing
to shortage of funds, only twenty-five prospective candidates for
the eighty-three constituencies in Lancashire, Cheshire, and the
north-west. Meanwhile Muir's attempt to raise a central fund had
made little headway. In October 1930 he issued an appeal to
supporters which was disarmingly frank :

> We no longer possess the lavish resources which were placed
> at our disposal during the past few years. The party funds
> are totally inadequate for the work that needs to be done.
> If our case is to be presented to the nation, we need at least
> £250,000 of new money for the assistance of candidates
> and propaganda work. . . . Many have withheld their aid
> from us in the belief that there is a very large unexhausted
> fund at the disposal of Mr. Lloyd George. This is not
> so. . . . The time has come when the Liberal Party must
> finance itself or cease to exist.[3]

A year later, with an election upon him, Muir wrote : " We

---

[1] Muir to Gladstone, 6 January 1929 (i.e. 1930), Herbert Gladstone Papers.
[2] *Liberal Magazine*, November 1930.
[3] *The Times*, 11 October 1930. Muir's private communications to the party
had an uncomfortable habit of getting into the press.

have practically no funds at our disposal, though we are doing our best to raise them." [1]

The running-down of the Liberal machine was one consequence of the party's loss of hope and lack of money. Another was the revival of public antipathy to Lloyd George. The Liberal Council, which had muted its feelings during the election (and might have gone on doing so had he brought about the hoped-for revival), swiftly returned to the attack. Phillipps announced that Lloyd George was " not an asset " to the party but " a positive liability ", and that his fund was " an offence to thousands of Liberals who care for the best traditions of our public life ".[2] Harcourt Johnstone wrote of " the miasma of bad faith which the leadership of Mr. Lloyd George connotes."[3] And Sir Charles Mallet devoted a whole book (*Mr. Lloyd George A Study*) to discussing its subject's shortcomings. But the most weighty denunciation came from Grey. For him the issue of the fund was decisive. He had helped to found the Liberal Council when the party accepted Lloyd George's money in 1927, and he warned Samuel soon after the 1929 election that unless Liberals stopped asking for more he would renew his protest.[4] On 14 January 1930 he did so : on behalf of the Liberal Council he condemned the party's dependence on a personal fund, and declined to acknowledge Lloyd George as party leader. In form this was rather irrelevant. Lloyd George was forcibly terminating the party's dependence on his fund, and it was not the Council's business to choose the Liberal leader. But Grey's point was clear enough. As long as Lloyd George remained in command, the followers of Asquith would keep themselves separate and hostile.

But it was not only followers of Asquith who felt that, in matters of finance, Lloyd George was behaving badly. The *Manchester Guardian* implied that misgivings about the fund existed among many Liberals outside the Council, and the *Daily News* cried out " Scrap The Fund ", claiming that Liberals of all sections were " absolutely sick to death of the squalid

[1] Memorandum by Muir (" private and confidential "), 7 October 1931, Lothian Papers ; *Manchester Guardian*, 10 October 1931. See comment on previous footnote.

[2] *The Times*, 12 June 1929.   [3] *ibid*, 16 January 1930.

[4] Grey to Gladstone, 3 August 1929, Herbert Gladstone Papers.

interminable controversy which has raged about this subject for years ".[1] And delegates at the N.L.F. conference in October 1929 expressed clear disapproval of the way money was being withheld and the party machine being dismantled—which in effect was disapproval of Lloyd George himself. One Liberal candidate was warmly applauded when he observed, somewhat darkly : " It was an atmosphere of insincerity and of hidden questions which was bringing the party into difficulties, and if the party could not read the writing the electorate could."[2]

III

For a while after the 1929 election, the parliamentary party seemed immune from the malaise which had descended on the rest of the Liberal forces. For one thing, Liberal M.P.s were in a special position. The Labour party under MacDonald was once more in office, but without a majority. So near had it come to securing one that Baldwin had resigned straight after the election, so that there had been no question of the Liberals putting Labour into office. But they were in a position to put it out. The Government to survive had to secure their support or at least their abstention, and this gave Liberal M.P.s an accidental importance which the party outside Parliament did not possess. Further, the parliamentary party was driven to a display of unity and decision by the example of its predecessor. Members felt that at all costs they must avoid the disunion of Liberals in the last Parliament. At the first party meeting after the election, in June 1929, the main topic discussed was the need for unity. According to Maclean's account, " there was a clear consensus of opinion that joint action was vital to our existence." E. D. Simon, the Manchester radical, even proposed that members be obliged to vote in accordance with party decisions, and Sir John Simon " smote his breast and declared that except on matters which could only be fitly decided in the sacred court of conscience—or words to that effect—no matter of opinion would induce him to do other than follow the crack of the whip."[3] A month later Maclean wrote : " The Party holds

---

[1] *Manchester Guardian*, 15 January 1930 ; *Daily News*, 1 November 1929.

[2] *Manchester Guardian*, 5 October 1929.

[3] Memorandum by Maclean, 14 June 1929, Herbert Gladstone Papers.

or rather clings together with a grip almost pathetic in its fear of division."[1]

But in December 1929 the front of unity in Parliament began to crack, and from then until the collapse of the second Labour government in August 1931 Liberal M.P.s passed from one upheaval to another. Newspapers told the story under headings like : " Divided Liberals ", " Liberal Split ", " Angry Liberals ", " A Liberal ' Crisis ' ", " A Fateful Party Meeting ", " Liberal ' Rebels ' Save The Government ", and " A Party Crisis." These events took heavy toll on the party outside Parliament : one federation protested to the chief whip in July 1930 that events like the recent dissension among M.P.s on the Finance Bill were having a disastrous effect on the rank and file, who were already facing very difficult tasks in the constituencies.

Underlying all these upheavals was a single issue. What attitude should Liberals adopt to the Labour government ? Two courses lay open. They could remain entirely aloof from it, judge its acts solely on their merits, and where it failed to give satisfaction vote against it and damn the consequences. Or, assuming it avoided reckless forays into " socialism ", they could grant it reasonable security of tenure, negotiate with ministers regularly, and try to evolve a joint Liberal-Labour policy. Lloyd George tried both these courses during the lifetime of the government. To begin with he came down strongly for the first of them. He feared that Liberals would become once more the " patient oxen " of 1924, prolonging the life of a government which treated them with contempt and awaited a suitable moment to slaughter them. If, he warned, Labour believed that they would not dare to vote against it, their criticisms would be treated with contempt. They must show themselves ready to carry their views into the division lobby.

The Coal Bill of December 1929 gave him a chance to apply this principle. The government had produced the measure after lengthy negotiations with owners and miners, and had achieved a considerable measure of conciliation between these interests. To the Liberal leaders this was small virtue. Both Lloyd George and Samuel had helped to produce schemes for solving the coal industry's problems, Lloyd George with *Coal and Power* in 1924, Samuel with the report of the Royal Com-

[1] Maclean to Gladstone, 21 July 1929, Herbert Gladstone Papers.

Herbert Gladstone

Margot Asquith

mission in 1926. They believed that the industry could only be saved by a bold policy imposed from above, including the statutory amalgamation of pits into economic units. The government's bill contained nothing so ambitious. In the view of the Liberal leaders, it evaded the real issues and penalised the consumer. So Lloyd George laid it down that the measure must be drastically improved or Liberals would vote against it. William Graham, Labour's President of the Board of Trade, went to considerable lengths to meet Liberal objections, but not far enough. So on 19 December 1929 Lloyd George led his party into the lobby against the second reading.

This occasioned the first Liberal " split ". Two Liberals voted with the government, and six others remained in the House without voting (some of them sat on the Liberal front bench so as to rally abstainers). It was a small breakaway, but it was enough. The government was saved by eight votes. Two months later, on 27 February 1930, the same thing happened. On a vital amendment to the Coal Bill, four Liberals voted with the government against their party and eight others prominently abstained. This time the government's majority was nine. These divisions caused a considerable upheaval in the Liberal ranks, and led to severe criticism of the defectors. Yet it was apparent that if Lloyd George persisted in opposing the bill, further exhibitions of disunity would occur. He decided not to run the risk. Without consulting his colleagues, he advised a party meeting in March 1930 to abstain from voting during further divisions on the bill. He offered the " transparently fictitious excuse "[1] that he did not wish to embarrass the government during the conference on naval disarmament. More plausible was the suggestion that he preferred Liberals to vote in neither lobby rather than in both.

Which Liberals caused these early breaches in party unity ? At first sight there was no clear pattern of division. The rebels against Lloyd George's policy included the radical E. D. Simon, previously an advocate of mandatory obedience to party decisions, and the near-conservative Sir William Edge, an ally of Lloyd George since coalition days. (Edge had been made a junior whip by Lloyd George, but now resigned the position). But despite the diversity of view among the rebels, there was one

[1] *The Times,* 22 March 1930.

distinct " group " acting together to save the Coal Bill. It consisted of Runciman, Maclean, and Leif Jones—all members of the Liberal Council. This seemed odd. By most standards they were well on the " right " of the party, and were expected to have less sympathy for Labour's measures than Lloyd George and the Liberal " left ". But this was not so. They saw considerable merit in the Coal Bill, not least when Lloyd George condemned it as an " owner's " bill. Runciman and Maclean had been in touch with several leading coal-owners during the preparations of the bill, and had urged them to adopt a conciliatory spirit.[1] They regarded the resultant measure as an important step towards pacifying the industry. Why should they assist in defeating it, just because Lloyd George and Samuel were wedded to proposals far more " socialistic " in character than anything the government was suggesting ?

Moreover, on general grounds the Liberal Council saw much to approve of in the government. Runciman and his associates were staunch Cobdenites : they held by the doctrines of free trade, retrenchment, and individual enterprise. And they recognised in Snowden, Labour's Chancellor of the Exchequer, a man after their own hearts. As Harcourt Johnstone put it : " Those of us in particular who are still free traders feel more confidence in Messrs. Snowden and Graham than in Mr. Lloyd George, with his patchy fiscal history and his roving political eye."[2] Indeed in July 1930 Leif Jones became so eloquent in praise of Snowden that Churchill spoke scoffingly of these twin Victorian dodos pledging each other in libations of cold water. (They were, of course, strict teetotallers as well as strict economists).

Lloyd George could not share this enthusiasm for Labour's performance (except in the field of foreign policy). He had feared that the government might prove too socialistic. He found that he could not induce it to become socialistic enough. Certainly it is a misconception to believe that the second Labour government failed because its dependence on Liberal support prevented it from carrying out the bold measures on which it had set its heart. It failed because no amount of Liberal pressure would induce it to adopt bold measures. Granted that it

[1] Memorandum by Maclean, 22 December 1929, Herbert Gladstone Papers.
[2] *The Times*, 16 January 1930.

encountered an appalling economic crisis, nevertheless it revealed neither the capacity nor the will to surmount it. The economic dogmatism of Snowden, the pusillanimity of MacDonald and J. H. Thomas, and the unhappy combination of doctrinal radicalism and innate caution among its followers, rendered it incapable of dealing with the crisis. Eventually in August 1931, overwhelmed by problems which it knew no method of solving— no method, anyway, which it was prepared to apply—Labour willed itself out of office. The last word on the government had been spoken five months earlier by W. J. Brown, a left-wing Labour M.P. who was resigning from the party : " It seems that we have spent twenty years destroying the Liberal Party in order to get a Government whose policy is less radical in relation to the needs of to-day than that of the Liberals was in relation to the needs of 1906-14."[1]

Yet for a year preceding its demise, Lloyd George, for all his misgivings, had been striving to make the Labour government a success. The Liberal crises over the Coal Bill had caused him to abandon his original policy of voting against the government regardless of consequences. Instead he adopted the alternative course : that of according the government general Liberal support, and seeking through consultations with ministers to guide them along desirable paths. His object from mid-1930 was to develop an agreed Liberal-Labour programme on matters like unemployment, agriculture, and electoral reform.

On the face of it this change of policy was not entirely fruitless. It resulted in measures affecting agriculture entirely satisfactory to Liberals. (Ironically the Labour minister with whom Lloyd George found himself negotiating was his old colleague Addison).

---

[1] *Liberal Magazine*, April 1931. The late Reginald Bassett, who dispelled so many myths about this Labour government, nevertheless accepted the myth that the government was seriously hampered by its dependence on the Liberals. He wrote that MacDonald in 1931 " was at the head of a minority Government which had been restricted essentially, though not exclusively, to the task of ' keeping things going '." (*Nineteen Thirty-One Political Crisis*, p. 338.) In what way the government was " restricted " by its minority position he did not say. On the contrary, the failure of the government lay within itself, and (despite many other shortcomings in the Labour movement) it was essentially a failure of leadership. This deficiency in leadership was as apparent in the August 1931 crisis as earlier. And, for good reason or bad, the individuals mainly responsible then abandoned their party to suffer the consequences of failure without them.

And early in 1931 MacDonald introduced an Electoral Reform Bill containing the important concession to Liberals of the alternative vote.[1] Yet in essentials the policy of co-operating with Labour failed utterly. It did not save the government, and it did not preserve Liberal unity. Lloyd George could not induce ministers to combat the rising menace of unemployment. During the summer of 1930 he laid before them a concrete scheme for this purpose, which required the raising of a national development loan. Snowden would not touch it. Borrowing to pay the dole was one thing; borrowing on a larger scale to provide employment was another. This refusal doomed the government. Unemployment was the one quite crucial issue it faced. If it failed here, it failed altogether. And by late 1930 it was not only seen to have failed, it was seen to be conscious of failure. In November, following a censure debate on unemployment, a Liberal journalist quoted Goethe's dictum that no one dies without consenting to die. This government, he concluded, was full of the consent to die; from the moment MacDonald sat down after as pathetically inadequate a speech as a Prime Minister ever made in a crisis of his fortunes, it did not seem likely that Parliament would be able to keep the government alive if it wanted to.[2]

Lloyd George's policy of Liberal-Labour co-operation was equally unsuccessful in preserving Liberal unity. If his opposition to the Coal Bill had caused one Liberal split, his support for the government caused another.

The earlier division had been—very roughly—between the followers of Cobden and the followers of Keynes, the former (although farther to the " right ") having more sympathy for the government than the latter. But when Lloyd George sought to revive the government with doses of Keynes, he caused the breakaway of a different section. They were stimulated less by economic dogmas than by a deep-seated revulsion against the Labour government. On a matter like free trade Labour might be entirely orthodox. But to these Liberals it did not feel orthodox. It lacked respectability : it possessed no background of wealth or breeding, could draw on no traditions of government,

[1] This measure passed in the Commons but had not got through the House of Lords when the government fell.

[2] *Manchester Guardian*, 10 November 1930.

was unstable, inexperienced, and somewhat vulgar. And it was
faced with a mounting economic crisis which its want of
respectability and refusal to act were converting into a crisis of
confidence. Such a regime might be permissible in times of
buoyancy and security. In time of crisis it was an unwarrantable
luxury. The situation required a government which was safe,
reliable, and trusted. The Conservatives, despite their relapse
into tariffs (and could that policy any longer be dismissed out
of hand ?), alone possessed these qualities.

There was a further reason why this section of Liberals began
looking to the Conservatives. Liberals were no less, although
no more, subject to the urge of ambition than members of other
parties.[1] Yet what prospect had they now of ever satisfying
their legitimate aspiration towards office ? The great attempt
at a Liberal comeback had failed, and at the next election the
party was expected to lose ground once more. Labour, although
dependent on Liberal support, had made it perfectly clear that
it would never admit Liberals, as Liberals, into its ministry, or
even cease electoral war upon them. (As it was Hutchison,
Ernest Brown, and Sir John Simon had only been secure at the
last election owing to the tacit abstention of Conservative
candidates). If a Liberal government lay outside the realm of
possibility, and a Labour government would never reward their
support with office, what hope had they of playing a part in
government ? Clearly the answer lay with the Conservatives,
if it lay anywhere.

The Liberals who took part in this new defection were of
mixed origin. Some, like Ernest Brown and Hore-Belisha, were
post-war Liberals who had entered politics as Asquithians but
had come to see Lloyd George as the saviour of Liberalism.
The failure of 1929 and his erratic course since, particularly his
volte-face over the Coal Bill, had disillusioned them. Others,
like Hutchison (who resigned as chief whip in November 1930)
and Sir Murdoch MacDonald, were allies of Lloyd George from
coalition days. They had gone along with him this far, but now

This consideration had been worrying Lloyd George before the election. He
feared that the party would lose its able young men if they had no prospect of
office, and said that the Liberals ought not to put Labour in until it agreed to
give posts to some of the more promising young Liberals. But as it happened
Labour took office without the Liberals being consulted. (Scott's diary, 7
December 1928, C. P. Scott Papers).

they were anxious to recover their coalitionist role, even if it meant deserting him. Yet the leader of the breakaway was an Asquithian by origin, of seemingly excellent Liberal credentials. He had left the cabinet in 1914 over British participation in the war, but had been persuaded to return ; he had resigned in 1916 over conscription, and had refused to come back ; and after the war he had condemned Lloyd George up hill and down dale for his alliance with the Conservatives. Yet even then there were some who doubted whether Sir John Simon was quite an ideal Liberal. Scott, who had seen much of Simon during the conscription crisis, had been dismayed at his infirmity of purpose and uncertainty of principle. And after talking with him in 1923, Scott summed him up thus :

Somehow, in spite of general political agreemt. I always feel slightly repelled by him. An affectation of cordiality which hasn't much behind it, great volubility in talking about what interests him & no attempt to talk about what interests you. An appearance of deference with no real desire to consult, except in so far as may be needful to find out what line you mean to take. Intellectually a Liberal without much of the stuff of it. A great contrast to Maclean . . . who has Liberalism in his bones & never thinks of himself.[1]

About one aspect of Simon's character there was general agreement : his great ability had marked him out for success, and he was determined to succeed. A typical, and entirely friendly, comment is this one by A. C. Murray in 1923 : " John Simon is doing very well, and working very strenuously. . . . He means to ' get there ' if he can ! "[2] Since the war two forces had stopped him from " getting there " : Lloyd George and the Labour party. They had helped to keep him out of Parliament until 1922, and his party out of office for longer than that. In 1923 Lloyd George had added insult to injury by returning to the party and replacing him as heir apparent to the Liberal leadership. Yet in the following years Simon, although keeping his distance from Labour and Lloyd George, had rarely expressed strong feelings against them. 1926 was an exception : he denounced the general strike so effectively as to hasten its

[1] *ibid*, 29 January 1923.
[2] A. C. Murray to Reading, 7 March 1923, Elibank Papers.

abandonment, and signed the famous letter refusing further confidential relations with Lloyd George. Perhaps these events revealed the real man. For although Simon's position soon became fluid again, by late 1930 he had resumed the stance of 1926. He could see no purpose in shoring up the Labour government (which had just dealt him the insult of exclusion from the Round-Table Conference on India), or of remaining associated with Lloyd George. In November 1930 he and Hutchison condemned the policy of co-operating with Labour, and in June 1931 they rejected the Liberal whip.

The burden of Simon's complaint was that Lloyd George's policy had changed. Instead of voting against the government where it clearly had failed, as on unemployment, Liberals were tempering their actions for fear of the consequences. The party, he warned, was " dying of tactics "; it should take a stand, come what may, for the things it believed in. In substance this charge was warranted. Lloyd George admitted that Labour had failed regarding unemployment, and that he was giving it another chance only because an election now would damage the Liberals and return a Tory government. But were tactics altogether absent from Simon's behaviour ? It was soon being rumoured that Liberal M.P.s who joined his group might expect to be free from Conservative opposition at the next election, as long as they accepted the full Conservative programme—including tariffs. Simon for one was prepared to pay this price. In Lloyd George's tart phrase, by early in 1931 he was lending " one of his countenances " to a tariff policy.

Simon's breakaway caused a fresh upheaval in the Liberal ranks. It came to a head in March 1931. A particularly bad example of Liberal cross-voting in Parliament caused the resignation of Sir Archibald Sinclair, who had succeeded Hutchison as chief whip. The issue raised by this incident— whether Liberals should vote contrary to party decisions—was soon submerged by the larger issue of Liberal policy towards the government. Five days before the crucial party meeting, Sinclair sent H. A. L. Fisher this account of the situation :

You have probably heard of the crisis which we are now facing in the House of Commons. The decision as to our future course of action will have to be reached next week. Broadly speaking the position is that the vast majority of the Party are working well together under Mr. Lloyd George's leadership on the lines of which you told me in your recent letter you strongly approved. Nevertheless there are certain Members of the Party—and among them some of the best known Liberals in the country such as Simon and Hutchison—who are definitely bent on turning out the Government and making an agreement with the Conservatives, and they are in a position to assure those who follow them that they will have no Tory opponent at the next General Election. They constitute a nucleus of disaffection and disloyalty in the Party ; their interventions in debate and constant opposition in the division lobby weaken the influence of the Party in the House of Commons, while their criticism of our policy as unprincipled as well as unwise bewilders and discourages our supporters in the country. Runciman is wholly occupied with his business interests and only appears in the House of Commons very occasionally to emphasise by vote or speech some difference with his Liberal colleagues.[1]

In Mr. Lloyd George's opinion our chief concern must be to carry out in this Parliament the mandate which we received at the last Election from over five million electors and obviously this can only be done by agreement with the Labour Party. The view, therefore, to which he is now inclining is that we should endeavour to come to some agreement with the Labour Party covering India, Disarmament, Free Trade, National Development and Unemployment and Electoral Reform ; and, while reserving our right as an independent Party to criticise or oppose the Government on matters not covered by the agreement, assure them of our general support so long as the agreed policy is being carried out.

Mr. Lloyd George has no desire to drum any Liberals out of the Party, and it is obvious that Members who have been returned to Parliament as candidates of Liberal Associations are entitled to receive the whip.

Nevertheless, there would be an advantage if we knew

[1] In the latter part of 1930 Runciman had considerably extended his business interests, and insisted that he would not again stand for Parliament. (This decision he subsequently reversed).

Liberal members of the National Government in August, 1931. Left to right: Sir Donald Maclean (President of the Board of Education), Lord Lothian (Chancellor of the Duchy of Lancaster), Sir Herbert Samuel (Home Secretary), Sir Archibald Sinclair (Secretary of State for Scotland) and Lord Reading (Foreign Secretary)

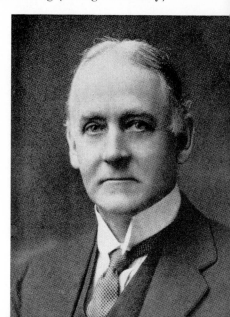

Vivian Phillipps

Lloyd George in the grounds of Churt, 1932

that there were forty or forty-five Members on whose loyalty
and cooperation we could definitely rely.[1]

In the event, this letter proved somewhat optimistic. Lloyd
George's scheme for an agreement with Labour was whittled
down almost to nothing, in an attempt to preserve party unity.
The final resolution was a very tame affair : it affirmed the
independence of the party, laid down Liberal policy, and agreed
to support " this or any Government " in putting this policy
into effect. Yet even in this innocuous form it was not accepted
by the " forty or forty-five Members " for whom Sinclair had
hoped. (Nevertheless, he agreed to resume as chief whip). Only
thirty-three members voted for the resolution, and seventeen
against it. The minority, as Lloyd George hastened to point out,
were not united. Only about seven were Simonites who wanted
immediately to turn out the government. The rest followed
Ernest Brown, who argued that Liberals should stand entirely
aloof from the government and not promise it even " general "
support. But these two sections moved irresistibly together.
When Simon and Hutchison resigned the Liberal whip three
months later, Brown did the same.

So by mid-1931 the parliamentary party was, as one Liberal
federation put it, " hard-pressed ". Its cardinal doctrine of
free trade was being everywhere assailed. As the *Manchester
Guardian* admitted on 21 May 1930 :

> The two " bad winters " which Mr. Bonar Law prophesied
> would be sufficient to kill Free Trade have lengthened into
> eight, and as the tide of economic prosperity recedes so do
> our Protectionists advance. There is no longer any doubt
> that we are now back at the old days of the fight with out-
> and-out Protection, with the ghost of Joseph Chamberlain
> looking benevolently on.

Chamberlain's ghost could afford to smile. Conservatives who
had resisted his policy in earlier days, like Churchill and Derby,
now renounced their free trade faith. They were joined by noteworthy Liberals, not all of them Simonites. Some of the party's
principal economic advisers of two years earlier, like Keynes,
Henderson, and Josiah Stamp, were advocating a revenue tariff.
And at the Liberal Summer School in 1930, E. D. Simon questioned the validity of free trade doctrine in a speech which,

[1] Sinclair to Fisher, 20 March 1931, Fisher Papers.

complained Muir, had embarrassed his work as chairman of a party already fighting under great handicaps. Furthermore, Liberal resources in the press were being woefully depleted. Between 1928 and 1931 two major Liberal dailies, the *Westminster Gazette* and the *Daily Chronicle*, passed out of existence, and so did the much respected weekly the *Nation*.

At the same time Liberal M.P.s could derive no comfort from either of the courses open to them. If they turned the government out they faced disaster at the polls. But the humiliations involved in keeping it in were becoming intolerable. They had to endure the sneers of Conservatives and Simonites ("Liberals Again Run Away" was a typical headline in a Conservative paper[1]). And the behaviour of some Labour ministers was well-nigh unendurable. The government's bill to amend trade union law caused Liberals much embarrassment. They let it through on the second reading in the hope of improving it in committee. Yet when they carried an amendment to which they believed ministers had assented, they were told by Jowitt, who was in charge of the bill, that the suggestion of ministerial approval was "a pack of lies".[2] Snowden's manners were no better. He averted a crisis on his land tax proposals in June 1931 by making concessions to the Liberals. But in announcing the fact to Parliament he indulged in a savage, purposeless attack on Lloyd George which brought relations near breaking-point. Lloyd George and his leading colleagues let it be known that they would attend no further conferences with ministers at which Snowden was present. How long the two parties could go on co-operating after this was problematical. One observer believed that, despite everything, the Liberals would continue to support the government. Another reported that, if only the Upper House would enact the alternative vote, the Liberal party was ready to throw in its hand.

Such was the state of the party when, in July 1931, Parliament adjourned for the summer recess. Its problems looked insoluble. But in August a way of escape apparently offered itself. For the Liberals, as for MacDonald, patriotism seemed to be the last refuge.

---

[1] *Daily Dispatch*, 29 January 1931.   [2] *The Times*, 16 April 1931.

IV

In August 1931 the Labour government broke up. MacDonald, instead of resigning, invited the Conservative and Liberal leaders to join him in a National government. Whilst Labour strongly opposed this move, they agreed. Samuel, Maclean, Sinclair, the elder statesmen Crewe and Reading, and several other Liberals took office. Lloyd George was not able to do so, for he had fallen seriously ill in July and remained out of action for several months. (How, otherwise, MacDonald and Baldwin could have avoided asking him to join the government must remain a tantalizing mystery). But even he gave his approval to the new government. As for the Liberal rank and file, their support was overwhelming. " Not a single letter of criticism has been received at headquarters from any local Liberal association. This is almost unique, I should think, in the history, or at any rate the modern history, of the organisation."[1] Such response was predictable. Liberals were getting rid of the decrepit Labour regime without bringing on themselves the election they dreaded. They were being asked to co-operate with a government on terms of dignity, and even to take office in it. And despite Labour's hostility, they could regard the new administration as genuinely " national " because no party possessed an independent majority and none, presumably, could dictate its policy. At long last the Liberal party seemed to have recovered a *raison d'être*.

Yet within a month the Liberals discovered the trap into which they had walked. The Conservative rank and file had welcomed the National government as a first step in getting Labour out. They never meant to forgo the second step : the election they were sure to win, and the tariff programme it would facilitate. By mid-September the Conservative drive for an election was mounted. By the beginning of October it had carried the day. The Liberals resisted it to the utmost, recognising that an election would destroy the government's " national " character by producing a one-party majority enforcing a one-party programme. But they were powerless. MacDonald was practically without a parliamentary following, and the Liberals

[1] *Manchester Guardian*, 2 September 1931.

had only three-score members—of whom the Simonites, having prepared themselves against the rigours of an election, were happy to discomfort Samuel by supporting the Conservatives' demand. If MacDonald and the Liberals proved too stubborn, the Conservatives could leave them high and dry, arguing— with reason—that the immediate financial crisis was over and that only long-term measures (i.e. tariffs) would now suffice. In face of this threat resistance to an election collapsed.

At this point the National government, in effect, ceased to exist. It became a coalition, overwhelmingly Conservative in composition but including small elements of " National " Labour and Simonite Liberals. Of this coalition the official Liberals were never, in any meaningful sense, members. If they remained nominally a part of it, that was because they had nowhere else to go.

20. CLOSING STAGES

The political situation is depressing and surely one of the oddest within our memories ? Ramsay leading the Tories, and people like Donald Maclean faced with the alternative of embracing tariffs or standing out against them *with L-G*, who has become a sort of Wee Free ! I am told the Tories have behaved with the minimum of tact, brushing aside the Liberals as of no account. . . .

Cyril Asquith to Gilbert Murray, 1 October 1931[1]

BY the end of 1931 the Liberals had entirely lost their bearings. Their own failure in 1929, the lamentable performance of Labour since, and the wretched outcome of the plunge into National government, had destroyed their sense of direction. In the next four years they struggled unsuccessfully to recover it.

The election in October 1931 was the Coupon election all over again, with Labour now in the unenviable position occupied by the Liberals in 1918. There were no actual coupons, partly because MacDonald was not attempting to rescue many of his old party and so did not need a device to label them, but mainly because he was in a far weaker position *vis-à-vis* the Conservatives than Lloyd George had been earlier. Nothing would have persuaded them in 1931 to relinquish the 150 seats they conceded to Lloyd George in 1918. Indeed MacDonald had cause to complain about the way they did treat his tiny group of " National Labour " candidates, whose number fell from thirty-five to twenty during the campaign as a result of Tory intransigence. Some Conservatives, he lamented, were using the national emergency for party purposes.

But despite the absence of coupons, the essence of the matter was the same in 1931 as in 1918. In both instances a party which had failed in a national crisis was being assailed by some of its own leaders at the head of a Conservative regime. In both instances the party being assailed could not seriously maintain

[1] Gilbert Murray Papers.

that it had a hope of recovering office. And in both instances the Conservatives as a result were in an impregnable position. The only hope for other parties lay in persuading them to stand aside. In 1918 the Liberals designated by Lloyd George, and in 1931 the Liberals associated with Simon, were usually able to secure their indulgence. The mass of Liberals were not. The fact that in 1931 Liberals were theoretically supporters of the government and were represented in it made no difference. Not even Liberal office-holders were immune from Conservative attack ; and if Baldwin regretted this, he publicly refused (except in the case of Samuel) to say so. As one free trader wrily observed, " Well, I didn't think the Tories would shoot their prisoners."[1]

At least the Liberal party in October 1931 was under no delusion about what was happening. Muir, the party chairman, issued a frank memorandum to Liberal associations at the start of the campaign. (It was marked " private and confidential " but soon got into the press.) " We have been plunged ", he stated, " into an unnecessary and dangerous election in the midst of a national crisis. The sole cause of this wild gamble with the nation's fortunes was the desire of the Conservative party to turn a national emergency to party advantage." He characterised the government's election slogan " A Doctor's Mandate " (a lame attempt to cover over cabinet divisions on tariffs) as a demand for a blank cheque, which would reduce parliamentary government to a nullity. Liberals must support the government, he said, as free traders or not at all. They could not hope for an arrangement regarding seats with the Conservatives, who " will do their best to destroy us, except, possibly, in the constituencies where we alone have any chance of defeating Labour." But without funds the Liberals could achieve little themselves. " We cannot hope to do well in this election ", Muir admitted ; " the dice are loaded against us."[2]

Yet he had no policy to offer except support for the National government—which meant, in most constituencies, support for protectionist candidates. A Labour government at this moment, he wrote, would be " a grave danger ". Liberals should concentrate on trying to capture Labour-held seats, and Tory seats

[1] *Manchester Guardian*, 13 October 1931.
[2] Memorandum by Muir, 7 October 1931, Lothian Papers.

where there was no danger of letting Labour in. His attitude reveals the extent of Liberal revulsion against Labour. Liberals were genuinely appalled at Labour's abdication in face of the economic crisis of August 1931. To a party still drawing inspiration from the Gladstone tradition of financial rectitude, such irresponsibility seemed hard to excuse. Nor was this Labour's only offence. From the outset, Labour members had dismissed the National government as a Tory front. Liberals could not easily forgive them for so soon being proved correct.

Only one prominent Liberal sought to revive the policy of Liberal-Labour co-operation. Lloyd George had given the new government a guarded endorsement for as long as it remained " national "—that is, abstained from an election. When resistance to an election was overriden, he expected Samuel and his colleagues to resign. Their failure to do so he regarded as a gross betrayal, which led him to sever all connection with the party machine. Here was fresh cause for Liberal embarrassment. In the first place Lloyd George, though withholding his fund for other purposes, had for over a year been promising headquarters a substantial contribution to an election. Now he refused to give anything. Secondly, he not only condemned the election as a Tory ramp (which in effect the other Liberal leaders were doing) but drew the conclusion they were seeking to escape : that victory for the government would mean tariffs before Christmas, and that Liberals wanting to preserve free trade had better vote for the only free trade candidates offering— those of the Labour party.[1]

Thus the Liberals went to the country offering three distinct positions : the semi-Conservative position of Simon ; the semi-Labour position of Lloyd George ; and the non-Conservative, anti-Labour position of the official party under Samuel. This variety of postures was scarcely warranted by the number of candidates available. Only 160 Liberal candidates were nominated, and they were divided into supporters of Samuel and supporters of Simon, plus seven independents who opposed the National government. (This last group included not only Lloyd George and his offspring but the thriller-writer, Edgar Wallace.) Many of the seats left uncontested had looked quite promising

---

[1] Lloyd George was prevented by illness from active participation in the campaign. But he issued a manifesto and delivered a broadcast address.

in 1929, including a considerable number where Liberals had come second in three-cornered contests. But in 1931 nowhere looked promising. The party attributed its paucity of candidates to a desire not to split the " national " vote, or to a lack of funds. More important than either was the utter hopelessness of its position.

In the outcome 72 Liberals were elected, while the Conservatives won an awesome 473 seats, and Labour dropped catastrophically to 52. On the face of it the Liberals had done thirteen better than in 1929. But from every standpoint they had lost ground. Their percentage of votes fell. In 51 constituencies fought by the three major parties in 1929 and 1931 (not quite a representative sample) the Liberal share of the poll fell by $7\frac{1}{2}\%$: from 33·1 to 25·7. The party only picked up seats by abandoning its traditional radical position and joining in the hunt against Labour—something the Conservatives could always do better. And it enjoyed a share of the pickings only through Conservative indulgence, that is through the absence of Conservative candidates. Compared with 1929, Liberals in this election lost thirteen seats, all to Conservatives, gained 26, all from Labour, and held 46. Of the 72 gained or held, only ten were contested by official Conservatives (five of these were in Wales and one in the Scottish highlands). The other 62 had no Conservative candidates. In some, admittedly, the Conservatives had little prospect of unseating the Liberals and so lost nothing by " playing the national game". But in the majority, the Conservative party stood aside to keep Labour out, or because it had secured such binding promises from the Liberals that they were Conservatives in all but name. Whereas in 1929 the Liberal party had won its seats in its own strength, in 1931 it secured most of them by grace of its traditional enemies.

There was a further contrast between 1929 and 1931. After the former contest, Liberals had congratulated themselves on the unity of their parliamentary party. After the latter, Liberal M.P.s were palpably divided into three hostile groups : 31 official Liberals, 37 Simonites, and four anti-government Independents.[1] The last-named group did not include Edgar Wallace. He had been heavily defeated at Blackpool by a

[1] In the case of a few Liberal M.P.s, it did not become clear until after the election whether they belonged with Samuel or Simon.

Conservative who, it was suggested, had it all over him when it came to chilling the electors' blood with far-fetched stories.

II

Immediately after the 1931 election, the National government was reconstructed. The changes made reflected the negligible role which Liberals were now expected to play in it. Snowden, still a free trader and hereafter associated with the Liberals, relinquished the Exchequer to an ardent protectionist, Neville Chamberlain.[1] Reading and Crewe, the Liberal elder statesmen, retired from the government, and no Liberals were called in to replace them. The Simonites, by contrast, at last entered into their reward. Simon, who hitherto had received no position (and had been disappointed when Samuel did not resign because of the election), now secured the key post of foreign secretary. And his newly-acquired ally Runciman became President of the Board of Trade. Snowden, strangely enough, backed this last appointment because he regarded Runciman as still a free trader. Yet from the formation of the National government Runciman had provided evidence to the contrary. He had advocated a ban on luxury imports, had offered the government a " free hand " on tariffs to restore the trade balance, and had thrown in his lot with the Simonites—whose distinctive characteristic was support for protection. As a " business " Liberal, his concern had always been as much for rigid economy as for free trade. Alliance with the Conservatives would secure him the former, even if it meant forgoing the latter.[2]

The meaning of these cabinet changes was clear. The Liberals were reduced to three positions (or four including Snowden).[3] It was not that their colleagues were trying to get rid of them. But as long as they were likely to be obliged to leave anyway, the smaller the upheaval caused by their departure the better.

[1] Snowden remained in the cabinet as Lord Privy Seal.

[2] There may have been another, personal, reason for Runciman's defection to the Simonites. Samuel relates in his *Memoirs* (p. 205) that when the National government was originally formed " Lloyd George, not being willing to let bygones be bygones, raised strong objection to one or two of my suggestions for junior posts . . . . those exclusions gave rise to difficulties afterwards."

[3] The number dropped by one in mid-1932, when Maclean died and his post went to a Conservative.

THE SEARCH FOR A SOLUTION

In January 1932 the cabinet decided, inevitably, on a policy of full-scale tariffs, and the Liberals sent in their resignations. But their colleagues, although unwilling to forgo tariffs to keep them, were prepared to modify the forms of the constitution. They persuaded the Liberals to stay by proposing the " agreement to differ ", suspending collective cabinet responsibility on the tariff issue. Under this arrangement, Liberal ministers while remaining in the government were free to speak and vote against its tariff policy. This arrangement rapidly became unworkable. Its justification was that ministers, although divided on tariffs, were agreed on everything else. The trouble was that the government was not doing anything else. Tariffs were its major accomplishment, and of them it was doing a great deal. So Liberals, by differing from it on this matter, were attacking it at the centre. What was more, the tariff issue was central not only to the government but to the Liberal party. Free trade, far from being just one aspect of Liberal policy, was Liberalism's *sine qua non*. Its importance ranged far outside the field of economics. It was the symbol of the great Liberal age, the meeting-ground of the party's diverse elements, the expression of the Liberal hope for a free society and international reconciliation. Liberals could not just " differ " from a government which was destroying it. They must view such a government with profound animosity.

During 1932, rank and file opposition to the " agreement to differ " became formidable. From the start this arrangement had been more acceptable to the older generation, like Grey, Howard, and Margot Asquith, than to the younger, like Muir, Hubert Phillips, and Violet Bonham Carter. Muir called it " the most astounding departure from Constitutional usage that we have yet heard of ", the " logical consequence " of deciding to hold an election after ministers had realised that they could not agree on fundamentals.[1] This view gathered considerable support. In March 1932 the League of Young Liberals called upon " all Ministers still using the name Liberal to come out of the Government forthwith ", and the Union of University Liberal Societies asked free trade ministers " to tender their resignations immediately or withdraw from the Party."[2] The annual meeting of the Manchester Liberal Federation, with

[1] *Liberal Magazine*, February 1932.   [2] *ibid*, April 1932.

only four dissentients, passed a resolution condemning " the reactionary and protectionist activities manifest in the National Government " and looking forward to the day when Samuel and his colleagues would " resign office and again champion the cause of Liberalism in the country "—this despite the presence of a Liberal whip who claimed that opposition from within the government carried twenty times the weight of opposition from without, and that no amount of agitation would make Liberal ministers do what they did not think was right.[1] Only with difficulty was the annual meeting of the N.L.F. restrained from passing a similar resolution. Even so, it repudiated " any obligation to support the policy of the present Government " and hoped that " the united strength of the Party, free from all entanglements ", would soon participate in the fight for free trade.[2]

In face of this pressure Liberal ministers could not stay in the government much longer. In September 1932 the resolutions of the Ottawa Conference, extending protection in yet another direction, gave them cause to resign. As one of the junior Liberal ministers, Lord Lothian, admitted, should they try to stay on, the N.L.F. and probably a majority of the party would go against them.[3] Yet even now Samuel and his colleagues did not know where to go. Part of them was drawn to the radical, anti-Conservative stance of 1929, part looked longingly to the national front of 1931. Lothian, in discussing the decision to resign, alternated between these positions and seemingly fell between them. On the one hand he was reluctant to break up " the national front agreement ", on the other he assumed that " they would in time have to try to co-operate " with Labour. He envisaged their ultimate task as " trying to infuse the Liberal spirit of reason and tolerance into the left parties ", but for the moment saw their role as " criticism and support " of the government " from an independent but friendly position ".[4] Consequently the Liberals, although resigning, remained seated

---

[1] Minutes of the Manchester Liberal Federation, 11 April 1932.

[2] *Liberal Magazine*, May 1932.

[3] Thomas Jones, *A Diary With Letters 1931–1950*, pp. 52–4. Lothian, formerly Philip Kerr and Lloyd George's private secretary from 1916 to 1921, was playing a considerable part in Liberal affairs at this time.

[4] *ibid.*

on the government benches. This looked like a further variant on the agreement to differ, an attempt " to infuse the Liberal spirit of reason and tolerance " not into the left parties but into the right. Sinclair gave colour to this when he said in October 1933 : " Because the Tories have been false to the National appeal, does that justify our being false ? "[1]

The Liberal rank and file could not appreciate these subtleties. The party could only advance by capturing seats from the Conservative hordes in Parliament, and it was not likely to do this while remaining in proximity to the government. So during 1933 pressure of the sort which had driven the Liberal leaders out of the government was exerted to drive them off the government benches. This time the annual conference of the N.L.F. actually passed an amendment criticising its parliamentary representatives. It said that, " whilst not wishing to usurp the responsibility of the Parliamentary Party and its leaders ", nevertheless " their appropriate place is on the Opposition Benches ". And the annual meeting of the Scottish Liberal Federation resolved that it " would welcome the passing of the Liberal party in the House of Commons into formal Opposition by way of making the political situation more clear to their supporters throughout the country."[2] Once more the party leaders gave way. In November 1933 Samuel announced that they would move on to the opposition benches.

III

During the next two years this decision boomeranged. For one thing, much as the Liberal leaders yearned for free trade, they could not pretend that in existing economic conditions they would instantly restore it. Moreover, just before the 1935 election an international crisis blew up in which they were obliged to support the government. In response to the Italian attack on Abyssinia, the Conservatives appeared to be embracing the doctrine of collective security through the League of Nations. This placed Liberals, who held the League very dear, in a cleft stick. They found themselves, to quote the *Liberal Magazine* for December 1935, " condemning and supporting the Government at the same time, though on different grounds ". Under

[1] *Liberal Magazine*, November 1933.   [2] *ibid*, June and November 1933.

such " peculiar handicaps ", " few people of experience expected better results " for the Liberals.

Yet the actual circumstances of the 1935 election probably affected their fate in only a handful of constituencies. The real problem was that since 1933 the party had failed to recover the *raison d'être* which it had lost when the National government ceased to be national. In a broadcast address on 16 November 1933, Samuel justified the Liberal decision to go into opposition on the grounds that there must be an alternative government available other than the Labour party—a party bound to precipitate another financial crisis, and containing " a powerful section " " careless of political liberty ". " Whenever the next general election comes we shall present a full complement of candidates to the constituencies throughout Great Britain ", and so " give the electorate an opportunity of returning a Liberal Government to power ". Muir at the same time stated : " We have got to fight all along the line at the next election. We at headquarters see our way to fighting at least 400 seats. We may not have much support financially, but 400 is the minimum we are going to fight."[1] These were pipe-dreams. The party no longer possessed the resources, in candidates, organisation, or enthusiasm, to fight on a national front. When the election came in 1935, only 161 Liberal candidates were available. Samuel in these circumstances could not talk of offering an alternative government. The most he could ask was that the Liberals should be " greatly strengthened ", thus becoming a " most useful factor " in safeguarding the country from " a complacent and idle Toryism " and " a reckless subversive Socialism ".[2]

Yet even had there been more candidates, did a valid position exist for an " alternative government " squeezed in between Labour and the Conservatives ? Whatever Liberals might say publicly, in private some of them doubted it. In September 1933 Lothian made this analysis of the Liberal situation :

From a party point of view Liberalism is in an almost hopeless position, so long as Baldwin is leader of the Conservative Party and Arthur Henderson the leading figure in the Labour Party. Both are democrats, liberally minded, supporters of disarmament and the League of Nations, and

[1] *ibid*, December 1933.   [2] Broadcast address on 6 November 1935.

constitutionalists. Both, too, are moderate tariffists, even friendly, in theory, to free trade. It is obviously as impossible for the Liberal Party to advocate an immediate and unilateral return to free trade in a world in which competitive economic nationalism has reduced the world price of almost everything below the cost of production, as it is for it to advocate a policy of immediate and unilateral disarmament. We have, therefore, no future by just talking what may be called the general principles of Liberalism and criticising certain aspects of the Government's policy. Apart from the stalwart remnant of the old guard the mass of voters will tend to vote for one or other of the two major parties, which at any rate have some hope of coming into power and are both, to-day, essentially liberal minded.[1]

This acute analysis was not intended as a counsel of despair. Lothian was suggesting that Liberals should seek another role in politics. Instead of trying to insert themselves between two " essentially liberal minded " parties, they should show themselves to be a manifestly different party. And to do this they must adopt a distinctive and constructive programme (which he proceeded to outline). Yet this was hardly a novel suggestion. Lloyd George had tried it in 1929. His failure then had thrown doubt on the whole notion that a programme, however meritorious and far-sighted, would convert the Liberal party into a separate third force. Anyway by the mid-1930s there was little opportunity to put forward a really distinctive programme. If anything, the country was suffering from a surfeit of them— if not of statesmen to carry them out. Nor did the Liberals now possess (as they had in 1929) a leader capable of supplying the crusading zeal necessary to put a big programme across. Samuel and his colleagues spoke much sense on matters of economic revival and international security. But their very balance, caution, and intellectual integrity conflicted with the sort of campaign which Lothian envisaged. Kenneth Clark, the director of the National Gallery, compared the Liberals with the school of " belated impressionists or pure painters "—a school which " still has the support of sensitive, educated people " but retained " no power over the general imagination." " Like Liberalism it depends too much on fine perceptions of

[1] Memorandum by Lothian, 7 September 1933, **Lothian Papers.**

CLOSING STAGES

right and wrong and shuns crude assertion or violent appeals to the emotions." [1] This was said a month before the 1935 election, and it summed up the Liberals' role in that contest. The manifesto and speeches of the Liberal leaders were full of " fine perceptions of right and wrong ". What they lacked were " crude assertion " and " violent appeals to the emotions."

[1] Quoted in *Liberal Magazine*, October 1935.

EPILOGUE

Lloyd George, no doubt,
When his life ebbs out,
Will ride on a flaming chariot,
Seated in state
On a red-hot plate
'twixt Satan and Judas Iscariot;
Ananias that day
To the Devil will say,
" My claim for precedence fails,
So move me up higher,
Away from the fire,
And make way for that liar—from Wales!"

Traditional

[H]is name now stands with Chatham, and with Chatham alone, as the greatest
of War Ministers in our history.

R. B. McCallum (writing in 1936) on Lloyd George [1]

In the 1935 election the Liberals once again suffered a set-back.
Their voting strength fell,[2] and their parliamentary representation was almost halved. Of the 31 seats secured by Samuel's
followers in 1931, seventeen were lost in 1935—eleven to Labour
and six to government supporters. Fourteen were retained,
and three were captured from Conservatives (by narrow majorities and in the absence of Labour candidates). This brought the
party's total to seventeen. In addition, Lloyd George's family
group of four retained their seats, and after the election took the
Liberal whip. This brought the total to 21. As for the Simonites,
they need not be considered. For some time their leaders had
been appearing at Conservative functions and supporting Con-

---

[1] McCallum, *Asquith*, p. 127.

[2] Only a small number of seats is available for comparison. There were
30 constituencies contested by the three major parties in 1931 and 1935, and
in them the Liberal share of the vote fell by 4%: from 29·4 to 25·3.

servatives against Liberals at by-elections, and all their seats
were secured with Conservative aid. So even though one of their
number, Clement Davies, eventually returned to the Liberals
and led the party after 1945, the Simonites may be fairly classified
with the Conservatives.

Thus by 1935 the Liberals, having been reduced to the status
of a minor party, were being hard pressed to maintain even
minor-party representation. Unlike the pre-1914 Labour and
Irish parties, they possessed no concentrated body of supporters,
and hence very few safe seats. Only in Wales, which returned
seven of their 21 members, did they retain a few apparent
strongholds. As for their three constituencies in Scotland and
their eleven in England, they were scattered over the country
without rhyme or reason.

But in truth the Liberals did not think of themselves as a
minor party representing some regional or sectional interest.
They might propose devolution for Scotland and Wales, but
they had no intention of becoming simply a party of Scottish
and Welsh nationalism. In the recent past they had constituted
one of the great parties of the state; and they could not turn
their backs on this past. However attenuated their parliamentary party, however formidable the problems of fighting on
a national front or distinguishing themselves from the two major
parties, they still saw themselves as a national party concerned
with national issues. The answer to their problems must lie
in these terms.

Yet by 1935 no answer had presented itself. The blows
suffered by Labour in 1931 had not redounded to their advantage. If Labour made only a limited recovery in 1935, the
Conservatives, not the Liberals, were the beneficiaries. For the
Liberal party, the search for a solution had thus far gone
unrewarded.

II

Among the defeated Liberals in 1935 were some of the party's
outstanding figures. Samuel, the party leader, Walter Rea and
Harcourt Johnstone, two of the whips, and Isaac Foot, one of
the principal representatives of West Country Nonconformity,
all lost their seats. Among junior members of the last Liberal

government, only Acland remained in Parliament ; among senior, only Lloyd George. And the latter never again played a prominent part in Liberal affairs.

Yet if Lloyd George was, to all intents and purposes, lost to the Liberal party from 1931, it is fitting that he should be the subject of a last word. Any leave-taking would be incomplete if it did not attempt a summing-up of an individual who has loomed so large in these pages.

The events of 1931 had appeared to open up a new phase for Lloyd George. From the time in 1930 when he had decided to support the Labour government, he had done so with—for him—surprising consistency. This, together with the feeble performance of Labour's own leaders, had caused one member of the government, George Lansbury, to urge him early in 1931 to join the Labour party. The events of the following August to October had seemed to facilitate this course. At no stage did he appear to like the National government, whereas to start with the Liberal party rejoiced at it. He was a leader becoming detached from his party; and the Labour party was now almost leaderless. In Parliament just before the dissolution, Herbert Morrison referred to Lloyd George's absence through illness as being deplored by everyone, but by none more than the Labour party. The rest of his sentence was drowned in a roar of Labour cheering. Soon afterwards, Henderson spent several hours at Lloyd George's sick-bed, with the result that Lloyd George repudiated the anti-Labour policy adopted by the Liberal party in the 1931 election.

This indeed was a tide in the affairs of one man. As the forces of radicalism lay prostrate, the country's greatest radical seemed about to find a new home and to give a new lead. As he bluntly told Samuel, " If I am to die, I would rather die fighting on the Left. "[1] But it all came to nothing. The chance was let slip, the flood-tide receded. Lloyd George withdrew to write his war memoirs, and to fight over again—always successfully—the battles of two decades before. (He fought some more recent battles while he was about it. The scathing denunciations of Grey and Samuel in his *War Memoirs* owed more to the events of the past few years than to anything that had happened during the war). When he returned to political activity in 1935,

[1] Samuel, *Memoirs*, p. 211.

it was not as a leader of Liberals or Labour. He produced yet another programme to cure the country's ills, and founded the Council of Action to propagate it. He took comfort in his ample financial resources, and talked about running 340 candidates. But when the election came there were no candidates, only questionnaires to the candidates of other parties. This was the *reductio ad absurdum* of the Beaverbrook-Lloyd George obsession with campaigns and programmes as a means of transforming the face of politics. Lloyd George had failed in 1929 when he had had only a weak party behind him. Now he was trying with no party at all. There was never the remotest prospect of success.

The Council of Action duly passed out of existence, and Lloyd George, with his enemies Baldwin and Neville Chamberlain in the ascendant, withdrew to the role of elder statesman. But in 1940 the chance of a comeback presented itself. Events in Europe shattered Chamberlain's career (aided by a sharp push in Parliament from Lloyd George himself) and brought the other leading political outcast of the 1930s, Churchill, to the premiership. For over thirty years he and Lloyd George had been nearer rivals than allies. But just as Lloyd George, when his ascendancy was unassailable in 1917, had given Churchill a hand up, now Churchill was happy to reciprocate. He offered Lloyd George a post in the war cabinet. At this moment every potential biographer of Lloyd George sharpened his pencil for a concluding flourish : " Now, at last, in a crisis as grave as December 1916, the nation recalled the pilot who had brought it through that earlier storm. Of course he was too old now to take the first place. But the national will to victory could not have been fully expressed without his presence in a position of authority. . . ." The purple passages, alas, had to be laid aside. The opportunity, now as in 1931, was rejected. He announced that he was " not going in with this gang." He seemed to think of himself as the Prime Minister after this one, even perhaps as a latter-day Lansdowne arranging a negotiated peace. On some occasions he offered hostility to Chamberlain (who retained a post in the government) as the reason for his refusal. But it was jealousy of Churchill, more than anything, which probably decided his course. This ended all prospect that he might ever again play a part in British affairs. So, in a haze of irrelevance, he stumbled from the stage of history, delivering one final blow to his biographers, two months before his death in March 1945, by accepting an earldom.

There is much that is hard to fathom about Lloyd George's conduct during these years. But the point that needs to be stressed is that this is true of more than his last phase. An element of incomprehensibility exists all through. The great error in trying to understand him, made by his contemporaries as well as by his biographers, is to imagine that there was always some purpose, some carefully-laid plan, underlying his every action. Too often he acted without plan or purpose.

One random example will help to show this : his speech to the N.L.F. annual conference in June 1926. It will be recalled that this was an important event for Lloyd George. A month earlier Asquith had broken with him because of his abstention from a meeting of the shadow cabinet. It was clear that the N.L.F. conference was not going to endorse this action. But a substantial Asquithian element was present. When Lloyd George entered to speak in support of a resolution on land reform, he appeared to be setting out to win his opponents over by showing that he was a leader above faction, anxious to restore the unity of the party. For much of his speech he came close to succeeding. There was no vocal opposition, and on several occasions he seemed on the point of carrying the whole gathering. Then he moved into his peroration. What, he asked, did the agricultural labourer want from the Liberal party ? The answer he gave was incredible : " Believe me," he stated, " he is not searching registers of shadow or other cabinets to see who has attended and who has not. If he did, believe me, he would have many surprises in the regular attendants and the regular absentees." These remarks split the meeting asunder. His reference to " shadow or other cabinets " produced an outburst of cheers and boos, and at the end of the first sentence someone shouted : " What about unity now ? " Lloyd George waded on. What the agricultural labourer was looking to Liberalism for, he began ; but it was no good. A voice answered : " Loyalty." But neither the interjector nor anyone else was now thinking of the agricultural labourer.

This performance was simply inept. No doubt there was something to be said for making a pugnacious speech. Certainly there was much to be said for making a conciliatory speech.

But a speech which began by appealing for unity and then tore open the wounds of conflict had neither point nor object.

Did Lloyd George know what he was trying to achieve by such conduct ? It is unlikely. The urge to act, and then find out where his action led, was a major element in his career. Yet this is not the popular conception of him. He is regarded as a master of artifice, moving with infinite cunning towards clearly-defined objectives. So it has been said that he unseated Asquith in 1916 by a " complex intrigue " conducted with " ruthless skill."[1] Such statements must be viewed with caution. Certainly Lloyd George was a compulsive, obsessive intriguer. But he did not always seem to know where his intrigues were supposed to be leading. And it is far from clear that indulgence in them assisted his advance to power. Indeed it is more probable that his passion for duplicity, instead of helping him to secure the premiership, was a major force in keeping him out of it.

In view of the widespread belief that, at least between 1914 and 1916, Lloyd George proved himself to be a master of intrigue, it is worthwhile looking again at his conduct during these years. If he was convinced that the war was being mismanaged, and that he alone could " save this nation ", then he needed to follow one of two courses. Either he must convert Asquith into a figurehead, a sort of Newcastle to his Chatham, or else he must drive him out of office. The first required the conciliation of Asquith. The second required a firm alliance between Lloyd George and the leading Conservatives. Lloyd George attempted neither. He alienated Asquith by his open disloyalty. Yet he had no sooner formed an alliance with the Conservative leader than he turned round and smashed it to pieces. Lloyd George's conduct in May 1915, just after he had established the conditions for Asquith's overthrow, probably had more to do with Asquith's retention of office until December 1916 than any other single factor.

It has often been remarked that Asquith gave Bonar Law only a relatively minor office when forming the first coalition. And it has been usual to puzzle over Asquith's motives, the assumption being that this action alienated Bonar Law and so contributed to Asquith's eventual overthrow. Yet there is no evidence that Bonar Law felt resentment against Asquith over

[1] David Thomson, *England in the Twentieth Century*, p. 47.

this matter. That he felt resentment is certain. But it was not against Asquith. It was against Lloyd George. For Lloyd George was Asquith's willing instrument in the manœuvre which kept Bonar Law out of the Exchequer and gave it to McKenna. If Lloyd George had stood with Bonar Law, Asquith would have had to capitulate. Instead Lloyd George threw his weight on the other side. In Bonar Law's view, it was Lloyd George who had cheated him, not Asquith. And this was the principal cause of his bitter resentment against Lloyd George for the next eighteen months—resentment which was decisive in enabling Asquith to survive that long.

Lloyd George's behaviour in this matter is of the same order as his address to the N.L.F. in 1926 : if it had not happened, one would not consider it possible. Asquith's speedy surrender to the demand for a coalition had revealed the power of a Lloyd George-Bonar Law combination. Why should Lloyd George then alienate his new ally just to secure the Exchequer for the Liberal who, above all others, hated him ? His motive was not to conciliate McKenna : he insisted on a statement being issued that McKenna was only serving as *locum tenens* for himself. Thus he succeeded in preserving McKenna as an enemy while converting Bonar Law into one. Whatever his reasons, it is not surprising that he soon came profoundly to regret this conduct.

Yet his bungling did not stop there. In September 1915 he formed an alliance with Curzon over the conscription issue. Now Curzon had designs on the Conservative leadership, so this antagonised Bonar Law further—it was he who first warned Asquith of what Lloyd George and Curzon were up to. But from Lloyd George's point of view, Curzon for Bonar Law was not a bad swap. There was a good chance that Lloyd George and Curzon together could oust both Asquith and Bonar Law. The trouble was that while this manœuvre was developing, Lloyd George became engaged in a ding-dong row with Curzon over the strategic issue of Salonika-versus-the Dardanelles. Thus another promising alliance came to an end. By the end of 1915 Lloyd George had scarcely a prominent Conservative ally left. Walter Long about this time was using the word " Judas " in regard to him.[1] And Bonar Law admitted " a little change of feeling in his party " towards Lloyd George on account of his " instab-

[1] Sir Percy Harris, *Forty Years In and Out of Parliament*, p. 69.

EPILOGUE

ility and lack of judgment ". Hence the Conservatives " were
on the whole more disposed to put up with Asquith." According
to Garvin in January 1916 : " One after another [Lloyd George]
had alienated every leading member of the Cabinet. Balfour,
with whom he was once intimate, Asquith & McKenna with
both of whom he was at enmity and now Bonar Law. . . . He
hd. become a sort of Ishmael."[1]

It may seem lamentable that during a great conflict such
personal considerations should have turned the Conservative
leaders against Lloyd George and " disposed " them " to put
up with Asquith." But it illustrates Lloyd George's deficiency
in political judgement that he did not recognise such things ; so
that it required another year of military calamities before Bonar
Law could be driven by his rank and file to resume the alliance
with Lloyd George which the latter had so wantonly destroyed.
Far from Lloyd George intriguing his way into power, it is a fair
guess that but for his obsession with sharp practice he would
have become Prime Minister at least a year before he did—and
he might even have accomplished this with the consent of
Asquith, or anyway with the consent of Asquith's party.

We err in calling Lloyd George a Machiavellian, if we mean a
man of deep purpose and ruthless practice. At times he came
nearer the Machiavel of the Elizabethan stage, who revelled in
intrigue for its own sake and indulged in duplicity so palpable
that only the exigencies of the plot caused anyone to be deceived
by him. Frequently Lloyd George's political manœuvrings
suggested that he knew neither his ultimate objective nor the
means of attaining it. And if he was often unscrupulous and
disloyal, these qualities were so apparent that they defeated
their own ends. Asquith after his fall comforted himself with
the conviction that Lloyd George had stabbed him in the back.
The truth was otherwise. A man with Lloyd George's reputation
for back-stabbing is not presented with any backs to pierce.
He dislodged Asquith by frontal assault, if only because no other
line of advance was open to him.

If these considerations help to explain the ill-repute into which
he ultimately fell, the barrenness of his later years, and the

[1] Scott's diary, 15 December 1915 and 27 January 1916, C. P. Scott Papers.
Scott's diary has been the major source for information in the last three
paragraphs.

opportunities he failed to grasp, they also throw light on his triumphs. For if he did not reach the pinnacle because of, but in spite of, his obsession with political tactics, it follows that he achieved it by sheer capacity. Time and again, Lloyd George proved himself to be the necessary man. Before the war radicalism and Nonconformity needed a leader, and Lloyd George, for all his shortcomings (not least in his personal morals), alone filled the bill. The same was true after 1926 : the " old gang " profoundly believed that the party had taken his side against Asquith's because he had " bought " it with his fund. But the fund was a stumbling-block to the party's acceptance of him, not the cause of it. The party turned to him because it needed his positive qualities so badly. He alone could hold out any hope of a Liberal revival ; he alone possessed the drive, the dynamism, the streak of daring, which might accomplish it. So it was during the First World War. Whatever his shortcomings, by the end of 1916 it was evident that he alone could bring spirit and resolution to the direction of the war effort. This is his ultimate justification. One may adapt some expressions which Pitt the Elder used of himself. In December 1916, when others had fallen short in the service of the state, Lloyd George was summoned by his sovereign and by the voice of the people to save this nation. That trust he faithfully discharged. Nothing that has been said in these chapters about his effect on the Liberal party is intended to detract from that mighty achievement.

III

In most senses the events recounted here are very much past history. The age of Lloyd George, MacDonald, and Baldwin seems remote. Quite apart from the passage of time, a world war has separated our day from theirs. Yet in one sense we have lived until very recently in the shadow of the events related in this book. In the half-century following August 1914 the Conservatives held office continually, with only one major interruption—the Labour government of 1945-1951. In part this was a consequence of the decline of the left. The left parties suffered from the loss of buoyancy and self-confidence which followed from Britain's decline as a world power and the experiences of the First World War, as well as from the twin phenom-

ena of economic growth and economic crisis which ran parallel
after 1914. The resultant urge to play safe proved largely to the
advantage of the Conservatives. So did the decline in " idealism ". This was partly a result of the circumstances just mentioned. But other forces helped to cause it : among them the
concession of votes to women, the emergence of bolshevism as
a world force (despite its basic irrelevance to British politics),
and the decline in religious belief—for contrary to a popular
view, periods of religious vigour are likely to be periods of
political radicalism, and periods of religious quiescence periods of
political conservatism.

Yet when this has been said, it must be added that, in terms
of elections, the left parties did not do as badly during these
fifty years as the succession of Conservative governments would
suggest. What happened was that election results of the sort
which kept the Conservatives out of power for a decade before
1914 scarcely interrupted their tenure of office after it.
Thus in 1923, 1929, and 1950 the left parties won substantial
electoral victories, which earlier would have assured them
of perhaps fifteen years in office. Yet these elections actually
kept the Conservatives out of power for only four years all
told. Before 1914 the Liberal and Labour parties so managed
their electoral affairs that between them they derived the
maximum advantage from votes cast against the Conservatives.
After 1914 this became impossible. During the First World
War Labour became convinced—and the decrepit state of
Liberalism even by 1918 seemed to justify the conviction—
that the Liberal party would soon be extinguished altogether
and that Labour would appropriate its entire following ; then
the " swing of the pendulum " would do the rest. By concentrating on destroying the Liberals, Labour was ensuring its
own victory " in the long run ", even though in the short run
the Conservatives benefited. The trouble with this view proved
to be that the short run went on and on. Even the 1945
election proved, as a fulfilment of Labour prophecies, to be a
false dawn. At every other election after 1914 when the anti-
Conservative parties did well, a sufficient number of electors
preferred Liberal to Labour (even though " a vote for the
Liberals is a vote wasted ") to deprive Labour of a secure
majority.

Yet after 1914 certain concepts became so potent in the thinking of the left that not even a succession of Conservative governments could bring a halt to the strife between Labour and Liberals. During the inter-war years it was fashionable to classify the Liberals as a " capitalist " party, which had involved Britain in an " imperialist " war, and was incapable of achieving " socialism " or of speaking for " the workers ". Whether these concepts had any basis in reality is an open question ; what is not in question is that they were believed to represent reality. The Liberal party fell, in short, because of a revolution in ideas occurring in the minds of men. The revolution may have begun before 1914. But only the war, and the action during it of certain Liberals best equipped to deflect the revolution, ensured that it would triumph.

After 1945 these concepts lost much of their hold, notwithstanding the charges of " socialist " and " capitalist " which the Liberal and Labour parties still felt obliged to level at each other. But the two parties continued to be heirs to the history related in these pages ; the Conservatives correspondingly were its beneficiaries. Thus whether one views the downfall of the Liberal party as triumph, or tragedy, or neither, depends ultimately on whether one regards the past half-century of Conservative rule as a blessing, or a misfortune, or a matter of complete indifference.

LIBERALS AND GENERAL ELECTIONS,
1914-1935

NOTE : statistics of seats held, gained, and lost are based on a comparison with the preceding general election, irrespective of what might have happened to these seats in the interval.

Number of Liberals in the House of Commons, August 1914   261

1918 ELECTION

Independent Liberals elected		27
Elected with the coupon	8	
Elected without the coupon	19	
Coalition Liberals elected		138
Elected with the coupon	128	
Elected without the coupon	10	
(*Total* Liberals elected with the coupon	136	
Total Liberals elected without the coupon	29)	
Total Liberals elected 1918		165

1922 ELECTION

Independent Liberals elected			56
Seats held			13
Seats gained :	from Conservatives	31	
:	from Coalition Liberals	10	
:	from Labour	1	
:	from Independent	1	
	Total gains		43
Seats lost :	to Conservatives	3	
:	to Coalition Liberals	2	
:	to Labour	9	
	Total losses		14
Coalition Liberals elected			60
Seats held			57
Seats gained :	from Independent Liberals	2	
:	from Labour	1	
	Total gains		3

Seats lost	:	to Conservatives	31	
	:	to Independent Liberals	10	
	:	to Labour	39	
	:	to Independent	1	
		Total losses		81
Total Liberals elected 1922				116

1923 ELECTION (*following Liberal reunion*)

Seats held				75
Seats gained	:	from Conservatives	69	
	:	from Labour	13	
	:	from Independent	1	
		Total gains		83
Seats lost	:	to Conservatives	16	
	:	to Labour	23	
	:	to Independent	2	
		Total losses		41
Total Liberals elected 1923				158

1924 ELECTION

Seats held				34
Seats gained	:	from Labour	8	
	:	from Independent	1	
		Total gains		9
Seats lost	:	to Conservatives	107	
	:	to Labour	16	
	:	to Communist	1	
		Total losses		124
Total Liberals elected 1924				43

1929 ELECTION

Seats held				24
Seats gained	:	from Conservatives	33	
	:	from Labour	2	
		Total gains		35
Seats lost	:	to Labour	17	
	:	to Independent	2	
		Total losses		19
Total Liberals elected 1929				59

Seats held			46
Seats gained :	from Labour	26	
		───	
	Total gains		26
Seats lost :	to Conservatives	13	
		───	
	Total losses		13

Samuel Liberals elected	31
Lloyd George Liberals elected	4
Simonite Liberals elected	37

Total Liberals elected 1931 (including Simonites)   72

Samuel Liberals elected			17
Seats held			14
Seats gained :	from Conservatives	3	
		───	
	Total gains		3
Seats lost :	to Conservatives	4	
:	to Simonite Liberal	1	
:	to MacDonald Labour	1	
:	to Labour	11	
		───	
	Total losses		17
Lloyd George Liberals elected			4
Seats held			4

Simonite Liberals elected			33
Seats held			30
Seats gained :	from Conservatives[1]	2	
:	from Liberals	1	
		───	
	Total gains		3
Seats lost :	to Conservatives[1]	1	
:	to Labour	6	
		───	
	Total losses		7

Total Liberals elected 1935 (excluding Simonites)   21

---

[1] These seats changed hands by agreement between the Conservatives and the Simonites, not as a result of contests between them.

LIBERAL CHIEF WHIPS, 1914-1935

I 1914—DECEMBER 1916

1914 Percy Illingworth
January 1915 John Gulland

II DECEMBER 1916—NOVEMBER 1923

(During this period both Asquith and Lloyd George had their chief whips.
In fact only Asquith's nominee was entitled to be described as chief
Liberal whip, but for convenience both are listed.)

Asquith		*Lloyd George*		
December 1916	John Gulland	December 1916		Neil Primrose
February 1919	George Thorne	May	1917	F. E. Guest
	(with J. M. Hogge)	April	1921	C. A. McCurdy
February 1923	Vivian Phillipps	December 1922		E. Hilton Young

III NOVEMBER 1923 (LIBERAL REUNION)—1935

January 1924 Vivian Phillipps
November 1924 Sir Godfrey Collins
November 1926 Sir R. Hutchison
November 1930 Sir Archibald Sinclair
September 1931 Goronwy Owen
November 1931 Walter Rea

ACKNOWLEDGEMENTS

The following individuals and institutions have very kindly granted me permission to quote from documents of which they hold the copyright :
Sir Richard and Lady Acland (Francis Acland's correspondence) ; Beaverbrook Newspapers, and the late Lord Beaverbrook (Lloyd George's correspondence) ; Mrs. Mary Bennett (H.A.L. Fisher's diary and correspondence) ; Birmingham University Library (Sir Austen Chamberlain's correspondence) ; Mr. Mark Bonham Carter (H. H. Asquith's correspondence) ; The Trustees of the British Museum (J. A. Spender's correspondence) ; Sir Donald Finnemore (W. Finnemore's correspondence) ; Lord Forres (Sir Archibald Williamson's correspondence) ; Lord Gainford (J. A. Pease's correspondence) ; Mr. C. A. Gladstone of Hawarden (Herbert Gladstone's correspondence) ; Mr. John Grigg (Sir Edward Grigg's correspondence) ; Mrs. Isobel Henderson (Gilbert Murray's correspondence) ; Mr. Albert Ingham (Minutes of the Leeds and Yorkshire Liberal Federations) ; Mrs. Harold Laski, and the Harvard University Press (extracts from *Holmes-Laski Letters*) ; Lord Lothian (Lord Lothian's correspondence) ; Mr. A. D. Maclean (Sir Donald Maclean's correspondence) ; Lord Melchett (Sir Alfred Mond's correspondence) ; Lady Mottistone, Mr. A. R. B. Haldane, and Mr. A. H. Noble (Lord Murray of Elibank's correspondence, and A. C. Murray's diary and correspondence) ; The Trustees of the National Library of Scotland (Lord Haldane's correspondence) ; Mr. H. R. Oldman (H. F. Oldman's correspondence) ; Mr. Maurice Phillipps (Vivian Phillipps's correspondence) ; Mr. G. Philip Robinson (Minutes of the Manchester Liberal Federation) ; Lord Rothermere (Lord Rothermere's correspondence) ; Mr. L. P. Scott (C. P. Scott's diary) ; Lord and Lady Thurso (Sir Archibald Sinclair's correspondence) ; Lord Wimborne (F. E. Guest's correspondence) ; Mr. Arthur Worsley and Mr. N. Stanton (Minutes of the Lancashire, Cheshire, and North Western Liberal Federation).

SELECT BIBLIOGRAPHY

The following are the main sources for this book :

A PRIVATE PAPERS

Francis Acland Papers, in the possession of Sir Richard and Lady Acland.
Asquith Papers, in the Bodleian Library.
Bolton Liberal Association Minutes, in the office of the Association.
John Burns Papers, in the British Museum.
Elibank Papers, in the National Library of Scotland.
H. A. L. Fisher Papers, in the Bodleian Library.
A. G. Gardiner Papers, in the possession of Mr. and Mrs. Clive Gardiner.
Lloyd George Papers (a selection only), in the possession of Beaverbrook
    Newspapers.
Herbert (Viscount) Gladstone Papers, in the British Museum.
Edward Grigg Papers, in the possession of Mr. John Grigg.
Haldane Papers, in the National Library of Scotland.
Lancashire, Cheshire, and North Western Liberal Federation Minutes, in
    the office of the Federation.
Leeds Liberal Federation Minutes, in the office of the Federation.
Lothian Papers, in the Scottish Record Office, Register House.
Manchester Liberal Federation Minutes, in the office of the Federation.
Milner Papers, in the Bodleian Library.
Alfred Mond Papers, in the possession of Lord Melchett.
Gilbert Murray Papers, in the Bodleian Library.
C. P. Scott Papers, in the British Museum.
Scottish Liberal Federation Minutes, in the library of Edinburgh University.
J. A. Spender Papers, in the British Museum.
Yorkshire Liberal Federation Minutes, in the office of the Federation.

B SERIAL PUBLICATIONS

A great many daily newspapers have been consulted for various aspects of
this book, as well as other periodical literature. Without enumerating the
particular issues that have been referred to, it would be pointless to list
them all.
    The following list is confined to publications which have been con-
sulted for the greater part of the period dealt with. All except *The Glasgow
Herald* and the *Manchester Guardian* originated in London.
*Daily Chronicle; Daily News; The Glasgow Herald; Liberal Magazine; Liberal
Yearbook; Manchester Guardian; Nation; Parliamentary Debates, House
of Commons (H.C. Deb.); The Times; Westminster Gazette.*

The number of books providing background information about the period under consideration is very large. The number dealing with the actual topic of this book is not. The list below is confined to books mentioned in the text or cited in footnotes. All of them were published in London, unless otherwise stated.

ADDISON, CHRISTOPHER, *Four and a Half Years*, 2 vols, Hutchinson, 1934.

ASQUITH, H. H., *The Paisley Policy*, Cassell, 1920.

BAKER, E. B., and BAKER, P. J. NOEL, *J. Allen Baker: A Memoir*, The Swarthmore Press, 1927.

BASSETT, R., *Nineteen Thirty-One Political Crisis*, Macmillan, 1958.

BEAVERBROOK, LORD, *Politicians and the War*, one-volume edition, Oldbourne Book Co., 1960.

BLAKE, ROBERT, *The Unknown Prime Minister*, Eyre and Spottiswoode, 1955.

Britain's Industrial Future, Ernest Benn, 1928.

BUTLER, D. E., *The Electoral System in Britain 1918-1951*, Oxford at the Clarendon Press, 1953.

CHURCHILL, WINSTON, *The World Crisis*, 5 vols, Thornton Butterworth, 1923-9.

Coal and Power, Hodder and Stoughton, 1924.

DANGERFIELD, GEORGE, *The Strange Death of Liberal England*, Constable, 1936.

DAVIES, JOSEPH, *The Prime Minister's Secretariat 1916-1920*, R. H. Johns, Newport Monmouthshire, 1951.

GARDINER, A. G., *Prophets, Priests, and Kings*, J. M. Dent, 1914.

GEORGE, DAVID LLOYD, *War Memoirs*, 6 vols, Ivor Nicholson and Watson, 1933-6.

GREY OF FALLODON, VISCOUNT, *Twenty-Five Years*, 2 vols, Hodder and Stoughton, 1925.

H.H.A. Letters of the Earl of Oxford and Asquith to a Friend, First and Second Series, Geoffrey Bles, 1933-4.

HALÉVY, ELIE, *A History of the English People in the Nineteenth Century*, 6 vols, Ernest Benn, 1952.

HARRIS, SIR PERCY, *Forty Years In and Out of Parliament*, Andrew Melrose, c. 1947.

Holmes-Laski Letters, edited by Mark Howe, 2 vols, Oxford University Press, 1953.

JENKINS, ROY, *Asquith*, Collins, 1964.

JONES, THOMAS, *A Diary with Letters 1931-1950*, Oxford University Press, 1954.

JONES, THOMAS, *Lloyd George*, Oxford University Press, 1951.

KEYNES, J. M., *The Economic Consequences of the Peace*, Macmillan, 1919.

Land and the Nation, Hodder and Stoughton, 1925.

Lloyd George by Mr. Punch, Cassell, 1922.

MALLET, SIR CHARLES, *Herbert Gladstone A Memoir*, Hutchinson, 1932.

MALLET, SIR CHARLES, *Mr. Lloyd George A Study*, Ernest Benn, 1930.

MASTERMAN, LUCY, *C. F. G. Masterman*, Nicholson and Watson, 1939.

MCCALLUM, R. B., *Asquith*, Duckworth, 1936.

MUIR, RAMSAY, *Liberalism and Industry*, Constable, 1920.

NEWTON, LORD, *Lord Lansdowne*, Macmillan, 1929.

NICOLSON, HAROLD, *King George the Fifth*, Constable, 1953.

OWEN, FRANK, *Tempestuous Journey*, Hutchinson, 1954.

The Parliamentary History of Conscription in Great Britain, preface by R. C. Lambert, George Allen and Unwin, 1917.

PERCY, LORD EUSTACE, *Some Memories*, Eyre and Spottiswoode, 1958.

PETRIE, SIR CHARLES, *The Life and Letters of the Right Hon. Sir Austen Chamberlain*, 2 vols, Cassell, 1939-40.

Raymond Chandler Speaking, edited by Dorothy Gardiner and Kathrine Sorley Walker, Hamish Hamilton, 1962.

RAYMOND, E. T., *Mr. Lloyd George*, Collins, 1922.

RIDDELL, LORD, *Intimate Diary of the Peace Conference and After 1918-1923*, Gollancz, 1933.

RIDDELL, LORD, *War Diary 1914-1918*, Ivor Nicholson and Watson, 1933.

ROYLE, CHARLES, *Opened Doors*, Meat Trades' Journal Co., 1949.

SAMUEL, VISCOUNT, *Memoirs*, The Cresset Press, 1945.

SNOWDEN, PHILIP VISCOUNT, *An Autobiography*, 2 vols, Ivor Nicholson and Watson, 1934.

SPENDER, J. A., and ASQUITH, CYRIL, *Life of Lord Oxford and Asquith*, 2 vols, Hutchinson, 1932.

STOREY, HAROLD, *The Case Against the Lloyd George Coalition*, Liberal Publication Department, 1920.

TAYLOR, A. J. P., *Politics in Wartime*, Hamish Hamilton, 1964.

TAYLOR, H. A., *Robert Donald*, Stanley Paul, n.d.

THOMSON, DAVID, *England in the Twentieth Century*, Penguin Books, Middlesex, 1965.

Towns and the Land, Hodder and Stoughton, 1925.

TREVELYAN, G. M., *Grey of Fallodon*, Longmans, 1937.

INDEX

Coupon, the (*1918*) election ; described : 139-40 ; statistics of : 140, 157-9 ; basis on which distributed : 140-9 ; Maurice debate and : 144-6 ; F. E. Guest and : 141-4, 147-8 ; Sir George Younger and : 141 ; extent to which determined outcome of *1918* election : 177-82 ; *mentioned* : 161, 191, 192, 232, 369

Cowan, W. H. (Lloyd George Liberal) : 78-9

Cowdray, Lord (Liberal newspaper owner) : 114-17

Cozens-Hardy, W. (Lloyd George Liberal) : 158

Craig, H. J. (Liberal M.P. and candidate) : 147-8, 149, 175

Crawfurd, H. E. (Asquith Liberal) : 309*n*, 321

Crewe, Lord (prominent Liberal) : 217, 367, 373

Croft, Sir H. Page (right-wing Conservative) : 158

Curragh incident (*1914*) : 111

Curzon, Lord (prominent Conservative) : 44, 72, 73, 93, 168, 386

Daily Chronicle (Liberal newspaper); attitude to Lloyd George : 113-14; acquired by him : 86, 117-18 ; sold by him : 338 ; demise of : 366 ; on Asquith coalition : 88-9 ; on free trade and Liberal reunion (*1923*) : 248-9 ; on state of Liberal party (*1924*): 271, 299 ; *other references* : 136*n*, 253, 260, 288

Daily Mail (right-wing newspaper) : 67, 262

Daily News (Liberal newspaper) ; and Lloyd George : 45, 78, 113 ; and Labour party : 172-3 & *n*, 217 & *n* ; attacked by MacDonald (*1923*) : 268 ; on Lloyd George Fund (*1929*) : 354-5 ; *mentioned* : 114

Dalziel, Sir Henry (Lloyd George Liberal) : 38, 53, 67, 79, 107, 117, 142*n*, 161

Dardanelles operation (Gallipoli) : 39, 50, 53-4, 65, 87, 387

Davies, David (prominent Welsh Liberal) : 114-15 & *n*, 118, 148

Davies, E. Clement (Simonite, then Liberal leader) : 381

Davies J. T. (Lloyd George's private secretary) : 281

Davies, Joseph (Lloyd George Liberal) : 119

Davies, R. H. (Asquith Liberal organiser) : 281, 339

Denman, R. D. (Liberal, then Labour) : 308

Derby, Lord (prominent Conservative) : 58, 258, 365
recruiting scheme (*1915*) : 74-5, 82

Dillon, John (Irish Nationalist) : 135, 160

Dodds, Elliott (post-war Liberal) : 319, 340

Donald, Robert (Liberal editor) : 102-3, 113-14, 117-18

Drummond, Eric (secretary to Asquith) : 60

Dunstan, R. (Liberal " pacifist ", then Labour) : 128

Edge, Sir William (Lloyd George Liberal, then Simonite) : 291, 292, 357

Edwards, Clement (N.D.P. member) : 158

Elections : *see* By-elections, General elections

First World War, *see* War

Fisher, H. A. L. (Lloyd George Liberal and historian) ; and *1918* election : 150 & *n*, 151-2, 178 ; as a Coalition Liberal : 153-4, 160, 198 ; and free trade : 191-2 ; and " fusion " : 197 ; and Conservatives : 204, 221, 226 ; and *1922* election : 229 ; and Liberal reunion : 250 ; and Liberal chairmanship : 320 ; *mentioned* : 108 & *n*, 259, 266, 282, 283, 321, 363

Fisher, Lord (First Sea Lord) : 51, 53, 55, 59

servatives : 351 ; *mentioned* : 38, 222, 291, 292

Gulland, John (Asquith Liberal) : 59-61, 98, 105, 106, 175, 188

Gwynne, Rupert (right-wing Conservative) : 221

Haig, Sir Douglas (military leader) : 37, 108, 109, 113 & *n*, 114

Haldane, Lord (prominent Liberal, then Labour) : 23, 26-7, 46-7, 49, 55-8, 59, 65, 67, 87, 125, 131, 209, 214, 219

Harris, John (radical Liberal) : 269, 273

Harris, Percy (Asquith Liberal) : 309

Hemmerde, E. G. (Liberal M.P., then Labour) : 145*n*, 146, 147

Henderson, Arthur (prominent Labour figure) : 197, 206, 267, 377, 382

Henderson, H. D. (Liberal editor and economist) : 124-5, 305*n*, 319, 324, 340, 344, 346, 365

Henry, Sir Charles (Lloyd George Liberal) : 86, 104, 114

Herald (Labour journal) : 128

Herbert, Sir Jesse (Liberal organiser) : 25*n*

Hewart, Sir Gordon (Lloyd George Liberal) : 121, 171*n*, 191, 200

Hirst, Francis (*laissez-faire* Liberal): 31 & *n*

Hobhouse, Sir Charles (prominent Liberal) : 175, 316, 328, 338

Hobhouse, L. T. (Liberal academic and journalist) : 90

Hogge, J. M. (Liberal independent, then Lloyd George) : 33, 35, 112, 161, 177, 189, 202 & *n*, 211, 243, 276, 308

Holt, R. D. (Asquith Liberal) : 84, 99, 175, 324, 340

Honours ; and party funds : 38, 113, 288, 289, 292

scandal (*1922*) : 221, 222, 323

Hopwood, Sir Francis (Liberal supporter) : 60

Hore-Belisha, Leslie (post-war Liberal, then Simonite) : 309, 310, 327*n*, 361

Horne, Sir Robert (prominent Conservative) : 284

House of Lords : and extension of life of Parliament : 62, 71, 75 ; mentioned : 17, 198, 234

Howard, Geoffrey (Asquith Liberal) : 61, 98, 111-12 & *n*, 119, 172, 175, 274, 297, 298, 374

Howard, S. G. (Lloyd George Liberal) : 146

Hudson, Sir Robert (Asquith Liberal organiser) : 211, 280, 293, 330, 339

Hutchison, Sir R. (Lloyd George Liberal, then Simonite) : 320, 337, 361, 363, 364, 365

Hutton, J. A. (Lancashire Conservative) : 258

Illingworth, A. H. (Lloyd George Liberal) : 162

Independent Liberals (" Free " Liberals, " Wee Frees ") : 170, 189-91, 202, 203, 205, 210-11, 214, 215, 219, 230, 231-5, 237-40, 251, 256-7, 287, 309, 319, 322

Ireland : 16, 18, 34, 69-70, 87 & *n*, 107-8, 137, 173, 192, 198, 202, 212-13, 221, 223, 335

Irish National party : 25, 50, 69-70, 87, 96, 127*n*, 381

Jellicoe, Sir J. (naval leader) : 37, 94*n*

Jenkins, Roy, *Asquith* ; views discussed : 54, 102 ; quoted : 72-3

John, E. T. (Liberal " pacifist ", then Labour) : 128

Johnstone, Harcourt (Asquith Liberal) : 332-3, 354, 358, 381

Johnstone, Joseph (Lloyd George Liberal) : 152

Jones, Harry (Liberal journalist) : 136*n*

Jones, Leif (Asquith Liberal) : 159, 164, 170, 175, 340, 349*n*, 358

Jowitt, W. A. (Liberal M.P., then Labour) : 351, 366

Liberal and Radical Candidates' Association : 320, 327, 328, 332-3
Liberal Central Association : 112, 314, 329, 337, 339
Liberal Council : 339-41, 346, 354, 358
Liberal funds : 112, 165, 250, 252, 288-98, 352-4, 370 ; *see also* : Lloyd George fund
Liberal " ginger " group (Liberal War Committee) : 36-8, 78-9, 96, 99, 100, 160
Liberal Industrial Inquiry : 328, 337, 344-5
Liberal Magazine (Liberal journal) : on formation of Asquith coalition : 55 ; on Conservative attacks on Liberal ministers : 55-6 ; on Lloyd George's popularity : 63 ; on course of the war : 65 ; on Lloyd George coalition : 106 ; on *1922* election results : 238 ; on *1923* election results : 257 ; on Liberals and Conservatives : 265, 300 ; on Million Fund : 316 ; on Lloyd George's *1929* campaign : 345
Liberal " pacifists " : 30-1, 99, 112, 128, 160, 164, 175
Liberal party : theories regarding its downfall : 15-19, 390
effects of First World War upon : 23-7, 30-48, 49-51 ; and Asquith coalition : 34, 40, 49, 58-61, 63, 78-85, 87, 97 ; and conscription : 40, 70-85, 97, 160-1 ; meeting of 8 December *1916* : 98-101, 112 ; and Lloyd George coalition : 96, 98, 100, 104-12, 164-70, 174, 181, 202-3 ; state of during *1917-18* : 104-31
division of (*1916-23*), explanations concerning : 159-63 ; extent of (*1917-18*) : 105-25 ; becomes complete (*1919-20*) : 187-200 ; reunion : 120-1, 202, 203, 226, 231 & *n*, 243-52 ; partial nature of : 251-2, 280-1, 294, 299, 313, 329
and *1918* election : 135-40, 149, 164-74, 175-83 ; stage of during

1918-22 : 205-19 ; and *1922* election : 226, 231-5, 237-40, 243 ; and *1923* election : 250-1, 253-64
poverty of : 289-94, 297-8, 301, 316-18, 338-9, 352-4, 370 ; shortage of candidates : 289, 292-3, 297, 299, 313, 315-16, 353, 377
state of, October *1924* : 278-9, 299, and *1924* election : 299-310, 319 ; parliamentary party after : 309-10, 314, 319-23
attempts to restore (*1925-6*) : 313-18 ; and controversy over land policy : 323-9 ; and quarrel over general strike : 331-6, 388 ; struggle for control of : 337-9 ; and return of Samuel (*1926-9*) : 341-2 ; reorganisation under : 341-3 ; and industrial programme : 328, 332, 344 ; and *1929* election : 345-7, 348-51, 378 ; state of, following election : 352-6 ; dissensions in parliamentary party (*1929-31*) : 348, 356-8, 360-5 ; and National government (*1931-5*) : 367-8, 373-7, 382 ; and *1931* election : 367-8, 370-3 ; and *1935* election : 376-7, 379, 380-1 ; position of party by *1935* : 377-9, 380-1
period *1914-64* surveyed : 388-90
and Labour party (pre-*1914*) : 16-17, 25*n*, 389 ; (*1914-18*) : 127-8 ; (*1918* election) : 164, 168, 171-3 ; (*1919-23*) : 188-9, 205-7, 216-8, 232-3, 263 ; decision to support first Labour government (*1924*) : 264-6 ; relations with : 264, 267-79 ; and second Labour government : 355, 356-66, 367 ; and Labour party (*1931-5*) : 370-1, 372, 377, 382 ; relations with Labour surveyed : 389-90 ; defection of members to Labour : 29-30, 31, 99-101, 128-30, 211, 219, 304, 308, 309, 340, 351 ;
and Conservative party : 164-5, 168, 231-2, 265, 321-2, 349, 361, 363, 364, 370, 372

412